The Pearson Guide to
Critical and Creative Thinking

Robert DiYanni

New York University

PEARSON

Boston   Columbus   Indianapolis   New York   San Francisco   Upper Saddle River
Amsterdam   Cape Town   Dubai   London   Madrid   Milan   Munich   Paris   Montréal   Toronto
Delhi   Mexico City   São Paulo   Sydney   Hong Kong   Seoul   Singapore   Taipei   Tokyo

Editorial Director: Dickson Musslewhite
Senior Acquisitions Editor: Debbie Coniglio
Editorial Assistant: Stephanie Ruland
Director of Marketing: Maggie Moylan
Senior Marketing Coordinator: Theresa Rotondo
Managing Editor: Melissa Feimer
Program Manager: Beverly Fong
Project Manager: Richard DeLorenzo
Senior Operations Supervisor: Mary Fischer
Operations Specialist: Eileen Corallo
Art Director: Blair Brown
Cover Designer: Maria Lange
Cover Image: Andrii Kondiuk/Shutterstock
Director of Digital Media: Sacha Laustsen
Digital Media Project Management: Learning Mate Solutions, Ltd./Allison Tuohy
Digital Media Project Manager: Amanda Smith
Full-Service Project Management and Composition: PreMediaGlobal/Revathi Viswanathan
Printer/Binder: LSC Communications
Cover Printer: LSC Communications

Credits and acknowledgments borrowed from other sources and reproduced, with permission, in this textbook appear on appropriate page within text (or on pages 347–348).

Library of Congress Cataloging-in-Publication Data
DiYanni, Robert.
  The Pearson guide to critical and creative thinking/Robert DiYanni, New York University.
    pages cm
  Includes index.
 ISBN-13: 978-0-205-90924-7
 ISBN-10: 0-205-90924-8
 1. Critical thinking. 2. Creative thinking. I. Title. BF441.D59 2015
 153.4'2—dc23

                                                                2014007092

Student Edition:
ISBN-10: 0-205-90924-8
ISBN-13: 978-0-205-90924-7

7 2019

Instructor's Review Copy:
ISBN-10: 0-205-93845-0
ISBN-13: 978-0-205-93845-2

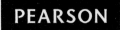

In Memoriam

This book is dedicated to the memory of my parents,
Edward Salvatore DiYanni (1921–1987) and *Lena Derrico DiYanni* (1921–1987),
who applied critical and creative thinking in every facet of their lives.

Brief Contents

v

Contents

7   Reasoning Badly: Thinking Fallacies   160

Preface

When we think about thinking, we often think first of "critical" thinking. The academic world values critical thinking highly—and for good reason. Critical thinking involves analysis and evaluation, interpretation and judgment. This kind of thinking is essential for developing and deepening our understanding.

To limit our thinking, however, only to critical thinking is reductive, even dangerous. To supplement and complement critical thinking, we need "creative" thinking, the kind of imaginative thinking that leads to new ideas and to innovation. Creative thinking is highly valued in higher education and in the world of work. Creative thinking completes and fulfills critical thinking. The two kinds of thinking go hand in hand. Either without the other is inadequate. We need both to become fully mindful thinkers who can creatively generate new ideas and critically evaluate them.

This book puts these two essential and complementary kinds of thinking together. It provides opportunities for developing the capacity to think both critically and creatively in practical and productive ways. Gathered here are thinking practices and strategies useful for academic courses, and for situations with friends, family, and colleagues in school, at home, and at work.

A few words about the book's organization: It is divided into five parts. Part One (Chapters 1 and 2) introduces basic concepts of critical and creative thinking, respectively. These preliminary chapters set up the more detailed and invigorating work in critical and creative thinking that follows. Part Two (Chapters 3–5) focuses on critical thinking with an emphasis on analysis; these chapters focus on language and visual images; they explore connections among critical reading, cogent writing, and careful thinking. Part Three (Chapters 6–8) continues the focus on critical thinking, but with an emphasis on argument. The first two chapters in this part concern logic; the third focuses on rhetoric. Part Four (Chapters 9–11) is about creative thinking, with an emphasis on how to generate ideas—how to think in new and fresh directions. These three creative thinking chapters are designed to develop the imagination. Part Five (Chapters 12–14) continues the emphasis on creative thinking (with some critical thinking considerations) by exploring aspects of design and innovation, and by examining ways technology and information impact our lives.

Learning to think critically and creatively can make a difference in our lives. Developing our critical and creative capacities can improve academic performance, strengthen work skills, enhance personal relationships, and enrich our perception of the world.

Developing thinking power—becoming adept at higher-order thinking—can make a difference in our lives. Not thinking well reduces the range, depth, and intensity of our lived experience. It limits our accomplishments. This book can help overcome such limitations, and thereby make a difference in how we perceive ourselves, how we understand others, and how we experience the world.

Acknowledgments

The Pearson Guide to Critical and Creative Thinking has had a long gestation. It began more than 30 years ago, when I was teaching English at Queens College, City University of New York. It was then that I began to reflect on the relationship among reading, writing, and thinking, which culminated in my first book, *Connections*, published in 1985. The idea for a book focused specifically on thinking, however, lay dormant for many years, until I was invited to teach a course in Critical Thinking at New York University (NYU) in 2002. That course, offered in an undergraduate program for adults returning for a university degree, provided the seedbed for many of the ideas presented in this book. I, therefore, wish to acknowledge Bob Boynton, who encouraged my efforts to produce *Connections*, and Peter Stillman, who helped me fashion that book with the interconnections among reading, writing, and thinking it explores. I also wish to acknowledge my colleagues and friends at NYU, particularly those in the McGhee Program, which houses the Critical Thinking course I still teach. Thanks, especially to Kathleen Hulley, Clinical Professor of Media Studies, who hired me to teach the course and who serves as coordinator for its multiple sections. As an outgrowth of my NYU Critical Thinking course, I was invited by Debra Szybinski, director of NYU's Office of Faculty Resources, to conduct a number of workshops for various NYU departments and schools, as well as summer seminars run through the Faculty Resource Network, which she also directs. I would like to thank Debra, and her associate director, Anne Lydia Ward, for the opportunities they have offered me to work with various elements of the NYU community.

I would like to acknowledge my friend, colleague, and mentor, Pat C. Hoy II, who served as Director of the Expository Writing Program at NYU for 20 years. Pat has long been a powerful influence on my own thinking about writing and its relationship to thinking. We taught together in the Harvard Expository Writing Program in the 1990s and more recently in Pat's program at NYU. I have learned much about teaching from Pat. In addition, I wish to thank three Expository Writing faculty members—Brooke Lewis, Clara Lewis, and Brian Schwartz—for their helpful suggestions on reviewing an earlier version of parts of this book.

Other colleagues and friends who offered valuable advice include William V. Costanzo, Professor of English at Westchester Community College, State University of New York. Bill and I had the privilege of codirecting an NYU Summer Seminar on Critical Thinking a few years ago. Our seminar brought together 22 faculty members from institutions around the United States and Puerto Rico. Like Pat Hoy, Bill Costanzo is himself an outstanding critical thinker, and I have benefited from our conversations in preparing and jointly leading our seminar. I would like to thank Bill as well for providing many incisive and insightful comments about this book's concepts and contents.

I would like to thank Donald Pardlow, a professor at Claflin University in South Carolina, for permission to use a writing assignment he created for logical thinking, included in Chapter 6. Thanks go also to Paul Sheehey of Scarsdale High School for permission to adapt his richly detailed description of the Odessa steps scene sequence from *Battleship Potemkin*, included in Chapter 4. Four Scarsdale HS art teachers deserve my thanks for contributing works of art accompanied by their artist comments, also included in Chapter 4; thanks to Maria DeAngelis, Nadine Gordon-Taylor, Dina Hofstetter, and Lisa Scavelli.

I should also acknowledge the inspiring work being done by two friends and colleagues, John Chaffee and Richard van de Lagemaat. John Chaffee, Professor of Philosophy at La Guardia Community College of the City University of New York, is the initiator and former director of a large program in Critical Thinking serving more than 4,000 students annually, as well as the author of a best-selling book, *Thinking Critically*, now in its tenth edition. Richard van de Lagemaat is the creator of *InThinking*, a Web site and on-site program devoted to promoting critical thinking, as well as author of a valuable book, *Theory of Knowledge*. Both John and Richard are major figures promoting higher-order thinking skills in the United States and Europe, respectively. I have learned much from both of these fine critical thinkers, teachers, and workshop leaders.

Among the many opportunities I have had in the past decade during which this book was simmering was an ECIS (European Council of International Schools) Conference presentation I attended in Dubrovnik, Croatia, given by Pat Bassett, former President of the National Association of Independent Schools. Pat's talk, which featured the work of Daniel Pink and Sir Ken Robinson, inspired me to begin gathering materials and pulling together my thoughts about critical and creative thinking.

ECIS is one of a number of international schools consortia that have invited me to give talks and conduct workshops about critical and creative thinking. I would like to thank the Executive Directors past and present of ECIS, CEESA (Central and Eastern European Association of International Schools), NESA (Near East South Asia Association of International Schools), MAIS (Mediterranean Association of International Schools), AAIE (Association for the Advancement of International Education)—Dixie McKay and Jeanne Vahey, David Cobb and Kathy Stetson, David Chojnacki, Reina O'Hale, Dick Krajczar and Elsa Lamb, respectively, for the invitations they extended me to work with their organizations, schools, and teachers. In this context I also wish to acknowledge a similar kind of encouragement and support from my friend and colleague Nancy Willard Magaud, vice president of the English Language Schools Association (ELSA) in France, another group I have had the privilege to work with many times in Paris during the past decade.

I have also had the special pleasure of working closely with Pat Carlisle, president of the de Bono Group. After Pat trained me in de Bono's thinking tools—parallel thinking, lateral thinking, and perception-broadening thinking—we presented workshops together for independent schools. I would like to thank Pat for deepening my understanding of the power of Edward de Bono's thinking tools.

I have had the opportunity to work closely with the Lincoln Center Institute of Aesthetic Education (now Lincoln Center Education). There I met Scott Noppe-Brandon and his Lincoln Center Institute colleagues, who introduced me to the work of Maxine Greene, the philosopher-educator whose work on releasing the imagination is the inspiration for much of what happens in schools worldwide that work with the Lincoln Center capacities for imaginative learning. I have also had the pleasure of working with the current Lincoln Center Education director, Russell Granet, an inspiring leader in critical and creative thinking through the arts.

I wish, also, to thank my Scarsdale colleagues who encouraged my work on critical and creative thinking: Dr. Joan Weber, Assistant Superintendent for Personnel and Administrative Services, who is the driving force behind Scarsdale's Lincoln Center partnership; Susan Taylor, director of the Scarsdale Teachers Institute, for whom I have had the privilege of conducting a number of workshops on critical and creative thinking; Diane Celentano, coordinator of the Scarsdale Lincoln Center initiative, who has been instrumental in ensuring the success of Lincoln Center program in all seven of its schools; Jerry Crisci, Director of Technology, whose skills and knowledge have deepened my understanding of technology; and Michael V. McGill, outgoing superintendent. A number of ideas in this book were tested out in venues under the leadership and with the partnership of these smart, talented, and highly collaborative colleagues.

And most recently, I have had the good fortune to work with John Moscaro and his administrative and faculty colleagues at the Morristown-Beard School, an outstanding independent school in New Jersey. John and his colleagues have given me the chance to explore together with them how critical and creative thinking can be fostered in secondary school students across a range of academic disciplines.

At various stages of this book's development, including its many drafts, I received thoughtful and productive responses from many people. I would like to thank the following for their input:

At Pearson, Dickson Musslewhite, Editorial Director, encouraged me early on with the idea for this book.

Pearson editors with whom I worked include Ashley Dodge, Editor-in-Chief, and Debbie Coniglio, Senior Acquisitions Editor, Beverly Fong, Program Manager, Stephanie Ruland, Editorial Assistant, Ben Ferrini, Manager of Rights and Permissions. Each of these individuals assumed an important role in the book's development. I wish to thank them all for their professionalism, their critical and creative thinking, and their faith in our joint work on the book. Debbie Coniglio, in particular, has been masterful in shepherding the book and its various supporting materials, print and digital, into development and timely production.

In addition, I would like to thank the talented teachers, Christopher Stahl and Christine Malvasi, New York University, who, under Debbie Coniglio's direction, developed some of the Web support applications for the book.

None of these good people should be held accountable for any errors contained in this book. Any errors are mine alone.

My final and most important acknowledgment of appreciation is to my wonderful wife, Mary Hammond DiYanni. Mary is a critical and creative thinker par excellence. I am fortunate beyond measure to have enjoyed her steadfast love and splendid companionship for more than four decades. My toughest critic, Mary has also been my most ardent supporter. I owe her not less than everything.

1
Developing Critical Thinking

No problem can withstand the assault of sustained thinking.
—VOLTAIRE

LEARNING GOALS

1.1 UNDERSTAND the basic elements of critical thinking.

1.2 IDENTIFY obstacles to critical thinking and how to overcome them.

1.3 INVESTIGATE the influence of perception on thinking.

1.4 EXPLORE the different ways knowledge is acquired and used.

1.5 APPLY critical thinking to personal, professional, and academic issues.

FOCUSING QUESTIONS

- How do you define thinking? What aspects or elements of thinking are most important to you? Why?
- How do you know what you think you know? That is, how do you acquire and evaluate knowledge?
- What inhibits your thinking, and what promotes your best thinking?
- What kinds of questions might be most useful to stimulate your thinking?
- What might you do to become a better critical thinker?

Chapter Overview

This chapter introduces the concept of critical thinking as a habit of mind, a way of considering both what we know and how we know what we know. Considered here, too, are various kinds of impediments or blocks to thinking, along with ways to overcome them. A major topic of the chapter is perception, which is approached from numerous angles—psychological, cultural, philosophical, and scientific. The central concerns of the chapter are how we acquire knowledge and how we can be assured of what we think we know—"how we know what we know." Because critical thinking involves analysis, analytical work is central throughout the chapter.

What Is Critical Thinking and Why Do We Need It?

⊙ **Watch** the **Video**,
What is Critical Thinking
and Why Do We Need It?
MyThinkingLab

critical thinking
The process of analysis, reflection, and evaluation that leads to reasoned conclusions and judgments.

interpretation
The concluding stage of the analytical process resulting in an idea about the meaning or significance of whatever is analyzed and interpreted, often, but not always, a text.

Critical thinking is a type of thinking in which we reflect and analyze to make decisions and solve problems. Critical thinking has been defined by Peter Facione and Carol Gittens in their book, *Think Critically*, as "reasoned judgment"—that is, a way of judging and evaluating based on logic and evidence. Critical thinking is purposeful thinking—thinking directed toward inquiring into a problem or situation and focused on arriving at a solution.

Critical thinking is not "negative" thinking; it does not necessarily involve criticizing ideas (although sometimes, being "critical" in this way can be an aspect of thinking critically). Nor is critical thinking used only for serious subjects or important issues; you can think critically about all kinds of things, from what kind of toothbrush to use or socks to wear to whether and whom to marry or what to do with your life.

Critical thinking involves analysis and **interpretation**. Some characteristics of critical thinking are the following: noticing deeply and carefully; making connections; asking probing questions; making distinctions; evaluating evidence; transferring and applying knowledge; thinking independently and interdependently. Our word *critical* derives from the Greek word *kritikos*, which means "judge." Critical thinking, not surprisingly involves making judgments, offering evaluations. Critical thinking is also associated with problem solving, logic, rationality, and convergent thinking.

Critical thinkers recognize the legitimacy and value of multiple points of view. They are able to embrace ambiguity, and they remain open to continued learning. To develop our capacity for critical thinking, we need to nurture certain tendencies, or dispositions, in ourselves—at least the following qualities and mental habits: open-mindedness, honesty, and flexibility; persistence and perseverance; reasonableness, diligence, and focus. In addition, a critical thinker is willing to reconsider ideas, to change his or her mind.

We need critical thinking in our everyday lives, in our academic studies, and in our professional and working lives. Critical thinking helps us make informed and sensible personal decisions. It anchors our academic studies in school, and it serves as a solid support system for the challenges we confront in the workplace. We need critical thinking to be responsible citizens and contributing members of society. We also need critical thinking to live more conscious and fully mindful lives.

Core Critical Thinking Capacities

Among the essential critical thinking competencies are analysis, interpretation, evaluation, and self-direction. Aspects of self-direction include self-awareness and **self-regulation**—managing our thinking and our motivation for thinking. Analysis is a method whose goal is interpretation, or understanding. Aspects of the analytical method include making careful observations, connecting and relating them, drawing inferences from them, and formulating a provisional or tentative conclusion. Essential also for thinking critically is evaluation, making informed and sound judgments. Both analysis and evaluation, or judgment, are key aspects of critical thinking.

self-regulation
The critical thinking skill by which one monitors one's cognitive activities.

Essential Critical Thinking Questions

Knowing how to ask good questions is an essential skill for both critical and creative thinking. For both types of thinking, in fact, learning how to ask the right kinds of questions is every bit as important as learning how to answer them.

Ask yourself the following questions for good critical thinking:

1. What do I already know?
2. What have I assumed?
3. What questions can I ask?
4. What does it mean?
5. What is the evidence?
6. What are my criteria?

Underlying all these questions is the most fundamental of all critical thinking questions: "How do I know what I think I know?" and "What evidence do I have for what I think I know?"

What Critical Thinkers Do

Critical thinkers exhibit a consistent set of behaviors; they:

- Identify important problems accurately and precisely.
- Raise key questions and formulate them clearly.
- Gather relevant information.
- Use concepts, theories, and models effectively.
- Recognize underlying assumptions and extenuating implications.
- Consider evidence honestly and fairly.
- Reason logically.
- Evaluate carefully and judiciously.
- Test conclusions and solutions against relevant criteria and standards.

Habits of Mind

Our intelligence is, in effect, the sum of our habits of mind—how we use our mental habits to think and solve problems. An organization called The Institute for Habits of Mind proposes the following six mental habits as essential for enhancing our ability to think critically and creatively.

- **Applying Past Knowledge to New Situations** Using what we already know, making connections between prior knowledge and new situations is essential for higher-order thinking. The American philosopher John Dewey reminds us that we learn by reflecting on our experiences. And the inventor Thomas Edison claimed that he never made mistakes; instead, he kept learning what didn't work until he finally figured out what did.

- **Thinking Independently and Interdependently** We need to learn to think for ourselves, to become independent thinkers, to see things from our own unique perspective. But although necessary, independent thinking is only half the story, for we also need to think collaboratively, to work with and learn from others. The process is reciprocal: We link our thinking with the thinking of others. We feed off others' ideas, and they feed off ours. We think both independently and interdependently.

- **Remaining Open to Continuous Learning** We continue developing our minds, learning all our lives. Doing this successfully involves being able to identify opportunities for continuous learning in every sphere of our lives. The mental habit of being "open" is essential, open to other perspectives and ideas, open to possibilities for intellectual growth and development wherever we find them.

- **Questioning and Posing Problems** Among the important tools for critical thinking is asking good questions and identifying problems by posing them accurately. Socrates is famous for asking probing questions and pushing those he questioned deeper into inquiry. Questions, of course, invite answers; in thinking about how to answer good questions, we learn the limits of our knowledge.

- **Taking Intellectual Risks** Developing the habit of taking risks, of moving outside our comfort zone can push us to think and learn in new and interesting ways. Taking risks involves the possibility of failure, of course, as well as being frustrated by uncertainty. Progress, however, depends on taking chances. As Robert F. Kennedy noted, only those who dare to fail greatly achieve great things. And the painter Vincent van Gogh wrote, "I am always doing what I cannot do, so that I may learn how to do it."

- **Sustaining Intellectual Curiosity** Curiosity, an eager seeking after information, knowledge, and understanding, is essential for all learning, but especially for continued learning throughout our lives. As children, we are immensely curious about all manner of things. Unfortunately, many of us lose that curiosity during our years of schooling. One of the greatest thinkers of all time, Leonardo da Vinci, considered curiosity to be fundamental to his life as an artist, scientist, and inventor.

EXERCISE

1. Select one of the habits of mind and provide an example from your experience when you put that habit into practice. Then explain why you think it's important to develop that particular habit of mind. Or, alternatively, challenge the proclaimed value of one of the habits of mind. Explain why you agree or disagree with whichever habit of mind you select. Consider as well, how you would go about assessing the trustworthiness, the credibility, of The Institute for Habits of Mind and its Web site.

To become useful, these six habits of mind need to be actualized as behaviors—as things done on a regular basis to develop our thinking capacities. In acting on these and other habitual thinking behaviors, we develop what Ron Ritchhart has called "intellectual character," a cohesive way of thinking that is distinctively our own. Ritchhart's notion of intellectual character includes our particular habits of mind, patterns of thinking, and general dispositions, all of which reflect how we, uniquely, think.

Developing an intellectual character requires inculcating good thinking habits, building on positive thinking dispositions, such as persistence, patience, and perseverance, over significant periods of time. Our intellectual character represents us as individual thinkers; it reflects our unique ways of engaging the world mindfully.

EXERCISE

2. Which qualities of Ritchhart's "intellectual character" do you possess, at least moderately? Which qualities do you need to work at developing? How might you go about doing that?

Overcoming Obstacles to Thinking

One of the biggest hindrances to developing the habit of critical thinking is to allow different kinds of obstacles to inhibit our thinking. To become a better critical thinker, we may need to overcome various obstacles that can block our thinking. In his book *Conceptual Blockbusting*, James L. Adams discusses a number of such blocks to thought. These include perceptual blocks, cultural blocks, intellectual blocks, emotional blocks, and polarizing blocks.

Perceptual Blocks to Thinking

Perceptual blocks inhibit our ability to make sense of what we are looking at. They interfere with our thinking by blocking what we can see. We can overcome perceptual blocks by continuing to look until we can begin making sense of what we are seeing.

In looking at a work of modern art, such as Pablo Picasso's painting *Guernica*, for example (available on the Internet), we may be puzzled upon a first encounter. However, once we take a few moments to look carefully at this famous and complex work of art, we begin to notice different aspects of the painting's details.

We notice a horse with its mouth open in what appears to be a seemingly agonized scream; we notice an extended arm with a hand holding a light. We notice various kinds of distortion of human and animal facial and bodily features. Making sense begins with this kind of noticing. It involves relating the details we see, considering why they have been put together in the painting. It involves asking questions about what we notice.

As we do our own noticing, we can also ask others what they see in the painting and what sense they make of it. We can also do some research to learn what Picasso attempted and achieved with this painting, and why he created it.

Learning to see new things requires patience, effort, and practice. We prepare ourselves to see; we learn how to look. One crucial element for improving our thinking, then, is to become more observant—to notice more widely and more deeply, to broaden and enrich our perception.

It is certainly true that to notice the special features of Picasso's *Guernica* or of Notre Dame cathedral in Paris, or to appreciate the moves of National Basketball Association star LeBron James, or the skills of movie star Matt Damon, we have to know something about painting, architecture, basketball, or acting, respectively. One pillar of observation, then, is knowledge. The more we know about something, the better we can see it, understand it, appreciate it. We may take pride in our knowledge of painting or architecture, of basketball or acting, a pride earned through a deepening of our knowledge. It is that deepened knowledge that enables us to "see" better than those who lack such knowledge.

EXERCISE

3. Choose something to look at that has been difficult for you to really see. It could be a work of art, something in nature, a person, a place in your neighborhood, even a room or portion of a room in your home, school, or workplace. Make an effort to look really closely and patiently and to discover at least three elements you had not noticed or appreciated before—and then to reflect on their significance. You may wish to do your close looking and deep noticing with Picasso's painting, *Guernica*. Or, perhaps this work makes you think of another image—a painting, photograph, sculpture, monument, building—you would like to work with.

Cultural Blocks to Thinking

Cultural blocks derive from our ingrained thinking habits or predispositions. Cultural blocks to thinking derive from our ethnic, racial, national, and intellectual traditions, as well as from our gender and social class. Chinese and Italians, Latinos and Native Americans, men and women, the wealthy and the poor have different life priorities largely because of their different experiences and their differing social, cultural, political, economic, and other backgrounds. Similarly, people of varied religions may be committed to quite different ideas about the role of children or animals in society, the degree of respect given to the elderly, the value of meditation, or the necessity of relating to the divine. Our perspectives on many issues, and even our ways of seeing the world, are influenced by such cultural factors.

Cultural blocks inhibit thinking. Some of these blocks, such as the biased attitudes of racial prejudice, sexism, and ageism, are dangerous and destructive. One of the benefits of collaborating with others is comparing our cultural assumptions with theirs. Recognizing and acknowledging our cultural blocks is the first step toward avoiding their interference with good thinking.

Intellectual Blocks to Thinking

Intellectual blocks involve obstacles to knowledge. We sometimes find ourselves unable to solve a personal, professional, or academic problem because we lack information or because the information we have is incomplete or incorrect. When buying a car, for example, we may be unaware of the performance ratings of different models, or of their differing repair records or safety features. We may have only one-sided information provided by dealers and their sales reps. If we lack a general knowledge of cars, we will very likely lack confidence when purchasing one.

On the other hand, we may know quite a bit about a particular subject but still lack the skill to express our ideas effectively. How many times have you said to yourself, "I really knew more than I was able to say (or write) for that presentation or that report, but I just couldn't organize my thinking and find the right words." To break through an intellectual block to thinking, we need either to acquire additional information or to deepen our understanding. Perhaps we may have to think harder, deeper, and more broadly about what we know—to consider other ways our knowledge can be used or applied or valued. We may also need to do some research.

Emotional Blocks to Thinking

Emotional blocks to thought occur when feelings inhibit our thinking. Such blocks include our fears and anxieties. Perhaps the biggest emotional block to thinking is the fear of being wrong. This fear is grounded in how we believe people will perceive us, especially how people might view us if we are mistaken. As a result, we may be reluctant to put forth ideas about which we are unsure. "What if I'm wrong?" we might wonder. "What if people think my comment is stupid?" Such blocks inhibit our ability to explore an idea; such emotional blocks impede our thinking. The solution is to develop confidence, to allow ourselves the luxury of being wrong, and to forgive ourselves for our mistakes. We need to recognize that mistakes are necessary for intellectual development, that not knowing all the answers is normal, and that error can lead to discovery. Such knowledge can alleviate our fears about being wrong.

Another emotional block to thinking is the inability to tolerate confusion, uncertainty, and ambiguity. Periods of confusion and uncertainty are often necessary for breakthroughs in thinking. We need to tolerate a degree of chaos in our thinking. In writing a report, for example, we shouldn't expect to decide on and refine our idea, plan the perfect organization, and write the ideal version in a single attempt. Exploring a subject, coming up with various ideas, experimenting with different organizational structures, and writing a few messy drafts is more often the reality than not, even for professional writers. The renowned American essayist and children's book writer, E. B. White wrote six drafts before he was satisfied with a single paragraph that he published about the 1969 moon landing in *The New Yorker* magazine. Few successful thinkers get things right the first time.

Polarizing Blocks to Thinking

To polarize refers to see things in terms of opposites—"polar opposites" we call them, such as "us" and "them," Republican and Democrat, liberal and conservative. Polarized thinking is "black-and-white" thinking, "either-or" thinking. Polarizing involves creating mutually exclusive categories that do not allow for compromise. Polarized categories, such as the following, inhibit both critical and creative thinking:

yes/no	friend/enemy
right/wrong	win/lose
true/false	intelligent/stupid
now/never	good/bad
us/them	diligent/lazy

We should avoid limiting our thinking with these and other polarized categories, and look, instead, for the middle ground between such opposites. One way to do that is to create a continuum that permits gradations between the opposing perspectives. Being simply either strictly "for" or "against" some plan, project, or idea limits our choices and misrepresents their complexity. We may want to say, in such a case, "Wait a minute. I am for this part of the plan or idea, and against that part." For instance, we may favor curtailing health care costs, but that does not necessarily mean that we support the president's plan for health care reform. Conversely, to oppose the president's plan does not mean that we are against controlling health care costs. Or we may be in favor of an economic stimulus package—just not the one that either Barack Obama or his opposition favors. Perhaps we favor elements of each of their plans, but we support neither plan in its totality. Often, our agreement and/or disagreement will reflect one or another gradation or shade of conviction that is neither "black" nor "white." "Yes, but" and "No, but" provide a structure for avoiding black-and-white, all-or-nothing polarized thinking.

We can also ask "to what extent" or "to what degree," which is more productive than seeing a situation as "all or nothing." To avoid "black-and-white," "either-or" thinking, ask the following question: "To what extent" is an idea acceptable, a book interesting, a film entertaining or provocative? Considering degree or extent pushes us to make distinctions, to explore and consider possibilities and shades of difference. It encourages listening to others' views and perspectives, thinking interdependently, and ultimately developing better critical thinking habits of mind.

How to Overcome Obstacles to Thinking

Obstacles to Thinking	*Ways to Overcome Obstacles*
Perceptual blocks	Practice observing and noticing
Cultural blocks	Become aware of cultural perspectives
Intellectual blocks	Study, review, research
Emotional blocks	Conquer fear of mistakes
Polarizing blocks	Identify the middle ground

EXERCISES

4. Identify two cultural blocks to thought that, if removed, would promote tolerance, improve social relationships, or enhance one of the environments in which you live or work.

5. Choose an assignment or project you are working on at school, at home, or on the job. Consider how an intellectual block limits or could limit your ability to complete the assignment or project effectively. Explain what you plan to do to minimize or eliminate the intellectual block to thinking.

6. Describe a time when you were fearful of presenting an idea or of volunteering for a project. Looking back on it now, consider what you might have done to overcome, or at least minimize, your fear. Alternatively, identify a current situation at school or at work that is affecting you because of an emotional block to your thinking. Think about what you can do to overcome this emotional block.

7. Choose one of the following sets of polarized terms. Draw a continuum, as shown in the example for love/hate. Identify three or four intermediate terms and place them on your continuum.

Example: Hatred . . . Love
Hatred Enmity Animosity Disaffection Indifference Affection Fondness Love

  a. Heroic . . . Cowardly
  b. Success . . . Failure
  c. Proud . . . Humble
  d. Good . . . Evil
  e. Weakness . . . Strength
  f. Wealth . . . Poverty

8. Identify your most difficult challenge at work, in school, or at home. Think of two different kinds of blocks to thinking that might be affecting your performance. Explain what you could do to improve matters.

A Model for Critical Thinking

In his book, *Theory of Knowledge*, Richard van de Lagemaat presents the following cyclical model for critical thinking: Question—Clarify—Support—Evaluate—Reflect—and then repeat the cycle. Using this model, we begin with what we already know—or think we know. As we think about these things and as we absorb new knowledge, we do each of the following things:

- *We ask questions*: What questions can we ask about this new knowledge?
- *We seek clarification*: What does the new knowledge mean for us?
- *We consider available support*: What is the evidence for this knowledge?
- *We evaluate*: What are the criteria by which we evaluate this knowledge?
- *We reflect*: What have we assumed and what can we consider about this knowledge?

The process is both cyclical and reciprocal, with each of these aspects of critical thinking carrying over and into one of the others. The circularity of the process suggests continuity—the process never really ends. We continue to question and clarify; we seek additional support; we evaluate and reevaluate; and we reflect farther and deeper on what we know. In the process of doing so, we deepen our understanding and develop and refine our critical thinking capacities.

Thinking about Thinking: How We Know What We Know

Underlying this model of critical thinking—or any model of thinking—is a basic question: "How do we know what we know—or what we think we know?" Alternatively: "Where does our knowledge come from?" Basically, we learn things in three ways: (1) through our individual experience of the world; (2) through reading and hearing from others; and (3) through figuring things out for ourselves. Experience, or empirical knowledge, comes to us through our senses—what we observe, feel, hear, smell, taste, and the like. Learning from others involves accepting authority, taking on faith what experts say about a subject. Figuring things out involves using reason to understand and arrive at conclusions. Some philosophers posit a fourth way of knowing, a kind of intuitive understanding of things that is independent of experience. This kind of knowledge, *a priori* knowledge, is somehow already there inside us, innate, or inborn; we just have to discover it.

Each of these ways of knowing, however, can lead us astray. Empirical knowledge, the knowledge derived from our senses, cannot always be trusted, for sometimes we don't see or hear accurately. Taking the word of others can lead us into error, if others are not truthful or if they are mistaken. Using reason, although often effective, can be a challenge if we don't reason logically, or if we base our reasoning on false premises or erroneous information. And *A priori* knowledge, which takes the form of **intuition**, can be proven wrong by empirical evidence.

intuition
An unexplained understanding that relies less on logic and reasoning than a sense or feeling about things.

Compounding the difficulty of being secure in our knowledge are a few additional difficulties. One is that our models of how the world works—physically, economically, socially, culturally, and politically—are often vastly oversimplified when they are not simply wrong. As Nate Silver points out in *The Signal and the Noise*, this problem of inaccurate models is magnified because our mistakes about complex systems are measured not by degrees or small margins of error, but rather by large orders of magnitude—the difference of a single zero between, say, 1,000,000 and 10,000,000. Silver notes that the gap between what we know and what we think we know is very likely widening, along with our reluctance to acknowledge this unpleasant probability.

EXERCISES

9. Apply van de Lagemaat's critical thinking process to a topic with which you are familiar but not an expert. Perform the tasks at each of the stages associated with his cycle of actions—question, clarify, support, evaluate, and reflect. And then repeat the process.

10. Give an example of a time when you were in error because of sense experience, being misled by others, reasoning from false information, or discovering that a self-evident truth you believed was contradicted by empirical evidence.

Focus on Perception: Perception and Knowledge

In the next few sections, we consider how perception—what we see or think we see—is central to what we know and understand, and also to how we think. Perception involves much more than simple "seeing," as the following discussion of the psychology of perception suggests. Seeing is more complex than it initially appears. Perception involves interpretation, and hence understanding—what we think we know.

The renowned art historian E. H. Gombrich has noted that we cannot "separate what we see from what we know." This is so for three interrelated reasons. First, we can't know more than we can see. That is, we can't understand something until we "see" it either literally or figuratively (as when you "grasp" or "see" an idea). Second, our ability to see (and understand) anything is grounded in prior experience. Our understanding is based on our prior knowledge and on the expectations that grow out of it. And third, our knowledge and seeing are linked because they are based on the conceptual categories we "think" with. We always see something "as" something we can categorize, something we know from experience or from general knowledge.

Seeing is also a kind of thinking, as another art historian, Rudolf Arnheim, has argued. For Arnheim, "observation is also invention"; when we see something, we make sense of it by making inferences about it, guessing about what it is and adjusting those guesses to conform to our changing perceptions. Seeing, thus, is an active, selective, and interpretive process, and not simply a kind of automatic, objective absorption of external reality.

How does this process of seeing work? When we see something, we begin "editing" it. Our brains highlight particular features of what we are looking at and suppress others. Without the brain's editing of visual stimuli, we would not be able to make sense of what we see. By selecting, classifying, and relating details, our brains enable us to see something rather than a jumble of confused nothings. When looking at an object rooted in the ground, its trunk rising and proliferating in branches filled with leaves, we see it "as" something—in this case a tree, a deciduous tree, the type of tree that sheds its leaves and regrows them each year. If our brains did not isolate the features it does and highlight them, we would register, as American psychologist William James has noted, "a blooming, buzzing confusion."

Up till now, we have been emphasizing one sense—sight. But perception generally refers more broadly to our awareness of things through our other senses as well. Perceiving through our senses gives us knowledge and experience of the world and of others. The senses are important in our everyday lives, our work, and in every academic subject area. Sight, for example, is essential in critical ways for scientific observation, for historical investigation, including eyewitness accounts, and for every aspect of architecture and the arts of painting, drawing, and sculpture, as well as for work in mathematics and music, language and literature—and much more. Hearing is essential for music, of course, and for theater, but it is also important for the study of literature—poetry especially—as well as for work in political science and rhetoric.

Perceptual Illusions

One of the dangers of perception is that sometimes things we look at appear different from the way they really are. Visual artists have long known how to make things appear "realistic"—the way they seem to us in everyday life—by using linear perspective. That's why the photograph of the train below looks right to us.

In looking at the four figures in the drawing (Figure 1.1), things appear strange because there has been no scaling of the figures between the front and back of the picture. In fact, the three figures are actually the same size—though the one in the rear looks larger than the one in the middle and the one in the foreground. Our eyes tell us that the figures differ in size; a ruler measurement will confirm that all thee are actually the same size.

Figure/Ground and Perception

When we look at objects, we tend to focus on some aspects or details rather than on others. We focus on the "figure" and not on the "ground" (or background). In reading these words, for example, we ignore the white background in favor of the black printed words. We ignore, too, the spaces between the words—*thoughifthosespaceswerenotthereitwouldbehardtoreadthewords*.

Some images can be confusing because they can be viewed, or "read" in more than one way at the same time. These figures or images are ambiguous and unstable.

FIGURE 1.1 Size and Scale

We can use figure and ground to look at the following two images—Figures 1.2 and 1.3. If we look first at Figure 1.2 and make the white part the figure to focus on and the black area the (back)ground, we see two faces staring at each other as if in a mirror. Switching the figure and ground, focusing now on the black figure as foreground, keeping the white as background, we see a goblet.

Similarly, in looking at Figure 1.3, we should be able to see both an old woman and a young one. To see images of both women, we need to shift our focus and interpret the black-and-white areas of the figure in different ways. To see the old woman, we imagine that the large black area at the bottom of the figure is a furry coat into which the woman has tucked her chin. The large white area to the top and right is a scarf that covers most of her head, with some black hair visible in the front of her head, just above her left eye, and her large downward pointing nose, as she looks forward and to the left. To see the young woman, who faces outward and the left rear of the drawing, we reinterpret the old woman's left eye as the young woman's left ear. The old woman's nose is now seen as the young woman's jaw and the left side of her face.

Perception and Expectation

Expectations influence what we see and how we see. What do we see in the following groups of words?

WE GO	OH HOW
TO	I LOVE
MIAMI	PARIS
IN THE	IN THE
THE WINTER	THE SPRING

Do they read: "We go to Miami in the Winter" and "I Love Paris in the Spring"? Or do they read: "We go to Miami in the the Winter" and "Oh How I Love Paris in the

FIGURE 1.2   Goblet/Faces

FIGURE 1.3   Old Woman/Young Woman

the Spring"—(though all in upper case letters)? Most of us, most of the time, would miss the second "the" in each case because that's not what we expect to find. Our brains edit out that second "the" because it is redundant, unusual, unexpected, and unnecessary.

We often see what we expect to see, and we don't see what may be in front of our noses, if we had not expected to see it. In a famous set of experiments, two psychologists, Christopher Chabris and Daniel Simons, asked participants to watch a video by focusing on two teams, one dressed in white, the other in black, as they bounced a ball back and forth. The participants were asked to count the number of bounces that went to the white-clothed and the black-clothed players. During the experiment, a person dressed in a gorilla costume walked in front of the camera. In one experiment the "gorilla" passed by quickly. In another, the "gorilla" stood for a couple of seconds before moving out of camera range. At the end of the experiment, the psychologists asked each of the participants whether they saw anything unusual during their viewing of the video. Fully half of them saw only the teams bouncing basketballs, completely missing the "gorilla." It made no difference whether the "gorilla" walked by quickly or paused for a few seconds. In fact, some of the participants in the experiment refused to believe that the "gorilla" was ever there at all—even after being confronted with the evidence on film. They simply did not believe they could have missed seeing something so obvious. But, in fact, they didn't see it. The original and subsequent examples of this selective attention test can be found on the Internet.

Alison Gopnik references Chabris' and Simon's "gorilla" research in the *Wall Street Journal*, while reporting on an article in the journal *Psychological Science* that demonstrates how experienced physicians missed a "gorilla" that had been included in slides of lung tissue that they were reading. The gorilla was faded in and out of the slides as the radiologists read them. But when they were asked if they had seen anything unusual in the slides they examined, 83% of the radiologists said they had not. Gopnik explains this phenomenon as a kind of "inattentional blindness" to which we are all prone. She raises a number of questions about the nature of knowledge and consciousness, concluding that we know less about our perceptions and that we have far to go "before we understand how consciousness works."

Perception and Culture

One additional perceptual filter is culture. Our cultural background helps us see things in certain ways, but it also prevents us from seeing things in other ways. Or at least it makes it more difficult to see things from another and different cultural perspective. That's one of the reasons we find so much misunderstanding and conflict in the world. And it's one of the prime reasons we need to develop our capacity to consider other perspectives than our own—other ways of seeing and understanding, and other ways of describing "reality."

Roger von Oech, who has written and consulted widely on thinking in the business world, in his *A Kick in the Seat of the Pants*, tells a story that reveals a difference in perception resulting from differing cultural expectations. During World War II, American soldiers dated English women, with the result that each accused the other of being sexually aggressive because of confused signals regarding kissing. According to American cultural norms of the time, kissing was about #5 on a sequence of 30 steps of courtship leading to sexual relations. Kissing, in the American sequence of events, was more or less a signal of early romantic interest.

In pre–World War II England, however, kissing was more like step #25 out of 30—a much more serious event and one that came much later in the courtship.

So when an American GI, dating an English woman decides, after a couple of dates, that it's time to kiss her to let her know of his interest, she's astounded, even dumbfounded. She's thinking, "this isn't supposed to happen until much later." And she might even feel cheated out of most of the courtship ritual that, from her perspective, should have preceded the kissing. But she has to make a decision: either cut this relationship off, or get ready for intercourse, since, in her mind, it's only a few steps away. The man, of course, is equally confused, since if the woman backs off after the kiss, he doesn't know why. Conversely, if she turns on the heat, he wonders whether she's being overly aggressive. The result is culture shock for both of them.

EXERCISE

11. Take a look at the following picture. How would you describe what you see? How do you think someone from a culture with very different social values might describe what they see in the picture? Consider, for example, how Asians and Westerners value differently self-expression and self-display on the one hand, and quietness and humility, on the other. How important do you think sociability and cheerfulness, enthusiasm and aggressiveness are in Western countries as compared with Asian countries—especially the Confucian belt countries—China, Japan, Korea, Vietnam? Look again at the picture and consider how an American student and a Chinese student might describe it.

In an experiment based on the "marine scene" depicted in Figure 1.4, people of Western backgrounds emphasized the fish swimming in the foreground. The picture, according to them, was about the fish. People of Asian cultural backgrounds, however, saw it differently. They put much more emphasis on the environment in which

FIGURE 1.4 Marine Scene

the fish were swimming. For them, it was less about the fish than about the relationship among all the elements of the picture. How people from these different cultural groups looked at the picture—or, more precisely, what they saw when they looked at it, differed significantly.

In *Drunk Tank Pink*, Adam Alter cites a number of psychological experiments that reveal how differently people from cultures that stress individualist ideals (Americans, for example) respond compared to those from cultures that emphasize collectivist ideals (Asians, for example). Participants viewed photographs of a tiger near a stream and jet fighter planes against mountains. Later they were shown photographs of the same tiger and the same jet planes, but against different backgrounds—the tiger on a grassy plain and the jets against a clouded sky. American students were much more likely to recognize that they had seen the central image—the tiger and the jets—than were Chinese students. Their difficulty in deciding whether they had seen the tiger and jets is explained by the "way" they had seen them—as parts of a whole, in context, rather than as isolated, foregrounded, central objects.

Cultural bias provides yet another way that culture filters what we see. If we prize our cultural heritage, we will tend to see mostly the good in it and downplay its less attractive features. We will tend to be attentive to its achievements and contributions and to ignore the less savory aspects of its history. Cultural biases include our national pride, our pride in our ancestry, our language, our geographical region, our city or town, our neighborhood.

Religion and gender also serve as filters akin to those of culture. What we see and understand, what we acknowledge and comprehend, is influenced by our experience as males or females, men or women, and by the beliefs we hold about the world. And so, with all these perceptual filters affecting what we see and think we know, it is imperative that we remain alert to their shaping influence. To strive for the open-mindedness necessary for critical and creative thinking, we need to begin by recognizing the complexity of perception and its relation to knowledge and to ways of thinking.

EXERCISES

12. Why do you think so many participants failed to see the "gorilla" in the experiment done by the psychologists Christopher Chabris and Daniel Simons? Do you think you would have seen it? How do you respond to the conclusions drawn by Alison Gopnik about the medical "gorilla" experiment?

13. Give an example of a time when you and a friend or family member perceived something in radically different ways. Explain why you think this difference of perception occurred. What were the filters affecting the differing perceptions?

14. Describe how people might see each of the following:

    a. A full moon as seen by an astronomer, an astrologer, a painter, a seaman, a lover.

    b. A forest as seen by a hiker, a logger, an environmentalist, a forest dweller, an urbanite, a biologist.

    c. A shopping mall as seen by a shopper, an advertiser, a merchant, a group of preteens.

    d. The Super Bowl football game as seen by an advertiser, a knowledgeable football fan, a knowledgeable golf or tennis fan, a college football player, a student of communications and media, an immigrant from Brazil, a believer in nonviolence.

15. How do you respond to the "kissing" scenario? What do you think the woman should have done? Why? Was there a way for the couple to have avoided the possibility of misunderstanding?

16. Describe a time when one aspect of your cultural background and experience influenced, or perhaps even caused you to see, experience, and/or understand something very differently from someone else. What did you perceive? What did the other person perceive? Why? How did the difference in perception affect your discussion and/or your relationship?

17. To what extent do you think we are influenced and affected by our cultural backgrounds and experiences, including the influence of our parents? To what extent is it possible, and perhaps necessary for us to think and act in ways counter to our cultural background?

18. Which of the following advertisement slogans do you think would appeal to Americans and which to Koreans and why?

    a. Seven out of ten people are using this product.

    b. The Internet isn't for everybody. But then you are not everybody.

19. In viewing Facebook pages of American and Japanese students, where would you expect to find more pictures of individuals without their friends? Whose pictures do you think would tend to be larger?

Being Wrong

In her book, *Being Wrong*, Kathryn Schulz identifies a number of reasons why we are often wrong, especially on those occasions we are absolutely convinced that we are right. Primary among these is what she calls "error-blindness." Error-blindness is necessarily invisible to us; hence our inability to see it. And even though other psychological factors contribute to error—arrogance, insecurity, stubbornness, and egocentrism, for example—blindness to our false beliefs seems to trump them all. Part of the reason for the power of "error-blindness" is that we are not really able to feel that we are wrong even when we are clearly in error. And since we can't see our mistakes, we conclude that we are right—as usual. Once we do see our mistakes, they become our past mistakes, what we once thought or believed but which we no longer accept as true.

Schulz cites an example presented by Sigmund Freud in *The Psychopathology of Everyday Life*, a book about why we make mistakes. Freud describes a time when he could not recall the name of a patient he had treated even though he had seen her for many weeks not long before his instance of forgetting. It turns out that Freud had misdiagnosed the patient as suffering from hysteria when in fact she was suffering from abdominal cancer, which killed her. On the other hand, Schulz provides an example from her own life when she made a mistake in pronouncing the name of the German poet Goethe (GER-tah) and had to be corrected by a professor, an episode that she never forgot.

There are still other ways we err in our thinking. In *Thinking, Fast and Slow*, Daniel Kahneman identifies numerous thinking biases we have that skew our thinking, mostly toward error. Kahneman argues that we are inclined to overestimate how much we understand about the world and, conversely, to underestimate the significance of chance in events. To this he adds that our confidence, actually an overconfidence, is increased by what he calls "the illusory certainty of hindsight." We just know we are right (even when we are wrong about things).

Kahneman explains our thinking processes as the operation of two parallel mental systems. The first of these, which he dubs "System I," operates quickly and

system I thinking
A form of thinking quickly and reactively without careful reflection and consideration.

system II thinking
A form of deliberative thinking that allows time for analysis and consideration of different approaches and alternative options.

automatically, even effortlessly. The other, "System II," involves effort and thought. System II thinking takes time; it involves computation and concentration, judgment and analysis. According to Kahneman, we mostly operate with our **System I thinking** habits in full force. We prefer the cognitive ease of this kind of thinking, as it is nearly effortless. That's why we prefer the quick thinking of "blink" to the cognitive strain, the mental effort involved with "think." "Just stop and think about it," we sometimes have to tell one another, when we are ready to make a decision. Or we ask, "Have you really thought this through?" In such instances, we acknowledge Kahneman's **System II thinking.** We need both of these thinking systems, but we need to be aware of when and where, how and why we use each of them. And we also need to be aware of the uses and the limitations of each system—of thinking fast, and of thinking slow.

Kahneman identifies a series of biases and heuristics that govern and influence much of our thinking. For example, he uses the acronym WYSIATI to stand for "What you see is all there is." When we believe WYSIATI, we are likely to make judgments and decisions on insufficient information, on a too-small sample, on inadequate evidence. When we do that, we often make mistakes. WYSIATI errors are related to overconfidence that the pattern we detect in the information and evidence we have is a pattern of value and importance, and that it is a pattern that explains things in a way that allows for accurate predictions about what will happen next. But this is less a matter of fact than a matter of faith. And our faith in WYSIATI often confirms what we want to believe, what we hope for, rather than what might actually be the case. WYSIATI confirms our biases.

The problem we have fundamentally about knowing how things really are and what we might predict from them about the future is that we don't really know what we don't know. As Kahneman puts it, we're "blind to our own blindness."

In a book about the failure of prediction and forecasting, *The Signal and the Noise,* Nate Silver offers three common reasons for the persistence of these kinds of errors. First, Silver says that we focus on signals—information and details—that convey a story or embody a picture of the world less as it is, than as we believe it to be. Second, he suggests that we exaggerate positive potential outcomes for ourselves while wildly downplaying risks, all the while ignoring the risks that are hardest to measure. Third, he notes that the assumptions we make about "reality"—the world as it is—are typically far rougher and cruder than we realize. We have a distaste for uncertainty and ambiguity, even when—especially when—ambiguity and uncertainty are an inescapable and intractable part of what we are trying to understand—earthquakes or economic behavior, for example, or the irrational exuberance people feel when they gamble.

EXERCISES

20. Select two of the following questions and answer each in a paragraph.

   a. To what extent can we trust our perceptions? To what extent is perception a reliable source of knowledge?

   b. Why don't we often see what is right in front of our noses? Why do we occasionally see things that aren't there at all?

   c. How can we prepare ourselves to see things from the perspective of others? To what extent is this possible?

   d. How does our description of what we see (or someone else's description of it) affect how we see it and respond to it?

   e. How can we minimize the role our emotions play in perception? And should we try to do this?

21. Why do you suppose that Freud could not remember his patient's name and that Schulz seems unable to forget her mistake about pronouncing the name of Goethe? To what extent do you think the forgetting and remembering are related to the seriousness of the incident?

22. What benefits can we take away from Daniel Kahneman's analysis of our propensity to overestimate our knowledge and our ability to predict what will happen in the future? How useful do you find his discussion of WYSIATI? Of his idea that we are "blind to our own blindness"?

23. What does Silver add to your understanding of the challenges that confront us as we attempt to understand how things work in the world?

Why Are Political Experts So Often Mistaken?

One example of error from the field of political science is identified in the journal *Critical Review*, in an issue devoted to *Expert Political Judgment* by Philip E. Tetlock, who describes the inaccurate predictions frequently made by political experts. Even with data and statistical models at their disposal, political analysts make mistakes in their predictions about a wide range of outcomes. Why might this be so? In part, it derives from the sheer difficulty of predicting the future. It also derives from the limitations of facts, data, and information, which need to be accounted for when designing and applying theories and methods. Finally, it can derive from the human tendency to be influenced by belief and ideology, which lead us (and the experts) to make predictions that conform to our (and their) beliefs and ideologies.

Political experts defend their mistakes by arguing that the real value of expert political **prediction** lies not in prediction per se, but in more subtle (and valuable) arts of interpretation and analysis. One of the ironies of the debates about Tetlock's analysis is this kind of **justification**, which Tetlock calls "nowcasting," or "predicting the present." Political experts may be poor forecasters of the future, but they can be valuable explainers of the present. By a simple act of extrapolation, the argument is made that knowing and understanding where we are politically is a necessary prerequisite for knowing what should come next, what political decisions might be made, and what policy directions might be taken.

The biggest obstacle for political forecasting (or indeed of any kind of prediction making) is uncertainty, particularly uncertainty in the long run. And because most things in life and the world at large are uncertain, they are fundamentally unpredictable. Weather forecasters, for example, are notorious for their inaccuracy when they venture out beyond strict limits—more than a few days. They are good at predicting the weather for the next day or two, worse at prognosticating a week or two, and clueless about weather specifics a few months or a year away.

Predicting the behavior of societal action, whether political or economic, social or cultural, is even more challenging. Nonetheless, economists issue forecasts about jobs and housing prices, criminologists predict trends in criminal activity, and political scientists are not shy about boldly predicting the behavior and fortunes of major world powers. Most of their predictions fail to materialize, but, ironically, that does not diminish either the confidence pundits have in their own knowledge or their confidence in their future predictive prowess.

The reason for such confidence is largely that experts know so much about the past and the present that they assume it is useful for predicting the future. A second reason is that people tend to be in awe of experts; we fail to call them on their missed predictions. We also want to believe in their ability to discern patterns of

prediction
A declaration in advance that something will happen; an expectation of something that is to come.

justification
The process of providing reasoned evidence to support, or "justify" an argument, decision, or choice.

⊙ **Simulate** the
Experiment, Politics and
Error **MyThinkingLab**

explanation. We have a hard time with randomness and an even harder time with uncertainty. And thus we are ripe for belief in the illusory power of prediction by experts of every stripe.

EXERCISE

24. Do you think someone who has become an expert in international relations, particularly the study of a particular region of the world, such as Southeast Asia, Latin America, or the Middle East, should be better at predicting possible outcomes of political developments in those places? Why or why not? Do you think that even if political experts are poor at predicting what will happen, they are of significant value in explaining present events, such as the protests in Egypt, Lebanon, Yemen, and Syria, where citizens are demanding more open and less autocratic societies?

Intuitions and Rationalizations

In *The Righteous Mind,* Jonathan Haidt argues that much of our thinking is driven by intuitions based on feelings. What we typically do in our thinking, Haidt claims, is to develop after-the-fact explanations—rationalizations primarily—for our beliefs. Further, he suggests that this post hoc justification for our beliefs is prevalent in all kinds of thinking, regardless of the subject of that thinking.

In short, we use thinking to confirm our beliefs rather than to consider them rationally; our reasoning is motivated by self-justification. Evidence that confirms what we believe, we accept. Evidence that contradicts what we believe, we reject.

Haidt goes so far as to suggest that the prominence we give reason in our own thinking and the thinking of others is a form of delusion. Our conviction that reason is paramount in thinking he calls "the rational delusion." And so an even-handed, fair-minded analysis and exploration of beliefs, ideas, and evidence is a rare exception rather than the rule. Thinking more often than not tends to confirm our beliefs by rationalizing our point of view. Haidt finds this to be the case almost without exception when moral issues and questions are at stake.

Haidt does not suggest that we are always mistaken about ideas or that it is necessarily wrong to follow our intuitions. He argues, instead, that we are wrong to believe that reason drives our thinking when the psychological studies he cites and those he has conducted himself provide evidence that intuition comes first and that reason follows.

The Pleasures and Benefits of Error

Although errors can be annoying, disconcerting, even painful, they can also be amusing, serendipitous, and even productive. Errors and mistakes are something we can smile about and laugh at en route to seeing and accepting ourselves as fallible beings. Errors can be amusing, and stories about our mistakes and faux pas, if nothing else, can serve as fodder for entertaining conversation.

Much of the comedy in drama and film turns on error. One of the most famous examples is Shakespeare's play *The Comedy of Errors,* which is based on an ancient Roman play, *The Menaechmi,* by the Roman comic dramatist Plautus. Both Shakespeare's adaptation and Plautus's original play turn on cases of mistaken identity and other forms of misunderstanding and error. Many television comedy shows during the last half-century also involve plots involving a wide variety of mistakes, errors, and misunderstandings, including *I Love Lucy*, *The Honeymooners*, *Laurel and Hardy*, *Abbot and Costello* (with the famous sketch, "Who's on First?"), as well as shows of more recent vintage, such as *Seinfeld*, *Friends*, *30 Rock*, and *The Office*.

Mistakes and errors can lead us to discoveries we would not have arrived at without them. And, in the best of circumstances, our mistakes can lead us to positive and productive outcomes. For artists, accepting, even embracing error, allows for exploration, risk-taking, and the confidence to make something new. In a way, all art gets things wrong in terms of misrepresenting things as they are. In the process, however, in changing things as they are and imagining them otherwise, artists create new ways of seeing and understanding.

For scientists, whose goal is objectivity pursued through rational means rather than the subjective and imaginative direction of the artist, error is often a route to truth. A scientific researcher takes the errors involved in an experiment to arrive at a satisfactory result, whether this leads to the development of a new drug or a new treatment for a disease, a new invention, a new model of car or appliance, or a better way to do just about anything. Every invention and every discovery includes error in its development. Perhaps the most amazing example is the error of mutation in biology, which leads to variation in a species, a mechanism for survival and a facet of evolution.

EXERCISES

25. To what extent do you think Jonathan Haidt is right in his claim that our thinking is more confirmatory than exploratory, and that we react with intuition and feelings that we subsequently seek to justify?

26. Do you think it is easier to convince people to change their minds by logical reasoning or by considering their intuitions and beliefs? What happens mostly in moral and political discussions when you dispute, criticize, attack, correct, or otherwise attempt to change someone's position or perspective? To what extent do you think Haidt's theory of thinking explains this behavior?

27. Identify a current television comedy or movie you have seen that turns on some kind of error or mistake. Explain what is amusing about that error and what the actors and director make of it. To what extent do you agree with Schulz that error can be useful, beneficial, and productive? To what extent do you find her examples persuasive?

The Perspective of Philosophy

Philosophy offers an approach to establishing knowledge and evaluating evidence. Epistemology, the branch of philosophy concerned with the study of the nature of knowledge, considers both the possibility of and the scope of knowledge. It investigates how we know what we know and what we think we know. Among the questions explored by epistemology are "What is knowledge?" And: "How can we justify our knowledge of what we think to be true?" These questions are fundamental to any attempt to think seriously about every aspect of our lives—from the choices we make on a daily basis to our major life decisions, from whom to trust to what to believe when we listen to political leaders. Knowledge and belief, mistrust and skepticism are part of our epistemological practice, as much as are confidence and certainty in what we think we know.

Epistemology, thus, provides a theory of knowledge. But we might also describe it as a theory of doubt. This is so because much of what we believe and think we know cannot be conclusively proven either rationally (through logical reasoning) or empirically (through sense-based evidence). The seventeenth-century French philosopher René Descartes, who first said, "I think, therefore, I am" ("*cogito, ergo sum*"), began his philosophical investigation by doubting everything. The one thing he could be certain of is that he could think (and doubt). Hence, because he could not doubt himself as a thinking being and a doubting being, he built his theory of knowledge on that supposition.

A second major question of epistemology is whether the objective world exists, or whether it is a figment of the imagination. The classic question about if a tree falls in a forest and no one hears it, does the sound actually exist?—represents one illustration of this question.

Knowledge, Certainty, and Belief

Knowledge is sometimes defined as "justified true belief"—a belief we have that turns out to be correct, accurate ("true") and for which we can provide evidence to justify our belief that it is true. How much evidence and what kind of evidence qualifies for a belief to be considered "true," for a belief to qualify as "knowledge?"

We might respond by saying that what we need are reasonably good grounds for our beliefs to be considered knowledge. This response assumes at least two things: (1) that we can't be certain of most of our knowledge; (2) that we can be mistaken even when we have good grounds for believing something to be true. The grounds we have for justifying our belief that something is true are the observations we make and the connections between them. The inferences we draw from those connected observations can be accurate or inaccurate, right or wrong—even when the "evidence" of our observations points reasonably in a particular direction.

Consider the following example, provided by Stephen Law in his book *Philosophy*. You hear water drops hitting the window and see them trickling down the glass against the background of a dark sky. A friend enters shaking a wet umbrella and leaving wet footprints across the floor while complaining about the rain. From these details, you possess excellent grounds for believing it is raining. Yet you might be wrong, as your friend may have placed a lawn sprinkler against the glass to simulate rain.

What seems like "knowledge" in this example is more like "error." We might wonder then what the opposite of knowledge can be—a question Marjorie Garber asks in her book *Loaded Words*. Among the prospects she offers are "ignorance," "uncertainty," undecidability," and "belief." Garber then wonders what the opposite of *belief* might be, offering options that include *unbelief, disbelief, doubt, certainty,* and *knowledge.*" In considering such a range of options and in thinking of the terms *knowledge* and *belief* together, we realize that there is more to their difference than a simple matter of seeing one as settled truth and the other as mere opinion. A further complication is that for some people *knowledge* is the term to be exalted as *truth*; for others *belief* warrants that honor.

As Garber says, these terms are both "loaded" and "empty." The terms are "loaded," because they convey multiple meanings and implications; the terms are "empty" because they mean so many different things in various disciplines and situations. As a result, they are not really adequate as terms of understanding. They simply don't help us understand very much.

Moreover, what was once "belief" or "knowledge" can become obsolete, such that what appears certain at one time—certain knowledge or justified true belief—can be superseded or be proven incorrect. One among many examples is the scientific theory of "phlogiston," which held sway in the eighteenth century as the explanation for why things catch on fire. Other examples include the policies and practices of National Socialism, or Nazism; the eugenics movement; the use of electroshock therapy for mental illnesses; theories of racial inferiority and superiority and their political implications—to cite a few. As with phlogiston, which served as the basis for understanding and explaining chemical reactions far beyond combustion, and which has been discredited, these other downgraded forms of knowledge serve as cautionary examples of how elusive a concept certain knowledge can be.

Moral Questions

Among the most important questions we can consider are those involving moral and ethical issues. In his book *Justice*, Michael Sandel asks to what extent we can reason our way through questions of justice and injustice, equality and inequality, and how we might go about doing so. He suggests that in considering difficult moral questions we begin with a view, an opinion, a conviction about "the right thing to do." He asks, for example, that you imagine you are driving a trolley car speeding down a track when you notice five workers standing up ahead on the track. You try to stop your trolley, but the brakes don't work. You assume that if you crash into the helpless workers they will be killed. At a glance, however, you notice a side track with only a single worker. If you turn the trolley onto that track, you will kill the one worker, but the others will live. Should you do this? If you say, "yes," what assumptions have you made about human life? What position are you deciding from?

But consider this slightly different scenario: You are now an onlooker from a bridge above the track, and there is no side track. A train is speeding toward those five workers and there is no driver to stop it. You notice standing nearby a large man, whom, if you pushed onto the track, could stop the trolley before it hit the five workers. What would you do? Why? Sandel asks us to consider the difference in these two difficult moral dilemma scenarios. And he invites us to consider how we would decide what would be the right thing to do in each case.

EXERCISES

28. How does the criminal justice system use epistemology in asking a jury to determine a defendant's guilt or innocence? What is the jury actually asked to do in a criminal trial? (That is, how does "doubt" factor into their decision? What place is "doubt" allowed to play in their verdict?)

29. In his *Theory of Knowledge*, Richard van de Lagemaat proposes that we think of belief and knowledge in terms of a continuum—a spectrum—that ranges from the impossible through the possible and on to the certain:

−10	−5	0	+5	+10
Impossible	Unlikely	Possible	Probable (BELIEF)	Certain (KNOWLEDGE)

Put the following different beliefs on the continuum:

a. Eating six walnuts a day is good for your heart.

b. American astronauts planted the American flag on the moon.

c. People are descended from apes.

d. Other universes exist; aliens exist in some of them.

e. There is life after death.

30. Whatever you decide about Sandel's two-trolley scenarios, to what extent would you want to discuss the moral implications of your decision with others? To what extent might such a discussion be a political discussion? To what extent might it be a religious discussion? How would we go about deciding with others what principles should underlie a decision about "the right thing to do" in such complex circumstances?

31. In 1980, a CEO earned, on average about 40 times what an average worker earned. In 2007, CEOs earned more than 340 times the salary of that same average worker. Also, for the period 2004–2006, CEOs at top US companies earned on average approximately twice the compensation of top European CEOs. Is there a moral issue here? Or is this simply a question of economic market supply and demand?

Small-Scale Ethical Challenges

In a collection of philosophical provocations, *The Pig That Wants to Be Eaten*, Julian Baggini offers a set of thought experiments. Among the *100 Experiments for the Armchair Philosopher*, (the subtitle of Baggini's book), are a number that present ethical dilemmas. One of them involves a bank error in your favor. Suppose, Baggini asks, in withdrawing $100 from an ATM, the machine mistakenly gives you $10,000 instead. When you look at the receipt for the transaction, it reads $100. Moreover, in checking your account balance at the ATM and again later online, you find that your account was debited for only $100.

You begin thinking that this is truly a lucky break and a real windfall for you. But you wonder whether, in time, a few days or weeks, the bank will catch the error. So you decide to put the money somewhere safe, just not in that account. After a few months, when no one notifies you, you consider the money yours. After all, you reason, "I didn't steal it; it was just presented to me." It was the bank's mistake. Besides, aren't banks insured for all kinds of losses, this one included?

Baggini argues that we should have qualms about this because the money doesn't really belong to us, and that we should return it. If a cashier returned you $20 in change instead of $10, would you keep it? Or would you identify the mistake, so it wouldn't come out of the cashier's earnings when the mistake was later found?

The principle at work, Baggini argues, is fairness; it's not fair to take advantage of others' mistakes, especially if they are going to be hurt by them. Furthermore, if we deal with a particular individual from time to time, we would feel guilty in taking advantage of his or her mistake even more. But that might not be the case with a "faceless" large corporation, like a bank.

On the other hand, if you think keeping the money is justified on the basis that the bank won't really "feel" the loss, you might also justify shoplifting items from stores, using the same argument. But Baggini claims that this doesn't seem right; it certainly involves your doing something yourself actively—going into the store and actually "stealing" merchandise. In the case of the ATM error, it just happened. That money just kept coming out of the machine; it's as if you had won the lottery. Or is it? What is the right, or ethical, thing to do in this situation?

Whose Ball Is It?

For a number of years, the *New York Times Sunday Magazine*, has carried a column under the heading "The Ethicist." In these weekly columns, Randy Cohen, the

Ethicist, presented two or three short letters he received, each of which focused on an ethical dilemma. In his capacity as ethicist, Cohen responded to the articles with something like "No"; "Yes"; "No, unless"; or "Yes, but."

One letter came from a woman who described how her husband and 11-year-old son had attended a major league Red Sox baseball game. At the game, when a foul ball was hit and not caught by the fielder, he tossed it to the boy, who had "coaxed" him to do so. Another father sitting nearby with his own son offered the boy who got the ball $30 for it so he could give it to his son, sitting with him. The first boy's father told his son to ask for $50. After a quick negotiation, they agreed on a price of $40. All parties seemed pleased with the transaction, including the woman's husband, who told her it was a good lesson for their son in "supply and demand." The woman, however, felt uneasy about the situation and wrote seeking the ethicist's response.

EXERCISES

32. The first question to ask about this baseball scenario is whether there is an ethical issue at stake here at all. What do you think? The second question is whether you agree with the boy's father about the lesson taught and learned regarding "supply and demand." Are there any other "lessons" being taught and learned in this little scenario? If so, what are they?

33. A third consideration is to look closely at the description of the scenario. What inferences do you make based on the details provided? What do you infer from the word *coaxed*? What might the 11-year-old boy have done to get the Red Sox player to toss him the ball? And what inference can we make about the player as he tossed the ball to the boy in the stands? To what extent do the inferences you make about these matters affect your judgment about the father's and boy's decision to sell the ball? Does it make any difference what price they sold the ball for? Why or why not?

34. What arguments would you make to support the mother's feelings of uneasiness at the transaction?

Looking Back and Looking Ahead

Revisit the learning goals that begin this chapter. Which of these goals do you think you have best achieved? What might you do to reach the remaining goals?

Return to the focusing questions at the beginning of the chapter. How would you answer those questions now? Which of them do you find most interesting and provocative and worthy of following up? Why?

In reviewing the list of resources that follows this section, identify the two that attract you most. Explain why these books or Web sites interest you. Consider looking into them for further developing and deepening your ability to think critically.

Take a look, too, at the MyThinkingLab resources on the Prentice Hall Web site. Included there are readings, images, videos, questions, exercises, and other provocations to help you develop your critical thinking prowess.

• •

Resources

Think Critically, 2nd edition, Peter Facione and Carol Gittens. Pearson, 2012.

Theory of Knowledge, Richard van de Lagemaat. Cambridge University Press, 2006.

Conceptual Blockbusting, James L. Adams. Perseus Books, 2001.

Intellectual Character, Ron Ritchhart. Jossey-Bass, 2004.

Art and Visual Perception, Rudolf Arnheim. University of California Press, 1971.

Art and Illusion, E. H. Gombrich. Princeton University Press, 1960 .

The Invisible Gorilla, Christopher Chabris and Daniel Simons. HarperCollins, 2010.

"Mind and Matter: The Gorilla Lurking Where We Can't See It," Alison Gopnik. *The Wall Street Journal*, August 10–11, 2013.

A Kick in the Seat of the Pants, Roger Von Oech. William Morrow Paperbacks, 1986.

Being Wrong, Kathryn Schulz. Ecco, 2011.

Thinking, Fast and Slow, Daniel Kahneman. Farrar, Straus and Giroux, 2011.

The Signal and the Noise, Nate Silver. Penguin Press, 2012.

The Righteous Mind, Jonathan Haidt. Pantheon, 2012.

Drunk Tank Pink, Adam Alter. Penguin Press, 2013.

Expert Political Judgment, Philip E. Tetlock. Princeton University Press, 2006.

Philosophy, Stephen Law. DK Publishing, 2007.

Loaded Words, Marjorie Garber. Fordham University Press, 2012.

Justice, Michael Sandel. Farrar, Straus and Giroux, 2010.

The Pig That Wants to Be Eaten, Julian Baggini. Penguin/Plume, 2006.

Habits of Mind Web site: http://www.habitsofmind.org/

Richard van de Lagemaat Web site: http://www.inthinking.co.uk

• •

2

Developing Creative Thinking

To cease to think creatively is but little different from ceasing to live.

—BEN FRANKLIN

LEARNING GOALS

2.1 UNDERSTAND the elements of creative thinking.

2.2 RECOGNIZE major obstacles to creative thinking and how to avoid them.

2.3 IDENTIFY strategies to think creatively and begin using them.

2.4 UNDERSTAND the value of key questions and how to generate them and build on them.

2.5 EXPLORE and practice techniques to become a more creative thinker.

Chapter Overview

This chapter introduces the concept of creative thinking as a complementary alternative to critical thinking. The chapter includes a number of ideas about creativity. A variety of techniques and strategies are provided to develop creative thinking capacities. The central notion of the chapter is that creative thinking can be fostered and enhanced through desire and with practice. The essence of creative thinking is making something new—a new product or process—often by combining elements of what already exists.

FOCUSING QUESTIONS

- What does creativity mean to you? To what extent do you see yourself as a creative person?

- What examples of creative thinking do you admire, and why?

- In what ways in your everyday life do you find creative solutions to problems?

- To what extent do you believe that creative thinking is important for you—and for all of us, and not just for especially talented creative types of people?

- What might you do to develop your creative thinking capacities?

What Is Creative Thinking and Why Do We Need It?

◉ **Watch** the **Video**,
What is Creative Thinking
and Why Do We Need It?
MyThinkingLab

creative thinking
The purposeful generation and
implementation of novel ideas.

alternatives
In creative thinking, an
additional choice or possibility
that fosters the generation of
new ideas.

imagination
The faculty of forming mental
ideas, images, or concepts
that are not perceived through
the five senses.

creativity
The use of imagination and/or
intuition in the production of
original things or ideas.

Creative thinking is imaginative thinking directed toward innovation. Creative thinking is based on questions that ask "what if," "why," or "why not," "how," and "how else?" Creative thinking is grounded in the consideration of **alternatives**, of other possibilities, other ways of seeing and doing. At the heart of creative thinking is **imagination**, which the American philosopher John Dewey defined as looking at things "as if they could be otherwise." The goal of creative thinking is to develop new insights, novel approaches, fresh perspectives, and alternative ways of understanding.

Some characteristics of creative thinking include the following: being open to new ideas; believing that alternatives exist; being able to defer judgment; being willing to generate multiple alternative approaches to solving problems; trying novel approaches and generating new ideas. Creative thinkers exhibit fluency and flexibility of thought; they use metaphor, analogy, and visualization to make connections and explore ideas from varied perspectives. Creative thinking is associated with imagination, innovation, originality, lateral thinking, divergent thinking, and "out-of-the-box thinking."

Creativity is the ability to build something from nothing. It is also the ability to think of a common idea in an uncommon way, the ability to move a concept, task, idea, or product in new directions. Creativity has been considered under the aspect of problem solving and as a type of improvisation, in the manner of jazz musicians creating something together that did not exist until they performed it in their unique manner. Richard Florida, in *The Rise of the Creative Class Revisited*, locates creativity at the "intersection of novelty, utility, and surprise."

Dispositions and attitudes that foster creative thinking include patience and perseverance, along with a speculative sense of wonder. They include curiosity, playfulness, and a positive frame of mind; they also require seeing mistakes as opportunities to learn, welcoming challenges and difficulties, and being willing to follow intuition and instinct. In addition, creative thinking involves self-direction and initiative, and a "can-do attitude," along with a desire to explore rather than prove, to consider rather than argue.

Why do we need creative thinking? We need creative thinking because it provides a necessary complementary balance to the analytical, rational, and logical powers of critical thinking. Where critical thinking utilizes our left-brain capacities, creative thinking uses our right-brain potentialities. We need both kinds of thinking skills if we are to develop our minds fully; we need both kinds of thinking to make full use of our mental capacities.

Core Creative Thinking Capacities

Among the core creative thinking skills are observing and noticing deeply; questioning and reflecting on what we notice; envisioning or picturing things mentally; wondering and speculating about what could or might be; asking questions upon questions upon questions; engaging with problems and challenges and patiently persisting and persevering with and through them. At the heart of creative thinking is imagination, which is of prime importance. A key factor in creativity is satisfying constraints. Limitations imposed by constraints release the imagination; a chef, for example, creates a new dish out of a limited number of ingredients, a department finds effective ways to work with fewer resources, a poet works within the confines of a highly prescriptive literary form.

Essential Creative Thinking Questions

Among the essential creative thinking skills are "How else can I view or consider this?" "What alternative explanations might there be?" "What would other people see or say that I might not have considered?" Creative thinkers ask, "why not" as often as they ask "why?" They regularly ask, "what if?" They worry less about whether something can be done than about how it can be done. They maintain a questioning attitude in a positive light—with an outlook that indicates promise and possibility and one that looks at problems and challenges from multiple perspectives.

What Creative Thinkers Do

Creative thinkers exhibit a wide range of behaviors; they:

- Ask persistent and insistent questions.
- Maintain a sense of wonder about the world.
- Are deeply and constantly curious.
- Play with things and with ideas.
- Experiment and explore.
- Collect and connect things.
- Tinker and tinker some more.
- Are positive and optimistic.
- Learn from error and failure.

Seeking Alternatives and Possibilities

One general definition of creativity is "the purposeful generation and implementation of a novel idea." Selling books online, now a commonplace event, exemplifies such an idea. So does buying songs singly, as compared with purchasing them bundled as "albums," which itself was once a new idea. Creativity involves the ability to think of a common idea in an uncommon way, and the ability to take a concept, task, idea, or product and move it in new directions. With creativity, something new and useful is generated, developed, and implemented.

A recent article in *Scientific American Mind* stresses the importance of keeping an open mind as an essential disposition that facilitates creative thinking. But what does it mean to keep "an open mind"? Generally, an open mind is one in which minimal rules and constraints guide the thinking process. According to recent psychological studies, creative thinking appears to benefit from a lessening of cognitive control—from fewer limitations and guidelines that direct our thinking. Interestingly, and paradoxically however, creative thinking can also be stimulated by an opposite situation, one in which constraints and limitations provoke fresh solutions to problems.

An illustration of how an open mind can stimulate creative thinking involves considering different ways of categorizing objects, as for example, thinking of different uses for an everyday object such as a safety pin, a brick, or a metal clothes hanger. A second and related example is to describe objects in unusual ways, as for example, in terms of features rather than functions, in terms of their elements or aspects rather than according to their primary purpose. And a third way to foster open-minded thinking is to consider how common tasks might be performed in an unconventional or unusual order—preparing a sandwich, for example, in an unconventional way. These and other mental exercises have been found by researchers to stimulate creative thinking in terms of developing what has been called "cognitive flexibility."

Among the most important aspects of creative thinking is developing a mindset that seeks alternatives, that looks for different ways of understanding a situation, arriving at a judgment, making a decision, solving a problem. In such cases, we frequently try to choose the best solution from a number of options. Often we need to generate the options or possibilities ourselves from which to choose. Cultivating a habit of seeking alternatives and possibilities is an important first step in the process.

Quota of Alternatives

Simulate the Experiment, Quota of Alternatives and APC (Alternatives, Possibilities, Choices) **MyThinkingLab**

One way to seek alternatives is to establish a quota, an arbitrary number of alternatives to be considered. In deciding on an approach to solving a problem or undertaking a project, for example, it is best not to settle on the first approach that comes to mind. Instead, we should set ourselves a quota—four or five possibilities, perhaps—before deciding on one of them. Similarly, in considering how to implement a chosen approach, we might set a quota of three or four different ways to do so.

The main reason for using a quota strategy to generate possibilities is that it gives us a chance to come up with something better (or at least different) than our initial idea. And in the event that that first thought is actually the best one, we have the comfort of having considered alternatives and found them not as useful. In addition, even if we select the first idea, thinking through other possibilities might influence the way the initial idea is developed, thereby extending or enriching it in an initially unforeseen way.

quota-of-alternatives
In creative thinking, a technique to push thinking beyond the first things that come to mind with the goal of discovering something surprising and interesting.

We can practice applying the **quota-of-alternatives** technique by considering the following scenario:

> Each weekday morning, a woman takes the elevator in her office building to the tenth floor. She gets out there and walks up the sixteenth floor, where her office is located. After work, she enters the elevator on the sixteenth floor and rides down to the first floor. She then exits and heads home.

One possible explanation for the woman's behavior is that she uses the bathroom on the tenth floor, the only floor between 10 and 16 with bathrooms. Another is that she stops to meet her supervisor, who works on the tenth floor. We can, of course, consider other explanations for the woman's elevator-riding behavior. To do so, we might set ourselves a quota that includes a few very likely possibilities and some others that are more far-fetched. The idea is to push ourselves beyond the conventional explanations for her behavior, to stretch our imaginations.

APC (Alternatives, Possibilities, Choices)

In his book *Serious Creativity* Edward de Bono uses the terms *alternatives, possibilities*, and *choices* more or less interchangeably. In some cases, one or another of these terms may seem more natural or readily helpful. They mean the same thing, essentially.

Why might it be useful to consider alternatives and different approaches to a question or problem? The main reason is that we often find more and better ideas when we consider such alternatives. It helps us develop our capacity for thinking;

it enables us to see more than two "sides"; it pushes us beyond simple and too easily satisfied explanations; and it increases our choices and encourages us to see more shades and shadows, to consider issues and ideas, problems and solutions along more of a spectrum of possibilities. In short, this simple tool stretches our thinking beyond what is typical, comfortable, or easy for us. It broadens our perception.

EXERCISES

1. In two minutes each, describe as many uses as you can for each of the following: a safety pin, a brick, a pencil, a thin flat piece of cardboard 8.5 × 11 inches.

2. Describe an unorthodox way of doing each of the following, that is, reorder the usual steps of the process: making a sandwich; eating a sandwich; cleaning a room; preparing to attend a social event; fulfilling a school or work assignment.

3. For each of the following, provide three alternative explanations or approaches.

    a. Discouraging people from driving their cars into the center of a city.

    b. Encouraging people to donate money to charity.

    c. Dealing with a school bully.

    d. Sustaining interest in a project over a long period of time.

    e. Meeting deadlines for work projects.

4. Set yourself a quota of alternatives for one of the following: improving your salary, saving money, losing weight, increasing the amount of reading, or exercise you do.

5. Describe the following figures as many different ways as you can. Identify at least five.

(a)   (b)

Broadening Perception

In addition to APC (alternatives, possibilities, choices), Edward de Bono's thinking tools include others that help broaden our perception, including expanding the possible ways we look at the world. De Bono notes that David Perkins of Harvard University has suggested that most errors of thinking are errors of perception, which is one reason these tools are especially important.

PMI (Plus, Minus, Interesting)

A thinking strategy useful for generating and evaluating ideas is PMI—plus, minus, interesting. This is another of de Bono's perception broadening tools; it encourages us to think beyond our normal binary analysis of pluses and minuses, positives and negatives as we consider an issue. De Bono adds the notion of "interesting," for aspects of an idea that are neither pluses nor minuses, but are, nonetheless, interesting to think about. This, in itself, is an "interesting" approach.

PMI, a perception-broadening tool, is designed to focus attention, first, only on the positive features of a subject, then only on its negative features, and finally on any interesting features (neither positive nor negative ones). Our usual tendency is to bounce back and forth between positive and negative aspects, and not even to consider anything else—"interesting" features, for example. PMI can enable the discovery of "interesting" aspects of a problem or situation, especially if we preface the search for them with words such as, "It is interesting to consider . . . ." OR: "I wonder whether . . . ."

While doing a PMI, a number of things can happen. We may change our minds about a subject or an idea. We may retain our original feeling about it. We might generate new ideas after considering the "interesting" aspects.

In doing a PMI, it is important to think in one direction at a time—first all the pluses, then all the minuses, and last the "interesting" notions. And then a further push to consider other "interesting" aspects of the topic.

EXERCISE

6. Do a PMI on one of the following proposals:

   a. Children should be paid to attend school.

   b. Teachers should be rewarded financially for successful student performance.

   c. Schools should be open year round, but on a four-day school week.

   d. US Presidents should be able to serve a single six-year term and only one such term.

   e. US Supreme Court Judges should have a 10-year term limit.

Reversing Relationships

Explore the **Concept**, Reversing Relationships **MyThinkingLab**

Another strategy for considering alternatives is to reverse relationships. Sometimes we refer to this as "flipping," "spinning," or considering another person's point of view. One possibility is to consider the opposing arguments for and against a public policy—first from say a liberal (or Democratic) perspective and then from a conservative (or Republican perspective). One example might be the legalization of illegal immigrants currently residing in the United States. This kind of mental shifting helps us understand the "logic" of conflicting viewpoints; it helps us better understand "the other side," so we can support our counterarguments.

reversing relationships
A creative thinking process that promotes considering the implications of an opposite perspective or point of view.

Reversing relationships can spur reconsideration and rethinking. It can broaden our perspective so that even if we wind up adhering to our initial point of view, we can at least begin to appreciate that there are other viable and reasonable ways of considering an issue. It might also have the benefit of enabling us to see that though we may disagree with the position of "the other side," there is some logic and merit to the way of thinking that led to that other position.

In addition, sometimes reversing relationships can lead us to new and deeper insights about a topic, or help solve a problem.

Our human ancestors once were preoccupied with getting to the water hole. At a later stage, they reversed this approach by getting the water to themselves. Something similar occurred with foraging for plants and hunting animals when both became domesticated, leading eventually to farms and slaughterhouses.

To create a work of art one typically thinks of building it up, adding materials, including sculpture. Michelangelo reversed that direction when he "subtracted" his David from a huge block of marble. Or consider how the following lines from a poem by Emily Dickinson reverse a typical way of thinking: "Much Madness is divinest Sense / … Much Sense—the starkest Madness." In what sense might it be true that what appears to be "madness"—something seemingly crazy—carries with it a kind of sense (and maybe even a "divine" sense)? And in what sense, conversely, might something seemingly sensible, possibly be considered the opposite—madness or craziness?

Reversing relationships in this way can spur us to think more creatively by enabling us to break away from fixed ways of thinking and from conventional ideas. As with setting a quota of alternatives, reversing relationships can help us generate new and different ideas.

EXERCISES

7. Provide an example to illustrate the "madness—sense" reversal suggested by Dickinson's poem. Consider how the following paradoxes illustrate reversing relationships: To save your life you must first lose it. To rise you first must fall. To lead you need to follow. To succeed you need first to fail.

8. Take one of the following pieces of "common sense," and reverse it.

   Example: If something's worth doing, it's worth doing well.

   Reversal: It's OK to do it poorly—at least at first. If you insist on doing it well, you may never do it at all. Worrying about how well you're doing anything can prevent you from stretching yourself and trying new things—which you probably won't do very well in the beginning.

   a. Patience is a virtue.

   b. Haste makes waste.

   c. Business before pleasure.

   d. Too many cooks spoil the soup.

   e. Curiosity killed the cat.

Cross-fertilization

With cross-fertilization, we apply the ways of thinking about one kind of activity to another. For example, we might use the vocabulary of football to talk about business or the vocabulary of war to talk about love (to make an "assault" or an "advance")—or the vocabulary of war to talk about football (throwing a "bomb," for example, or "blitzing" the quarterback). We might take concepts from the graphic arts—color, line, pattern, texture—and apply them to music, literature, or fashion. Or we might take a concept from physics—for example, the concept of centripetal force or escape velocity—and apply it to a problem in economics or social psychology.

Cross-fertilization is a special kind of analogical thinking, a way of seeing relationships between things that are not normally related. Like other creative thinking techniques, cross-fertilization involves an act of imagination. Its method, essentially, is to force what Michael Michalko has described as a kind of "conceptual blending," by combining elements from different realms, domains, areas of reference. The purpose of cross-fertilization is to shake up conventional thinking patterns and push thinking in new and unexpected directions. Cross-fertilization is closely related to analogical thinking and **metaphorical thinking,** which also involve making connections among disparate things.

Shifting Attention

Still another strategy for developing a capacity for creative thinking is to shift attention from one facet of a problem, one aspect of a situation, to another. In writing a report about the effects of excessive drinking, we might think of large-scale social effects—of the impact of alcoholism on work productivity and its cost to businesses, or its impact on the cost of health care nationwide. A shift of attention from this kind of macroconsideration to a smaller-scale microaspect could help generate additional ideas.

We might consider, for example, the costs of alcohol abuse to a drinker's family and friends—to his or her personal relationships. We might also consider the effects on the drinker both physically and psychologically. Still another shift would be from the effects of alcoholism to its causes. Considering causes sends our thinking in another direction; it helps generate new ideas by coming at the topic or problem from another angle. Why do people turn to alcohol in the first place, we might ask? Whether all these aspects are eventually included in the report doesn't matter. What's important at this stage is to generate ideas to think about. And for this process, **shifting attention** can be helpful.

Consider how the shift of attention in the following anecdote leads to the solution of the problem:

> As a man is driving home from work, his car comes to a halt. Lifting up the hood, he notices that he has a broken fan belt. He looks for something he can use to replace the fan belt so he can drive a short distance to a service station, where he can have the car repaired properly. His solution: He remembers that he is wearing a tie, which he takes off and ties tightly in the fan belt position. He drives to the nearest station and replaces the fan belt. With the money he saves on a towing charge, he buys a new tie.

Michael Michalko refers to this kind of shift as a change in "perceptual positions," and he suggests that our perceptual positions influence and even determine how we see things. Rotating our perceptual positions so that we can see things from multiple perspectives, in particular from another person's point of view, is an especially useful habit to develop. Michalko offers the following thought experiment as an example:

> Suppose you have the opportunity to reduce the human error associated with hospital procedures, including mistakes in diagnosis, medicine dosages, and hospital-induced infections. Consider how different experts, such as a football coach, a prison warden, an airline pilot, an orchestra conductor, and a priest, might approach this challenge.

cross-fertilization
The process of bringing ideas and approaches to thinking from one discipline to bear upon another. Using concepts of physics (gravity, for example) to think about literary characters; or using concepts from the visual arts (color and texture) to describe music.

metaphorical thinking
In creative thinking, a form of analogical thinking that seeks unusual connections to promote the discovery of fresh ideas.

shifting attention
An analytical technique and problem-solving strategy that involves turning one's focused attention from one aspect of a situation, text, or problem to another.

In a book, *The Checklist Manifesto*, which includes a solution to this problem, Atul Gawande explains how introducing a checklist for hospital operating room procedures cut the death rate from hospital-induced infections to zero. The improvement was due both to creating a checklist of sterilization procedures, including scrupulous and frequent hand sanitizing, and to ensuring that the checklist procedures were followed assiduously and enforced vigorously by nurses. Enforcing the checklist procedures requires both critical and creative thinking because even though logically one would be hard pressed to disagree with the Gawande's argument for checklist procedures, creative thinking is needed to implement them because people are set in their ways and getting them to change their behavior can be challenging.

EXERCISES

9. Explain how each of the following cross-fertilizations might work—what the idea is for each analogy.

    a. School as entertainment; school as confinement.

    b. Shopping as an addiction; shopping as socializing.

    c. Moviegoing as escapism; moviegoing as intellectual stimulation.

    d. Work as play; work as fulfillment of an obligation.

    e. Marriage as a partnership; marriage as an adventure.

10. Use a shift of attention to solve the problem presented in the following story, a version of which can be found in Edward de Bono's *New Think*.

    A merchant owed a large sum of money to a moneylender who was attracted to the merchant's beautiful daughter. The moneylender offered to cancel the debt if the merchant would permit him to marry his daughter. The moneylender proposed that they allow chance to determine whether this should happen. He suggested that a black pebble and a white one be placed into an empty bag. The girl would pick one of the pebbles by reaching into the bag. If she picked the black pebble, she would become his wife and the debt cancelled. If she picked the white pebble, she would remain with her father with the debt also cancelled.

    When the merchant agreed, the moneylender bent down to select the two pebbles for the bag. The girl noticed that he chose two black pebbles instead of one black and white pebble. With the two black pebbles in the bag, the merchant asked the girl to pick out the pebble that was to decide her fate and that of her father. What should she do?

11. Read a short story or news article that describes a relationship between two characters. Focus your attention closely at first on only one character, considering that character as the more important of the two. Do some thinking about that character and how you use the information to form an opinion and come to a judgment about him or her. Then shift your attention to the other character. Think, now, of that second character as the more important one. Follow through the same way to arrive at a judgment about this other character. And finally, shift your attention from each character individually to consider the relationship between the characters. Your focus now is what happens between them—on their relationship rather than on either character individually.

Denying the Negative, Pursuing the Possible

Write the Response,
Denying the Negative,
Pursuing the Possible
MyThinkingLab

If critical thinking tends toward evaluating and ultimately rejecting ideas, creative thinking inclines more to encouraging them. Some kinds of thinking say "no," whereas other kinds say "yes." For example, instead of thinking of approaches to a problem as not being workable—as unrealistic or inadequate, silly or stupid, for example—we might think more positively. We can say "yes, perhaps," rather than "no, never." We can deny the negative.

We need to be careful not to reject an idea out of hand, regardless of how unpromising it may seem at first. A poor idea taken seriously can lead to a better idea, even when, and especially if, the lesser idea is rejected. Reaching a dead end on an idea for developing a new product or process, for example, might lead to another path or approach—if we keep our minds open throughout the process. Asking "what if" and "why not" enables us to entertain possibilities and discover promising options through **denying the negative** and pursuing the possible.

denying the negative
A creative thinking strategy that avoids a negative attitude and instead encourages pursuing possibilities.

The concept of possibility is available with the smallest and most ordinary of everyday behaviors. Consider, for example, how often we describe things in terms of what they are not. We say in response to someone asking how we're doing, "not bad" or "nothing to complain about." We invite people to lunch with "why don't we get together soon for lunch?" How much better it sounds to say, "Let's do lunch tomorrow or the next day." And "I'm feeling pretty good, how about you?" Changing the way we speak to avoid negative attitudes and emphasize positive ones influences how we feel and how we think.

The Eight Commandments of Ideation

In *Disciplined Dreaming*, Josh Linkner describes what he calls "The Eight Commandments of Ideation," eight ways of igniting ideas. Linkner describes these as sparks that flame ideas into life. Here are his commandments—what to avoid when we are in the process of generating ideas.

1. *Thou Shall Not Judge.* Withhold judgment when generating ideas. Premature judgment kills ideas.
2. *Thou Shall Not Comment.* In listening to others' ideas, withhold comment. Let ideas be heard, however far-fetched they might sound.
3. *Thou Shall Not Edit.* Editing is analyzing, a useful and important function—but not when ideas are in development. Save editing for later.
4. *Thou Shall Not Execute.* Analyzing the practicality and viability of an idea is essential, but not when generating ideas.
5. *Thou Shall Not Worry.* Fear kills ideas. Fear is also contagious.
6. *Thou Shall Not Look Backwards.* Past experience is no guarantee of future failure—or success.
7. *Thou Shall Not Lose Focus.* Focus is central to good idea generation. Losing focus hampers creative thinking.
8. *Thou Shall Not Sap Energy.* Energy and positive spirit are essential to creative thinking. Negative thinking and negative people sap positive energy.

EXERCISES

12. For part of one day—a morning, afternoon, or evening—record how often you hear people using the negative, how often they deny and reject ideas, options,

and possibilities. Notice, too, how often you do this yourself. On at least one of these occasions, consider how what is being denied may be possible after all. Let the unpromising possibility sit for a while; then consider some ways it might be viable—perhaps by making some adjustments using one of the other creative thinking strategies: quota of alternatives, reversing relationships, using analogy, shifting attention.

13. Select one of Josh Linkner's eight commandments of ideation. Give an example of a time when you either applied Linker's advice or did the opposite. Explain what happened. Then try to add two more "commandments" to make them the 10 commandments of ideation.

Scamper

SCAMPER is a creative thinking strategy—really a suite of techniques—that appears in the writings of a number of creative thinking consultants. Letter by letter, SCAMPER stands for the following techniques:

scamper
An acronym for a set of thinking procedures to generate ideas: substitute, combine, adapt, magnify (or minify), put to uses, eliminate, reverse, or rearrange.

S = Substitute—What can be substituted?

C = Combine—What and how can it be combined with other things?

A = Adapt—How can it be adapted?

M = Magnify, Minify—How can it be enlarged or reduced?

P = Put to other uses—To what other uses can it be put?

E = Eliminate—What aspects or elements can be eliminated?

R = Rearrange and Reverse—What can be rearranged; how can it be reversed?

SCAMPER is based on the idea that everything new modifies something that already exists. Petroleum becomes chemical feed that becomes synthetic rubber that eventually winds up as car and truck tires, which may emerge as the soles of sandals. We can follow here Josh Linkner's illustration of each SCAMPER technique with reference to breakfast cereals.

Substitution is a technique we simply can't do without. When we don't have what we need, we search for something to replace it. We can substitute people and processes, rules and materials, locations and times, and approaches—pretty much anything. Cereals: Corn Flakes with substitute ingredients = Bran Flakes.

Combining things is a fundamental principle—perhaps the essential fundamental principle of creative thinking. We can combine purposes and units, appeals and uses, people and programs, and more. We can make alloys (metals), blends (wines), assortments (candies), and ensembles (musicians), among many other combinations. Cereals: Combining Bran Flakes and Raisins = Raisin Bran.

Adaptation is the essence of survival. Without adapting to changing conditions and circumstances, we don't survive. Some questions we can ask include "What else is like this?" "What other ideas does it suggest?" "What parallel does the past suggest?" "What different contexts can be used?" "What else can be incorporated?" Adapting the chocolate chip cookie to a cereal yields cocoa crisps.

Magnification and Minification—making it larger or smaller. Can some aspect of your idea be exaggerated or weakened, enlarged or shrunk? Cereal: Wheat Biscuits cereal became Mini-Wheats.

Putting the idea to another use involves changing the context. How many uses can we find for the common red brick? How about for a peanut? George Washington Carver discovered more than 300 uses for the humble peanut. Cereal: Rice Krispies cereal morphed into Rice Krispies Treats.

Eliminating, subtracting something from the idea can often be useful. Trimming, cutting, whether we're pruning trees or shedding pounds, can result in renewal. Spotlighting an aspect and backgrounding other elements is a way to eliminate distraction. What can be understated, simplified, reduced, cut? What is not really necessary? How can it be condensed or streamlined? Cereals: Many cereals offer reduced fat, and reduced calories, Special K, for example.

Rearranging things is another form of combination. What components can be interchanged? What sequences can be adjusted? What schedule or pacing changes can be made? Baseball managers shuffle lineups; basketball coaches run players in and out of games; composers rearrange music for different instrumental combinations. Cereal "rearrangements" include products such as Honey Bunches of Oats and Just Bunches.

Reversing a perspective helps us see things in new ways. Asking about opposites can clarify what we are looking at. Dark clarifies light; losing amplifies winning; positive spin counters negative spin. Can we flip it, spin it, turn it around, turn it upside down, and turn it inside out? Can we reverse roles? Is an "Un-Cereal" coming?

EXERCISE

14. Choose some aspect of your workplace or home that you would like to improve. Use SCAMPER to generate ideas for improving it. You might try using SCAMPER with an existing product or service, such as e-book readers, mail delivery, customer service.

The Creative Habit

In her book, *The Creative Habit*, dancer and choreographer Twyla Tharp argues that creativity can be learned, developed, and fostered through habitual effort. She suggests that we can make creativity a habit. Tharp does not claim that we can all become geniuses like Leonardo and Michelangelo, Mozart and Beethoven, Tolstoy and Dostoyevsky. But she does claim that by focused attention and sustained concentration over time, we can dramatically increase our creativity. Her book provides both guidelines and practices for doing so. And it includes numerous personal examples and stories of creative breakthroughs that are both entertaining and inspirational.

Tharp advocates a number of key principles to develop "the creative habit." Among them are rituals, creative DNA, memory, the box, scratching, accidents, spine, skill, failure, and something she calls "the long run." A few words about each of these will show just how richly varied a set of practices Tharp provides.

1. *Rituals.* Creativity requires preparation, and the best and most consistent kind of preparation, according to Tharp, is ritual. She reminds us that we employ rituals all the time in our everyday lives and suggests that we develop rituals of preparation for creative thinking and activity as well. The great cellist Pablo Casals began each day by playing a prelude and fugue from Bach's solo keyboard work, *The Well-Tempered Clavier*, as his ritual of preparation. The modern composer Igor Stravinsky also played a Bach fugue on the piano as his entry into the world of music each morning. Twyla Tharp herself begins her days by hailing at cab at 5:30 a.m. and heading for the gym to do a two-hour workout as her preparation for dance and choreography. We all need some kind of ritual

as a way to get started each and every day—and as a habit to keep us going over the long haul.

2. *Creative DNA.* Tharp advances the notion that each of us is born with something like a "*creative code* hard-wired into our imaginations." Each of us has a talent for something that brings out our uniquely expressive creative powers. It might be the way we dribble and shoot a basketball, or how we handle a needle and thread; how we design and cook a meal; how we solve problems in mathematics or science; how we arrange flowers, plan a vacation, or express ourselves verbally or musically. Our creative DNA marks our unique and peculiar way of being in the world; it inhabits and exhibits our sense of style, our particular way of walking, talking, writing, and thinking. It is something we can learn to respect and appreciate in ourselves the better to develop, nurture, and cultivate that creative DNA.

3. *Memory.* Tharp urges us to harness our memory, which she compares to a muscle that can be strengthened with practice. A rich and well-stocked memory can be a solace in times of difficulty; it can provide entertainment in times of boredom; it can lend coherence and meaning to our lives. Tharp describes different kinds of memory that we can harness and develop. One type is muscle memory of the kind that dancers exhibit in physical movement and musicians display in performing on their instruments. Another is what Tharp calls "virtual memory," which lets us project ourselves into the past to recapture and reexperience former emotions, or to project ourselves into the future to visualize a successful outcome for some project or course of action we are undertaking. She describes "sensual memory," which is triggered by the senses, the smell or taste of warmly baked bread, for example, and the associations we have with them. She also highlights "institutional memory," possessed by those who have worked in a place for a long time.

4. *The Box.* For every creative project, Twyla Tharp gathers materials for potential use and deposits them into a file box. She labels her box with the project name. Into the box go slips of paper with random ideas, clippings from magazines and newspapers, CDs, videotapes, photographs, pictures of artworks, books, excerpts from books, and more. Using such a box is a practical and functional way to keep connected to a project. Research notes are always available in the box. Things put into the box at one time can be mingled with others that have been dropped in later to create new connections that stimulate fresh thinking. Of course, we have to go beyond simply putting things into the box. We also need to pull things out and begin working with them, perhaps combining different items, to see what ideas might be stimulated.

5. *Scratching.* In answer to the question "where do you get your ideas," Tharp suggests "scratching." For her, "scratching" is a form of inquiry that involves looking around for a spark, for any little bit of energy to jump-start thinking. Scratching is a way to think by starting small. It's the beginning of an improvisation, the hunt for the scent of inspiration. A writer might scratch by recording a snippet of overheard conversation to trigger imagining the dialogue's backstory. A musician might play around with a little three- or four-note motive, a bit of melody that can be developed into a phrase and then a theme and then a symphonic movement—as Beethoven did with his famous dah-dah-dah-**dah** motive in the first movement of his Symphony #5. Scratch around in various places. Put yourself in motion. Read. Write. Engage in conversation. Take a walk. Visit a museum. Look around. Listen. Some productive thinking might come of it.

EXERCISE ———————————————————————

15. Which of the first five strategies that Twyla Tharp uses to spark her creative thinking do you find most interesting—and potentially of use? Why? How might you use this strategy to spur your own creative thinking?

6. *Accidents*. Like many others who write about creativity, Tharp values and validates the potential for accidental discovery—for times when errors and mistakes can lead to productive results. And like those others, she also advocates the necessity to be prepared to take advantage of such happy accidents. She suggests that we have to be prepared to be lucky; we have to learn to recognize an opportunity, to keep our eyes and ears and minds open and receptive, and then to seize that opportunity when it appears. She gives the example of the creator of the General Electric advertising slogan, which conveys the idea that GE makes things that make life good. Playing with this concept and thinking of different ways to express it enabled the copywriter who created the GE slogan prepared himself to recognize what was eventually created: "We bring good things to life."

7. *Spine*. By "spine," Tharp means the core idea for a work or project, the essential notion that motivates and animates it. The spine is our goal, our intention, our central concept or idea. For Buster Keaton's slapstick comic routines, it was to get the last laugh. For Michael Jordan shooting a basketball, it was to jump up above the defender. For French novelist Gustave Flaubert, it was to get the words of his novel *Madame Bovary* exactly right. It's easy to drift from that spine as we gather material for a project, as we explore it and work out its implications. It's important to keep reminding ourselves what the goal is, what we are trying to do, and then to evaluate the project in light of its "spine," and to revise it according to its essential purpose and direction.

8. *Skills*. Acquiring the skills to perform a work, the knowledge to develop a project demands effort and practice. Skills are a necessary foundation, an essential prerequisite for any creative output. Skills, though, are not enough. Although necessary, they are not sufficient; something more is needed. But we won't make progress unless the fundamentals have been developed solidly and confidently. We can't compose an intricate piece of music, perform a complex series of dance movements, produce an emotionally powerful film, or create an exceptional four-course meal, without mastering the fundamentals of music, dance, filmmaking, or cooking. Learning and disciplining ourselves to develop those fundamental skills, practicing them, and keeping them sharp and fresh provide the essential baseline and foundation for working passionate and creative magic. For Tharp, combining skill with passion is the very essence of the creative life.

9. *Failure*. None of us likes to fail. It's painful. It's humbling. It's dispiriting. Even so, failure can be instructive, illuminating, inspiring. Tharp reminds us that failure is unavoidable, especially for creative efforts and attempts. Even Leonardo da Vinci failed at times, as when he tried unsuccessfully to harness the River Arno in Florence. Each of us has failed in the past, and we will fail again in the future. But that simple fact should reveal that we are trying new things, attempting things we have not yet done or cannot quite do—yet. Without romanticizing failure, we need, as people say, to simply "get over it." And then get on to the next new thing. That's Twyla Tharp's advice. And it's sound, sane, and sagacious. Consider what happened with Apple CEO Steve Jobs in his mix of failures and successes. Jobs failed in his first attempt as CEO of Apple Computer; he was fired by the company he cofounded. And he failed in his venture with NeXT

Computer (though the operating system he developed there he put to use later at Apple). But then he succeeded at Pixar by developing award-winning animated films, such as *Toy Story*, and then again spectacularly at Apple with the development of the iPod, iPhone, and iPad, as well as the iMac computer.

Twyla Tharp also offers some insight into failure beyond her encouraging ideas. She suggests that we think about what causes a failure. Is it a failure of nerve? A failure of judgment? A failure of skill or of concept? Perhaps, the failure stems from denial—a denial to listen to the good advice of others, or to our own best instincts. And once we determine the cause of failure, it's then time to do something to fix it, change it, address it, remedy it—and then get beyond it.

10. *The Long Run.* By "the long run" Tharp means the arc of creative development, the creative trajectory of one's life and career. Although creative thinking and creative production have been shown to peak in the prime years of middle age—after the rich learning curve of youth and before the decline and trailing off of creative energy in later years—there are exceptions to that pattern. Tharp cites a number of exemplary creative individuals who continued to produce fresh and original work all their lives, with their late work as vibrant and original as their earlier masterpieces. Such a catalog includes Mozart and Schubert (both of whom died young), Verdi and Wagner (who lived much longer), and many who lived the normal lifespans for their times, Rembrandt, Dostoyevsky, Yeats, Cezanne, Picasso, Matisse, Kurosawa, Balanchine. Each of these creative artists kept learning, continued to experiment and explore, to take creative risks, to try new things—with amazing results.

Tharp herself continues to produce ballets. She describes herself as not feeling like a "master choreographer" until she was 58 years old and after completing here 128th ballet. Twyla Tharp exemplifies how creative thinking can permeate a life and how creative production can continue over a long arc of time and learning. Her book *The Creative Habit* was first published in 2003, when she was 62. A dozen years later, she is still in creative mode, choreographing dances and writing about her experience as dancer, teacher, choreographer, and creative thinker. She is an example and an inspiration for the rest of us.

EXERCISES

16. Choose one of Twyla Tharp's additional five strategies (accident, spine, skills, failure, the long run) for developing the creative habit. Consider how you could apply and adapt her suggestions to prepare yourself to be more creative, to develop your creative potential more fully.

17. Provide an example of a time when a chance meeting, an accidental encounter, or otherwise unplanned connection started you thinking in a new way—gave you an idea that you made use of, perhaps helped you solve a problem, or create a new approach to a problem.

Developing Creative Confidence

In their coauthored book, *Creative Confidence*, brothers Tom and David Kelley claim that having confidence in our ability to be creative is fundamental to improving our creative capacity. They claim that creativity is a muscle than can be strengthened with disciplined and regular practice. We can nurture our creative potential with effort and through experience.

We should not confuse being creative with being artistic, say the Kelleys. Nor should we believe that creativity is a fixed trait, an unalterable, immutable power that can never be increased. The authors cite the research of Carol Dweck, especially her book *Mindset*, which contrasts people who believe that their intelligence is fixed (along with their creativity), and those who see themselves as capable of becoming more intelligent (and more creative). We have all heard people say that they are not the creative type. Some of us have said this ourselves, and perhaps believed it, as well. Such an attitude hinges on what Dweck calls a "fixed mindset." She describes the benefits of a contrasting "growth mindset," one that allows for continued growth, not just in knowledge but in intelligence, and also as the Kelleys claim, in creativity.

In synch with Carol Dweck, Tom and David Kelley want to argue us out of the belief in a fixed mindset that includes an assumption that we are not creative. They claim, instead, that everybody can be creative. However, it takes effort; it requires overcoming insecurity about our abilities and talents; it requires us to develop our imagination, become more curious, and exhibit some courage in the face of obstacles, difficulties, challenges, and failures.

What if, we might ask—just, what if we believed with the Kelleys that "creativity isn't some rare gift to be enjoyed by the lucky few"? What if we agreed with them that creativity is "a natural part of human thinking and behavior"? Might a belief in the possibility and even the actuality of our creative potential become a self-fulfilling prophecy? Might a conviction of our creativity lead to self-efficacy? And might developing the habit of self-efficacy encourage us to set our sights higher, to try harder, to persevere in the face of difficulty, even failure?

According to the Kelleys, creative confidence improves our ability to make better choices. It enables us to more easily push ourselves in new directions. It enables us to become better problem solvers, to collaborate more productively, and to approach challenges with confidence.

We can choose to be creative. We can get beyond simply "trying" and as the Nike ad asserts, "just do it." Instead of waiting and wondering, we can act, we can get moving, we can do something to become at least a bit more creative. Tom and David Kelley have some suggestions to help us get started.

Here are a few:

1. Choose a project or activity you are interested in doing, and break it down into small steps. Take the first small step. Tackle a doable piece.

2. Lower the stakes. If your project or activity requires significant investments of time and/or money or other resources, scale it down. Also, in beginning to work at it, consider what you do initially as an experiment.

3. Establish a milestone, or series of milestones that you can celebrate once they are reached.

4. Set mini- and multiple deadlines for small segments of the project or activity.

5. Don't worry about perfection at first. Just produce something to get your creative juices flowing. Revision can come later as you make progress.

6. Seek help from others. Perhaps create a support network.

EXERCISE

18. To what extent have you victimized yourself by believing in a fixed mindset about your abilities, including your creative abilities? To what extent are you made hopeful and do you find helpful what the Kelleys suggest about your creative potential. Which of their suggestions do you find most promising, and why?

Idea Killers and Idea Growers

In his book, *Little Blue Reasoning Book*, Brandon Royal presents a series of comments people often make that express diametrically opposed attitudes toward ideas. The first set of comments reflects attitudes that stifle and kill ideas; the second set conveys attitudes that generate them. Many of these are, sadly, all too familiar—especially those in the first set.

Idea Killers

- We tried this before (and it didn't work).
- It would cost too much.
- It would take too much time (and/or too much effort).
- That's not my (your, his, her, our) job.
- That's not how we do things here.
- That sounds crazy. It's impossible.
- What we have (do) now is good enough.
- My mind is made up—definitely.
- Maybe next year.
- If it ain't broke, don't fix it.

Idea Growers

- Let's review the options.
- Is there anything we haven't yet considered?
- What other ways might there be to do this?
- Where else can we get more information?
- How could we improve?
- I've changed my mind.
- Let me ask you for some ideas about this.
- Is this what you mean?
- Who else has a suggestion?
- Wouldn't it be fun (interesting) if we . . .
- I'd like to get your help (thinking) about something.

EXERCISES ————————————————————

19. Which three of the Idea Killers seem most destructive of fresh thinking? Why?

20. Which three of the Idea Growers appeal to you most why? Which do you tend to hear more—the idea grower or idea killer comments? How do you account for this?

Creative Questioning

Effective thinking, both critical and creative thinking, involves asking questions. The kinds of questions we ask are important, as are the ways that our initial questions lead to others. Good questions direct our thinking, encourage exploration, and open our minds to varied possibilities. In their book, *The 5 Elements of Effective Thinking*, Edward B. Burger and Michael Starbird suggest that questions can be an "inspiring guide to insight and understanding." Creating useful and productive questioning enlivens our curiosity, provokes our thinking, and excites our imaginations.

But what are the characteristics of good questions? First, good questions are open-ended; they admit of more than a single answer. Second, good questions generate other questions; they lead beyond themselves. Third, good questions produce rich and varied answers; we can judge a question by the kinds of answers it evokes. Fourth, good questions jump-start our thinking—they stimulate, engage, and provoke. Neil Postman, in *The End of Education*, puts it like this: "The value of a question is determined by the specificity and richness of the answers it produces and by the quantity and quality of the new questions it provokes."

Some examples of questions that meet these criteria are these:

- What do we mean by a fact? Is a biological fact different from a historical fact or a mathematical fact? Can facts change? Can something once considered a fact be dethroned and shown to be a fact no longer?

- What is the relationship between fact and truth? How would we begin to answer that question?

- How should science be taught in the high school and university curriculum? How many sciences? In what order? To what extent should the teaching and learning of the sciences be integrated with one another? To what extent should science be integrated with technology? With other subjects? Which ones? Why?

- Is history a science? Is dance a language? What is a saint? What counts as an experiment? How would you go about answering these questions?

- How do we know what we know? How can we compensate for the limitations of reason, the inaccuracies of perception, the reliability of what we read and hear?

In *Microtrends*, Mark J. Penn examines the small forces behind big changes. He analyzes data, looking for changing patterns in religion and politics, social and family life. Penn argues that a number of forces are converging—the Internet, the global economy, the fragmentation of communication—to create a new sense of individualism that is transforming society. America (and the world) is splitting into thousands of small niches, readily evident by the proliferation of hundreds of cable TV channels. He wonders what societal effects might result from these proliferating interest groups, including the kinds of opportunities and threats they pose. Here is a sampling of Penn's questions:

- Though more people are retiring, more retirees are returning to work. What is the explanation for this trend—and what are its consequences?

- Why are there more women than men in colleges and universities? Why are there more African-American women than African-American men in higher education, and what consequences result from these facts?

- What are the implications for a Western world that is graying and in a declining population spiral? To what extent will power shift from the West to other parts of the world—and from Europe and the United States to China, India, and Latin America?

- What factors other than the size and ages of populations in different parts of the world need to be examined to answer that question about a power shift?

Learning to ask useful questions is a skill, even, perhaps an art. The better our questions, the better chance we have to develop our capacity for critical and creative thinking, because questioning is a key element in all thinking.

In *What?*, a book of twenty short chapters constructed entirely of questions, Mark Kurlansky asks, "What was the first question" in human history? He doesn't answer it, really, but he does offer a couple of possibilities, including "Where is the food?" a practical question linked with survival. Kurlansky suggests that it is questions that matter rather than answers, that we are still trying to answer most of the really interesting and important questions about ourselves, and that many, if not all the really significant questions, will never be fully answered.

Kurlanksy focuses on "what" questions, on "how" and "why" questions. "What," he asks "is at the heart of intellectual pursuit? Is it 'what' "? Or, as he suggests, is it "why" rather than "what"? "Why," Kurlansky suggests is the key question of science and "what" the central question of history. But in the process of saying that, he wonders whether that is not an oversimplification. And then there are the questions of "when" and "how," which are important to both history and science, respectively. And yet Kurlansky asks, "Why is the question 'What' so fundamental" to knowledge and understanding? "How," he asks, "do we know anything for certain? Aren't even our beliefs, our opinions, subject to change?"

EXERCISES

21. Which two of Postman's questions interest you most? Why? How would you begin to answer them?

22. Choose one of Penn's questions and begin to answer it. Identify three or four additional questions that his questions and your preliminary answers generate as you go.

23. What other basic questions would you add to Kurlansky's "what," "why," "when," and "how"? Why would you add each of them?

Questioning Routines

A number of educators have developed approaches to questioning that strive for breadth and depth. One approach provided by James Barell in *Developing More Inquiring Minds* uses the abbreviation pattern KWHLAQ. These are Barell's questions:

- What do we *Know* or think we Know?
- What do we *Want* to know or find out?
- *How* are we going to get that information or knowledge?
- What have we *Learned* from our efforts?
- How can we *Apply* what we have learned?
- What additional *Questions* do we have?

Notice how this set of questions ends with a question that leads to further questions. Questioning, like learning, and like thinking, never really ends. To understand and embrace that reality is a requirement of critical and creative thinking. There's no question about it.

Another approach to questioning is a set of strategies of inquiry developed in conjunction with Project Zero at Harvard University, a wide-ranging initiative designed to improve teaching and learning, with an emphasis on critical and creative thinking. One part of the Project Zero program, "Visible Thinking" emphasizes the use of thinking routines connected with the four ideals for thinking: *understanding, truth, fairness,* and *creativity*. Two of the visible thinking routines that focus on "thinking for understanding" are *See, Think, Wonder* and *Think, Puzzle, Explore*.

The first of these thinking routines, "See, Think, Wonder," is especially useful for thinking about visual art and images. In using this routine, we ask ourselves, "What do I see?" We take some time looking so we can notice as much as we can. What follows is the question: "What do I think about what I see?" Here we consider our perspective or stance toward what is being viewed. These initial thoughts are followed with an additional question: "What do I wonder" in looking at this object? Here we let our minds wander toward notions that have, perhaps, less of a firm grounding, but which can lead to further connections and insights.

The second thinking routine, "Think, Puzzle, Explore," is designed to deepen thinking. In using this thinking routine, we first consider what we think we know about the object, issue, topic, or problem. We take stock. Then we ask ourselves what is puzzling about it. What questions do we have about it? What don't we understand? What might be confusing? And finally, we consider how to explore the object, issue, topic, or problem further. What might be done to extend and deepen our thinking and understanding?

EXERCISE

24. Use the KWHLAQ questions or one of the Project Zero thinking routines to think about one of the following: a painting, photograph, sculpture, or work of architecture; a poem, short story, novel, play, or movie; a scientific or mathematical formula or discovery; a historical figure or event; a religious or philosophical question or problem; a musical, dance, or theatrical work; a print advertisement or television commercial; a television show of any genre; a political, social, or economic idea or theory.

Looking Back and Looking Ahead

Revisit the learning goals that begin this chapter. Which of these goals do you think you have best achieved? What might you do to reach the remaining goals?

Return to the focusing questions at the beginning of the chapter. How would you answer those questions now? Which of them do you find most interesting and provocative and worthy of following up? Why?

In reviewing the list of resources that follows, identify the two that attract you most. Explain why these books or Web sites interest you. Consider looking into them for further developing your capacity for creative thinking and its complementary relationship with critical thinking.

Take a look, too, at the MyThinkingLab resources on the Prentice Hall Web site. Included there are readings, images, videos, questions, exercises, and other provocations to help you develop your creative thinking prowess.

• •

Resources

New Think, Edward de Bono. Avon, 1968.

Edward de Bono's Thinking Course. Edward de Bono. BBC Active, 2005.

"Fire Up Your Creativity," Evangelia G. Chrysikou. *Scientific American Mind*, volume 23, number 3, 2012.

Creative Thinkering, Michael Michalko. New World Library, 2011.

Disciplined Dreaming, Josh Linkner. Jossey-Bass, 2011.

The Checklist Manifesto, Atul Gawande. Metropolitan Books, 2011.

The Creative Habit, Twyla Tharp. Simon & Schuster, 2003.

Creative Confidence, Tom Kelley and David Kelley. Crown Business, 2013.

The End of Education, Neil Postman. Vintage Books, 1995.

The 5 Elements of Effective Thinking, Edward B. Burger and Michael Starbird. University of Princeton Press, 2012.

Microtrends, Mark J. Penn. Twelve, 2009.

What?, Mark Kurlansky. Walker and Company, 2011.

The Little Blue Reasoning Book. Brandon Royal. Maven Publishing, 2010.

Making Thinking Visible, Ron Ritchhart, Mark Church, and Karin Morrison. Jossey-Bass, 2011.

• •

3

Analyzing Language

The limits of my language means the limits of my world.

—LUDWIG WITTGENSTEIN.

FOCUSING QUESTIONS

- How do you think language might be related to thinking? To what extent are words essential for thinking?

- What are some differences between and among the ways scientists, politicians, and advertisers use language?

- What kinds of words and phrases carry an emotional charge for you, and why?

- Why do you think it's important to pay close attention to the words people use (and you yourself use) in speaking and writing?

- How might detailed attention to aspects of language enhance your critical thinking skills?

LEARNING GOALS

3.1 UNDERSTAND the relationship between language and thought.

3.2 UNDERSTAND the ways language conveys ideas and feelings, especially through denotation and connotation.

3.3 EXPLORE the workings of metaphorical language to convey and generate ideas.

3.4 RECOGNIZE some ways language influences perception and perspective.

3.5 APPLY a critical analysis of language to deepen your understanding of texts.

Chapter Overview

This chapter considers aspects of language, including the denotation and connotation of words, metaphor and meaning, and the relationship of language to thinking. Some tools for analyzing language are provided, such as S. I. Hayakawa's "reports, inferences, and judgments." Some attention is given as well to the relationships among language, history, and culture. An approach to the critical analysis of texts focuses on making observations and connections among details, then drawing inferences and interpretive conclusions from them. Using tools of analysis, we can better understand and appreciate how language creates, embodies, and expresses meaning. The central idea of the chapter is that language is a complex and richly textured medium of thought and expression.

Language Saturation

We are surrounded with language. Words swirl all around us, from radio and television, from our iPods and computers, from Facebook and Twitter, from our conversations real and virtual. Perhaps because we hear so much language, we tend to take it for granted. We use language all day long, mostly without paying much attention to how we say what we say or to how we hear what is said. Speaking and hearing language is something we do almost without thinking. To some extent, of course, this is an exaggeration, as we have to do at least some thinking when we talk and listen. But we certainly can become much more conscious of our own language and the language of others; we can become more attentive to what we read, what we hear, and what we say and write.

The connections between language and thought are deep and pervasive. Language is an instrument of thought. We use language to think with—though it is not our only form of thinking, as we also think with images and sounds. Words are tools for thinking. We think by means of concepts in the form of words, which represent objects or things. When we talk about shoes, for example, we need not have any particular shoe in mind, though we certainly could if we liked. We use the word *shoes*, itself an abstraction, to refer to the concept of things we wear on our feet, from sandals to sneakers to stiletto heels.

Watch the **Video**,
Language Saturation/Words
MyThinkingLab

Words

Words are important units of meaning in all languages. Words are the smallest building blocks of language that make sense to us, though some linguists would argue that syllables and even smaller segments of sound carry significant meaning as well. Words name our experiences, convey our feelings, and explain our thoughts. They express our hopes and fears; they communicate our frustrations and our satisfactions, our disappointments and our accomplishments. Words inform and entertain us; they

(Enter Hamlet.)

HAMLET

To be, or not to be, that is the Question:
Whether 'tis Nobler in the minde to suffer
The Slings and Arrowes of outragious
Or to take Armes against a Sea of
And by opposing end them: to
more; and by a sleepe,

move us to laughter and tears. From combinations of the 26 letters of the alphabet have come all of English and American literature, including Melville's *Moby-Dick*, Twain's *Adventures of Huckleberry Finn*, Shakespeare's sonnets and plays, including *Macbeth* and *Hamlet* as well as Shakespeare's character Hamlet, who, when asked "What do you speak my Lord," replies: "Words. Words. Words."

We start, then, with some notions about words.

General and Specific, Abstract and Concrete

General words identify broad categories, such as *country, president, books*; specific words identify individual people or objects, such as *Egypt, President Lincoln, The Oxford English Dictionary*. Abstract words identify ideas and concepts that cannot be perceived by the senses (*education, generosity, fatherhood*); concrete words identify something perceptible by the senses (*desk, fifty-dollar bill, dad*). (Of course, as "words," even these more specific and concrete terms are abstractions, which stand for the objects their particular combinations of letters represent.) But you get the idea that words can be "more or less" general and abstract, and "more or less" specific and concrete. Sometimes we refer to this degree or extent property of words as a "ladder of abstraction," which we can illustrate with the following example, which goes from general to specific, from abstract to concrete:

living creature

animal

mammal

quadruped

cow

Holstein

Bessie

The relation between abstract and concrete language is critical for thinking. Abstract and general terms represent ideas and attitudes; we use them to explore relationships, such as causality and priority and contingency. Concrete and specific words clarify and illustrate general ideas and abstract concepts. Our thinking with, in, and through language switches back and forth between abstract concepts and concrete instances; it oscillates between general ideas and specific examples.

EXERCISE

1. Convert the following abstract/general sentences into sentences that use more concrete and specific language.

   Example: Abstract/General: Technology has revolutionized communication.

   Concrete/Specific: The invention of the smartphone has enabled people to make and receive calls and surf the Web from virtually anywhere.

   a. Deal makers use their cell phones to have virtual meetings while traveling.

   b. The transportation system throughout Holland is excellent.

   c. Standards of violence and morals in films have loosened in recent decades.

   d. The music industry has been radically transformed in recent years.

The Meaning of Average: What Is an Average?

Neither a word's definition nor the concept it represents is always simple or straight-forward. For example, when we encounter a reference to an "average" salary, an "average" height, the "average" cost of a house or apartment, the "average" life span of a man or woman, we don't always know just what "average" means in these situations. Consider, for example, the average salary at a company. Does that "average" refer to the average salary of all workers in the company, including for example, the CEO, who may earn more himself than everyone else combined, and whose salary skews the average significantly upward? Does that average include the salaries of temporary and part-time employees, which would skew the average salary downward? Averages tend to flatten and smooth out discrepancies, to suggest scenarios of typicality that more often than not, are misleading. Consider, for example, the average salary of a group of people enjoying dinner in a modestly priced restaurant. In walks Bill Gates of Microsoft, and suddenly the "average" salary increases dramatically thousands of times.

Averages rarely represent either a middle state or a typical state of affairs. Too many factors enter into the computation of averages, including very high and very low outliers reflecting extremely low or high numbers that skew the mean. This is particularly true in looking at salaries of people working in a single company—especially investment banks and Internet companies, but also professional sports teams, where the compensation of the top earners are hundreds of times, and in some cases thousands of times what more typical employees earn. Similarly, it is necessary to ask just what is being counted in the computation of the average—and what the numbers really signify.

EXERCISE

2. Think about how the average life span of men and women (separately and together) vary under the following sets of conditions: people living in the nineteenth century in Europe or in Africa; people living in the twentieth century on these continents; people living in the United States in the last decade of the twentieth century; men of African-American heritage in the United States in the last half of the twentieth century; women of upper-class socio-economic status living in east coast US cities in the last half of the twentieth century. What other additional kinds of questions need to be asked about "averages" in terms of an "average" life span to get a clear understanding of the concept?

Denotation and Connotation

Words have different kinds of meanings. Among the most important are denotation, or denotative meaning, and connotation, or connotative meaning. A word's **denotation** is its dictionary meaning; its connotation refers to the associations of thought and feeling it evokes in us. Denotations of words tend to be neutral and more or less objective. **Connotations** are personal and more subjective. Consider the word *dictator*, for example. What do you feel when you hear the word *dictator*? What (or who) do you think of when you hear it? Why? Or consider another word—*father*. What do you feel when you hear the word *father*? What do you think of, what do you feel—and why?

denotation
The dictionary definition of a word; a word's agreed-upon meaning.

connotation
The personal associations words possess for us, rather than their dictionary definitions.

EXERCISE

3. What do you feel and think of when you hear the following words:

mother

magnesium

mountain music

mercy killing

metatarsals

mystery

misery

money

master

mistress

Did you experience stronger feelings at the sight and sound of some of these words rather than others? Which ones elicited from you the strongest responses? Why?

The denotative or dictionary meaning of *dictator* is "a person exercising absolute power, especially one who assumes absolute control without the free consent of the people." However, in reading or hearing the word *dictator*, we might conjure up images of a particular individual, a specific place, as well as feelings and emotions. We might think of the Holocaust, for example, and of images of emaciated people, of skulls and skeletons of those killed in the gas chambers of Auschwitz and Dachau.

The word *dictator* elicits a range of associations that are primarily negative because the dictators we know from history have done horrible things—think not only of Hitler, Stalin, and Mussolini, but also of Idi Amin, of Roman emperors like Caligula, of Trujillo, of Perón, and of contemporary African dictators, for example. The word *dictator* acquires its meaning then in part from history, with many dictators behaving like ruthless tyrants. (The word *tyrant*, too, has negative connotations, though in Greek, *tyrannos* simply means *king*.)

The English word *dictator* also gets its meaning from a Latin word meaning to speak: *dicere*, the source of the English word *dictate*, which means to speak or tell. (Dictators, in the simplest sense, are people who speak, telling others what to do and not to do. Their word is law; disobeying their word is often punishable by death.)

The key point, however, is that words can have powerful connotations that go well beyond their denotative meanings or their original meanings. *Dictator* is a clear example. The second point to remember is that our experience of a word like *dictator* will vary, depending on our knowledge of dictators, and perhaps our experience of living under a dictatorial regime. Those who have experienced life under a dictator and later moved to a place of greater freedom will have a very different understanding of *dictator* than those who have always lived in liberty. Their understanding will include a strong emotional element.

Not all words have the kind of powerful connotative associations as *dictator*. Words like *magnesium* (a chemical element) and *metatarsals* (the small bones in your toes) have much weaker connotations. These are scientific and technical terms; as such they tend to have meanings limited almost exclusively to their denotations. Such terms convey more precise information than more common and familiar words; they lack the connotative power, the subjective emotional charge of a word like *dictator*, or of *mother*, for example.

Think of the difference—and feel the difference—for example, between the technical term *myocardial infarction* and the more familiar *heart attack*. *Myocardial infarction* identifies a particular kind of cardiac event; it's a term doctors use to distinguish the type and severity of an episode of cardiac arrest. Though a specific term, *myocardial infarction* is abstract and offers little in the way of connotative resonance. The term *heart attack*, on the other hand, evokes images of a person clutching his chest, sweating, gasping for breath, perhaps fainting and falling down. The words *heart attack* individually and together are concrete and highly visual; the images the term evokes are strong and emotionally powerful.

EXERCISE

4. Identify the denotation (dictionary meaning) and the connotation (the personal associations) you have for each of the following:

vacation

school

home

hydrogen sulfate

quadratic equation

electromagnetic field

baseball field

silk

prunes

eagle

Which of these words drew the strongest response from you? Which words were the most connotatively resonant—with the largest number and widest range as well as the most intense personal associations and responses? Why? Which words drew the least intense and extensive connotations—perhaps even no personal responses or associations at all? Again, why or why not? Where did those connotations come from?

Perhaps you did not know the meaning of some of the more technical words. And even if you did, their abstractness probably did not elicit much in the way of personal associations and feelings. This makes sense, if you think about it, as technical language exists to define things precisely so there is no misunderstanding about what a term refers to, what it means. $E = mc^2$ in any language; $a^2 + b^2 = c^2$ on every continent; H_2SO_4 is the formula for hydrogen sulfate. Period. Our personal associations with such terms are largely irrelevant. When we work with scientific concepts and mathematical equations, we need to avoid the complications of connotations. Thus the terms used in those disciplines are stripped down as much as possible to a singular meaning.

Everyday language, however, is less about fact and information and technical matters and much more about feelings and attitudes. Most words carry positive or negative charges—biases—with them. We need to be aware of what those biases are, of how words that might seem objective may carry with them a hint or even a strong judgment, whether favorable or unfavorable. These positive and negative associations of words are particular manifestations of their connotations. Advertisers and political speechwriters, among others, are adept at deploying words rich in connotative resonance in an attempt to influence our perceptions about their products and their candidates, respectively.

EXERCISE

5. Identify whether the following words carry primarily positive or negative connotations for you. Compare your responses with those of other classmates. Explain any differences you might find.

a.	adventurous	reckless
b.	average	outstanding
c.	average	mediocre
d.	stubborn	firm
e.	shy	reserved
f.	sensitive	touchy
g.	playboy	eligible bachelor
h.	athlete	jock
i.	clever	conniving
j.	clever	intelligent

Perhaps it was easy for you to decide about the positive or negative connotations of these words. Did you notice, though, how a word's connotations shift with its context? For example, when *average* is placed alongside *outstanding*, average has a negative connotation, but when placed alongside *mediocre*, its connotations, in comparison, are more positive. That's one other thing to keep in mind about words—their meaning in context. Something similar happens when we place *clever* alongside *intelligent* and then compare it with *conniving*. Suddenly the word *clever* shifts from being a negative to a more positive-sounding word.

Perhaps you are ambivalent about which is the positive and which the negative term in one or the other pairing. How about *playboy* and *eligible bachelor*? On one hand, you might say that *eligible bachelor* is the more positive term, as its connotations include such things as "single and available" (for marriage), "dependable," "reliable," "well off financially," "socially desirable," and the like. On the other hand, it depends on what a person is looking for. Someone might not be much interested in an "eligible bachelor" type because her connotations for him are "stuffy," "conceited," "boring," "conservative," "traditional," and the like.

What are the connotations of *playboy*? Someone, perhaps, who likes to "play around," "love 'em and leave 'em"; someone who is "unreliable," "undependable," "unfaithful," and the like. On the other hand, the playboy may also be someone who is "fun," "interesting," "unpredictable"; someone with a nice sporty car, who takes great vacations; someone who spends money lavishly, is good-looking, and so on. So, the next point about words is that their connotations do not just point in one direction—their connotations are neither completely positive nor entirely negative. It depends on a person's point of view. A group of middle-aged female students was once asked which term, *playboy* or *eligible bachelor*, had positive connotations for them. They replied *playboy*, because, they said, they would prefer to go out with a playboy. When asked with whom they would want their daughters to go out, they answered immediately in unison: "an eligible bachelor."

EXERCISES

6. Read the opening stanza of the following poem, in which the biblical Adam, the first human, gives names to the animals. The italicized words taken from the first book of the Bible, Genesis, serve as an epigraph for the poem.

Adam's Task

John Hollander

"And Adam gave names to all cattle, and to the fowl of the air, and to every beast of the field . . . " Genesis 2:20

> Thou, paw-paw; thou, glurd; thou, spotted
> Glurd; thou, whitestap, lurching through
> The high-grown brush; thou, pliant-footed,
> Implex; thou, awagabu.

How does this first stanza show evidence of the poet's linguistic imagination at work? What kinds of names does Adam give the animals in this stanza? How do you imagine the difference between a "paw-paw" and an "implex"? Between an "implex" and a "glurd." Which do you think can run faster? Why? In what part of the world do you think an "awagabu" might live? Why?

7. Here, now are the next two stanzas of Hollander's poem.

> Every burrower, each flier
> Came for the name he had to give:
> Gay, first work, ever to be prior,
> Not yet sunk to primitive.

> Thou, verdle; thou, McFleery'spomma;
>
> Thou; thou; thou—three types of grawl;
>
> Thou, flisket; thou, kabash; thou, comma-
>
> Eared mashawk; thou, all; thou, all.

How many different kinds of names for the animals does the poet use in all three stanzas? Why, for example, is "McFleery'spomma" not simply "pomma"? And what might be the principle behind a name like "comma-eared mashawk"? What do you think might be the difference between a "grawl" and a "flisket"? Which might be the "burrower" and which the "flier"? How is the title of the poem related to a later quotation: "Then work, half-measuring, half-humming, / Would be as serious as play?" What kind of imaginative thinking is at work (and at play) in these lines?

Connotation, Race, and Gender

As you have very likely noticed in your everyday experience, certain words convey disdainful, derogatory, racist, and sexist attitudes. To call an African-American man "boy" demeans him and denies his manhood. To call a Latino or Hispanic individual a "spic" or an Italian American a "wop" is similarly to denigrate them. Unfortunately, there are many more such racist terms for these groups and others, including Jews, Muslims, gays, and various other religious and social groups. Derogatory terms dehumanize and can lead on occasion from verbal abuse to physical violence.

Connotation also comes into play with gender terms. To refer to a woman as a "broad" or a "skirt" or a "piece of tail" defines her in physical terms. Adding adjectives like *dumb* broad or *hot* piece in the first instance diminishes her intelligence and in the second intensifies her sexual allure. (Corresponding terms for guys might be *jock, hunk*, and *stud*.) And even when not overtly derogatory or disdainful, terms for the sexes may still contain strongly suggestive implications about differences in sexuality, status, power, and privilege between men and women.

Consider, for example, the terms *master* and *mistress*. At one time, in the eighteenth and nineteenth centuries, for example, those terms were commensurate in their suggestion of importance and power. The master and the mistress of a household and estate were in charge together of its many separate aspects. (Think, e.g., of the "master" and "mistress" of *Downton Abbey*, the popular television show.) Today, however, those uses of the words *master* and *mistress* are no longer applicable. Nonetheless, the word *master* continues to have positive connotations—as in being able to "master" a process or a skill, such as designing a computer application or playing the piano. Not so, however, with the word *mistress*, which has very different sexual connotations that include submission and service to a person of power.

Loaded Words

In her book, *Loaded Words*, Marjorie Garber explores the concept of how language can be "loaded"—in various senses of the word. Garber notes that there are few words more loaded than the word *loaded*, itself. Its meanings include being "charged, burdened, laden," as in loaded shopping carts, loaded lives, plants or trees loaded or laden with fruit. But loaded also conveys other connotations as in being "weighted," as in loaded dice; in being "inserted," as in loaded cameras and loaded guns; in being "fully equipped," as in loaded cars or computers. Other common notions associated

with the word *loaded* are being drunk, wealthy, and talented. (The television commentator for the final heat of the 2012 London Olympics 110 meter hurdles described the field of finalists as "loaded" with premier caliber sprinters.)

Garber also discusses the ways in which questions can be "loaded." Loaded questions are dangerous questions; they anticipate a particular kind of reply; they often seem to push into a corner the person to whom a loaded question is asked. "Loaded," in this sense suggests bias and partiality. These negative connotations of the word *loaded* complement its more positive connotations, its associations with people and objects that possess an abundance of desirable features, qualities, or attributes—or of large amounts of money, power, or talent.

EXERCISES

8. Consider the types of bias conveyed by the following occupational terms. What word might you use in place of each?

    a. anchorman

    b. chairman

    c. mailman

    d. policeman

    e. stewardess

9. Consider the connotations of the following gender terms. What are the implications of each? Which words are positive and which negative in connotation?

bachelor	spinster
actor	actress
lady	gentleman
lady	woman
gentleman	man

10. The following stanza from John Keats's poem "Ode to Autumn" contains a number of words suggestive of being "loaded." Identify those words, and explain whether the loaded words are positive or negative in connotation, and why.

> Season of mists and mellow fruitfulness,
> Close bosom-friend of the maturing sun;
> Conspiring with him how to load and bless
> With fruit the vines that round the thatch-eaves run;
> To bend with apples the moss'd cottage-trees,
> And fill all fruit with ripeness to the core;
> To swell the gourd, and plump the hazel shells
> With a sweet kernel; to set budding more,
> And still more, later flowers for the bees,
> Until they think warm days will never cease;
> For Summer has o'erbrimm'd their clammy cells.

11. In what respects might the following words be considered "loaded"? Think of a number of different meanings and connotations for any four of them.

mad   knowledge   belief   doubt   intelligence   fame   celebrity

fair   just   theory   authentic   professional   genius   patriotism

The Power of Words: Connotation in Action

⊙▸ **Simulate** the
Experiment, The Power of
Words: Connotation in Action
MyThinkingLab

Why should we care about such differences between and among words? Isn't it enough to simply know what the words mean? Perhaps you have heard the story of Kitty Genovese, who was murdered in 1964, in Kew Gardens, Queens, New York, as she returned home from her job late one night. According to newspaper reports, about 3:00 a.m., Miss Genovese had parked her car and headed toward her apartment when a man assaulted her. She screamed for help, and some neighbors in the apartment building adjacent to the parking lot turned on their lights. A few came to their windows to see what was happening. One yelled, "Let that girl alone!" Some, thinking it was a lovers' quarrel, returned to bed. Frightened by the commotion, the attacker ran off, but not until he had stabbed her a number of times. When the neighbors turned off their lights and went back to bed, he returned and stabbed her again, repeatedly. She cried for help again, and again lights went off and the attacker ran off. Bleeding profusely from her wounds, she made her way into the vestibule of her building. The attacker found her there and continued his assault. Finally, one of the neighbors called the police. But it was too late and Kitty Genovese was pronounced dead at the scene of the crime.

This incident sparked considerable public interest. It received extensive press coverage, with newspaper and magazine articles appearing for weeks and even months afterward. Most who hear about this murder ask questions like these: "Why didn't somebody help her?" "Why didn't someone at least call the police from the start?"

You can find out more about the incident and the press response from news accounts in the New York newspapers for March 14, 1964, and also in a *New York Times Magazine* article, "Thirty-Eight Who Saw Murder Didn't Call the Police," by Martin Gansberg, published on March 27, 1964. A book by A. M. Rosenthal of the *New York Times, 38 Witnesses*, was published that year, as well. The 1975 movie,

Death Scream and a 1996 *Law and Order* episode, "Remand," are based on the incident, as is a 2000 book, *Acts of Violence*. In 2014, Kevin Cook published *Kitty Genovese*, in which he disputes a number of facts in the books from the 1960s. Our interest here, however, is in the language of the headlines from three newspapers—the *New York Times*, the *New York Herald Tribune*, and the *New York Daily News*. Here are the first two of these headlines:

> **New York Times:** Queens Woman Stabbed to Death in Front of Home
> **New York Herald Tribune:** Help Cry Ignored, Girl Dies of Knifing

EXERCISES

12. What do you notice immediately about the language of these two headlines? Which headline relies more on the denotation of words—the dictionary meanings, and which uses words that have stronger connotations—personal associations? How, for example, do the connotations of *girl* differ from those of *woman*? Do you think the difference today might be greater or less than the difference between the connotations of those words in 1964? How does each headline make you feel about the victim? Which headline "grabs" you more—affects you more deeply, emotionally? Why?

    Here, now, is the headline from *The Daily News*: Queens Barmaid Stabbed, Dies.

13. What does the word *barmaid* suggest? To what extent does it alter your response to Kitty Genovese and her murder? What is implied in the *News* headline about Kitty Genovese that is not implied by the language of the other two headlines from the *Times* and the *Tribune*?

14. Which of the three headlines seems the most "objective" and neutral in how it refers to the incident?

    Can we say that the *Times* headline is the fairest and most neutral in a reasonably objective way? Might we say that there is a stronger emotional charge generated by the other headlines from the *Daily News* and the *Herald Tribune*? Though these two headlines differ in what each suggests about Kitty Genovese, in how each "portrays" her, they do share a common feature: they both rely on heavily charged language, on loaded words that carry strong connotations—and, in the case of the *News*, a strong negative judgment.

15. Suppose you had read only one of these headlines. What would your perception of the event have been? Having read three headlines, what is your perception of the event now?

16. Write two more headlines for this event—without using the words *girl*, *woman*, or *barmaid*. In one headline, try to use neutral language that avoids a judgment. In the other use some language that evokes either sympathy for the victim or conveys a harsh judgment of her.

Here, now, are the first lines of each of the articles that follow the headlines for the three newspapers. First, the *NY Times* article's opening sentence:

> A 28-year-old Queens woman was stabbed to death early yesterday morning outside her apartment house in Kew Gardens.

That sounds fairly neutral, doesn't it? It uses words with a low connotation quotient, words that are direct and factual. The sentence conveys information, pretty much in the style and manner of the *New York Times* headline quoted earlier. And here is how the *Tribune*'s article about the murder begins:

> The neighbors had grandstand seats for the slaying of Kitty Genovese. And yet, when the pretty diminutive 28-year-old brunette called for help, she called in vain.

That's much more engaging, isn't it—and more shocking, too? It's much more emotionally charged. We might ask a number of questions about this sentence. Among them: Why is the victim described as "pretty"? Is that relevant? Why is she referred to as a "brunette"? How necessary is that detail? (Have you ever read an account of a man's murder in which information about his hair color or physical attractiveness was included?)

EXERCISES

17. What do you make of the first detail of the *Herald Tribune* article: the neighbors watching from "grandstand seats"? What is implied about the neighbors with that detail? And what is the effect of the words *called for help* and called in vain? What effect would be achieved if you substitute *cried for help* and *cried in vain*?

18. How would you characterize the differences in the journalistic philosophies or approaches taken by the *New York Times* and the *Herald Tribune*? Why do you think each newspaper approached the story the way it did?

And, finally, the first sentence of the story printed in the *New York Daily News:*

> An attractive 28-year-old brunette who had given up a more prosaic life for a career as a barmaid and residence in a tiny Bohemian section of Queens was stabbed to death early yesterday.

19. How does this article's opening sentence reinforce the negative judgment made by the *Daily News* headline: Queens Barmaid Stabbed, Dies? What words, in particular, convey a negative view of the victim? Why?

The Prevalence of Metaphor

In addition to the connotations of words as bearers of meaning beyond their literal denotative definitions, it is important to consider how metaphor works in language. Metaphorical language is richly suggestive, filled with implications. Like connotation, metaphor is a property of language that pays dividends for us to understand. (That last phrase includes a financial metaphor.)

When we need a way to explain the intensity of our feelings or a particular state of mind, we reach almost instinctively for metaphor—a form of comparison. We do it regularly, though we are often unaware of the metaphors we use. We talk, for example, of tables with "legs," of river "beds," of a "wild-goose chase" to mean something that doesn't involve a chase at all. We tell someone to "get off my back," or "go jump in the lake"—or to go a place that is, reputedly, very hot. When we speak this way we are speaking figuratively rather than literally. And the figure of speech we are using in these cases is metaphor—saying one thing in terms of another.

To see how prevalent metaphorical expression is in our lives and how persistently we use metaphor to think with, consider the following examples of how we talk about love. They have been adapted from *Metaphors We Live By* by George Lakoff and Mark Johnson.

> I could feel the electricity between us.
>
> They gravitated toward one another.
>
> Her eyes drew him to her.

These ways of talking about love see love as a physical force. What about these next examples? How do they talk about love?

> This is a sick relationship.
>
> We've been getting back on our feet.
>
> The children have never fully recovered from the divorce.

In these, love is described in terms of a medical condition, an illness.

EXERCISES

20. Add one example each to the two for "Love is a physical force," and "Love is a patient."

For these additional ways of talking about love, provide two examples.

  a. Love is war.

  b. Love is magic.

  c. Love is madness.

  d. Love is a disease.

  e. Love is a prison.

Provide one example for each of the following metaphors.

  f. Ideas are food.

  g. Ideas are money.

  h. Ideas are tools.

  i. Time is money.

  j. Time is a commodity.

21. Explain how the following poem uses comparisons.

In Hardwood Groves

Robert Frost

The same leaves over and over again!
They fall from giving shade above
To make one texture of faded brown
And fit the earth like a leather glove.

Before the leaves can mount again
To fill the trees with another shade,
They must go down past things coming up.
They must go down into the dark decayed.

They *must* be pierced by flowers and put
Beneath the feet of dancing flowers.
However it is in some other world
I know that this is the way in ours.

Metaphor and Meaning

The word *metaphor* means to transfer or carry across. (*Meta* is Greek for *across*; *phor* is Greek for *carry*.) The word *transfer* can be broken down the same way:

trans is Latin for *across* (think of *translate* or *transcribe*); *fer* is Latin for *carry* or *bear* (think of *ferry* or *conifer*—a cone-bearing tree). Metaphor involves a transfer of meaning, a carrying across from one area of meaning to another. The heart of metaphor is resemblance (notice the metaphorical word *heart*) stating how one thing is like another, seeing one thing in terms of another.

Metaphors make connections, often of a kind and with a power otherwise impossible to achieve. When the metaphorical connection is made with the words *like* or *as* or *as though*, the comparison is sometimes called a "simile" instead of a "metaphor." However, the concept and effect are much the same, overall. The essential characteristic, in either case, is that one thing is compared to another, one thing is seen in relation to something else, one concept is transferred to another.

EXERCISES

22. Identify the metaphorical connections in the following examples. Explain what is being described in terms of what else—and what the effect of the comparison is. In thinking about the examples, try to explain how the metaphorical connection helps you understand what's being said.

    a. 'Tis with our judgment, as our watches, none
        Go just alike, yet each believes his own.—Alexander Pope

    b. I wandered lonely as a cloud
        That floats on high o'er vales and hills—William Wordsworth

    c. O my Luve's like a red, red rose,

        That's newly sprung in June.

        O my Luve's like the melodie

        That's sweetly play'd in tune.—Robert Burns

23. The following passage is densely packed with metaphors. Try to unpack the lines, identifying each metaphor and what it implies. What, for example, are we to make of the candle? What does it represent? And what is the "tale" told by an "idiot"? By way of context: The lines come form Shakespeare's play *Macbeth*; they are spoken by Macbeth, who, goaded on by his wife, Lady Macbeth, has risen to power by murderous means. The passage comes at the point in the play when Macbeth has just discovered that his wife has killed herself.

    > Out, out, brief candle!
    >
    > Life's but a walking shadow, a poor player
    >
    > That struts and frets his hour upon the stage
    >
    > And then is heard no more. It is a tale
    >
    > Told by an idiot, full of sound and fury,
    >
    > Signifying nothing.

Metaphor and Ideas

Another aspect of metaphor is the way metaphors help generate ideas. One way to do this is to think of metaphors that involve some kind of action. Think, for example, of how solving a problem might be like interpreting a poem or organizing a dinner party. Think how giving a presentation is like skiing down a mountain or planting a garden. How might managing a project be similar to planning a vacation?

Thinking of a challenge you confront at work, in school, or at home, as an obstacle course presents a very different scenario than seeing that challenge as a game or as an opportunity. Seeing a weight-loss plan as a military campaign directs our thinking one way; seeing it as an opportunity to become a more creative cook and a chance to discover new foods and tastes results in very different dieting experiences.

Metaphors matter. Our metaphors affect and direct the way we experience the world. In his notebooks, Leonardo da Vinci connected the unconnected for creative inspiration. He found images and ideas hidden in the stains on walls, in the ashes of a spent fire, in the shape of clouds, even in mud. He forced himself to imagine connections between unlike things, sometimes throwing a sponge filled with paint against a wall to see what patterns might stimulate his imagination so that he could make a visual and metaphorical connection. One time he was watching the ripples spread by a stone thrown into water when he heard the sound of church bells. He realized then that sound travels in "waves," like the image in the water that he observed.

Leonardo bears out Aristotle's claim that making metaphors is an indication of creative genius. But Leonardo went further. He amended Aristotle by suggesting that it is impossible for the human mind not to see connections among things. We all make connections; we are all metaphor makers, just not at the same brilliant level of Leonardo.

EXERCISES

24. Explain the differing implications of the following metaphors:
    - Marriage as a legal and economic structure
    - Marriage as a form of friendship, companionship, and support
    - Marriage as an adventure and a journey
    - Marriage as a partnership
    - Marriage as an experiment
    - Marriage as a prison

25. Select a term from column A to match up with a term from column B to forge a metaphorical link. Then explain the implications of the metaphor you create.

A	B
Writing	Praying
Reading	Working
Thinking	Traveling
Studying	Conversing
Singing	Swimming

Metaphor and Politics

Among the most prevalent of metaphors in everyday life are political metaphors. Governing a state or nation has been compared to steering and guiding a large ship. This metaphor implies that the political leader is the pilot or captain of this "ship of state." It also implies that the ship can be steered through various kinds of troubled waters with different kinds of dangers lurking beneath the surface. The captain and his crew are responsible for ensuring that the ship of state sails safely to destinations that enrich the lives of its passengers and that it return securely to port.

As interesting as this metaphor is and as prevalent as it has been historically, it lacks the descriptive and explanatory power of social science explanation. To complement this historical-metaphorical model of politics, political scientists present a version of politics as a process. We can think of the political process from two perspectives—from that of experience (what it is like for us as individuals), and from the perspective of science (what it is like as a system).

Politics as a system also relies on a metaphor—on a mechanism, an aspect of engineering. In considering politics from this mechanical system perspective, the political leader is a kind of engineer with his aides serving as various kinds of technicians, specialists in overseeing different aspects of systems operations. One of those facets involves the collection, analysis, and dissemination of information or politically relevant data. We might consider, for example, data about the relationship of voting patterns to certain variables, such as level of education, religious affiliation, or ethnicity.

Another metaphorical view of politics is based on the idea that people behave in ways that maximize their own interests. This view considers people as rational thinkers who analyze political complexities and vote in accord with what is best for them as individuals and as members of important groups to which they belong. In many national elections, particularly those in the United States, voters tend to consider the state of the economy, particularly how well they are doing under the present administration, and what economic and financial implications would result if they were to vote for a new administration. Each of these political metaphors directs our thinking in different ways and to differing purposes.

EXERCISE

26. What aspects of politics would you identify as experiential and which aspects as part of a system that could be studied methodically? What are the benefits and drawbacks of considering politics from the perspectives of experience and of system? What are the advantages and disadvantages of the metaphors of politics as ship of state and politics as a mechanism?

Metaphor and the Mind

In an essay "Metaphors are in the Mind," in John Brockman's book, *This Explains Everything*, Benjamin Bergen reminds us just how important metaphor is by claiming that metaphorical language rather than being haphazard is, instead, "systematic and coherent." Bergen suggests that it's mostly abstract things that we describe in terms of more concrete things with metaphors. Political campaigns are "horse races." Morality is being "clean." Understanding something is "seeing" it. "I see what you mean," we say; and "Let's try to shed some light on the problem."

An even more significant claim made by Bergen is that we don't just talk metaphorically, we think metaphorically. When we speak of understanding in terms of seeing, we actually think of understanding as seeing. In thinking about morality in terms of cleanliness, we equate morality with cleanliness. Morality *is* cleanliness. Bergen argues further that we speak metaphorically because we think metaphorically. It is the thinking with metaphors that drives our use of metaphor in speech.

The connotations of words affect how we perceive things. Metaphor helps us understand things in different ways and convey our ways of seeing and understanding to others. Connotations imply attitudes and feelings. Metaphor enables writers to take their thinking in unexpected directions. But there is even more to the way language is connected to our thinking.

Language and Thought

Our minds, as John Searle notes in *Mind, Language, and Society*, are linguistically structured. For all but the very simplest thoughts, we need a language to think our thoughts. If thought involves language, so too, does language involve thought. We think in our native language, which filters the way we "see" and experience the world. (And if we speak other languages, we actually see and experience the world in somewhat different ways because of the way those other languages "carve up" and filter our experience of the world.) This philosophical notion is based on the concept that we construct reality rather than simply absorb it. From this constructionist perspective, we experience reality uniquely, as distinctive individuals. And yet we also experience reality in concert with others, based on the language we speak and the culture of which we are a part. But how far this idea of cultural and linguistic relativism holds, and what implications this idea actually has, remain in dispute among linguists and cultural historians.

For example, if a language lacks a future verb tense, does that mean that its speakers have no sense of the future—no concept of futurity? This is unlikely. Just think about English, which can be used to express a future notion without a "will" or "will have" verb. "I am going there tomorrow," we might say, and use the present tense verb *am* and the present participle *going* with the word *tomorrow* to convey future time. Or, to take another example: As the German language has a very tightly organized logical structure, does that mean that German speakers are more logical and more organized thinkers than speakers of Swedish, French, Hindi, or Swahili, for example? What about languages that have many more words for colors than others? Does a speaker of one of those color-rich languages see a painting by van Gogh or Matisse differently from a speaker of a color-poor language?

In *Through the Language Glass*, Guy Deutscher considers these and other questions about the relationship between languages and the ways people think. He challenges the notion that we all think pretty much the same way no matter what language(s) we speak, regardless of our mother tongue. Deutscher contends that different languages can and do lead their speakers to different ways of thinking.

Different languages (and cultures) name the rainbow in different ways; thus, their speakers "see" the rainbow differently. Different languages also classify things differently, and even "sex" them differently. Deutscher contends that it makes a difference whether the word for *sea* or *moon* in a language is masculine, feminine, or neuter. The different genders of the moon and the sea lead speakers of different languages to perceive them in significantly different ways. Deutscher, however, is careful to explain that every language has ways to conceptualize "reality," that all languages develop relationships between specific and general, concrete and abstract. But they do not all make those connections the same way.

Reports, Inferences, and Judgments

We are concerned in this chapter with how language is linked with thought—how our literal and metaphorical uses of language communicate thoughts and feelings,

Write the Response,
Reports, Inferences, Judgments
MyThinkingLab

attitudes and ideas. We have suggested that attending to the connotations of language and to its metaphorical uses can help us better understand what others are saying and suggesting and what we ourselves think.

An additional tool for sharpening our ability to understand the connection between language and thought is a set of terms—*reports, inferences*, and *judgments*.

Here is an excerpt from an article in a magazine. What do you notice about the details included? To what extent has the writer stuck to facts alone?

> In the United States, one in four children is born into poverty. The United States is the world's wealthiest country, but the vast majority of that wealth is held by a small percentage of the population. The combined wealth of the top one percent of American families is nearly equal to that of the entire bottom ninety-five percent. Such inequality is surely at odds with a country built on principles of equality and democracy.

Did you notice that the first three sentences present facts? And did you detect something different about the fourth sentence—that it departs from facts to suggest an attitude, a point of view about the facts? The words *surely at odds* convey the writer's attitude, his point of view; he suggests that inequality of wealth among different segments of the US population goes against, or contradicts, the principles on which the country was built—"principles of equality and democracy."

In his classic book, *Language in Thought and Action*, S. I. Hayakawa distinguishes usefully between and among reports, inferences, and judgments. (The previous sentence expresses an opinion; the word *usefully*, is a tip-off.) A **report** is a declarative statement that can be verified. It's a statement of fact. Report statements, or reports for short, can be right or wrong, correct or incorrect; their intent, nevertheless, is to identify something noted and believed. To test a report we attempt to verify it; we check its accuracy. If we say that the price of gasoline increased throughout the country in the past week, we could verify that statement by checking with agencies that monitor that kind of information. Given the proper resources, if a statement can be verified—proven true or false—it's a report.

An **inference** is an interpretive statement about the unknown based on what is observed. An inference is the recognition of an implication, what is implied or suggested by something noticed. We infer one thing on the basis of something else. For example, we might infer that someone is afraid of spiders based on the following observations: She screams when she sees one; she faints if she notices one crawling on her; she stammers when she tries to say the word *spider*. Those last three statements are reports, in Hayakawa's terms; they are declarative statements that can be verified. In considering the implications of those three statements, our inference that she is afraid of spiders seems quite reasonable.

We make inferences all the time; it's virtually impossible not to do so. We may infer the wealth of a person from the cut of his or her clothes, from the kind of watch or jewelry worn, from a home address, job title, and the like. We might be wrong or right; the more information on which we base our inference, and the more accurate the information, the likelier it is that our inferences will be correct. It's important to know that we are making inferences when we do, so that we don't confuse inferences with reports, or statements of fact. The quality of an inference is directly related to the quality of the reports or facts on which it is based.

report
A declarative statement that can be verified as true or false, accurate or inaccurate.

inference
A statement about the unknown made on the basis of the known; the recognition of an implication, what is implied or suggested by something noticed.

A **judgment**, in Hayakawa's terms, is a conclusion. Judgments are often expressed as opinions with the added element of approval or disapproval. Judgments can cloud our thinking, as we tend to jump to conclusions—to judge quickly with very little evidence in support. To confuse judgments with reports is a major obstacle to clear thinking. In saying, for example, that "the new Apple iPhone 5 is a great device," or that "the iPhone 5 is a dud," you are making a judgment. To say: "the iPhone 5 contains a more powerful camera and a unique shared video feature" is a report: so is "the iPhone 5 has a wraparound antenna that drops calls more frequently than other iPhone models." These statements can be verified, can be checked, and shown to be correct or incorrect, which makes them reports, declarative statements about what is observed.

On the other hand, to accuse someone of being a "liar" or a "thief" is to make a judgment (and also a prediction that he or she will lie or steal again). It's an opinion expressed with a strong dose of disapproval. To verify any of these accusations, we would have to acquire some facts. We would need to uncover information, such that what the person said contradicts what all others have said, and/or that it contradicts what his or her telephone records show. Or that he or she has been convicted twice for theft, and has served a year in prison on those convictions. (Of course, he or she might have been wrongly convicted; the evidence may have been planted, and so on. But even so, the decision to convict was based on reports. In some cases those reports are either erroneous or deliberately falsified.)

The biggest danger of judgments is that when they are made prematurely, without evidence, they can be wrongheaded, even dangerous. Judgments typically stop thought because judgments are essentially conclusions. Once we come to judgment (or conclusion), our minds have been pretty much made up. Therefore, we need to be aware when we are making judgments, and we need to be sure that we are basing them on reports, on accurate factual statements, and not just on opinions or on other judgments.

judgment
A conclusion that expresses approval or disapproval.

EXERCISES

27. Identify the following statements as reports, inferences, or judgments. Explain your reason in each case.

    a. She goes to the opera only to show off her jewelry.

    b. Stock prices were up slightly today in light trading.

    c. The Ukranian people do not want war.

    d. Beauty is only skin-deep.

    e. An apple a day keeps the doctor away.

    f. Mixing beer with wine or scotch leads to a terrible hangover.

    g. America has never lost a war.

    h. $a^2 + b^2 = c^2$

    i. A credit score of 650 is good.

    j. Eat blueberries and walnuts, as both foods are healthy for your heart.

28. Explain how you would verify two reports in the previous exercise. Explain how you would provide supporting evidence for one inference and for one judgment you found in the exercise.

29. Look through the preface, introduction, or first chapter of one of your text-books—or of any nonfiction book you have handy. Read the first three paragraphs and identify the sentences as reports, inferences, or judgments.

30. Return to the Kitty Genovese discussion earlier in this chapter. Review the three headlines from the newspapers and also the first lines of each story from those same newspapers—*the New York Times*, the *New York Herald Tribune*, and the *New York Daily News*. To what extent do those headlines and opening lines of the stories include reports and to what extent inferences and judgments? Which words and phrases do you think depart from reports?

Language and Critical Analysis

What we have been doing throughout this chapter, although we have not yet identified it as such, is "critical analysis." We focused on words in an effort to identify not just their denotations, or dictionary meanings but also their connotations, or emotional reverberations. We identified judgments conveyed by the language used in the headlines and the opening sentences of their respective stories. We also raised larger questions about the relationship between language and culture, and between language and thought.

In the process, we looked not just at this word or that. Instead, we looked for patterns—as in the connection between what we noticed about the language of a particular newspaper's headline and what we noticed about the language of its accompanying story's opening sentences. We will now delve more deeply into what we mean by critical analysis.

An Approach to Analysis

analysis
A process of identifying and considering the parts of something to better understand its structure and meaning.

When we **analyze** a text, whether visual or verbal, we isolate and look closely at its parts, focusing on one element at a time. We observe details. Then we make connections among those details, looking for patterns and relationships among them. Building on those connections we make inferences, which are based on what we have noticed and linked in our observations. And from those inferences, we arrive at an interpretive conclusion.

> In sum: Observations lead to Connections, which lead to Inferences, which lead to Conclusions. This process is then repeated, so that the analytical work is both cyclical and recursive.

Our goal in doing analysis is to understand what we read or view, to grasp how its parts fit together, to make sense of it as a whole. Our analysis of a text can only be as good as the evidence that supports it. And that evidence begins with what we observe, what we notice, what we "see." Noticing carefully and deeply is the foundation for thinking and the basis for thoughtful and persuasive interpretations. Let's follow the process through from the beginning. We start with observation.

Observing Details

The kinds of observations we make about a text will depend on the kind of text we are reading or viewing. In reading a scientific report, we observe the data it includes, the argument it develops, and the evidence marshaled in its support. In reading a psychological abstract, we attend to the purpose and limits of the study or experiment, along with the research field it exemplifies. In reading a historical document, we notice its date and place of composition, its social and cultural and political contexts, and more. In reading a work of literature, we notice details about plot and character, setting and point of view, diction and **imagery**, sentence patterns, sound patterns, structure and tone, and more.

imagery
Descriptive detail in a text that triggers visual, auditory, tactile, and other sense stimuli.

To demonstrate what observing details looks like in reading an essay, a work of nonfiction that advances an idea, we analyze the following excerpt from an essay by Susan Sontag, "A Woman's Beauty: Put-Down or Power Source?" Even before reading the excerpt, we might notice something about the language of Sontag's title, which focuses on beauty, specifically the beauty of women. We might notice, too, that the title sets up a dichotomy, or opposition, between two ways of considering women's beauty. And we might notice further that the essay's title is a question. This question, we expect, will be answered in the essay. But the question gets us thinking even before we begin reading what Sontag has to say. Here is one paragraph from Sontag's essay:

> To be called beautiful is thought to name something essential to women's character and concerns. (In contrast to men—whose essence is to be strong, or effective, or competent.) It does not take someone in the throes of advanced feminist awareness to perceive that the way women are taught to be involved with beauty encourages narcissism, reinforces dependence and immaturity. Everybody (women and men) knows that. For it is "everybody," a whole society that has identified being feminine with caring about how one *looks*. (In contrast to being masculine—which is identified with caring about what one *is* and *does* and only secondarily, if at all, about how one looks.)

Let's make a few observations about this paragraph. You probably noticed how Sontag contrasts remarks about women and men. (Twice, in fact, she puts those contrasts in parentheses—and she uses the word *contrasts* explicitly both times to cue the differences for us.) You noticed, too, very likely, how she italicizes certain words: *looks* with respect to women, *is* and *does* with respect to men. These words also present a contrast between men and women, a contrast that judges women as being superficial, concerned with their appearance, while men are concerned with presumably more important matters—doing things.

The italics emphasize the importance of the contrast, highlighting Sontag's claim that women are concerned with their appearance and men with their accomplishments. Noticing these details is essential for understanding what Sontag says about women. With these comments we have already started to make some connections among the details we have noticed—as for example, the various ways Sontag uses a contrast with men to explain her view of women and beauty.

Connecting Details

It is not enough to observe details. To understand what is being said and suggested, we also need to make connections among those details. In doing so, we see one detail or element in relation to another. The connections we make among a text's details are an important step toward making sense of it—making meaning from it. Here, now, is another paragraph from Sontag's essay. As you read, keep noticing details, and then make some connections between and among those details. And think about some connections you can make between this second part of the excerpt and the first part, the opening paragraph.

> It is not, of course, the desire to be beautiful that is wrong but the obligation to be—or to try. What is accepted by most women as a flattering idealization of their sex is also a way of making women feel inferior to what they actually are—or normally grow to be. For the ideal of beauty is administered as a form of self-oppression. Women are taught to see their bodies in parts, and to evaluate each part separately. Breasts, feet, hips, waistline, neck, eyes, nose, complexion, hair, and so on—each in turn is submitted to an anxious, fretful, often despairing scrutiny. Even if some pass muster, some will always be found wanting.

EXERCISES

31. List two observations about the language Sontag uses in this paragraph. Make two connections among the observations you made within the paragraph. Make one connection between this paragraph and the earlier one. In the process of doing this exercise, you may wish to circle or underline some key words that jump out at you—words that convey an opinion or a judgment, especially. Let's now look at one last additional bit of Sontag's essay—one more short paragraph.

> In men, good looks is a whole, something taken in at a glance. It does not need to be confirmed by giving measurements of different regions of the body; nobody encourages a man to dissect his appearance, feature by feature. As for perfection, that is considered trivial—almost unmanly.

32. What does this paragraph add to the others? What observations can you make about it? What further connections can you establish between this third paragraph and the two previously quoted paragraphs?

Making Inferences

Let's use this last short paragraph from Sontag's essay, in conjunction with the other two paragraphs to think a bit about the inferences Sontag is making and the inferences we are making in reading what she writes. First, however, we need to say a bit more about inferences. Remember that an inference is a statement based on an observation, on something noticed. Inferences drive our interpretations. They push us toward understanding and explanation. We can't develop an interpretation without making inferences.

Here are a few examples of inferences Sontag makes:

- She infers that a concern for beauty is linked with narcissism and immaturity.
- She infers that this vision of women, along with their dependence on men, is common knowledge.
- She infers that society as a whole has made women this way—overly concerned with their appearance, with what lies on the surface rather than with what lies beneath it.
- She thinks that women's obligation to be beautiful is a way to make them feel inferior to men.
- She believes that the ideal of women's beauty oppresses women.

And now here are some inferences we might make on the basis of our first group of inferences. These constitute an added layer of inferences.

- Sontag thinks there is a double standard in play with regard to men's and women's beauty.
- She judges this standard to be unfair to women, and thus wrong.
- She suggests that few women can meet the high standards for beauty imposed by society on women.
- She seems to approve of the way masculine beauty is evaluated—as a sum of a man's features.
- She seems to suggest that this more holistic approach to beauty would be a better one to apply to women.

Arriving at an Interpretation

Much of our interpretive work is accomplished when we make inferences. An interpretation is a way of explaining the meaning of a text. In making an interpretation, we connect our inferences into a coherent form of understanding that we can explain first to ourselves and then to others. So, just as you connected your observations to begin making sense of Sontag's text, you connect your inferences to arrive at an interpretation of it.

Your interpretation can be further elaborated or developed. It can be altered, even revised, based on further thought, deeper and more extensive observations you make, discussion of the text with others, what you read about it, and so on.

When we arrive at an interpretation, we look back at the text's details to reconsider our initial observations and to review the connections we made among them. Consider now whether your inferences about Sontag's text are justifiable, whether you can offer textual details as evidence to support those inferences. And look to see if you notice anything further, and if you can make other inferences—observations and inferences than can be incorporated into your interpretation.

For example, in reading Sontag's passage, you might first conclude that she is blaming women for their predicament. You might interpret her comments to suggest that women are complicit, even responsible for their situation. And you might argue that it is up to them to change things—if, that is, they want such a change. You might interpret Sontag's remarks as a condemnation of women's preoccupation with their beauty as a sign of self-absorption and triviality. On the other hand, you might decide later, after rereading the passage a few times, and after some discussion with others, that Sontag blames society as a whole for this superficial emphasis on women's beauty. And that though women may share in the blame, their responsibility is less than that of men, who expect and even demand that women be concerned with their physical appearance to the detriment of other important aspects and qualities, such as their courage, their social skills, and their moral and intellectual attributes.

EXERCISE

33. Read Sontag's complete essay. Then write a paragraph that summarizes what Sontag says in it about women and beauty. Write a second paragraph that explains how she presents her ideas. That is, analyze how she organizes her thoughts, and analyze her sentences, selection of detail, and her language—her word choices, or diction. Follow with a third paragraph that offers your own thinking about what Sontag says about women (and men). To what extent do you agree or disagree; to what extent would you modify or qualify what she says? Why?

A Woman's Beauty: Put-Down or Power Source

SUSAN SONTAG

For the Greeks, beauty was a virtue: a kind of excellence. Persons then were assumed to be what we now have to call—lamely, enviously—*whole* persons. If it did occur to the Greeks to distinguish between a person's "inside" and "outside," they still expected that inner beauty would be matched by beauty of the other kind. The well-born young Athenians who gathered around Socrates found it quite paradoxical that their hero was so intelligent, so brave, so honorable, so seductive—and so ugly. One of Socrates' main pedagogical acts was to be ugly—and teach those innocent, no doubt splendid-looking disciples of his, how full of paradoxes life really was.

They may have resisted Socrates' lesson. We do not. Several thousand years later, we are more wary of the enchantments of beauty. We not only split off—with the greatest facility—the "inside" (character, intellect) from the "outside" (looks); but we are actually surprised when someone who is beautiful is also intelligent, talented, good.

It was principally the influence of Christianity that deprived beauty of the central place it had in classical ideals of human excellence. By limiting excellence (*virtus* in Latin) to *moral* virtue only, Christianity set beauty adrift—as an alienated, arbitrary, superficial enchantment. And beauty has continued to lose prestige. For close to two centuries it has become a convention to attribute beauty to only one of the two sexes: the sex which, however Fair, is always Second. Associating beauty with women has put beauty even further on the defensive, morally.

A beautiful woman, we say in English. But a handsome man. "Handsome" is the masculine equivalent of—and refusal of—a compliment which has accumulated certain demeaning overtones, by being reserved for women only. That one can call a man "beautiful" in French and in Italian suggests that Catholic countries—unlike those countries shaped by the Protestant version of Christianity—still retain some vestiges of the pagan admiration for beauty. But the difference, if one exists, is of degree only. In every modern country that is Christian or post-Christian, women *are* the beautiful sex—to the detriment of the notion of beauty as well as of women.

To be called beautiful is thought to name something essential to women's character and concerns. (In contrast to men—whose essence is to be strong, or effective, or competent.) It does not take someone in the throes of advanced feminist awareness to perceive that the way women are taught to be involved with beauty encourages narcissism, reinforces dependence and immaturity. Everybody (women and men) knows that. For it is "everybody," a whole society, that has identified being feminine with caring about how one *looks*. (In contrast to being masculine—which is identified with caring about what one *is* and *does* and only secondarily, if at all, about how one looks.) Given these stereotypes, it is no wonder that beauty enjoys, at best, a rather mixed reputation.

It is not, of course, the desire to be beautiful that is wrong but the obligation to be—or to try. What is accepted by most women as a flattering idealization of their sex is a way of making women feel inferior to what they actually are—or normally grow to be. For the ideal of beauty is administered as a form of self-oppression. Women are taught to see their bodies in *parts*, and to evaluate each part separately. Breasts, feet, hips, waistline, neck, eyes, nose, complexion, hair, and so on—each in turn is submitted to an anxious, fretful, often despairing scrutiny. Even if some pass muster, some will always be found wanting. Nothing less than perfection will do.

In men, good looks is a whole, something taken in at a glance. It does not need to be confirmed by giving measurements of different regions of the body; nobody encourages a man to dissect his appearance, feature by feature. As for perfection, that is considered trivial—almost unmanly. Indeed, in the ideally good-looking man a small imperfection or blemish is considered positively desirable. According to one movie critic (a woman) who is a declared Robert Redford fan, it is having that cluster of skin-colored moles on one cheek that saves Redford from being merely a "pretty face." Think of the depreciation of women—as well as of beauty—that is implied in that judgment.

"The privileges of beauty are immense," said Cocteau. To be sure, beauty is a form of power. And deservedly so. What is lamentable is that it is the only form of power that most women are encouraged to seek. This power is always conceived in relation to men; it is not the power to do but the power to attract. It is a power that negates itself. For this power is not one that can be chosen freely—at least, not by women—or renounced without social censure.

To preen, for a woman, can never be just a pleasure. It is also a duty. It is her work. If a woman does real work—and even if she has clambered up to a leading position in politics, law, medicine, business, or whatever—she is always under pressure to confess that she still works at being attractive. But in so far as she is keeping up as one of the Fair Sex, she brings under suspicion her very capacity to be objective, professional, authoritative, thoughtful. Damned if they do—women are. And damned if they don't.

One could hardly ask for more important evidence of the dangers of considering persons as split between what is "inside" and what is "outside" than that interminable half-comic half-tragic tale, the oppression of women. How easy it is to start off by defining women as caretakers of their surfaces, and then to disparage them (or find them adorable) for being "superficial." It is a crude trap, and it has worked for too long. But to get out of the trap requires that women get some critical distance from that excellence and privilege which is beauty, enough distance to see how much beauty itself has been abridged in order to prop up the mythology of the "feminine." There should be a way of saving beauty *from* women—and *for* them.

Looking Back and Looking Ahead

Revisit the learning goals that begin this chapter. Which of these goals do you think you have best achieved? What might you do to reach the remaining goals?

Return to the focusing questions at the beginning of the chapter. How would you answer those questions now? Which of them do you find most interesting and provocative and worthy of following up? Why?

In reviewing the list of resources that follows, identify the two that attract you most. Explain why these books or Web sites interest you. Consider looking into them for further developing and deepening your thinking about language and critical analysis.

Take a look, too, at the MyThinkingLab resources on the Prentice Hall Web site. Included there are readings, images, videos, questions, exercises, and other provocations to help you develop your capacity for critical thinking and critical analysis.

• •

Resources

Notebooks, Leonardo da Vinci. Ed. H. Anna Suh. Black Dog & Leventhal, 2009.

The Night Mirror, John Hollander. Atheneum, 1971.

Language in Thought and Action, S. I. Hayakawa. Harvest, 1991.

Loaded Words, Marjorie Garber. Fordham University Press, 2012.

This Explains Everything, Ed. John Brockman. Edge Foundation, HarperCollins, 2013.

Mind, Language, and Society, John Searle. Basic Books, 2000.

Through the Language Glass, Guy Deutscher. Macmillan, 2011.

Metaphors We Live By, George Lakoff and Mark Johnson. University of Chicago Press, 2005.

Politics: A Very Short History, Kenneth Minogue. Oxford University Press, 2000.

Thirty-Eight Witnesses, A. M. Rosenthal. University of California Press, 1964.

"A Woman's Beauty: Put-Down or Power Source." Susan Sontag. In *Women's Voices*. Ed. Pat C. Hoy II et al. McGraw-Hill, 1989.

• •

4
Analyzing Images

An image, painted, sculpted, photographed, built and framed, is also a stage, a site for performance.

—ALBERTO MANGUEL

LEARNING GOALS

4.1 DISTINGUISH among signs, symbols, images, and icons, and what they communicate.

4.2 ANALYZE and explain how advertisements work to appeal to viewers through words and images.

4.3 EXAMINE how visual images convey information, ideas, attitudes, and feelings.

4.4 EXPLORE connections between and among visual images.

4.5 UNDERSTAND basic elements of moving images (movies), including the use of montage.

Chapter Overview

This chapter invites consideration of a series of images, including pictures, images, icons, signs, symbols, and other forms of visual representation. It includes and references a variety of visual texts, such as advertisements, political cartoons, works of art, photographs, paintings, and still images from a film. Throughout the chapter are repeated invitations to look and look again—to notice deeply, make connections, develop inferences toward a deeper understanding of how images influence both our feeling and our thinking. The central notion of the chapter is that images convey meaning in a multitude of ways. Because images are so prevalent, we need to understand them and use them effectively in communication.

FOCUSING QUESTIONS

- How do you distinguish between the terms sign and symbol? How is the word *icon* related to "sign" and "symbol"? What other terms might be related to these?

- How important are visual elements in print advertisements? What should be the relationship of a print advertisement's language to its visual images?

- Have you read any graphic novels or manga books? If so, which ones are your favorites and why? If not, why don't you read visual works?

- Which are your favorite works of visual art—paintings, photographs, sculptures, cartoons, comics, graphic novels, manga, films? What about them engages you?

The Prevalence and Power of Images

⊙ **Watch** the **Video**, The Prevalence and Power of Images **MyThinkingLab**

We are bombarded with visual images nearly as much as we are inundated with verbal information. We carry images on our PDA devices, on our computers, on Facebook, and other network pages. Images populate our books and magazines and newspapers, whether we read their print or electronic versions. Images are all around us in the form of ads, commercials, pictures, photographs, and more. In fact, much of the information that we receive comes our way via images.

For this reason, we need to become both more conscious of and more critical about the prevalence of images in our lives. Images, like words, communicate information, convey feelings, and express ideas and ideals. To understand what images communicate, convey, and express, however, we need to improve our ability to analyze and interpret them. The common saying that "an image is worth a thousand words" suggests that it can take a thousand words to explain what is implied in an image. And although that may seem like an exaggeration, it bears a considerable amount of truth.

Also like words, images have the power to bring us to tears as well as incite us to laughter. Images stimulate our interest, engage our curiosity, prod us to action. Images can turn us on and turn us off; they can excite and disgust us, inspire and terrify us. We have all seen photographs that make us smile or make us cry, that amuse and amaze and astonish us. And we have seen films that delight and entertain, that provoke our thinking, stimulate our imagination, and engage our deepest feelings. For all these reasons and more, a close look at images is warranted.

Image, Icon, Symbol, Sign

image
A general term for any pictorial representation.

What is an image? The simplest answer is that an **image** is a kind of picture—a visual representation of something. A photograph, for example, is an image of a person, place, object, or event. A photograph is static, a snapshot of a moment in time. That limits a photo's usefulness for narrative, for telling a story that unfolds over time. Of course, we can narrate a story with multiple photographs, streaming them in such rapid succession that they appear to move; hence our term *moving pictures*. Our interest here is in what and how images communicate—in their fundamental expressive power.

We begin with a few basic questions: Are images always symbolic? And if so, in what ways are they symbolic, or representative? What's the difference between a symbol and an icon? According to American philosopher Charles Sanders Peirce, icons bear a likeness to the things they represent, whereas symbols are more arbitrarily determined. And how is a sign similar to and different from an image, an icon, and a symbol?

EXERCISE

1. Take a look at the following images. Identify each. Consider what each image depicts. You may wish to discuss your explanations of the images with other classmates.

Let's sort out the terms *image*, *icon*, *symbol*, and *sign*. We can begin by identifying the images that accompany Exercise 1. You see five pictures. First, you see a set of four interlinked ellipses pitched at different angles, positioned around a black dot in the center. This picture represents atomic energy, with the central dot representing

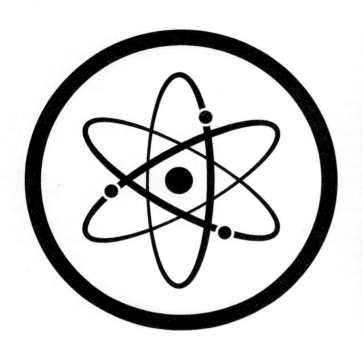

an atom. The second image depicts a woman whose pose might very well seem familiar—Leonardo da Vinci's *Mona Lisa*. Third, you see a pair of figurines, male and female, dressed in tuxedo and wedding dress—figurines that would be placed on top of a wedding cake. Next to this newly "married couple" is the head of an eagle, and beside the eagle, an old-fashioned black rotary-dial, landline telephone.

It is hard not to see each of these pictures as symbolic—as representing something beyond themselves, particularly when they are placed alongside one another. The first image, we have already suggested, represents atomic or nuclear energy, but we could go further and imagine it symbolizing the power of the atom for constructive and destructive purposes, as in the explosiveness of an atom bomb. The image of the woman seems a bit mysterious, and with her hint of a smile, we might suggest that she conveys the mystery not just of the woman depicted in Leonardo's, but of "woman" more generally. This, of course, is just one interpretation, but that's what the images seem to ask of us—to make "sense" of them in this interpretive manner. The bride and groom figurines represent a wedding, and more generally, marriage—and perhaps certain aspects of marriage, such as love and romance, fidelity and family.

What about the eagle? As a powerful bird, a raptor that perches atop the avian food chain, the eagle can represent strength and force. As a wild bird, it can symbolize freedom and independence. It's no accident that the bald eagle is used to represent the United States, with its celebrated history of independence and its tradition of freedom. Those, of course, are some positive associations of the image. We might also see the eagle as a violent predator, whose strength and power allow it to terrorize and cannibalize other smaller and weaker animals. However, you look at the eagle, it is a complex symbol and not just a simple image. This is so because of the associations we bring to it, which derive both from its nature and behavior and from historical events associated with the American nation it has come to symbolize. These associations of the eagle image correspond to the connotations of the word *eagle*.

And the telephone? What does that telephone signify or represent? Communication comes to mind, of course. And because this example of a telephone is something of a relic of the past, it can stand for an earlier time—and perhaps for associations we have with that time. Yet, however much we reflect on this image of the telephone, it lacks the symbolic resonance and the range and depth of reference the eagle represents. So we can say that some images have symbolic properties—they suggest meanings, ideas beyond themselves, and further, that some images have more intensive and more extensive symbolic power than others.

EXERCISES

2. Look through the following five additional images. Find one that you think has powerful symbolic reverberations—in the manner of the eagle. Explain what the image symbolizes. Identify another image from this second group of five that also has symbolic significance. Explain what this second image symbolizes.

3. What does each of those images represent? Should we call all of these images symbols, too, as we did for the previous images? Why or why not? Might we call some of them signs rather than symbols? What's the difference between a sign and a symbol?

4. Looking at the graphic that opens this chapter, identify each of the objects depicted. Are these pictures signs or symbols? Why? Where do you find such pictures? As you scan through them from one row to the next what additional observations can you make about the overall set of images—the graphic as a whole?

The Vocabulary of Comics

In his book, *Understanding Comics*, Scott McLoud distinguishes among the terms *image*, *icon*, *symbol*, and *picture*. His most general term, *image*, refers to anything pictorial, including *icons*, his second broadest category. Icons can represent many kinds of things; they serve different representational purposes. But those purposes are narrow, and the meanings of the icons are highly specific. McLoud depicts 10 sets of icons, beginning with the alphabet and including such things as numbers, the $ and % signs. These we understand as communication icons, whether that communication uses language, numbers, or some other representational system, such as musical notation. So, images are "pictures," and icons are highly specific designators of things such as letters, dollar signs, musical pitch and duration of sound, and so on.

Some images (and icons), however, are symbolic, like our eagle and McLoud's examples, which include the yin-yang symbol and the American flag—among others.

These symbolic images differ from the communication icons in the chapter opener graphic. They also differ from the icon that signifies "ladies room" and the simple smiley-face figure that signifies being "happy." The yin-yang symbol and the American flag are more complex signifiers. They possess the complexity of signification, the range and depth, the intensity and extensiveness of the eagle image discussed earlier. These images are symbols; they are not necessarily pictorial, nor are they simple indicators like the dollar sign or a musical note, which represent something more specific and confined in meaning.

⊙▶ **Simulate** the **Experiment**, The Vocabulary of Comics **MyThinkingLab**

Symbols can be contrasted with signs. We will use the term *sign* for the simple icons with a single meaning, and we will use the term *symbol* for the more complex representational icons. A "sign" points, but only in a single direction: "Men's room here"; "Information found here"; "Currency exchanged here"; and so on. Symbols, contrastingly, represent a range and variety of associations or ideas. Think of a sign as an arrow pointing in a single direction. Think of a symbol as a series of ripples from a center, radiating meanings in multiple directions.

McLoud defines **pictures** as images that are designed to resemble their subjects. This pictorial representation is a matter of degree, as with a picture drawn to represent a human figure in the manner we find in comics. So the degree of likeness between a picture and what it designates varies, as, of course, does the quality, detail, and iconic content of its representational intent.

We can say, along with McLoud, that "images" in the form of "icons" called **symbols** represent concepts, as well as, more broadly, ideas and philosophies. Symbols also carry with them feelings and other personal associations.

picture
An image meant to resemble its subject but in a simpler, less detailed form.

symbol
A complex icon that represents more abstract concepts, ideas, and values.

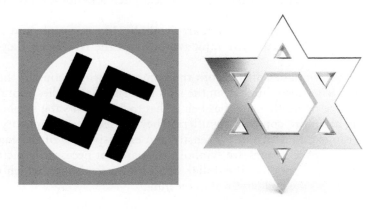

The Nazi swastika and the Jewish star mean vastly different things emotionally to those in any way connected historically or personally with the Holocaust than to those not so linked. (In the same way that the connotations of the words *Nazi*, *swastika*, *Holocaust*, and *dictator* resonate with different degrees of emotional intensity for people who have had various kinds of experience, directly or indirectly, with what those terms refer to historically.)

One last point to make about this array of terms is an additional note about the word *icon*. We tend to use **icon** in a special way when we designate a particular object, person, place, or event, as "iconic." For example, we think of the Statue of Liberty as iconic; that is, it is seen as a quintessential image of America, of freedom and opportunity. The Eiffel Tower is iconic for France and things French, as the Leaning Tower of Pisa or the Roman Colosseum are for Italy and things Italian. Certain foods operate iconically, as well. Pizza and pasta, for example, are iconic for Italian cuisine, baguettes and steak frites for French cuisine, tamales for Mexican cuisine, and the like. Socrates is the "iconic" philosopher, the *Mona Lisa* the "iconic" painting, the Olympics the "iconic" sports competition, Gettysburg the "iconic" Civil War battle, and so on.

icon
An image that represents a person, place, thing, or idea. An icon may also refer to a popular or well-known object, such as the Eiffel Tower, which stands for France.

EXERCISES

5. Identify three additional examples of "iconic" people, places, objects, or events. Explain why the person, place, object, or event, is "iconic" in the sense previously explained.

6. Create your own icon to represent a place or concept. You might want to do this in collaboration with a partner.

7. Look at some logos or symbols associated with brands of automobiles. What does Mercedes use? Lexus? Jaguar? Audi? How about Ford, Chevrolet, Cadillac, Jeep? Choose two of these car brand logos and explain why you think they do or do not work very well in terms of their symbolic suggestiveness.

8. Identify the logos for two products you frequently use. Provide alternate logos for each. Explain the logic or rationale for the logos you create.

Images with Words: Analyzing an Advertisement

When we analyze an advertisement, we look carefully at its words as well as its image(s). To the extent that the advertisement is successful, its images and words work together, reinforcing each other. We can look at an advertisement to see how it uses images and words to convey a message directed toward a purpose—to sell something. In considering both the ad's image and its language, we identify its appeal. In doing this, we ask ourselves not only what the ad is selling, but also how it makes its sales pitch.

Look carefully at the advertisement for Allen Edmonds shoes. Consider both its picture(s) and its words.

Write the Response, Analyzing an Advertisement MyThinkingLab

EXERCISE

9. Describe the three types of shoes pictured in the ad. What situations would be appropriate for wearing each style of shoe? In what sense are the names provided for each style of shoe appropriate for it? What's the difference among "Vincent," "Vince," and "Vinny," as names? When would the individual use

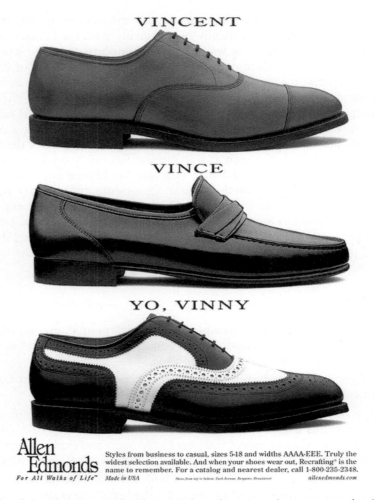

VINCENT

VINCE

YO, VINNY

Allen Edmonds
For All Walks of Life™   Made in USA

Styles from business to casual, sizes 5-18 and widths AAAA-EEE. Truly the widest selection available. And when your shoes wear out, Recrafting® is the name to remember. For a catalog and nearest dealer, call 1-800-235-2348.

Shoes from top to bottom: Park Avenue, Bergamo, Broadstreet   *allenedmonds.com*

each of those names—or when might others use those names for him? And how might each of the shoe styles be said to "fit" each of the names?

a. Who is the likely audience for this ad? Where do you think it might have appeared?

b. What might be the social and cultural implications of the ad? To what extent would this ad be understood in other parts of the world in which English is spoken?

c. Do you think this is an effective ad? Does the language used throughout the ad reinforce the image of the shoes? Why or why not? Do you think the ad could be effectively translated into other languages—perhaps one of the languages with which you are familiar?

d. Do you think anyone might be offended by this ad? Are you offended by it? Why or why not?

Observations and Analysis: Allen Edmonds Shoe Ad

Here are a few observations about the image and the words used in the Allen Edmonds advertisement. Let's start with the picture. Its size is the first thing we notice, as it dominates the page. Its color is equally striking. The shine and shading of the shoes make them look expensive, along with the stylish design—the elegant stitching of the top shoe, the clean lines and low-slung flow of the middle shoe, and the extravagant detailing and stark black-and-white contrast of the bottom shoe.

We might notice, too, that each shoe casts a shadow under itself, and that though the three shoes are the same size from left to right, they differ in height. We notice a balance in the top-to-bottom positioning of the shoes, which would be thrown off if the middle shoe were put on the top or the bottom. We "read" the shoes from top to bottom, and so the black-and-white wingtip, the most detailed and unusual shoe is best placed where it is—last.

Other visual details include the white space that forms under the heel of each shoe and the lift at the toe of each. You might notice that the middle shoe rises slightly less than the top- and bottom-tie shoes, whose shape and styling echo each other more than they do that of the middle loafer style.

About the words of the ad, we can begin with a visual detail: the elegant print used for the names, which is echoed in the "Allen Edmonds" brand name in the lower left—though the spacing for the names is wider. That spacing works to suggest the elegance of the shoes stretched across the width of the ad. The names are centered carefully, as we would expect. That centering, the spacing of the letters, the shine and shading, the use of light and shadow, white and black—taken together, the position of the words and the stylish and elegant font, match and reinforce the sense of style conveyed by the shoes themselves.

The three names used convey different aspects of the person addressed. "Vincent" is the most formal. It's the name used for serious situations, and the shoe that accompanies the name "Vincent" makes a good match for it. "Vince" is more informal. It's not buddy-buddy sounding, but it suggests a more relaxed atmosphere than Vincent. "Vinny" suggests a social closeness that Vince does not. And with the "Yo," added, we know we enter a world of close friends, probably guys who grew up together—perhaps from the Jersey shore.

Looking more closely at the ad's language, we notice under the brand name the phrase, "For All Walks of Life" followed by a TM for trademark. That phrase, a familiar saying, plays off the fact that the shoes are for walking. It also reinforces the fact that we wear different kinds of shoes for different occasions—work and leisure, for example. And those names and shoes and "walks of life" all mesh, with the upshot that Allen Edmonds has everything we might need in the shoe department. The company has it covered—and in style (for men, that is). That idea is reinforced in the paragraph of print at the bottom and to the right of the brand and slogan. That paragraph provides information, facts, including the range of sizes and widths, as well as a wide range of styles, only suggested by the three shoes pictured in the ad. The information is practical and useful; it includes a phone number to call for a catalog and a Web site, to locate dealers who sell Allen Edmonds shoes. It's a kind of call to action, an invitation to purchase some Allen Edmonds shoes.

Yet there is more. The small, italicized print, "*Made in the USA*," is an appeal to patriotism as well as to quality. We can add these appeals to those of style, elegance and "cool," which the ad makes with its depiction of the shoes, its three names, and its font style. These are its sales pitches. There is a further appeal to thrift and quality with the words: *And when your shoes wear out, Recrafting is the name to remember.* Allen Edmonds shoes, the ad suggests, are built to last, such that they can be "recrafted." Not "resoled" or "reheeled, or "rebuilt," but "recrafted," which suggests the quality and craftsmanship of an artisan. Also implied is that the shoes were originally "crafted" and not merely made or manufactured.

There is an additional appeal in the even tinier italic print, which reads: "*Shoes from top to bottom: Park Avenue, Bergamo, Broadstreet.*" "Park Avenue" suggests wealth, as Park Avenue is where the rich live and where the big banks are located (in New York City, at least). "Bergamo" suggests Italian style and elegance; the relaxed leisure of the Italian Lake District, in Lombardy, in northern Italy. And "Broadstreet" suggests a casual place where you can go out on the town. Each of the shoe names matches a place name; each shoe name reinforces the shoe's style and fits well with the names "Vincent," "Vince," and "Vinny," respectively.

We might pursue our analysis further by considering the advertisement's social and cultural implications. For example, the ad is pitched to men, not just in the shoe styles it pictures, but in the kind of taut, direct language it uses. There is no indication that Allen Edmonds makes shoes for women, nor is there any kind of appeal to women who might assist a man in purchasing quality shoes.

There is also a clear ethnic slant to the ad, in its use of a name associated with Italians, particularly its use of "Yo" with the nickname "Vinny." (You may know the movie "My Cousin Vinnie," about an Italian lawyer.") The ad, thus, incorporates ethnic stereotypes.

And culturally, we certainly might wonder about how well this ad could travel. What would English-speaking readers from other countries and cultures need to understand if the ad were to make sense to them? To what extent might it be found offensive, we might also wonder.

EXERCISES

10. Choose your own advertisement for analysis. Subject it to as close a level of scrutiny as you can. Describe and analyze its use of visual images. Analyze and explain how the ad's language works to make its appeals. And consider as well the ad's social and cultural contexts.

11. Either individually or in collaboration with a partner, create your own advertisement. You can develop an ad for a product currently available, for one that is no longer on the market—or for a product of your own invention. Be sure to think about your audience for the ad, where it might be placed, and what its appeals should be. Include in your ad both image(s) and words.

Images, Ideas, and Emotion

In this section, we consider a number of images, different kinds of images designed for different purposes. We begin by imagining (making a mental image of) the moon. Close your eyes and do that for a moment. When you have a "moon" (a full moon) in your mind's eye, you should then think about what the moon reminds you of—what you associate with it. Then continue.

What did you think of when you mentally envisioned the moon? Madness, perhaps—lunacy? Or perhaps romance. Perhaps you thought of something else. What other associations do you have with the moon? Where do these associations come from?

Now picture in your mind an image of a baby and an image of a computer. Put the words *work* and *play* on them. Which word did you associate with the computer and which with the baby? Why? Now imagine the words reversed, as perhaps one of your classmates linked them with their mental images of baby and computer. (You can find an HSBC ad that does this at http://www.unboundedition.com.)

So what does the baby represent? Work or play? And what about the computer? Is it linked with play or work? It depends, doesn't it—on who is answering the question—and on what that person is experiencing at the time. It depends, in short, on "context."

You may have probably seen images like these before—paired in this way. They can be found at airports around the world, lining hallways and corridors and the runways to the entrance of the plane. Among other things, they remind us that there is more than one way to look at something. Different people see the same thing in different ways, and we ourselves can see things differently at different times and under different circumstances. That's certainly true with regard to computers and babies.

HSBC Images

Now imagine another advertisement with an apple presented three times side-by-side. On each apple a different word is printed. One apple reads "organic"; another reads "imported"; and a third reads "engineered." There is a difference between such an advertisement with its triple image and an advertisement with a double image of two different things, like the baby/computer ad.

One difference is obvious, of course. This ad uses a single image—the same apple (or other visual item) three times. It presents three different perspectives on what the apple (or other object) signifies. One way of seeing the apple is as an organic product, grown according to certain standards and conditions. Another way is to think of the apple as imported produce. And a third is as an engineered product. Each of those words conveys a different attitude about the apple. Each of those terms calls up different emotional responses from reader/viewers. Just as the moon can be thought of under different guises, and just as we can respond to the moon in various ways, so, too do we respond to the different contexts of the advertised apple and its varied symbolic implications.

EXERCISE

12. Explain how the imagined apple ad differs from the baby/computer ad. How does the baby/computer ad do its work on us? Do you prefer one of these types of ad more than others? Why or why not?

You noticed that the first HSBC images were in binary mode, offering a two-sided perspective—flipping the images of moons, or of babies and computers, alternating between two ways of seeing each, two ways of conceptualizing the image (the moon) or pair of images (baby and computer). We considered each image (moon and baby and computer) from an "other" side, something of an opposite side—a kind of counterperspective. Other examples of HSBC ads that work in binary mode include one that pictures people camping in a tent alongside people lounging on a cruise ship. The words *holiday* and *hell* are printed on each, suggesting that one person's holiday (camping, for example) is another person's hell.

But with the apples, we have moved to a different mode—a ternary mode offering a triple perspective that moves beyond the back-and-forth, either-or thinking of the binary-coded images of computer and baby.

EXERCISE

13. What do you think the computer/baby ad is promoting? What about the apple ad? To what extent might either ad be selling or promoting more than one thing or idea?

Look, now, at another such triple image from another HSBC ad, this time of a man with a shaved head. You can find this image at http://www.psychologytoday.com.

EXERCISES ————————————————————————

14. What is your response to this image of the three shaved heads with different words under them? Did your perception of and reaction to the image shift just a bit when you saw the second and third terms for the shaved head—"soldier" and "survivor"? Does something affect you emotionally when you view the second and/or third term(s) of this triple image that was not operative in the previous apple triple image? If so, what is it? How can you account for it?

15. Jot down a few thoughts you have in response to this last image of the three shaved heads. You can include both emotional and intellectual aspects in your response. Then jot down some thoughts about our process of looking at these different images accompanied by carefully chosen words.

So what have we been doing in looking at and thinking about these images—these advertisements, really? We have been analyzing them with the purpose of interpreting them—have we not? Essentially we have been doing these things:

- Making observations (Noticing)
- Identifying connections (Relating)
- Making inferences (Inferring)
- Drawing conclusions (Concluding)

These four aspects of interpretation are bulleted rather than numbered to suggest that they are recursive—they cycle and loop back upon each other. The interpretive conclusions we reach are always provisional; we can change our interpretations, and we often do just that.

A Political Cartoon

Let's consider a political cartoon that appeared on April 21, 2005, in the *New York Times*—on the op-ed page, as an accompaniment to an article, entitled "War Isn't Fought in the Headlines." You can find this ad at http://nytimes.com/2005/04/21/opinion/21hammes.html.

EXERCISES ————————————————————————

16. Take a moment to jot down at least five details you notice about the image. Begin with some observations. (Observations are statements that can be verified.)

17. Now, make some connections among your observations. Try to focus on relationships—mostly comparative and contrasting connections. From there you can proceed to a few inferences. (An inference is a statement about the unknown based upon something observed.)

- What, for example, do you call the weapons each figure holds?
- What do you make of the way those weapons are being held?
- What about the attire of the figures? Their postures and gestures?
- What do you notice about the patterns of lines that appear above their heads in the "cartoon-bubble" that conventionally indicates speech or thought?
- What kind of speaking or thinking is represented by those different patterns of intersecting and overlapping lines?

18. Once you have some provisional answers to these questions, you are ready to develop an interpretation, a tentative conclusion about how you understand and interpret the image—how you explain it to yourself—and to others. Write a paragraph of 7 to 10 sentences that offers your interpretation of the image and caption: War Isn't Fought in the Headlines.

Commentary

Here are some observations about the process of interpreting the image and caption:

We know a good deal about the image because we have taken time to observe each of its elements. And we have asked a number of questions about the details of the image, including its relationship to the underlying caption. What might we infer from what we have noted and queried so far? We might infer, for example, that the two soldiers are indeed foes, one an American Army infantry (or perhaps a Marine, or even an allied soldier) and the other an Iraqi or Afghan insurgent (or perhaps a foreign Taliban mercenary insurgent). We might infer that the figure on the left is about to attack the one on the right—or we might infer that he is defending himself from the other figure, a trespassing invader of his homeland.

About the line drawings above each figure we might infer that they represent radically different kinds of language and thinking. This inference could lead to another: that these adversaries not only do not understand each other or think like each other but that they speak mutually incomprehensible languages, possess diametrically opposed values, and have radically different understandings of the world.

About the caption beneath the figures we might infer that war is fought, on the one hand, on the ground of a particular country and, on the other, in the heads of the enemy combatants. This last possibility is suggested by considering the last word of the caption, "headlines." If we break that word into its component parts "head" and "lines," we get a literal rendering of what is pictured above the figures—"lines" that reflect what is going on in the "head" of each. The more diagrammatic lines above the American, or western, soldier could be seen as reflecting an orderly, logical, analytical mode of thinking and operating. The less-patterned, seemingly less-orderly lines above the head of the insurgent could be understood to reflect a more emotional and chaotic kind of thinking and acting.

Armed with these inferences, we are now ready to push toward an interpretation. Arriving at an interpretive conclusion about such a suggestive image isn't easy. But our conclusion, remember, does not have to be final; it can remain tentative and provisional—and probably should. What are some ways that we might formulate our understanding of this piece as a conclusion, however tentative and provisional?

We might conclude, perhaps, that it suggests the mutual incomprehension at the heart of the cultures and worldviews of the soldier-figures depicted. The minds of these soldier-figures, like the worlds they inhabit, are dramatically different. We might thus conclude that there does not appear to be much hope for dialogue between them, that any kind of real understanding is impossible. We might conclude, at least provisionally, that the drawing, with its accompanying caption, suggests that wars are fought by those whose languages, ways of thinking, values, and conceptions of right and wrong differ so dramatically that the conflict between them has little likelihood of ever really being resolved.

This, of course, is only one interpretation of the image and caption. Very likely, as you were making your own observations, connections, and inferences, you were developing your own perhaps different interpretation—though there may be some overlapping elements, as well. It is interesting to consider how someone from another culture would interpret this image—someone from the Middle East, or perhaps someone from Iraq or Afghanistan who is living through the war in those places. Without question, there is more than one way to "see," this image, more than one way to understand and interpret it.

Comparing Representational and Abstract Images

In his book, *ABC of Reading*, about poetry, American modernist poet and critic Ezra Pound recommends that we study poems in the manner of biologists comparing specimens. Here are Pound's own words: "The proper METHOD for studying poetry and good letters is the method of contemporary biologists, that is careful first-hand examination of the matter, and continual COMPARISON of one 'slide' or specimen with another."

We will follow Pound's suggestion by putting up for your inspection and thoughtful consideration some specimen works of contemporary art. Four works are included, presented two at a time for comparison. The first two are photographs of works of art, one a painting by Nadine Gordon-Taylor, the other a sculpture by Maria DeAngelis. The second pair includes two photographs as works of art. The first of those is a black-and-white photograph by Dina Hofstetter and the second a color photograph by Lisa Scavelli.

EXERCISE

19. Take a look at the first pair before continuing. What details do you notice about each work? What do you think you are looking at? How would you describe what you see? And what first thoughts do you have about each? What title would you provide for each image?

The painting, *Ancient Rose Hawk* (Figure 4.1), depicts a red-tailed hawk set against the backdrop of a large red rose. Hovering behind the hawk is a figure in blue that appears to embrace the raptor. This work of art, of course, is an imaginative rendering of the artist's concept. It is also, however, representational in that it clearly depicts recognizable objects—a rose and a red-tailed hawk. And yet the work is not a mere representation of a hawk and a rose. What's imaginative is its conjunction of hawk and rose within the form the artist has constructed, a form that also incorporates additional colors, details, and images, such as stars and the hovering blue figure. So, although we can identify elements of the work as representational or even realistic, the work as a whole transcends those representational details to create something imaginative and somewhat mysterious.

EXERCISE

20. Read what the artist, Nadine Gordon-Taylor, has written about her work, and consider how her explanation alters the way you see and think about *Ancient Rose Hawk*.

> In this image you see a beautiful red rose opening its center to allow the Red-Tailed Hawk to emerge. It is leaving the starry dimension of the Ancients and coming back to our dimension to offer their wisdom. A gold ring encircles the hawk's body.

FIGURE 4.1   *Ancient Rose Hawk*, Nadine Gordon-Taylor

A totem, the Red-Tailed Hawk is associated with visionary qualities and with nobility, dignity, and pride. Ancient Native Americans recognized it as a messenger from the ancestors. With its keen eyesight, it represents close attention and scrupulous perception. With its soaring ability, it manifests a broad perception and a higher plane of experience.

Although roses are well-known symbols of love, beauty, and romance, they also served as an ancient sign of secrecy. Roses were also used as legal tender, as was rose water.

The circle represents the sacred, the universal, and the divine. It has no beginning and no end and thus symbolizes the infinite. Gold, associated with the sun, has long been both a symbol and a token of wealth, but it is also linked with prosperity and happiness.

Another image, one that we can pair with *Ancient Rose Hawk* pictures a welded steel sculpture entitled *Sol* (Figure 4.2); it is less representational and more abstract than the rose-hawk image. The form of the sculpture, although not realistic or strictly representational, nonetheless reminds us of things we know or have

FIGURE 4.2   *Sol*, Maria DeAngelis

seen. That is, this abstract work of art reminds us of elements in the natural world through its details and its overall form.

EXERCISE

21. How does the following explanation by the artist, Maria DeAngelis, affect your perception and alter your understanding of her work?

> My involvement and love for artistic processes that are transformative through fire has been a cornerstone of my creative work. I am drawn to materials such as steel, clay and glass for their organic qualities, originating from the earth, and their inherent ability to change structurally through heat.
>
> My sculptural imagery tends towards the abstract to express the dynamic quality of movement in space. Taking my inspiration from nature, I am interested in expressing the essence of each element through the repetition of shape and form. In a way, like photography, a welded sculpture can capture a moment, frozen in time, still movement.
>
> In *Sol*, my intention was to express the sun's radiating heat, light, and energy. The length and width of the sun's rays vary to create a dynamic quality, with some of the rays undulating outward and emphasizing the feeling of moving centripetally, out from the center. Some of the rays are cut into and cut through to create texture and light, emphasizing the movement and dynamism, increasing the visual energy. A grinding wheel was used to create the circular lines in the center to emphasize the roundness and "glow" of the sun itself.

FIGURE 4.3 *Light Tide*, Dina Hofstetter

Two Photographs

Here now is a second pair of artworks. Both are photographs, one in black and white, the other in color. The black-and-white photograph was created as one of a series in which the artist, Dina Hofstetter, explores the qualities of light. This photograph, like DeAngelis's sculpture, is an abstract artwork, yet it, too, can be related to the natural world, something Hofstetter suggests in her title for it, *Light Tide* (Figure 4.3).

EXERCISE

22. Read Dina Hofstetter's artist's statement, and then consider how your perception and/or understanding of her work may be altered.

Things As They Were

The word photography is derived from two Greek words: *photos* (light) and *graphos* (drawing). While no photographic image, film or digital, exists without light, this image focuses on light as subject matter, as physical presence. I began shooting the series one morning as light poured through my bedroom window and reflected off a plastic storage container and onto the wall. I quickly realized that I could "draw" dramatic patterns on the wall by shifting and tilting the plastic, thereby redirecting the light. Each image has been manipulated to some extent with Photoshop. In some the manipulation involves contrast or size only. In others the light has been transformed into a negative or sepia image to impart a sense of solidity and/or age. The title of the series of images of which this is a single example, is a quote from Neale Eltinge Howard: "Astronomers work always with the past, because light takes time to move from one place to another; they see things as they were, not as they are."

Here, now, is a color photograph to pair with Hofstetter's black-and-white *Light Tide*. Just as Hofstetter's photograph is one of a series, so too, is this color

FIGURE 4.4 *Reflective Sky,* Lisa Scavelli

photograph taken by Lisa Scavelli, *Reflective Sky* (Figure 4.4). Though a still image, the artist has animated it along with the others in the series. And just as the other images considered in this section display characteristics of both representation and abstraction, so, too does this color photo. See what you can make of it before reading Scavelli's artist statement.

EXERCISES

23. Read the following artist statement by Lisa Scavelli. Then consider how your perception of her image and/or your understanding of it has been altered.

When I begin to work on a piece of artwork, I usually get inspired by something I see. For example, when I hiked to the top of Turkey Mountain, in Yorktown

Heights, NY, the first thing I saw was the sun's reflection in a puddle. I was so out of breath from the climb that I felt a little dizzy. That's when the thought occurred to me that the reflection of the sun made me feel like I was upside down.

I stooped down as low as my body would allow me to go, and I shot the image with my Canon Rebel XT. On the hike down the mountain, I began to visualize what I could do with the image once I uploaded it to the computer. The words "upside-down" and "right-side-up" kept coming to mind, and I decided to create a mirrored image of the landscape, allowing the viewer to experience the feeling I had while on top of the mountain. I altered the colors in Adobe Photoshop to express a more unrealistic reality, as if one were actually in an upside-down, right-side-up world.

24. Find on the Internet sculptures entitled *The Kiss*, by Auguste Rodin (1876–1957), a nineteenth-century French Romantic sculptor and by Constantin Brancusi (1840–1917), a twentieth-century Romanian modernist sculptor. Compare and contrast the two works in terms of their abstract and representational qualities. Consider the following questions as you look closely and think about these two very different renditions of a kiss.

  a. What is the dominant impression created by each sculpture? How does the sculptor create that impression?

  b. What geometric forms do you discern in each sculpture? How has each sculptor used that geometric form and to what effect?

  c. To what extent do you think Brancusi's work derives from and comments on Rodin's sculpture? How would you characterize the relationship between these two works of art?

  d. Do you think that one of these sculptures conveys the essence of a kiss better than the other? If so, how and why? If not, why not?

  e. Which of these sculptures would you prefer to have in your home? Why? To what extent are the terms "representational" and "abstract" useful in viewing and thinking about Rodin's and Brancusi's sculptures?

  f. Select two other images of couples kissing—in paintings, photographs, or other artistic media. Compare and contrast the depictions of the kiss in those images with one another—and then with Rodin's and Brancusi's sculptures.

Two Powerful Images

We have been analyzing images, primarily to consider what we think about them. Images, however, can also be approached another way, in terms of the emotional impact they convey. The following image—a photograph—was taken by the professional photographer Eugene Smith and included in *Minamata*, a book of photographs, which first appeared in *Life* magazine in 1972. The book is titled after the Japanese fishing village, Minamata, where Smith had gone at the behest of friends. What he found there profoundly disturbed him—a village ravaged by industrial pollution, which had already much earlier—in the 1950s—reached catastrophic dimensions. Smith lived in the village for a number of months. He got to know the people, gaining their trust, as he began photographing these victims of mercury poisoning from factory wastes in the area. The photographs played a major role in the struggle against the perpetrator of this destruction—the Japanese Chisso Corporation.

One photograph, in particular, has become famous: *Tomoko in Her Bath*. You can find this image at http://www.masters-of-photography.com.

EXERCISES

25. What are your feelings on seeing this picture? To what extent does this photograph tell the "truth" or at least "a" truth about what happened in Minamata? To what extent is this picture "photojournalism" with an agenda—with a strong social bias and a clear political purpose? How do you feel on hearing the story of what lies behind this work of art?

26. Look again closely at Smith's photograph. Jot down half a dozen specific details that you notice—observations. What do those details get you thinking about? Where and how do they direct your thinking? What does your noticing and thinking make you "wonder about"? How would you finish this lead: "I wonder how . . . why . . . whether . . . ?"

Eugene Smith on His Photograph of Tomoko in Her Bath

Smith's picture seems very much a composed work—a "composition," and not just a lucky hit of a snapped shot produced with little if any plan or purpose. And so we might consider Smith's image of "Tomoko in Her Bath" a work of art. Here is part of an interview with Eugene Smith and what he said about taking the photograph of Tomoko in Her Bath.

Interviewer: "How did the famous picture of the mother washing her daughter come about?"

Eugene Smith: "By that process of getting to know the individuals. We looked after the child at times when the parents were on protests. They lived about a ten-minute walk from your house. Every time we went by the house, we would see that someone was always caring for her. I would see the wonderful love that the mother gave. She was always cheerful, and the more I watched, the more it seemed to me that it was a summation of the most beautiful aspects of courage that people were showing in Minamata in fighting the company and the government. . . . One day I said to Aileen, my wife, "Let's try to make that photograph." I imagined a picture in which a child was being held by the mother and the love was coming through. . . . I wanted to show her caring for the child. And she said, "Yes," I'm just about to give Tomoko her bath. Maybe that will help you. . . . I could see the picture building into what I was trying to say. I found it emotionally moving, and I found it very difficult to photograph through my tears."

Here, now, is what the scholar and critic Robert Scholes has written about this picture in *Protocols of Reading*. After discussing the political and photojournalistic significance of the picture, Scholes writes the following:

"Smith's concept and his message preceded the image itself. 'I could see the picture building into what I was trying to say,' Smith tells us. Learning to read visual images is partly a matter of understanding how the visual and conceptual are linked in consciousness. In this case, I should like to suggest, Smith knew what he was looking for because he knew one of the most persistent and elaborate linkages of image and concept in our cultural history: the iconographic code of the pietà: the image of the *mater dolorosa*, holding in her arms the mutilated body of her crucified child."

And so, Smith's powerful photograph, taken by a twentieth-century photojournalist, a document he used strategically in a political and economic struggle on behalf of the victims of a corporate polluter backed by a national government, is also, simultaneously, an iconic image of maternal love, which is linked inextricably with another iconic image, Michelangelo's *Pietà*, brilliantly executed more than 350 years earlier by the 25-year-old Italian genius.

FIGURE 4.5 Michelangelo's Pieta

Each of these images is a work of art in its own right. Each called upon the artist's deepest resources of skill and of feeling. Michelangelo's sculpture and Smith's photograph speak to each of us across the centuries and across cultures, provoking thought and eliciting feeling. Images have the ability to do both.

Images have the power to affect us deeply. They persuade us, inspire us, amaze us, move us. We should take as much care in thinking about our viewing of images as we do in thinking about what we read and what we hear. Looking at images thoughtfully and critically has its basis in noticing, the kind of deep noticing essential for all good thinking, whether critical or creative.

Moving Images: The Power of Movies

Throughout the chapter, we have been focusing on still images—photographs, paintings, icons, and symbols—and other visual aspects of communicating with one another. We take a brief look here at images that move—moving images, images from a film, more commonly known as movies.

As critical viewers of film, or movies, we should be alert for visual patterns, just as we are when viewing paintings, photographs, sculptures, and buildings. And we should think about the effects these visual patterns create. We can be alert, for example, to how a director arranges the actors in a scene; we can be attentive to how a sequence of scenes creates a particular design, or conveys an idea or a feeling. Consider, for example, the ways the *Star Wars* films or the *Lord of the Rings* films handle battle scenes, alternating long shots of vast armies with close-ups of individual details, such as torsos and faces.

Another aspect of the moving images in films is the physical movement of actors. Think, for example, of slapstick's exaggerated movement in comic films, whether classic Laurel and Hardy or Three Stooges films or contemporary comedies, which also rely on exaggerated physical movement and physical predicaments and situations. Or think of the way physical movement plays out in action films, whether the acrobatics of performers in films like *Crouching Tiger, Hidden Dragon* and the carefully choreographed *Kill Bill* fight sequences, or the aerial acrobatics of films involving fighter plane battles, such as those in *Top Gun*.

Film Editing and Montage

Film editing is a highly complex and extremely important art. Editing affects the look and feel of a film as well as its pacing and rhythm. How a camera lingers on a shot or over a scene, the way it moves slowly or quickly across a wide shot affect the emotional as well as the visual implications of a film. Differences in editing dramatically affect our experience as viewers.

Film shots are edited to create continuity in the action—or perhaps discontinuity and disruption. It depends on the effect the director wants. One important aspect of editing is "montage," sequences of rapidly appearing images to suggest the lapse of time or the passing of events—or even of simultaneously occurring events. The great Russian filmmaker Sergei Eisenstein was a master of montage. His silent film *Battleship Potemkin* contains one of his most famous examples, the Odessa Steps sequence. Four images from that montage appear here on pages 96–98.

Analyzing Film Editing

- How fast or slow are the shot sequences? How consistent are the shot sequences throughout the film? With what effects?
- Does the film employ much cutting between and among scenes, or is it relatively fluid and continuous in its changing scenes?
- How are changes of time and place indicated?
- What kinds of juxtapositions of scene do you notice, and with what effects?
- Are techniques of montage used? For what purposes, and with what effects?

EXERCISE

27. Borrow, download, or rent Sergei Eisenstein's classic film *Battleship Potemkin*. Analyze the way Eisenstein uses montage, especially in the Odessa Steps sequence, which begins with a caption: "Suddenly."

Montage refers to sequences of rapidly appearing images to suggest the lapse of time or the passing of events—or even of simultaneously occurring events. Here are four images from the montage that constitutes the Odessa Steps sequence.

Following these images, we consider a segment of the film. An outline of film shots describes the action with timings. Even from just reading the description and timings without seeing the film, you can get a sense of what happens and how Eisenstein uses montage to convey dramatically the emotions of the character and to elicit the emotions of viewers of his film. The abbreviations *CS, MS, LS,* stand, respectively, for *close-up shot, middle shot,* and *long shot. Panning* refers to the way a camera pivots to slowly sweep across a scene and capture images in a smooth focused manner.

The Odessa Steps Sequence—Battleship Potemkin

(:01–:15) The sequence begins with a title: "Suddenly." A rapid series of images follows: flashes of a girl's head; feet as they move down the steps; a man

without legs and a woman with a parasol; a long shot looking down the steps, with a statue in the foreground; a line of soldiers.

(:16–:43) A wide angle shot from the bottom of the steps; the crowd rushes down. A shot is fired (not seen); CS a man's knees sag forward; MS a man throws out his arm; a man collapses on the steps; knees, completion of the collapse.

(:44–2:18) More soldiers advance; camera reveals a portion of the crowds wildly racing down the steps, including the woman with the parasol and a one-legged man on crutches; LS of a tree moving softly in the breeze; another volley is fired; one victim is a child (seen earlier with his mother); CS child is stepped on by the panicking crowd; the mother pauses; looks around; cries out CS; turns back to her son; picks him up and cradles him in her arms.

(2:19–4:17) Another woman addresses a portion of the crowd: "Go—beseech them" in a caption; the people huddle together fearfully; they rise; the one-legged man appears; shouting, the mother carries her son up the steps; the scene slows as the mother confronts the advancing soldiers with their rifles pointed; the line of soldiers halts momentarily in shadow; an officer's arm appears; the mother sinks to her knees; they fire and she falls backwards.

(4:18–6:42) A volley is fired, then another; horse-mounted Cossacks below the steps charge those escaping; a young mother is caught with her carriage on the steps; MS she frantically leans over and kisses the baby, then turns around; CS her face in fear; MS she stands braced, shielding the carriage; cut-in CS shows the baby; then . . .

LS (feet only) a line of soldiers halts and . . .

LS (looking along the line of rifles) . . .

CS the mother cries out and . . .

CS her head sways backward . . .

CS the baby carriage wheels hover at the top step . . .

CS her head sways forward . . .

CS her hands clutch at her chest . . .

LS the massacre continues at the foot of the steps;

CS her hands, fingers are covered with blood;

CS her eyes close; her head sinks out of the picture frame;

MS she sinks down against the baby carriage;

LS a line of soldiers proceeds down the steps and away;

MS baby in the carriage;

CS the carriage wheels hover on the top step;

LS (feet only) a line of soldiers advances;

LS (along rifle) they continue to advance;

MS the mother tries to move forward;

MS she sinks back against the carriage;

CS the carriage wheels move;

MS the mother sinks back further, helplessly;

MS the carriage jolts down the steps;

CS MS the carriage moves forward;

CS the carriage wheels move as the mother's head falls against it;

CS the carriage wheels move on;

CS the other woman shouts.

The carriage jolts down the steps. The school teacher and a young man, both with glasses, look on horrified. The carriage reaches the bottom of the steps and tips over. The young man screams; a Cossack slashes with his sword and the image is repeated and followed by a CS of another Cossack; the sequence concludes with the school teacher shot, her glasses broken, and blood pouring from her eye.

EXERCISES

28. Describe your experience of viewing *Battleship Potemkin*. How does Eisenstein create a sense of energy and urgency—of excitement and of danger?

Take a look at the still shots that form part of the film sequence of images in action. What aspects of the Odessa Steps sequence are captured in those still images from the film?

29. Think about one of your favorite films, one you know well and may have seen more than once, perhaps numerous times. What particular scenes stand out in your memory?

Which characters and situations do you remember most vividly? What do you recall of how the filmmaker establishes the time and place—the setting of the film (and perhaps its changing settings)? What do you recall of the film's use of music and other sound effects? Do you remember close-up shots of the actor's faces? If so, what purpose do those close-ups serve? Perhaps there were close-up shots of scenery, buildings, or other details of setting—the time and place of the film's action.

The Attraction of Movies

In *The Power of Movies*, Colin McGinn claims that movies have enthralled us more intensively and in ways that differ from the captivation other arts exercise over us. Movies have both an individual appeal and mass appeal, more mass appeal, especially than other artistic mediums. McGinn claims, further, that this mass appeal of movies crosses cultures, so that the same powerful appeal is felt by viewers all over the world.

William V. Costanzo begins *Great Films and How to Teach Them* by asking, "What if all the motion pictures ever made were suddenly to disappear? What would we have lost?" You might answer, of course, that you would retain a visual memory of your favorite films, new and old, classic and contemporary. But what if, Costanzo muses, "all recollection of them vanished too." What then? If you were to make a list of your favorite films and select just one scene from each that has indelibly impressed itself on your memory, it is likely that the list would be very long indeed. And it is equally likely that the visual memory you have of those scenes is powerfully locked in. And it is quite likely also that those scenes have become part of the way you see and understand the world, even, as Costanzo notes, "how you have been trained to observe the world."

So in answer to the question, we would have to say that given such a hypothetical disaster a great deal would be lost—and not just for each of us individually. Costanzo reminds us that because the images we hold in our minds have been "shared around the world, their loss would deeply diminish our global heritage."

EXERCISES

30. To what extent do you agree with McGinn about the power and mass appeal of movies? And whether you agree with him fully or just in part, what do you think accounts for the powerful appeal of movies? What is there about movies that so attracts, engages, and enthralls us?

31. What do you think of Costanzo's suggestion about losing the record and memory of movies? Would we lose the ability to mentally focus, filter, and edit? What do you think of his further notion that we would lose not only the motion pictures but the loss of the stories the movies tell, the issues they publicize, the tools of the trade and how they are used? To what extent do you think critical and creative thinking would be diminished?

Looking Back and Looking Ahead

Revisit the learning goals that begin this chapter. Which of these goals do you think you have best achieved? What might you do to reach the remaining goals?

Return to the focusing questions at the beginning of the chapter. How would you answer those questions now? Which of them do you find most interesting and provocative and worthy of following up? Why?

In reviewing the list of resources that follows, identify the two that attract you most. Explain why these books or Web sites interest you. Consider looking into them for further developing your thinking about images and deepening your understanding about how to view them critically.

Take a look, too, at the MyThinkingLab resources on the Prentice Hall Web site. Included there are readings, images, videos, questions, exercises, and other provocations to help you develop your critical thinking prowess.

Resources

Understanding Comics, Scott McLoud. William Morrow, 1994.

ABC of Reading, Ezra Pound. New Directions, 1934, 1951.

Protocols of Reading, Robert Scholes. Yale University Press, 1991.

Minamata, Eugene Smith. Center for Creative Photography, 1981.

Battleship Potemkin, Sergei Eisenstein, 1925.

The Power of Movies, Colin McGinn. Vintage, 2007.

Great Films and How to Read Them, William V. Costanzo. NCTE, 2004.

5

Reading, Writing, Thinking

Reading is to the mind what exercise is to the body.
—RICHARD STEELE

Write something worth reading or do something worth writing.
—BENJAMIN FRANKLIN

FOCUSING QUESTIONS

• What kinds of reading and writing do you do most often? What kinds of reading and writing do you do for yourself—outside of school or for work assignments?

• What are your greatest challenges in reading and writing? What are your greatest pleasures in reading and in writing?

• To what extent do you read print materials and to what extent do you read digital text? How would you characterize the differences in these kinds of reading? What kinds of writing do you do in response to each?

• How are reading and writing related to thinking? How might reading and writing aid thinking?

LEARNING GOALS

5.1 EXPLORE the reading process and develop strategies for critical reading.

5.2 RECOGNIZE and understand how writing can enrich reading and stimulate thinking.

5.3 APPLY reading and writing skills to deepen thinking and the comprehension of texts.

5.4 UNDERSTAND and practice an active approach to reading, writing, and thinking that includes observations, connections, inferences, evaluations, and conclusions.

Chapter Overview

This chapter provides guidance in critical reading and writing—in thinking critically about what writers say, suggest, and imply, and then writing cogently in response to your reading. Techniques and strategies for active reading are presented along with texts upon which to practice reading, writing, and thinking—a few paragraphs about weasels, the first section of an essay about the hot dry winds of Los Angeles, an essay about the experience of growing up black and female, and an essay about gender roles and attitudes. The central idea of this chapter is that reading, writing, and thinking are inextricably intertwined; they reinforce and stimulate one another. Working through this chapter will increase your ability to understand, evaluate, and write cogently and thoughtfully about what you read.

Why Read?

Why read, you might ask? Reading allows us to discover ideas, develop our opinions, and think new thoughts. Reading helps us see familiar things in new ways. Through reading we connect with the minds and hearts of others. We come to know what other people think, and how they feel about things. Reading is also one of life's pleasures. We might consider reading as a reward for using our intellectual capacities, an end rather than a means to an end. We can read for the pleasure of reading itself, for its intrinsic rewards.

Watch the **Video**, Why Read? / Kinds of Reading / Why Write? / Kinds of Writing **MyThinkingLab**

The Pleasures of Reading

To suggest that reading can bring pleasure is not to deny that it can be hard work as well. We know from experience that reading can be frustrating as well as enjoyable, enervating as well as exhilarating. Reading has its pains as well as its pleasures.

What do we read and why? We read about topics that interest us, about people and places, about activities we enjoy. We read newspapers for information and magazines for pleasure. We read to amuse ourselves, to escape, to deepen our understanding of an issue, to solve problems, to satisfy our curiosity. Mostly, we do these kinds of reading for ourselves. We also read to learn about subjects and fields that, for one reason or another, we need to study. Some of this reading we may do for a job or career, some for academic courses, and some out of our own interest and desire.

We read in different ways at different speeds depending on our purpose and on the complexity of what we are reading. We also read in different ways, depending on whether we are reading printed text or Web-based text. Printed text is linear; we read it left to right, down the page, and one page after another. Web-based text can be read that way, but only up to a point, as there are links to click and other nonlinear texts and images beckoning to us.

Whatever our purpose and whether we read print on pages or words and images on screens, reading makes us more aware of our world; it deepens our understanding of ourselves. It broadens us, extends our experience, enlivens our imagination. Reading provokes our thinking and stimulates our feelings. It challenges our assumptions and, at its best, surprises us, enlightens us, delights us. Reading helps us make sense of our lives and our world.

Kinds of Reading

When we talk about reading, we are usually talking about reading texts—words on a page or a screen. But we also read people; we read their faces and gestures, their postures and moods. We read the natural world as well—waves and clouds, landscapes and animals. We read paintings. We read films. We read buildings. We read battlefields, ballparks, and other public spaces.

Astronomers read the sky, architects read the land on which a house will be built; cardplayers read one another's faces and gestures; parents read their children's faces for signs of joy and fear. Lovers read each other's bodies, and doctors read the bodies of their patients. Fortunetellers read tealeaves, tortoise shells, birds, stars, and lines in hands. Scientists read tree rings, laboratory slides, graphs, charts, and data patterns.

A baseball pitcher reads his catcher's signs, and base runners read their coaches' signals. A quarterback reads the alignment of the defense; hockey players and basketball players, soccer and lacrosse players read one another's moves on ice and court and field. All these kinds of reading and more involve looking at things, noticing them, and making sense of them based on what is observed. All these kinds of reading are forms of analysis and interpretation. We focus here primarily on reading texts made of words. Our interest is in how reading stimulates and extends our thinking.

EXERCISE

1. What kinds of reading do you usually do? Do you read mostly printed or Web-based texts? What kinds of reading do you enjoy most and least? Why?

   What strategies have you developed to become a more active, engaged, and effective reader? To what extent have you experienced some of the benefits of reading?

Why Write?

We write because we have to and because we need to. We are required to write for our courses and for our jobs. We need to write for ourselves, to find out what we think. How do we know what we think until we see what we have to say through writing. Writing, like reading, fosters thinking. To write well, we have to think about what we want to say and how best to convey that thinking. In the process, we may find ourselves thinking of things we didn't know we were going to write when we started. That is so simply because the act of writing itself stimulates thinking.

The Pleasures of Writing

It might sound strange to talk about the pleasures of writing. We normally think of writing as difficult and challenging—as a kind of work. But writing also has its pleasures, such as the pleasure of discovering something we didn't know we knew and only find out in the process of writing. Another pleasure of writing is the pleasure of using our minds actively and imaginatively. Considering ideas, exploring them, and finding ways to express them effectively are among the basic pleasures of writing. And, of course, seeing something that we have written in finished form, completed to our satisfaction, and perhaps to the satisfaction and even pleasure of others—those, too, are other pleasures that writing brings.

Kinds of Writing

There are many kinds of writing, from jotting notes and making lists, to writing to provide information and offer explanations; from writing to entertain and express our feelings, to writing designed to develop our thinking and communicate what matters to us.

One of the most important kinds of writing done in many college courses is writing about reading—writing about historical events, perhaps using primary sources such as original documents; writing about literary works, including poems, stories, novels, plays, and essays; writing about texts in philosophy and religion, experiments in social and natural sciences, performances of music and drama and film, visual images of painting and photography, business cases, architectural and engineering design and construction. When we write about such things, we need to read them attentively, to notice things we might overlook on a more casual noticing. When we write about texts we need to do a more active kind of reading and noticing.

Writing, like reading, is an active process. It requires intellectual energy. It demands attention to meaning and to evidence needed in support of that meaning. For the evidence needed to support our views and ideas, we rely on our experience of life, on our observations about the world, and on our reading.

Active Reading

In one of his lecture/essays, "The American Scholar," nineteenth-century American writer, Ralph Waldo Emerson writes: "There is then creative reading as well as creative writing." For Emerson, reading is active and purposeful; it bears fruit in thinking and writing. "First we read," he notes, "then we write." The sequence is natural, for some readers almost inevitable.

In another essay, "History," Emerson urges that "the student is to read history actively and not passively; to esteem his own life the text, and books the commentary." As Robert Richardson points out in a commentary on Emerson's thoughts on reading and writing, Emerson's ideas strengthen the reader's authority and weaken the authority of books themselves. Emerson encourages active reading as a springboard to individual thinking.

What is active reading, anyway? Active reading is a kind of reading in which we focus intently not only on what is written but on how it is written. Active reading requires attention to details of language and structure, to words and images, to how sentences and paragraphs are related to one another. In reading actively, we seek the overall form or structure of the text—whether an article, essay, story, political debate, scientific analysis, philosophical argument, or something else. When we read actively, we think about the author's idea—whether we agree or disagree, and why. We consider whether we wish to accept, reject, or partially accept, to qualify, what the writer says—and why.

Active Reading—An Example

The goal of active reading is understanding. We aim to comprehend the writer's idea, to absorb the writer's meaning. We can demonstrate the process of active reading with the opening paragraph of an essay about weasels.

> A weasel is wild. Who knows what he thinks? He sleeps in his underground den, his tail draped over his nose. Sometimes he lives in his den for two days without leaving. Outside, he stalks rabbits, mice, muskrats, and birds, killing more bodies than he can eat warm, and often dragging the carcasses home. Obedient to instinct, he bites his prey at the neck, either splitting the jugular vein at the throat or crunching the brain at the base of the skull, and he does not let go. One naturalist refused to kill a weasel who was socketed into his hand deeply as a rattlesnake. The man could in no way pry the tiny weasel off, and he had to walk half a mile to water, the weasel dangling from his palm, and soak him off like a stubborn label.

Thinking about Dillard's "Living Like Weasels"

We begin our active reading with observations about the opening paragraph of "Living Like Weasels."

Dillard's first sentence is abrupt. It announces succinctly that a weasel is wild. But what does this mean to us at this point? How is a weasel "wild"—in what ways? The second sentence is a question, one that invites us to consider what a weasel thinks about—or possibly that we shouldn't bother because we can't know or because weasels don't think. How we take this sentence depends, in part, on how we hear it. Here's one way: "Who knows what he *thinks*?" Here's another: "Who knows *what* he thinks?" And yet another: "Who *knows* what he thinks?"

EXERCISE

2. What do you make of these various ways of hearing Dillard's sentence? What does each way of hearing the sentence emphasize? What are the implications of these different ways of hearing Dillard's sentence?

Dillard's next two sentences of the opening paragraph provide information—that weasels sleep in dens where they can remain for up to two days at a time. There's nothing really surprising here. But what about that other bit of information—how the weasel sleeps—with its tail draped over its nose. That draped tail is a lovely surprise, a visual detail offered to delight as well as to inform. It enables us to picture or see the weasel in our mind's eye, and to take pleasure in its unique sleeping style.

The fifth and sixth sentences of the opening paragraph reveal the weasel as hunter—stalking prey, killing it, dragging it to his den, where the weasel eats it and then, presumably, sleeps. When we are told that the weasel is obedient to instinct and are shown exactly how he kills—either by splitting the jugular vein or by crunching his victim's brain—we remember the essay's opening sentence: "A weasel is wild." And we begin to understand in a new way just what this "wild[ness]" means. Although we "understood" it before, on our initial reading of the sentence, we now have a deeper understanding of the weasel's wildness, an understanding that combines intellectual comprehension with emotional apprehension.

EXERCISES

3. How do you respond to Dillard's details about the weasel's method of killing its prey? Are you amazed? Engaged? Appalled? Amused? Shocked—something else? Do you think Dillard needs this degree of detail? How would less detail affect your response and your understanding? How important do you think the word *instinct* is here? Why?

4. Dillard's opening paragraph concludes with an anecdote about a naturalist bitten by a tenacious weasel. The anecdote makes a point, to be sure. But it does more. What effects does the anecdote achieve? How does Dillard achieve those effects with her choices of details and of language—of words and images?

Connecting and Relating Paragraphs

We can now turn to Dillard's second paragraph and consider how this additional paragraph affects our understanding of and response to the first. Consider, as you read, how this second paragraph develops what Dillard gives us in her opening paragraph. Consider how the second paragraph extends and enlarges the idea of that first paragraph.

And once, says Ernest Thompson Seton—once, a man shot an eagle out of the sky. He examined the eagle and found the dry skull of a weasel fixed by the jaws to his throat. The supposition is that the eagle had pounced on the weasel and the weasel swiveled and bit as instinct taught him, tooth to neck, and nearly won. I would like to have seen that eagle from the air a few weeks or months before he was shot: was the whole weasel still attached to his feathered throat, a fur pendant? Or did the eagle eat what he could reach, gutting the living weasel with his talons before his breast, bending his beak, cleaning the beautiful air-borne bones?

EXERCISE

5. Read the second paragraph again. Do the same work of analysis you did in reading the first paragraph; attend closely to words, sentences, images, meta-phors, anecdotes, and selection of details. And then do a third reading of the paragraph (aloud) for sound effects. Imagine that you are reading a poem, listening for ways the writer plays with repeating sounds of vowels and conso-nants. Circle, underline, and otherwise mark the repeating sounds you notice.

Going Deeper into Dillard's Essay

Our questions at the beginning of this second paragraph of Dillard's essay necessarily invite our responses both intellectual and emotional. In asking what strikes us about the details and the language of the paragraph, we move from subjective responses to more objective considerations. We move backward, in a way, from our initial responses to a set of observations about the essay's rhetoric—how it affects us, how it works on us. We might observe, for example, that the second paragraph begins with an image very much like the one that ends the opening paragraph. The tenacious weasel holds on, fiercely, in one instance to a man's hand and in another to an eagle's throat. We might also observe that the second paragraph begins with statements and ends with questions. We might notice, further, that it includes a reference to another written text (something that occurs in the first paragraph, too). Finally, we observe that the writer speaks personally, using the personal pronoun "I," perhaps revealing her own desire to have seen the amazing thing that she had only read about.

We should also note the vivid, precise verbs Dillard uses in her description of the eagle gutting the living weasel, bending his beak and cleaning the weasel's bones. (This image brings the image of the first paragraph to life with its string of participles—*gutting, bending, cleaning*.) We also hear a repetition of vowel sounds, a kind of litany of eagle and weasel, words that nearly rhyme, and whose "ea" sound is echoed in *eat, reach, beak*, and *cleaning*. And we hear an added echo with the alliterative "b"s of the last sentence: The eagle's talons "*before his breast, bending his beak, cleaning the beautiful air-borne bones.*"

To hear the poetry of this paragraph, you really do need to read it aloud.

EXERCISES

6. What connections can you make between these two opening paragraphs and this final paragraph of Dillard's essay?

I think it would be well, and proper, and obedient, and pure, to grasp your one necessity and not let it go, to dangle from it limp wherever it takes you. Then even death, where you're going no matter how you live, cannot you part. Seize it and let it seize you up aloft, even, till your eyes burn out and drop; let your musky flesh fall off in shreds, and let your very bones unhinge and scatter, loos-ened over fields, over fields and woods, lightly, thoughtless, from any height at all, from as high as eagles.

7. What observations can you make about Dillard's style in this paragraph? What do you notice about her sentences—about her words and phrases? What do you think Dillard means when she writes that it would be "proper," "obedient," and "pure" "to grasp your one necessity and not let it go?" What do you understand by her reference to "your one necessity?" What idea is implied in this paragraph?

The Interpretive Impulse

We have been doing a close analysis of the excerpted passages from the beginning and ending of Annie Dillard's essay "Living Like Weasels." We have been scrutinizing Dillard's language and style to better understand her idea. To acquire a fuller sense of her idea, of course, we need to read the entire essay and to consider what Dillard's structure and details contribute to her essay's central idea. We get a hint of this idea in the essay's final paragraph. But there is more, both more to the idea itself and more evidence in its support.

In analyzing Dillard's text, our goal has been to understand her idea, to follow her thinking. That is the essential work of interpretation that we do with any text we read. Interpretation is an essential aspect of our lives, and not just in the classroom. We all share an impulse to make sense of our experience, to understand what happens to us in our daily lives. When we make a new acquaintance, move to a new place, undertake a new responsibility, or undergo a new experience, we have to adjust to the strangeness of the event. We do this, primarily, by relating our new experience to what we already know. That's how we make sense of the unfamiliar, adding to our storehouse of experience.

Something similar happens when we read. Making sense of what we read is similar to making sense of experience in other ways. It's something like doing detective work. Like a detective studying clues, looking for patterns, and formulating a hypothesis, readers create a network of meaning from what they notice about a text. Good detectives and good readers use similar critical, analytical skills to develop their interpretations. They make careful observations and develop dominant impressions based on what they have noticed.

Interpretation is a dynamic act of thinking and an ongoing one. We make sense of a text as we read it; we make additional or alternative sense of it as we reflect on it later. Interpretation of any text is formed and re-formed as we read and think, reread and rethink.

Here is an opportunity to engage further in the interpretive act, with the first section of an essay, "Los Angeles Notebook," by Joan Didion. Its six paragraphs are printed one at a time, with intervening questions. Think about these questions as you read the passage. The questions have been headed with the word *exercise* to suggest that you need to exercise your capacity to read and think critically as you work your way through Didion's text.

Throughout these paragraphs, Didion works by implication rather than by stating things explicitly. She expects her readers to make inferences based on the details she provides. To make those inferences, we need to be alert and active readers, noticing carefully and making connections among the details we observe.

1   There is something uneasy in the Los Angeles air this afternoon, some unnatural stillness, some tension. What it means is that tonight a Santa Ana will begin to blow, a hot wind from the northeast whining down through the Cajon and San Gorgonio Passes, blowing up sand storms out along Route 66, drying the hills and the nerves

to flash point. For a few days now we will see smoke back in the canyons, and hear sirens in the night. I have neither heard nor read that a Santa Ana is due, but I know it, and almost everyone I have seen today knows it too. We know it because we feel it. The baby frets. The maid sulks. I rekindle a waning argument with the telephone company, then cut my losses and lie down, given over to whatever it is in the air. To live with the Santa Ana is to accept, consciously or unconsciously, a deeply mechanistic view of human behavior.

EXERCISE

8. What words and phrases contribute to the mood of the opening paragraph? How would you characterize this mood? How does Didion know when a Santa Ana wind is coming? What does she mean by saying that the hot, dry wind of the Santa Ana dries out not just the hills, but people's nerves, as well? What do you think she means by a "mechanistic view of human behavior"?

2   I recall being told, when I first moved to Los Angeles and was living on an isolated beach, that the Indians would throw themselves into the sea when the bad wind blew. I could see why. The Pacific turned ominously glossy during a Santa Ana period, and one woke in the night troubled not only by the peacocks screaming in the olive trees but by the eerie absence of surf. The heat was surreal. The sky had a yellow cast, the kind of light sometimes called "earthquake weather." My only neighbor would not come out of her house for days, and there were no lights at night, and her husband roamed the place with a machete. One day he would tell me that he had heard a trespasser, the next a rattlesnake.

EXERCISE

9. The second paragraph contains two kinds of details—details about the external world and details about human behavior. Identify examples of each, and then explain what the two types of details have in common. How are these details related to those of the first paragraph?

3   "On nights like that," Raymond Chandler once wrote about the Santa Ana, "every booze party ends in a fight. Meek little wives feel the edge of the carving knife and study their husbands' necks. Anything can happen." That was the kind of wind it was. I did not know then that there was any basis for the effect it had on all of us, but it turns out to be another of those cases in which science bears out folk wisdom. The Santa Ana, which is named for one of the canyons it rushers through, is *foehn* wind, like the *foehn* of Austria and Switzerland and the *hamsin* of Israel. There are a number of persistent malevolent winds, perhaps the best know of which are the mistral of France and the Mediterranean sirocco, but a *foehn* wind has distinct characteristics: it occurs on the leeward slope of a mountain range and, although the air begins as a cold mass, it is warmed as it comes down the mountain and appears finally as a hot dry wind. Whenever and wherever *foehn* blows, doctors hear about headaches and nausea and allergies, about "nervousness," about "depression." In Los Angeles some teachers do not attempt to conduct formal classes during a Santa Ana, because the children become unmanageable. In Switzerland the suicide rate goes up during the *foehn*, and in the courts of some Swiss cantons the wind is considered a mitigating circumstance for crime. Surgeons are said to watch the wind, because blood does not clot normally during a *foehn*. A few years ago an Israeli physicist discovered that

not only during such winds, but for the ten or twelve hours which precede them, the air carries an unusually high ratio of positive to negative ions. No one seems to know exactly why that should be; some talk about friction and others suggest solar disturbances. In any case the positive ions are there, and what an excess of positive ions does, in the simplest terms, is make people unhappy. One cannot get much more mechanistic than that.

EXERCISE

10. In this long paragraph, Didion refers to a sentence written by Raymond Chandler in one of his detective novels. How is this reference related to the hearsay about the Indians? How are the scientific facts and the cross-cultural details of this paragraph related to what Didion describes in the first two paragraphs?

4   Easterners commonly complain that there is no weather at all in Southern California, that the days and the seasons slip by relentlessly, numbingly bland. That is quite misleading. In fact the climate is characterized by infrequent but violent extremes: two periods of torrential subtropical rains, which continue for weeks and wash out the hills and send subdivisions sliding toward the sea; about twenty scattered days a year of the Santa Ana, which, with its incendiary dryness, invariably means fire. At the first prediction of a Santa Ana, the Forest Service flies men and equipment from northern California into the southern forests, and the Los Angeles Fire Department cancels its ordinary no-firefighting routines. The Santa Ana caused Malibu to burn the way it did in 1956, and Bel Air in 1961, and Santa Barbara in 1964. In the winter of 1966–67 eleven men were killed fighting a Santa Ana fire that spread through the San Gabriel Mountains.

EXERCISE

11. The first three paragraphs gradually build to a crescendo of detail that reveals a connection between a natural, elemental force and a set of human reactions—the hot dry Santa Ana wind and how people behave under its influence. In this fourth paragraph, what do you think Didion is suggesting by accumulating details from nature, history, science, and human behavior? Why might she have included so many different kinds of detail? What additional details does she provide in paragraph 4? And what is her point in saying that there are two violent extremes of weather in Southern California?

5   Just to watch the front-age news out of Los Angeles during a Santa Ana is to get very close to what it is about the place. The longest single Santa Ana period in recent years was in 1957, and it lasted not the usual three or four days but fourteen days, from November 21 until December 4. On the first day 25,000 acres of the San Gabriel Mountains were burning, with gusts reaching 100 miles an hour. In town, the wind reached Force 12, or hurricane force, on the Beaufort Scale; oil derricks were toppled and people ordered off the downtown streets to avoid injury from flying objects. On November 22 the fire in the San Gabriels was out of control. On November 24 six people were killed in automobile accidents, and by the end of the week the *Los Angeles Times* was keeping a box score of traffic deaths. On November 26 a prominent Pasadena attorney, depressed about money, shot and killed his wife, their two sons, and himself. On November 27 a South Gate divorcée, twenty-two, was murdered and thrown from a moving car. On November 30 the San Gabriel fire was

still out of control, and the wind in town was blowing eighty miles an hour. On the first day of December four people died violently, and on the third the wind began to break.

EXERCISE

12. How does paragraph 5 continue the implications and argument of paragraph 4? What is the purpose of the statistics included in this paragraph? How are these facts related to the examples of paragraph 2? What conclusion does Didion seem to be leading toward?

6   It is hard for people who have not lived in Los Angeles to realize how radically the Santa Ana figures in the local imagination. The city burning is Los Angeles's deepest image of itself: Nathanael West perceived that in *The Day of the Locust*; and at the time of the 1965 Watts riots what struck the imagination most indelibly were the fires. For days one could drive the Harbor Freeway and see the city on fire, just as we had always known it would be in the end. Los Angeles weather is the weather of catastrophe, of apocalypse, and, just as the reliably long and bitter winters of New England determine the way life is lived there, so the violence and the unpredictability of the Santa Ana affect the entire quality of life in Los Angeles, accentuate its impermanence, its unreliability. The wind shows us how close to the edge we are.

EXERCISE

13. What are the purpose and point of this paragraph? Does it present any new information? How are the bitter New England winters related to the Santa Ana wind? What "edge" do you think Didion is referring to? What do you understand by a "mechanistic view of human behavior"?

Aspects of Style

In working through these six paragraphs, we have been thinking about details and their implications. As you read through Didion's six paragraphs and followed through with the exercises, you were making connections among those details and drawing inferences as you moved toward an interpretation.

We next look more closely at Didion's *style*—the choices she makes among words, sentence patterns, images, allusions, and comparisons to see how they work together with her anecdotes and selection of detail to convey her tone and meaning.

Diction and Anecdote

We can look first at Didion's *diction*, her choice of words. It is by means of her diction that Didion suggests the tensions among people in Los Angeles when the Santa Ana wind arrives. She writes, for example, that there is something "uneasy" in the air, that there is an "unnatural" stillness. She further describes its ominousness as "*whatever* is in the air." The vagueness here is deliberate; the mysterious cause of the tension increases the intensity of people's reactions. That intensity and anxiety are reflected in other aspects of Didion's language, such as her description of the sea as "ominously glossy" with an "eerie absence of surf." Further, the heat is described as "surreal" and the "earthquake weather" swings in "violent extremes." It's no wonder people are on edge.

Besides her striking diction, Didion includes a selection of anecdotal evidence—details to suggest how weather influences people's strange behavior. She mentions how Indians would throw themselves into the sea during a Santa Ana, how a resident stays in a dark house, unwilling to come outside. She notes how a man roams his yard with a machete. She describes fights breaking out, murders contemplated. And she reports on the high incidence of accidents and deaths during the time of the hot dry Santa Ana. Taken together, this proliferation of details create a sense of foreboding, of impending catastrophe.

EXERCISE

14. Which of Didion's word choices do you find particularly striking and memorable? Why?

Details

Didion does more, however, than create a sense of ominousness and catastrophe. In her selection of diction and detail, she helps us see just how powerfully weather can affect people's behavior. Her accumulation of details is relentless. She piles them up in an attempt to persuade us that there is a "mechanistic" quality to human behavior, to convince us that we are conditioned, at the mercy of nature's forces. But her essay is not a traditional argument, a logical attempt at persuasion. Her method is different. It is more oblique, less direct and more an invitation to consider the implications of her carefully selected accumulating details than an explicit and objective argument. To that end she includes not merely historical and scientific "facts" but also hearsay and anecdote along with her own personal experience. Didion is a witness; she serves as our eyes and ears.

EXERCISE

15. What effect does Didion achieve by combining objective evidence in the form of facts and statistics with anecdote and subjective impressions?

Sentences and Allusions

The form of Didion's sentences reinforces her argument. She employs repetition of a phrase in parallel structure: "something uneasy . . . some unnatural stillness . . . some tension." She balances sentences and keeps them short for a strong, hard-hitting effect: "I know it . . . everyone knows it . . . We know it. We feel it." Didion also varies the length of her sentences and diversifies their forms. The short sentences in the opening paragraph are effective partly because they follow a series of longer ones. The contrast of long with short strikes us forcibly, conveying Didion's sense of certainty and establishing her authority.

Didion also uses *allusions* or references that provide an emotional punch to her descriptions. She alludes to Raymond Chandler, a writer of detective fiction, whose murder mysteries are set in California. She also refers to Nathanael West's novel *The Day of the Locust*, which ends with an apocalyptic description of Los Angeles in flames, an image Didion sees as the city's most forceful vision of itself. These two allusions call up images, mental pictures of destruction. They affect the emotions more than the intellect. Our response to them, as too much else in the essay, is one of emotional apprehension as well as intellectual comprehension. We become worried about how nature can affect us.

Diction and Comparisons

Didion's comparisons, largely submerged comparisons in the form of metaphors, contribute to the effects of "Los Angeles Notebook." She mentions an *incendiary* dryness that dries people's nerves to the *flash point*, when they *rekindle* arguments and feel *close to the edge*. The incendiary dryness is both literal and metaphorical. Literally, it is so dry when the Santa Ana blows that spontaneous combustion can occur. Fires simply break out from the combined effects of intense dryness and heat. But the word *incendiary* also suggests a fiery explosion not only literally, but also figuratively, as people explode into anger and wreak devastation. *Flash point* is literally the temperature at which an object can burst spontaneously into flames. Metaphorically, it is the point at which human beings lose control and burst into acts of violent destruction.

We have been especially conscious of Didion's diction, sentence structure, selection of detail, allusions, and uses of language, especially metaphor and other figurative language. We have been considering how appropriate Didion's style is to her subject, how effective her style is in conveying not just an intellectual concept or idea but also an emotional effect—how we feel as well as what we think.

An Approach to Reading and Writing

When we read a text of any kind, we do essentially three things: We respond, we interpret, and we evaluate. In responding to a text, we react emotionally, impressionistically, subjectively. In interpreting a text, we analyze it so as to understand more objectively what the writer says and suggests. In evaluating a text, we consider both how effective it is and what values it embodies.

In writing about a text, we may respond informally in writing that is personal and subjective—an analogue to our preliminary experiential reading. However, we can also write about a text more formally, more analytically and objectively. This kind of writing can result in an interpretation, in which evidence from the text provides support for our interpretive idea. And, as with reading, we can also write in the evaluative mode through making judgments about the text and through considering the values it reflects or embodies.

Reading to Understand a Text

One of the first things that happen in reading is that we respond in terms of our particular background and previous experience. These include both our experience of living in the world and our experience of reading. We bring to our reading a sense of who we are along with the knowledge we have accumulated. As we read, we form impressions that begin to coalesce. Consider what happens as you read the opening section of Zora Neale Hurston's essay "How It Feels to Be Colored Me."

"How It Feels to Be Colored Me"

ZORA NEALE HURSTON

I am colored but I offer nothing in the way of extenuating circumstances except the fact that I am the only Negro in the United States whose grandfather on the mother's side was *not* an Indian chief.

2   I remember the very day that I became colored. Up to my thirteenth year I lived in the little Negro town of Eatonville, Florida. It is exclusively a colored town. The only white people I knew passed through the town going to or coming from Orlando. The native whites rode dusty horses, the Northern tourists chugged down the sandy village road in automobiles. The town knew the Southerners and never stopped cane chewing when they passed. But the Northerners were something else again. They were peered at cautiously from behind curtains by the timid. The more venture-some would come out on the porch to watch them go past and got just as much pleasure out of the tourists as the tourists got out of the village.

3   The front porch might seem a daring place for the rest of the town, but it was a gallery seat to me. My favorite place was atop the gate-post. Proscenium box for a born first-nighter. Not only did I enjoy the show, but I didn't mind the actors knowing that I liked it. I usually spoke to them in passing. I'd wave at them and when they returned my salute, I would say something like this: "Howdy-do-well-I-thank-you-where-yoa-goin'?" Usually automobile or the horse paused at this, and after a queer exchange of compliments, I would probably "go a piece of the way" with them, as we say in farthest Florida. If one of my family happened to come to the front in time to see me, of course negotiations would be rudely broken off. But even so, it is clear that I was the first "welcome-to-our-state" Floridian, and I hope the Miami Chamber of Commerce will please take notice.

4   During this period, white people differed from colored to me only in that they rode through town and never lived there. They liked to hear me "speak pieces" and sing and wanted to see me dance the parse-me-la, and gave me generously of their small silver for doing these things, which seemed strange to me for I wanted to do them so much that I needed bribing to stop. Only they didn't know it. The colored people gave no dimes. They deplored any joyful tendencies in me, but I was their Zora never-theless. I belonged to them, to the nearby hotels, to the county—everybody's Zora.

5   But changes came in the family when I was thirteen, and I was sent to school in Jacksonville. I left Eatonville, the town of the oleanders, as Zora. When I disem-barked from the river-boat at Jacksonville, she was no more. It seemed that I had suffered a sea change. I was not Zora of Orange County any more, I was now a little colored girl. I found it out, in certain ways. In my heart as well as in the mirror, I became a fast brown—warranted not to rub nor run.

Whatever we might understand from this passage, our response to what Hurston describes is affected by what we know either theoretically or experien-tially about being "colored," by what we know about racial and regional differences in the United States (and elsewhere), and by what we know about changes people undergo as they experience life. Our experience of this passage will also be affected by moments when we learned something about our own race, ethnicity, social class, or other aspect of our identity. As we read this passage, we also begin to gain a sense of Hurston the writer, as well as of Zora, the "little colored girl." We begin to sense something of the writer's wit as well as of the little girl's vulnerability.

But it is not just our personal past experience that comes into play during our reading. There is also our experience of negotiating the text itself—the way we make our way through it, picking up cues and clues as to what is important, to what Hurston is saying and suggesting. When Hurston notes, for example, that her young self found out "in certain ways," that she was colored, we expect that she will describe those ways later in her essay. We might also expect that those "certain ways" were somewhat painful for her when she notes that as a young girl, she found this fact of life out in her "heart as well as in the mirror."

During our reading, we also bring our emotional response to the text—to what Hurston describes of her youthful experience. These emotional and subjective responses are inevitable, just as are those preliminary impressions we form as we read. These responses and impressions might change as we read further. For the time being, however, they are real and they are ours, and we need to recognize and acknowledge them.

EXERCISE

16. What are your first impressions of Hurston as a writer and as a young girl? What details contribute most powerfully to your impressions?

What emotional response do you bring to Hurston's essay so far?

To what extent has your past experience and your prior knowledge affected your response. What specific aspects of your knowledge and/or your experience are relevant?

Writing to Understand a Text

When we understand a text we are able to make sense of it, to explain it to ourselves. In doing so, we follow its argument and consider its implications. In writing to understand a text, we attempt to open ourselves to it, allowing the text to stimulate both our feelings and our thoughts. Consider, for example, the first impressions you had of Hurston's text, along with your emotional response to it can form the basis for your initial writing about it.

Annotating

One way to begin writing about a text is to understand it by making "annotations," brief notes within or around the text. **Annotation** is a way to increase our involvement with a text by writing about it as we read it. When we annotate, or make notes about, a text we respond actively to it. Usually annotations are made in the margins around a text, but they can also be made within it—by underlining words, circling phrases, bracketing sentences and paragraphs, drawing arrows, or adding question marks, exclamation points, or other abbreviations.

Annotating a text offers a convenient and relatively painless way to begin writing about it. Our annotations can get us started, helping us zero in on what's important to you. They can also signal textual details that may puzzle or disconcert us.

In annotating a text, we begin to clarify our understanding of it. The act of writing such notes, however brief, encourages a focus both on the writer's idea and on our reaction to it. Annotation stimulates our thinking, with the pen becoming an extension of our mind. A further advantage of annotation is that if we write no more, we have at least marked up the text for rereading and subsequent perusal. And if we need to write about the text in a more formal way later, our annotations have signaled key passages, noted significant details, and raised important questions for subsequent consideration.

Here is a sample annotation from another essay—Gretel Ehrlich's "About Men"—an essay about cowboys. We present the first paragraph of Ehrlich's essay and some sample annotations.

1   When I'm in New York but feeling lonely for Wyoming I look for the Marlboro ads in the subway. What I'm aching to see is horseflesh, the glint of a spur,

Simulate the **Experiment**, Annotation / Ehrlich on Cowboys **MyThinkingLab**

annotation
The process of making brief notes within and around a text.

romanticize
The process of idealizing something, such that it becomes both unrealistic and unpersuasive.

a line of distant mountains, brimming creeks, and a reminder of the ranchers and cowboys I've ridden with for the last eight years. But the men I see in those posters with their stern, humorless looks remind me of no one I know here. In our hellbent earnestness to **romanticize** the cowboy we've ironically disesteemed his true character. If he's "strong and silent" it's because there's probably no one to talk to. If he "rides away into the sunset" it's because he's been on horseback since four in the morning moving cattle and he's trying, fifteen hours later, to get home to his family. If he's "a rugged individualist" he's also part of a team: ranch work is teamwork and even the glorified open-range cowboys of the 1880s rode up and down the Chisholm Train in the company of twenty or thirty other riders. Instead of the macho, trigger-happy man our culture has perversely wanted him to be, the cowboy is more apt to be convivial, *quirky*, and *softhearted*. To be "tough" on a ranch has nothing to do with conquests and displays of power. More often than not, circumstances—like the colt he's riding or an unexpected blizzard—are overpowering him. It's not toughness but "toughing it out" that counts. In other words, this macho, cultural artifact the cowboy has become is simply a man who possesses resilience, patience, and an instinct for survival. "Cowboys are just like a pile of rocks—everything happens to them. They get climbed on, kicked, rained and snowed on, scuffed up by wind. Their job is 'just to take it,'" one old-timer told me.

Annotations left

She cites images of the cowboy, clichés about cowboys

Chisolm Trail—where's that? Important?

Cowboys work in teams—not solo

"toughness" vs. "toughing it out"

Annotations right

Visual details

Romanticizing—central issue?

Macho cowboy—cultural stereotype?

A really hard job—cowboying!

EXERCISE

17. Annotate paragraphs 1 to 5 of Hurston's essay, using the sample annotations of Ehrlich's paragraph as a model for what you might do with Hurston's paragraphs.

Questioning

Now that you have read the opening paragraph of Ehrlich's essay and considered how it could be annotated, return to that paragraph and ask a couple of questions about what Ehrlich says there. You can raise questions about Ehrlich's details, her idea, her evidence, perhaps about her uses of language, like the term *rugged individualist*. What do you think she is suggesting with that term?

Asking questions about the text is one way to become engaged with its idea and its evidence. You might choose to focus some of your questions on whether Ehrlich's idea about cowboys is applicable to American men more generally. Ask some questions about both the first paragraph and this next one.

2   A cowboy is someone who loves his work. Since the hours are long—ten to fifteen hours a day—and the pay is $30 he has to. What's required of him is an odd mixture of physical vigor and maternalism. His part of the beef-raising industry is to birth and nurture calves and take care of their mothers. For the most part his work is done on horseback and in a lifetime he sees and comes to know more animals than people. The iconic myth surrounding him is built on American notions of hero-ism: the index of a man's value as measured in physical courage. Such ideas have perverted manliness into a self-absorbed race for cheap thrills. In a rancher's world, courage has less to do with facing danger than with acting spontaneously—usually on behalf of an animal or another rider. If a cow is stuck in a boghole he throws a loop around her neck, takes his dally (a half hitch around the saddle horn), and pulls her out with horsepower. If a calf is born sick, he may take her home, warm her in front of the kitchen fire, and massage her legs until dawn. One friend, whose favor-ite horse was trying to swim a lake with hobbles on, dove under water and cut her legs loose with a knife, then swam her to shore, his arm around her neck, lifeguard style, and saved her from drowning. Because these incidents are usually linked to someone or something outside himself, the westerner's courage is selfless, a form of compassion.

EXERCISES

18. Respond to the following questions, then add one of your own.

Do you think that Ehrlich really means to suggest that cowboys need to be maternal—that they need to develop the kind of caring instincts of mothers for their children? Do you think that things have changed very much since Ehrlich published this essay in 1985? Why or why not?

19. Respond to the following question, and then add one of your own.

Do you think that the compassion Ehrlich describes as essential for cowboys is something that western men possess more than men from the middle, south-ern, or eastern parts of the United States?

Free Writing

Our initial impressions of a text, recorded with annotations and questions, will often lead to further thoughts about it. We can develop our preliminary thinking with free writing. As with annotating and questioning, free writing is a way to record observations, reactions, and feelings about a text without worrying very much about organization. Free writing, especially, is characterized by a freedom from form. It requires simply writing down what comes to mind. The point is to get some thinking going, some thoughts flowing, to get some initial ideas down on paper or computer and not worry about logical organization just yet. Free writing is an opportunity to explore preliminary thinking to see where it might lead.

Annotation, questioning, and free writing precede the more deliberative work of analysis, interpretation, and evaluation and the more formal ways of writing associated with them. Annotation, questioning, and free writing provide ways to prepare for writing essays, papers, and reports. These three informal writing tech-niques work well together; the brief, quickly jotted annotations can be comple-mented with a second look via questions, and then developed further with the more leisurely paced, longer elaborations of free writing.

Here are the next three paragraphs of Ehrlich's essay on cowboys followed by an example of free writing in response to them.

EXERCISE ——————————————————————————————

20. Before reading the free-writing sample, annotate Ehrlich's passage for practice and jot down some questions you have about it. Each of those ways of writing can better prepare you for the free writing sample.

Ehrlich—"About Men" Continued

3   The physical punishment that goes with cowboying is greatly underplayed. Once fear is dispensed with, the threshold of pain rises to meet the demands of the job. When Jane Fonda asked Robert Redford (in the film *Electric Horseman*) if he was sick as he struggled to his feet one morning, he replied, "No, just bent." For once the movies had it right. The cowboys I was sitting with laughed in agreement. Cowboys are rarely complainers: they show their stoicism by laughing at themselves.

4   If a rancher or cowboy has been thought of a "man's man"—laconic, hard-drinking, inscrutable—there's almost no place in which the balancing act between male and female, manliness and femininity, can be more natural. If he's gruff, hand-some, and physically fit on the outside, he's androgynous at the core. Ranchers are midwives, hunters, nurturers, providers, and conservationists all at once. What we've interpreted as toughness—weathered skin, calloused hands, a squint in the eye and a growl in the voice—only masks the tenderness inside. "Now don't go tell-ing me these lambs are cute," one rancher warned me the first day I walked into the football-field-sized lambing sheds. The next thing I knew he was holding a black lamb. "Ain't this little rat good-lookin'?"

5   So many of the men who came to the West were southerners—men looking for work and a new life after the Civil War—that chivalrousness and strict codes of honor were thought of as western traits. There were very few women in Wyoming during territorial days, so when they did arrive (some as mail-order brides from places like Philadelphia) there was a stand-offishness between the sexes and a for-mality that persists now. Ranchers still tip their hats and say, "Howdy ma'am," instead of shaking hands with me.

Free-writing Sample: Gretel Ehrlich, "About Men"

Androgynous? Cowboys as half-men and half-women? Cowboys are maternal and pa-ternal, manly and womanly? Motherly and macho? Tough and tender. Surprising and more complex than usually thought of. Is this specific to cowboys alone? More gener-alizable to other men? Is it profession-linked, this doubleness? Cowboys have a multi-tude of responsibilities. Ehrlich seems to understand them. They seem to accept her. She respects and likes them. Does she want to be "one of them"? Where is she from? Fonda and Redford in the movie—what's an "Electric" horseman? Have to check that out.

EXERCISE ——————————————————————————————

21. Do a piece of free writing in response to Hurston's essay, paragraphs 1 to 5 and a second free writing about paragraphs 6 to 8 of Hurston's essay, "How It Feels to Be Colored Me," which follow. Write for 10 minutes without stop-ping for each set of paragraphs. Try not to pick up your pen or to take your eyes off the computer keyboard. Just let the words flow.

6   But I am not tragically colored. There is no great sorrow dammed up in my soul, nor lurking behind my eyes. I do not mind at all. I do not belong to the sobbing school of Negrohood who hold that nature somehow has given them a lowdown dirty deal and whose feelings are all hurt about it. Even in the helter-skelter skirmish that is my life, I have seen that the world is to the strong regardless of a little pigmentation more or less. No, I do not weep at the world—I am too busy sharpening my oyster knife.

7   Someone is always at my elbow reminding me that I am the grand-daughter of slaves. It fails to register depression with me. Slavery is sixty years in the past. The operation was successful and the patient is doing well, thank you. The terrible struggle that made me an American out of a potential slave said "On the line 1" The Reconstruction said "Get set 1"; and the generation before said "Go 1" I am off to a flying start and I must not halt in the stretch to look behind and weep. Slavery is the price I paid for civilization, and the choice was not with me. It is a Bully adventure and worth all that I have paid through my ancestors for it. No one on earth over had a greater chance for glory. The world to be won and nothing to be lost. It is thrilling to think—to know that for any act of mine, I shall get twice as much praise or twice as much blame. It is quite exciting to hold the center of the national stage, with the spectators not knowing whether to laugh or to weep.

8   The position of my white neighbor is much more difficult. No brown specter pulls up a chair beside me when I sit down to eat. No dark ghost thrusts its leg against mine in bed. The game of keeping what one has is never so exciting as the game of getting.

Reading to Interpret a Text

When we interpret a text, we explain it to ourselves and make sense of it. In interpreting, we do not entirely disregard our subjective impressions, but we do try to become more objective, to think less of our personal reactions than of what the writer is saying. Our interpretation of a text such as Hurston's essay, involves one way of understanding it, one way of making sense of it. Other ways of understanding the essay, other interpretations are possible; they, too, make sense. Our interpretation should rely, primarily, on an intellectual comprehension rather than on our emotional response to the text or only of our subjective impressions of it. To comprehend the idea of the text is the goal of interpretation. Consider, from the standpoint of interpretation, the next section of Hurston's essay, paragraphs 6 to 8.

What can we say about these paragraphs? We can make the following observations, at least. Hurston suggests that she does not regret being black. In fact, she is delighted with her race, because she says, "no one on earth ever had a greater chance for glory." She sees being "colored" as an opportunity rather than a drawback, and she announces her satisfaction by distinguishing herself from those who see themselves as "tragically colored." Moreover, "no brown specter" and "no dark ghost" haunt her, as they do for those with a heritage of guilt for legal and moral crimes committed against black people.

But it is not just the idea Hurston expresses that is important. It is her attitude toward her idea and the tone in which she expresses it that matter, as well. Hurston appears to relish her chance to shine; she is thrilled to think about the opportunities she has in "the game of getting." She is also not one to weep over the past. Rather, she is "off to a flying start" toward success and the enjoyment of her life. As she puts it, she is "busy sharpening [her] oyster knife."

EXERCISE

22. What other details seem important to you in making sense of Hurston's idea and her attitude in paragraphs 6 to 8? What do you understand about Hurston's essay so far? What specific details in her essay lead you to think about it the way you do?

Elements of Interpretation

Interpretation involves four interrelated acts:

- Observing details
- Connecting details
- Making inferences based on related details
- Formulating an interpretive conclusion

Before explaining each of these aspects of interpretation—and asking you to do some work using them on Hurston's essay—you need to read the final portion of Hurston's essay.

9   I do not always feel colored. Even now I often achieve the unconscious Zora of Eatonville before the Hegira. I feel most colored when I am thrown against a sharp white background.

10   For instance at Barnard. "Beside the waters of the Hudson" I feel my race. Among the thousand white persons, I am a dark rock surged upon, overswept by a creamy sea. I am surged upon and overswept but through it all, I remain myself. When covered by the waters, I am; and the ebb but reveals me again.

11   Sometimes it is the other way around. A white person is set down in our midst, but the contrast is just as sharp for me. For instance, when I sit in the drafty basement that is The New World Cabaret with a white person, my color comes. We enter chatting about any little nothing that we have in common and are seated by the jazz waiters. In the abrupt way that jazz orchestras have, this one plunges into a number. It loses no time in circumlocutions, but gets right down to business. It constricts the thorax and splits the heart with its tempo and narcotic harmonies. This orchestra grows rambunctious, rears on its hind legs and attacks the tonal veil with primitive fury, rending it, clawing it until it breaks through to the jungle beyond. I follow those heathen—follow them exultingly. I dance wildly inside myself; I yell within, I whoop; I shake my assegai above my head, I burl it true to the mark *yeeeeoowww!* I am in the jungle and living in the jungle way. My face is painted red and yellow and my body is painted blue. My pulse is throbbing like a war drum. I want to slaughter something—give pain, give death to what, I do not know. But the piece ends. The men of the orchestra wipe their lips and rest their fingers. I creep back slowly to the veneer we call civilization with the last tone and find the white friend sitting motionless in his seat, smoking calmly.

12   "Good music they have here," he remarks, drumming the table with his fingertips.

13   Music! The great blobs of purple and red emotion have not touched him. He has only heard what I felt. He is far away and I see him but dimly across the ocean and the continent that have fallen between us. He is so pale with his whiteness them and I am so colored.

14   At certain times I have no race, I am *me*. When I set my hat at a certain angle and saunter down Seventh Avenue, Harlem City, feeling as snooty as the Lions in front of the Forty-Second Street Library, for instance. So far as my feelings are concerned, Peggy Hopkins Joyce on the Boule Mich with her gorgeous raiment, stately carriage, knees

knocking together in a most aristocratic manner, has nothing on me. The cosmic Zora emerges. I belong to no race nor time. I am the eternal feminine with its string of beads.

15   I have no separate feeling about being an American citizen and colored. I am merely a fragment of the Great Soul that surges within the boundaries. My country, right or wrong.

16   Sometimes, I feel discriminated against, but it does not make me angry. It merely astonishes me. How *can* any deny themselves the pleasure of my company! It's beyond me.

17   But in the main, I feel like a brown bag of miscellany propped against a wall. Against a wall in company with other bags, white, red and yellow. Pour out the contents, and there is discovered a jumble of small things priceless and worthless. A first-water diamond, an empty spool, bits of broken glass, lengths of string, a key to a door long since crumbled away, a rusty knife-blade, old shoes saved for a road that never was and never will be, a nail bent under the weight of things too heavy for any nail, a dried flower or two, still a little fragrant. In your hand is the brown bag. On the ground before you is the jumble it held—so much like the jumble in the bags, could they be emptied, that all might be dumped in a single heap and the bags refilled without altering the content of any greatly. A bit of colored glass more or less would not matter. Perhaps that is how the Great Stuffer of Bags filled them in the first place—who knows?

Making Observations

All interpretation begins with observation. In Hurston's essay, we observe how the writer describes her experience. We notice how she uses language and how she organizes her essay.

- She writes as an adult looking back on her childhood and adolescence, and how she includes a few scenes from her adult life.
- She describes her experience of living and being in different places—Eatonville, Jacksonville, New York City.
- She describes scenes in those places. She describes her feelings. She mentions changes and contrasting states of affairs.
- She uses comparisons in describing how she thinks about herself.

EXERCISE

23. Identify two scenes that Hurston describes. What does she convey in each?

   Identify three places where she describes her feelings. What are those feelings in each case? Identify one place where she indicates change or contrasting states of affairs. What is the significance of that change or contrast? Identify three comparisons she uses. What is the effect of each of those comparisons? What does Hurston communicate to us through each comparison?

Establishing Connections

Once we have made a number of observations, or as we are doing so, we begin making connections between and among them. The business of making connections is a personal one. We look for three kinds of connections:

1. Connections among textual details;
2. Connections between the writer's text and our own lives; and
3. Connections between the writer's text and other texts we have read.

We might consider, for example, the relationship between the two scenes Hurston describes—her serving as an unofficial welcoming committee for Eatonville, and her experience of listening to music in the cabaret. What, in each case, is her relationship to the white people she is with? We might consider the extent to which differences exist for Hurston between Eatonville and Jacksonville. How can we account for the difference in feeling she has about these places? And we might consider, also, the extent to which what Hurston describes echoes in some way our own experience. This establishes our personal relationship to Hurston and her essay. In addition, in reading Hurston's essay we might make connections with other reading we have done—a poem or another essay about personal identity, for example, or a short story or novel about coming to terms with being "different" racially, from others, or different in some other way.

EXERCISE

24. Make one additional connection for each of the following: (1) a connection among textual details; (2) a connection between the text and your life; (3) a connection between Hurston's text and something you have read or seen.

Making Inferences

When we make an inference, we reasonably conclude that something is the case based on evidence—on what we have observed, and on connections between and among our observations. Our inferences, however, may be correct or incorrect. Among the inferences we might make about Hurston's essay are the following:

- Hurston writes about her blackness without bitterness.
- She seems proud of her race.
- She values herself and is confident in her abilities.
- She sees herself as a performer, on center stage.
- She experiences pain in her discovery of her blackness.
- She is irrepressibly optimistic.
- She sees white people as bearing the weight of the race problems in America.

EXERCISE

25. Select three of the bulleted inferences from the preceding list. Either agree with the inferences made about Hurston, disagree with them, or qualify the inferences made about her essay. Then find evidence in the text to support or challenge those inferences.

Drawing Conclusions

In thinking about the inferences we have made about Hurston's essay, we move toward developing a conclusion about it—an interpretation. This interpretive conclusion is provisional and tentative. It can change based on our rereading of the essay, on our having thought more about it. Perhaps we will change our thinking a little or a lot based on conversations we have about it with friends or classmates or through a discussion with our teacher in class or in conference. Interpretations are always provisional, tentative, and thus subject to change.

One way to clarify our thinking about a text is to write about it. To develop our interpretation of Hurston's essay, we can ask ourselves questions such as whether

Hurston's description of her experience is believable and persuasive; whether it might extend to others beyond herself. We might consider, for example, the extent to which Hurston's resilience transcends racial and other boundaries, and whether she captures any particular truths about racial prejudice.

EXERCISE

26. What conclusions do you draw now, tentatively and provisionally, from your reading of Hurston's essay? What is your present interpretation of it?

Writing to Explain a Text

When we write to explain a text, our concern is largely one of making our understanding of it clear to others. Such writing will be based not only on our impressions of the text, but also on our interpretation, our considered understanding, of it. In writing to explain a text, we need to be less personal, less informal, and less subjective than when we make annotations, develop questions, and engage in free writing for ourselves.

The work of annotating, questioning, and free writing about a text, however, is useful and essential preparation for more formal kinds of analytical writing. In fact, that preliminary work actually provides steps toward more formal explanatory writing. The observations made with those less formal procedures, the connections noticed, the patterns discovered, and the questions raised—all are crucial for developing our thinking further. They help us to move toward the next important step— developing an idea about the text.

When we write an interpretation or explanation of the meaning of a text, our goal is clarity. This clarity is twofold. First, it involves clarity of understanding. (We need to know, in short, what we think.) Second, it requires clarity of explanation. (We need to convey our thinking clearly to others.) One way to begin clarifying our understanding of a text for others is to write a double-column notebook entry about it; another is to summarize it and/or to paraphrase a crucial part of it. We describe and illustrate each of these techniques in the next section.

Keeping a Double-Column Notebook

Keeping a double-column notebook is yet another way writing can aid our understanding and explaining of a text. In this type of notebook, we record thoughts about the texts we read, raise questions about them, and make connections with other things we have read, seen, or otherwise experienced. The double-column notebook can also provide a place to collect and copy sentences, phrases, words, and ideas we might wish to preserve. In it we can record our growing understanding of the significance and value of what we read. It can also serve as an arena to develop our thinking about issues that emerge from our reading. This writing strategy forms a bridge between the quick subjective personal response writing of annotation and free writing (writing for oneself) on one hand, and analysis and interpretation (writing for others), on the other hand.

To create a double-column notebook page, simply draw a vertical line down the center of the page. One side of the page is for "taking" notes, to record what we notice about the text. On this side, the goal is to capture what the writer is saying. On the other side, we record our own thinking about the text. That side is for "making" notes, recording our responses and questions. We make connections with other things we have read, seen, heard, and otherwise experienced. We can challenge the text here, as well. In the process of both "making" and "taking" notes, we create a dialogue with and about the texts we read. We begin to create what we might call an "intertextual" web.

Here is an example of a double-column notebook entry for a portion of Gretel Ehrlich's essay about cowboys. First, we present the final three paragraphs of Ehrlich's essay and then the sample double-column notebook entry.

6   Even young cowboys are often evasive with women. It's not that they're Jekyll and Hyde creatures—gentle with animals and rough on women—but rather, that they don't know how to bring their tenderness into the house and lack the vocabulary to express the complexity of what they feel. Dancing wildly all night becomes a metaphor for the explosive emotions pent up inside, and when these are, on occasion, released, they're so battery-charged and potent that one caress of the face or one "I love you" will peal for a long while.

7   The geographical vastness and the social isolation here make emotional evolution seem impossible. These contradictions of the heart between respectability, logic, and convention on the one hand, and impulse, passion, and intuition on the other, played out wordlessly against the paradisiacal beauty of the West, give cowboys a wide-eyed but drawn look. Their lips pucker up, not with kisses but with immutability. They may want to break out, staying up all night with a lover just to talk, but they don't know how and can't imagine what the consequences will be. Those rare occasions when they do bare themselves result in confusion. "I feel as if I'd sprained my heart," one friend told me a month after such a meeting.

8   My friend Ted Hoagland wrote, "No one is as fragile as a woman, but no one is as fragile as a man." For all the women here who use "fragileness" to avoid work or as a sexual ploy, there are men who try to hide theirs, all the while clinging to an adolescent dependency to cook their meals, wash their clothes, and keep the ranch house warm in winter. But there is true vulnerability in evidence here. Because these men work with animals, not machines or numbers, because they live outside in landscapes of torrential beauty, because they are confined to a place and a routine embellished with awesome variables, because calves die in the arms that pulled others into life, because they go to the mountains as if on a pilgrimage to find out what makes a herd of elk tick, their strength is also a softness, their toughness, a rare delicacy.

Double-Column Notebook

Taking Notes—Representing Text	*Making Notes—Commenting/Questioning*
Ehrlich debunks the stereotypical image of the cowboy without denying that cowboys are tough, strong, silent individualists.	Is Ehrlich's own image of the cowboy overly romanticized, idealized? In making cowboys maternal, does she make too much of their gentleness?
She uses direct quotes from cowboys as one kind of evidence. She refers to images from popular culture—the Marlboro ad and a film, as examples of cowboy manliness.	Ehrlich's historical explanation may be an oversimplification, though its broad outline makes sense.
She provides social and historical context about cowboys and women.	Is her historical analysis correct?

Add some additional NOTES here   Add some Comments/Questions here

EXERCISE

27. Add some additional notes and some more comments/questions to the Double-Column Notebook example for Ehrlich's essay.

    Write a double-column notebook entry for one section of Hurston's essay: paragraphs 1 to 5; paragraphs 6 to 8; or paragraphs 9 to 17.

Summarizing and Paraphrasing

A summary is a succinct account of a text. It compresses and condenses the text it summarizes, and thus is shorter than the original. A paraphrase differs from a summary, which squeezes out the essence of a text briefly. Paraphrase means "to explain alongside"; it is more extensive than a summary, and generally closely approximates the length of the original text. A paraphrase also follows the structure of the original text, which a summary may not do.

A paraphrase is inclusive; a summary is selective. In addition, a summary encompasses the whole of a text—it is an overarching encapsulation of the text. A paraphrase, on the other hand, focuses on a key moment of the text, a briefer segment. A summary telescopes much into little; a paraphrase puts a small slide of the text under a microscope. Both summary and paraphrase are essential components of analysis. Both are necessary in developing an interpretation of a text.

Here is a sample **summary** of Ehrlich's "About Men."

> In her essay "About Men," Gretel Ehrlich disabuses readers of some common misconceptions people have about cowboys. Ehrlich identifies a series of clichéd images and ideas, such as that cowboys are "strong and silent," "tough" and solo individualists who "ride[s] away into the sunset." These clichés she demolishes by providing evidence to support a more complex view of cowboys as tough and tender, rugged but compassionate, manly yet maternal. Ehrlich includes brief anecdotal evidence along with quotations from cowboys she has known and worked with to support her more complex, less romanticized image of the cowboy than the pop culture iconic "Marlboro man" once commonly found on poster ads and in television commercials. In the process, she helps us appreciate how hard the life of a cowboy is, how much cowboys rely on each other, how deeply they are committed to the animals in their care, and how well they embody an ethic of community and compassion.

And now here is a sample **paraphrase** of the final paragraph (paragraph 8) of "About Men":

> In the final paragraph of her essay "About Men," Gretel Ehrlich describes how the writer Ted Hoagland conveys the sense of fragility of the male cowboy. It is

summarize
The process of condensing and restating in brief form the argument, ideas, and structure of a text.

paraphrase
A restatement or reformulation of an idea, argument, text, or portion of a text, in different words, that follows the order and organization of the original.

a fragility that cowboys try to hide as they depend on women to perform traditional female household tasks. For Ehrlich the cowboy's "vulnerability" is real, authentic. Her final long sentence reveals the doubleness of a cowboy's experience—strength combined with softness, toughness mingled with a delicate sensibility. This complex feeling, Ehrlich suggests, is a consequence of the cowboy's love of his work, his appreciation of animals, and his deep reverence for the natural world.

EXERCISE

28. Write a 8-to-10 sentence summary of Hurston's essay, "How It Feels to Be Colored Me." Write a one-paragraph paraphrase of Hurston's essay.

Evaluation—Judging and Considering Values

Evaluation consists of two different kinds of assessment:

evaluation
The process of considering values—political, social, religious, and the like—during the analysis and interpretation of texts. Also, in argument, a judgment expressing favor or disfavor, approval or disapproval, agreement or disagreement.

1. A judgment about the work's achievement, including the power and persuasiveness of its ideas;
2. A consideration of the social, cultural, moral, and other values the work reflects and/or embodies.

When we evaluate an idea, we consider its accuracy as a description, its validity as an argument, its persuasiveness and interest as a proposal, and its credibility as an imaginative construction. Evaluation depends on interpretation. Our understanding of a work's idea influences our evaluation of it.

Let's consider some questions we might raise in an evaluation of Hurston's "How It Feels to Be Colored Me." We might consider, for example, how engaged we are by the essay, or how broadly it reflects the feelings of other African Americans. Does Hurston's description accurately reflect your experience or your knowledge? To what extent does it broaden or deepen your understanding? Do you agree that being colored provides greater opportunities than not being colored? Why or why not? What do you think of Hurston's celebration of her race?

Other criteria that emerge in evaluating texts involve moral, cultural, ethical, and other kinds of values. Such values shape and influence our response to and our evaluation of texts. Because value-based judgments are largely inescapable, we should not avoid them, but rather become aware of what part they play in the judgments we make.

In assessing the personal values of the writer and the cultural values reflected in the work, we bring our own values into play. It is precisely for this reason that it is important to consider the values Hurston's essay reflects. Considering those values brings a clearer understanding of them and a better understanding of our own values.

Evaluation also involves our appraisal of the social, cultural, and moral ideals a work supports or endorses. Our social values reflect our attitudes toward the beliefs and customs of communities. Our cultural values reflect our racial, ethnic, and family heritage, and are affected as well by our gender and our language. Our moral values reflect our ethical norms—what we consider to be right and wrong, good and evil. These values are influenced by our religious beliefs and may reflect our political convictions.

EXERCISE

29. What is your overall assessment of Hurston's essay? Is it an effective piece of writing? Have you learned something from reading it? To what extent does it make you think? Has reading it actively deepened and broadened your understanding in some way? What values—social, cultural, moral, and more—are at play and at stake in Hurston's essay?

Writing to Evaluate a Text

Much like evaluation in reading, writing to evaluate a text involves two different kinds of evaluation: (1) making a judgment about its quality and its value for us; (2) assessing the social, cultural, moral, and other kinds of values the text embodies and perhaps endorses. To evaluate a text, we have to understand it. We need to be clear about what we think it says and suggests. Evaluation, thus, is grounded in interpretation. In writing to evaluate, we also have to write to understand.

Our first challenge in evaluating a text is deciding on appropriate criteria for evaluation. These criteria form the basis of our critical judgments of the text. Often our criteria are implicit. It is when we consider specific examples of texts and our judgments of their relative merit and value that our criteria can be made explicit.

EXERCISES

30. Do you find Ehrlich's thinking about cowboys persuasive? To what extent do you accept her evidence—her personal testimony? Do you think she achieves her aims in this essay—to help us better understand the complex nature of cowboys? What cultural values are central for Ehrlich's argument? To what extent do your own values—your own sense of what a "man" is—mesh with those espoused by Ehrlich?

31. Write a response to Ehrlich in which you question, challenge, qualify, or debate her celebration of the androgynous male. Evaluate Ehrlich's argument, and explain how or why it might be modified to account for your own thinking about her idea. Consider the social and cultural values at play in Ehrlich's essay, along with the values associated with gender roles.

32. What social, cultural, and other values are at play in Hurston's essay? Consider the ways these values connect with racial and gender attitudes revealed in her essay.

33. Write a response to Hurston in which you question, challenge, qualify, or debate her celebration of herself. Evaluate Hurston's argument, and explain how or why it might be modified to account for your own thinking about her idea. Consider the social and cultural values at play in Hurston's essay, along with the values associated with race and gender.

The Value of Reading

So far throughout this chapter, we have been engaged with the process and practice of critical reading and writing. In this section, you are invited to consider some broader questions about the nature, purposes, and value of reading.

❇ **Explore** the **Concept,**
The Value of Reading
MyThinkingLab

In *A Reader on Reading*, Alberto Manguel claims that reading "defines our species." Reading, Manguel suggests, is a threshold activity; once we learn to read, we become members of the human tribe—the tribe of readers. That's why so much emphasis is placed on learning to read in the earliest grades. Reading serves as an initiation into the world of the book, the world of thinking, the world of the mind, the world of the imagination. Negotiating the symbolic language of words and meanings is a distinctive human attribute. Reading is an essential part of who we are as human beings.

Manguel describes reading as cumulative; the books we read grow with each new reading, building upon what we have read before. Moreover, we might add, the books speak to one another and affect one another, combining in various ways in our minds, affected, of course, by what we can remember of them over time. They form, as Robert Scholes notes in *Protocols of Reading*, an "intertextual web," one that enables us to construct ourselves as intelligible beings. According to Scholes, we are never really outside the web of our reading; this web of textuality is the environment in and through which we create ourselves.

Scholes agrees with the French thinker Roland Barthes, whom he quotes approvingly to the effect that when we read, we write the text of the work and we "write" the reading of the text within the text of our own lives. Scholes suggests that in reading texts, we read the book of ourselves, connecting those texts with our thoughts and lives. Reading, that is, becomes entangled and intertwined with our actual lives—our lives outside of reading. And living, we might add, becomes entangled with our reading lives. Reading and living stimulate, reinforce, and support each other. That reciprocal connection between reading and living, suggests Scholes, "is what reading is all about."

EXERCISES

34. To what extent do all the things you have read and continue to read in print and online mix and mingle to affect what you know, how you think, who you are? To what extent do you agree with the suggestions of Manguel and Scholes about the ways in which reading affects us, develops us, makes us who we are?

35. To what extent do you think "you are what you read"?—rather than, for example, "you are what you eat." How might we think of eating as a metaphor for reading? To what extent, do we, for example, "devour" books, or perhaps "nibble" at them? How does the following sentence from an essay by the Renaissance writer and thinker Francis Bacon speak to the connection between eating and reading? What is Bacon saying about reading by means of this metaphor?

> "Some books are to be tasted, others to be swallowed, and some few to be chewed and digested."
>
> —Francis Bacon, *Essays*, "Of Studies"

In *Protocols of Reading*, Scholes describes what he calls "an ethic of reading." By this he means that, as readers, we have a responsibility to the texts we read. Our major responsibility lies in giving the texts and authors we read their due. We need to hear them out, letting them have their say, whether we agree with their views or not, whether their ideas are difficult or accessible, no matter who wrote the books, when they were written, or why. We need, in short, to respect the integrity of the texts we read.

One aspect of this ethic involves not expecting something from a book that it does not intend to provide. When we read a novel, we may hope for a happy ending, but a writer is not obligated to provide one. To criticize the book for lacking that happy ending offends the ethic of reading. And when we read a detective novel or a work or fantasy or science fiction, it is unjust to expect or even demand that it be realistic. Its genre requires that it do and be something other than realistic.

Sven Birkerts in *The Gutenberg Elegies* describes reading a different kind of challenge when readers engage texts today. Birkerts sees reading as a "discipline" that includes a focused, serious engagement with a text. He believes that with the advent of multiple technologies, we are less and less able to do this kind of disciplined reading because the distractions of instant information and the constant stream of data have diminished and fragmented our attention. Birkerts believes that the electronic millennium we have entered has altered the way we think and how we perceive the world and ourselves. He claims that recent developments in technology have created an erosion of language, a simplifying of sentences, and a blandness of language generally, resulting in a shallower, less nuanced, and less richly textured discourse.

EXERCISES

36. To what extent do you share Birkerts's concerns about the consequences of the electronic millennium? Do you think he overstates the effects of electronic reading and living? To what extent do you believe you have a responsibility to the texts you read, whether in print or electronic form? Do you think that Scholes is right to suggest that there is an "ethic" of reading? Why or why not?

37. How do the following observations made by Henry David Thoreau in his book *Walden* relate to what Scholes and Birkerts say about reading?

   a. "How many a man has dated a new era in his life from the reading of a book?"

   b. Books must be read as deliberately and reservedly as they were written.

   c. "To read well, that is, to read true books in a true spirit, is a noble exercise, and one that will task the reader. . . . It requires a training such as the athletes underwent, the steady intention almost of the whole life."

   d. "A truly good book teaches me better than to read it. I must soon lay it down, and commence living on its hint. What I began by reading, I must finish by acting."

Digital Reading

Today, we do much of our reading on digital devices—smartphones, computers, tablets, and dedicated electronic readers, such as the Kindle, Nook, and iPad. And although books and magazines as well as newspapers continue to be published in print versions, digital reading is increasing, particularly among the young. One way of gauging the rise of electronic reading is to chart the growth of e-book readers and of e-book sales compared with sales of printed books. (And it is clear that every year more e-books are read and sold than the year before.) Another is to note indicators that acknowledge the importance of

Write the Response,
Digital Reading
MyThinkingLab

electronic books, such as the *New York Times* best-seller lists, which has separate sections for print books and e-books, along with a section that combines sales of books in both formats.

As with any new technology, the new reading technologies tend to coexist with the older ones. And though we no longer read texts very often in the form of scrolls, there are still readings of scrolls, especially for religious purposes. The Torah or first five books of the Bible, as both Jews and Christians know them, are still printed in Hebrew as scrolls and used in Jewish ritual, most notably perhaps the tradition of the bar mitzvah and bat mitzvah, in which a young man and young woman, respectively, assumes full-fledged religious adult membership in his or her congregation. Just as we continue to listen to radio though we have television, and watch movies in theaters though we have streaming Netflix video on our personal computers, so too, it can be argued we will continue to have bound books even as e-books increase in numbers and volume.

We should consider, nonetheless, how reading in print differs from reading on-line, and how reading books and magazines in print differs from reading them in an electronically transmitted, digitized format. What are some of these differences? And what are their implications for different kinds of reading?

In a *New York Times* op-ed piece for April 11, 2013, Verlyn Klinkenborg, who acknowledges having read hundreds of books on his iPad, suggests that the e-books he reads disappear not just into cyberspace but from his vision as well. As a result, the physicality and hence the substantiality of those books are effaced. He notes that registering the size and heft and shape of physical books, their typography and page layout, all help him to remember that he has indeed read those books. The e-books he reads he is more likely to forget having read, and having no physical books to see on his bookshelves, he is not reminded of having read them. Klinkenborg admits that both e-books and physical books "stir us into reverie," that they "revise our consciousness," as they entertain, inform, and even change us. But e-books make reading even more ephemeral than reading print books, whose physical presence testifies to their having been read and makes the imaginative act of reading substantial.

EXERCISE

38. How does your experience of reading printed materials, books especially, differ from reading them in electronic form? What do you see as the benefits and drawbacks of electronic reading of digitized texts? To what extent do you use different reading strategies when you shift from print to e-text, and vice versa? Do you prefer one form of reading over the other? Why or why not?

In *The Rise and Fall of the Bible* (available in both print and e-book versions), Timothy Beale reflects on the influence of electronic reading of the world's best known and most voluminously published book, the Bible. Beale considers how the impact of the digital revolution and the end of the dominance of print culture will change the meaning of the word and of the very idea of the book, including the idea of the Bible as a special book, "the book." Beale's speculations about electronic reading, however, are not limited to the Bible. The three dimensions of reading he describes—its hypertextual, processual, and collaborative nature—have much wider implications for reading.

The most frequently discussed is "hypertextuality," the fact that any text can be linked to multitude of other texts and images. One result is the proliferative nature of texts as they flow and overflow into one another, blurring the line between text and context. Beale's "processual" notion suggests how texts are in complex networked relationships with other texts. They are, thus, always in the process of being formed, deformed, and reformed. The processual implications for texts are that they are subject to alteration via editing, adaptation, and other forms of combination. The collaborative aspect of reading reminds us that not only are the texts themselves connected in expanding and changing networks, but so too are their readers. The most obvious examples are wikis and blogs, as well as the numerous interactive social Web sites, most notably perhaps, Facebook.

EXERCISE

39. What has been your experience of using various forms of digitized reading and writing? To what extent has your experience of using different forms of electronic media for communication—both reading and writing—involved similar and/or different strategies? Do you have one preferred form for electronic reading (and writing)? Why or why not?

Looking Back and Looking Ahead

Revisit the learning goals that begin this chapter. Which of these goals do you think you have best achieved? What might you do to reach the remaining goals?

Return to the focusing questions at the beginning of the chapter. How would you answer those questions now? Which of them do you find most interesting and provocative and worthy of following up? Why?

In reviewing the list of resources that follows, identify the two that attract you most. Explain why these books or Web sites interest you. Consider looking into them for further deepening your understanding of the connections between reading and writing and how they are inextricably linked with thinking.

Take a look, too, at the MyThinkingLab resources on the Prentice Hall Web site. Included there are readings, images, videos, questions, exercises, and other provocations to help you develop your critical reading, writing, and thinking abilities.

Resources

The Pleasures of Reading in an Ideological Age, Robert Alter. Norton, 1990.

First We Read, Then We Write, Robert D. Richardson, ed. University of Iowa Press, 2009.

"Los Angeles Notebook I," in *Slouching Toward Bethlehem*, Joan Didion. Farrar, Straus and Giroux, 1968.

"Living Like Weasels," in *Teaching a Stone to Talk*, Annie Dillard. Harper Perennial, 1982.

"About Men," in *The Solace of Open Spaces*, Gretel Ehrlich. Penguin, 1986.

"How to Be Colored Me," Zora Neale Hurston. *Women's Voices*. Ed. Pat C. Hoy et al. McGraw-Hill, 1989.

A Reader on Reading, Alberto Manguel. Yale University Press, 2011.

Protocols of Reading. Robert Scholes. Yale University Press, 1991.

Essays, Francis Bacon. Penguin, 1986.

Walden, Henry David Thoreau. Penguin, 1983.

The Gutenberg Elegies, Sven Birkerts. Faber and Faber, 1994.

The Rise and Fall of the Bible, Timothy Beale. Houghton Mifflin, 2012.

"Books to Have and to Hold," Verlyn Klinkenborg. *The New York Times*, August 11, 2013.

• •

6

Reasoning Well: Sound Thinking

Truths of reasoning are necessary and their opposite impossible; truths of fact are contingent and their opposite possible.

—GOTTFIED LEIBNITZ

LEARNING GOALS

6.1 UNDERSTAND the basic language and concepts of reasoning, including inductive and deductive reasoning, syllogisms, and enthymemes.

6.2 RECOGNIZE and analyze the logical relationship between claims and the evidence used to support them.

6.3 IDENTIFY and evaluate the assumptions and implications embedded in arguments.

6.4 EXAMINE strong and weak arguments, including those based on analogy and authority.

6.5 EXPLORE the nature and function of causality and evaluate the element of causality in arguments.

FOCUSING QUESTIONS

● How would you characterize the way most people "argue"? Why do you think so many everyday arguments conclude in stalemates?

● How do you evaluate the persuasiveness of a person's arguments? To what extent do you consider the evidence that supports an argument's conclusions?

● What do you think might help to enable people with opposing ideas to "argue" in a more productive way?

● What might you do to become a more logical thinker, to improve your ability to reason responsibly and effectively?

Chapter Overview

This chapter focuses on argument through a consideration of reasoning: It addresses aspects of logical thinking, and it emphasizes the consideration of ideas in a rational manner. Key concepts include (1) the nature and structure of arguments; (2) claims and evidence; (3) assumptions and implications; (4) inductive and deductive thinking; (5) syllogisms and enthymemes; (6) categorical, hypothetical, and disjunctive syllogisms; and (7) authority, analogy, and causality. The chapter's focus is on thinking responsibly in evaluating complex situations and issues.

👁 **Watch** the **Video**, The Pervasiveness of Argument / What Is an Argument? **MyThinkingLab**

The Pervasiveness of Argument

Arguments swirl all around us. Everywhere we look and listen some form of argument is occurring—in advertisements and brochures, on Web sites and blogs, in classrooms and meeting rooms, on television and radio, in books, magazines, and newspapers whether in print or electronic form. We hear arguments among politicians attempting to persuade voters to support a particular policy, to favor one program rather than another. We, in turn, are courted by those same politicians to cast our votes for them, as they make arguments about their performance, their, goals, and intentions. And we make and defend our own arguments about all manner of things in our personal, academic, and professional worlds. In these and myriad other ways argument forms part of the fabric of our lives.

What Is an Argument?

An argument in the sense we mean here is not a heated exchange of remarks, often insulting. The verb *to argue* as used here is not synonymous with *to quarrel* or *to bicker*. An argument in the sense we explore in this chapter is not a disagreement or a dispute, however intense. Simply put, an argument is a claim or statement that is supported by evidence. When we argue in this sense, we are asserting a claim, maintaining that something is the case and providing reasons to buttress our assertion.

Arguments at their best are grounded in thoughtful reasoning, in logical thinking. The primary goal of argument is to persuade, to convince someone or some group of people to consider something—a claim, a perspective, an idea—one way rather than another way.

An argument may present a position or claim while offering only a small amount of supporting evidence for it. Such arguments may overlook possible objections, alternative views, what we think of as "the other side." These arguments may use logic casually and carelessly. For example, in arguing that we should have use of the family car for a weekend trip, it is unlikely that we would think about anything more than our reasons for needing the vehicle, though our case would be strengthened if we also considered our parents' perspective, including questions they might ask and objections they might raise—and how we would answer them.

Successful arguments are careful and thorough; they consider potential objections, and they apply logical thinking rigorously. Such arguments attempt to present careful reasoning clearly and thoughtfully. For example, in making an argument in favor of a flat rate tax policy, we might do research into the history of tax policy, consult experts, consider thoroughly the implications of the policy advocated, provide supporting evidence, and take into account opposing arguments and how we might refute or at least qualify them.

The nature of the topic partly determines the approach, as does the complexity of the claim, and the necessity for doing research to support that claim. We might wish to argue the merits of Derek Jeter versus Lou Gehrig as the best Yankee hitter of all time. In doing so we would consider such things as their batting averages over their entire careers, along with the number of times they won batting titles, the number of times they were selected as most valuable player, their on-base percentages, and their extra-base hits, including home runs. We might also consider the extent to which they were successful in "clutch" situations—times when the game was on the line.

Or we might wish to argue the extent to which the architect Frank Lloyd Wright has influenced future architects and the extent to which the houses he built have defined a major architectural style and deserve to be celebrated as the most important ever built by an American architect.

Both the argument about the greatest Yankee hitter and the argument about the most influential American architect can be treated seriously and thoroughly. Each claim, one from popular culture and the other from the realm of architecture, requires support in terms of substantiating evidence, if the argument is to be taken seriously.

Argument Basics: Claims, Evidence, Assumptions, Implications

Arguments are collections of statements, some of which (the premises) support the conclusion, or claim. Every argument is based on a claim, or assertion; if there is no claim, there is no argument.

The **premises** of an argument provide the evidence that supports it. The *Oxford English Dictionary* defines **evidence** as "the available facts . . . supporting . . . a belief." Without evidence, there is no argument—only a claim, which may be stated as an opinion. For an argument, we need both evidence and a claim the evidence supports.

Arguments stand or fall based on the evidence that supports the claims they make. What counts as evidence? Examples provide one type of evidence; illustrations that clarify; comparisons or analogies that illuminate; reasons that explain; facts, data, and statistics that inform; stories that convey experiential truth; logical connections among accurate and factual premises—these and more provide evidence for an argument's claim.

An argument's claim or **conclusion** can be identified on occasion by certain key words that signal it. Some of these words are *in conclusion*, *so*, *therefore*, *thus*, *hence*, *consequently*, *as a result*, *my position is that*, and the like.

An argument's evidence can also be identified on occasion by other key words that signal support is being presented to substantiate the claim or conclusion. Some of these words are *as suggested*, *as indicated by*, *as shown by*, *because*, *for*, *given that*, *since*, "*the reason is . . . ,*" and the like. In the case of both an argument's claim or conclusion, and its evidence or support, guiding words are not always present. When they are present, however, it makes it a bit easier to identify premises and conclusions.

Assumptions about what people believe and what values they uphold underlie many arguments. An **assumption** is what is being taken for granted—something the speaker or writer believes does not need proof or evidence in its support.

An argument's claim and its evidence are always explicitly stated. Its assumptions, however, are implicit—that is, they are unstated. Assumptions exist in the mind of the writer or speaker. They need to be discovered, or uncovered, and made explicit if an argument is to be fully understood, and more importantly, if it is to be contested and perhaps refuted.

For any argument to be convincing, the premises must be true. Consider the assumptions behind the following two arguments:

1. Ms. Jones will bring a new perspective to the state government. As the outsider candidate, she is the choice we need. We should elect her.

2. Mr. Johnson has served the city for more than a decade. He knows the system and has the experience to get things accomplished. We should elect him.

Simulate the **Experiment**, Claims, Evidence, Assumptions **MyThinkingLab**

argument
The assertion of a claim or conclusion that is supported with evidence in the form of information, data, numbers, or reasons.

premises
In an argument, statements explicitly asserted or assumed that comprise an argument's reasons; premises provide justification for the conclusion.

evidence
Proof or support for an argument claim in the form of facts, data, information, and reasons.

conclusion
What an argument asserts; the claim of an argument. Also, the idea or meaning derived from the process of interpretation.

assumption
What is taken for granted in an argument.

The unstated assumption behind the first premise in argument A is that outsiders make better political representatives than people who have held office for a long time. It relies on the belief that fresh ideas are better than current ones, and that it is time for new ideas. The second argument relies on the opposite premise (also an assumption): that experience is more important than a new perspective, with the further implication that a new and inexperienced representative will not be able to get things done.

implication
A possible outcome or extension of the premises and conclusion of an argument.

Implication refers to the ways in which an argument's claim or conclusion might affect other areas beyond the limits of the argument itself. In *Good Arguments*, Connie Missimer describes implications as "possible outcomes that follow from an argument." An outcome of an argument is a kind of practical upshot or consequence resulting from it. Implications further an argument's practical consequences and extend its reach.

Consider, for example, the argument that because of the increasing age at which people in the United States marry (premise 1); along with the fact that women are remaining in the workforce for longer periods (premise 2); that average family size will decrease (claim). That's the argument.

What are its implications? One implication is that there will be fewer people in the workforce to support an aging population—and thus the next generation of workers will have a higher tax burden to bear. Another implication is that there might be generational conflict resulting from the difficulties faced by the working population in sustaining the entitlements of the aged. This conflict might lead to social unrest, perhaps expressed in violent demonstrations. As you can see, one implication can lead to another, and then another.

The notion of implication is important not only for argument, but also for analysis and interpretation. Whenever we engage in the act of interpretation, we are, essentially, explaining implications—we explain what is implied in and by a text, an image, an object, an event, an argument. The text, image, object, event, or argument carries with it a set of unstated meanings or significances; we "read" into and out of texts, images, objects, events, and arguments meanings, which are, simply, a sum of the implications we think they possess.

Implications, in the sense just described, offer interpretive possibilities—potential outcomes of meaning. Implications, of course, might also involve outcomes of action, as for example, with respect to an aging population, the extent to which advertising might change to address the needs of that population, or the extent to which more doctors might specialize in geriatric medicine to accommodate the aged, or more facilities for assisted living would be constructed.

EXERCISES

1. Analyze the following arguments by identifying their claims, evidence, and assumptions.

    a. Because Michael earned a high score on his college entrance exam, he will certainly be successful in his academic work in college.

    b. South Korea is the most technologically advanced country in the world. More South Koreans own computers and smartphones than any other country in the world.

    c. I shop at ShopRite rather than A&P because prices are 5% lower there.

    d. We should reduce our prison population because imprisoning people doesn't solve the problem of crime.

    e. We should celebrate art that shocks because it brings change and new approaches.

2. Identify some possible outcomes, some implications positive and negative, of the following brief arguments:

   a. Banning fraternities and sororities from college campuses because they are exclusionary.

   b. Majoring in a subject that will increase your likelihood of getting a job soon after graduation rather than studying a subject you truly enjoy.

   c. Delaying marriage and a family until your mid- to later-thirties because of lucrative and highly competitive employment.

   d. Borrowing heavily for your undergraduate and graduate education without the opportunity for grants, scholarships, or a part-time job.

   e. Taking a year off from school—delaying the completion of your degree by a year or two—to work, travel, or do both.

Going Further into Evidence: Claims, Warrants, Backing

We can consider further the notion of evidence and its relationship to an argument's claims. In *The Uses of Argument*, Stephen Toulmin identifies three elements common to most arguments: a claim, support, and a warrant.

A **claim** is simply a thesis or central idea of an argument that is being proposed or defended. It's an assertion, a declarative statement. Toulmin suggests that a claim should be a conclusion whose merits we attempt to establish after we have tested the evidence.

Support is the evidence—details, examples, facts, statistics, and the like. Support provides the "grounds" for the claim. Grounds may also include proof of expertise.

A **warrant** is the "bridge" that connects the claim and its various kinds of supporting evidence. Like the second premise of a syllogism, the warrant links the claim to the support by showing the grounds or data and reasoning to be relevant.

A fourth related term Toulmin uses is **backing**, additional data and other assurances that strengthen the authority of the warrant.

Toulmin identifies three types of claims: claims of *fact*, claims of *value*, and claims of *policy*. *Claims of fact* refer to a truth that requires significant research to be substantiated. *Claims of value* express acceptance or denial of a standard of taste or of morality. *Claims of policy* assert that a particular policy or way of doing business should be adopted. Claims of policy require evidence that strongly suggests their likelihood of success. Perhaps they have worked somewhere else, somewhere similar to the community where the policy being proposed is claimed to work.

A warrant, according to Toulmin, can be either implicit or explicit. An implicit warrant is similar to an enthymeme—a syllogism with one of its parts implied rather than explicitly stated. A warrant is a type of assumption. For example, if we wish to claim that the Harry Potter movies are the greatest fantasy films ever made, we need to consider the assumptions, or warrants, that our audience might have about the type of movie—the film genre—that the Harry Potter movies exemplify. We need to consider other fine films of that fantasy genre, such as the *Lord of the Rings* trilogy or the *Star Wars* trilogy, and provide comparative and contrastive analysis of the strengths and weaknesses of one group of films against the others.

claim
In argument, an assertion or conclusion that requires evidence in its support.

support
In argument, the evidence that provides the grounds for a claim.

warrant
In argument, a term introduced by Stephen Toulmin to indicate the "bridge" that connects a claim and its supporting evidence; warrants show how the data or reasons supporting a claim are relevant.

backing
Data and other assurances that strengthen the authority of a claim.

What assumptions do people make about why such movies become successful? Might one assumption have something to do with plot—a movie's convolutions and complications of its action, keeping the story interesting with plot twists and turns? Might another assumption have something to do with characters—with their human interest, their complexity, and the relationships they have with one another? And might a third assumption have something to do with the setting and the various visual effects used to create a complex and believable alien world or alternate reality? If we think that one of these, the last, for example, is the most important indicator for a great fantasy film, that warrant or assumption needs to be accepted by our audience for the argument to be persuasive. A warrant such as this can itself become an argument claim, in which case we would need to explain why—provide reasons why—this claim merits our attention and ultimately our conviction.

Additional terms used by Toulmin are *qualifier*, *reservation*, and *rebuttal*. A *qualifier* limits and restricts the range of a claim. Such words as *probably*, *usually*, *most*, *sometimes*, and the like indicate the relative strength of the warrant. A *reservation* explains the terms and conditions the qualifier necessitates. And a **rebuttal** identifies objections to the warranted claim. Rebuttals suggest conditions that might refute the claim. A rebuttal is itself an argument and may include a claim, warrant, and backing.

rebuttal
In argument, showing how an opposing argument is deficient, weak, or otherwise unpersuasive.

EXERCISES

3. Identify each of the following as a claim of fact, a claim of value, or a claim of policy. Explain what kinds of evidence you would use to support or refute each claim. What assumptions and implications would you associate with each claim? What warrants?

   a. The popularity of reality television has decreased the willingness of media executives to develop, fund, and support more imaginative television shows.

   b. Rather than sending men and women into outer space, we should be using those resources to fix the problems with public schools.

   c. Global warming is a misnomer; what is happening is less a result of human energy use and more a simple experience of long-term climatic change.

   d. Social harmony is more important than personal freedom.

   e. It is necessary that people be allowed to curse and use foul language on occasion, because such uses of language let off steam that might otherwise result in violence.

4. On a topic of your choice, create one example each of a claim of fact, a claim of value, and a claim of policy. Then explain how you would provide evidence in their support.

Inductive and Deductive Reasoning

Argument involves careful reasoning. We can distinguish two different but interrelated kinds of reasoning—*inductive reasoning* (inductive thinking) and *deductive reasoning* (deductive thinking). Inductive reasoning often (but not always) begins with a limited number of observations. In such cases, it continues with additional observations until arriving at a general claim or conclusion based on those specific observations. **Inductive reasoning** involves making **inferences**, reasoning from past occurrences and regularities to future ones. Inductive thinking offers probability rather than certainty.

Deductive reasoning is an argument in which the premises guarantee the truth of the conclusion. In a deductive argument, the premises provide support for the conclusion such that, if the premises are true, it would be impossible for the conclusion to be false. An *inductive argument* is one in which the premises provide reasons supporting the likely or probable truth of the conclusion. In an inductive argument, the premises are intended only to be so strong that, if they are true, then it is unlikely that the conclusion is false.

The difference between deductive and inductive argument derives from the relation that exists between the premises and the conclusion of each type of argument. If the truth of the premises *definitely* establishes the truth of the conclusion, then the argument is deductive. If the truth of the premises *possibly or probably* establishes the truth of the conclusion, then the argument is inductive. Deductive arguments are assessed in terms of **validity**, the extent to which the relation between their premises and conclusion are logically valid. Inductive arguments are assessed in terms of reliability, in terms of their likelihood as being sound and believable.

The following is a deductive argument:

Oslo is either in Norway or Sweden. If Oslo is in Norway, then Oslo is in Scandinavia. If Oslo is in Sweden, then Oslo is in Scandinavia. Therefore, Oslo is in Scandinavia.

Although this argument begins with a statement about a specific place, it is deductive because its structure requires that if the premises are true (and they are) there is no way the conclusion can be false.

The next argument is also deductive, even though it reasons from specific to general; it is deductive because the truth of the premises *guarantees* the truth of the conclusion.

The members of the Williams family are Susan, Nathan, and Alexander. Susan wears glasses. Nathan wears glasses. Alexander wears glasses. Therefore, *all* members of the Williams family wear glasses.

Inductive arguments can deal with statistical data, generalizations from past experience, appeals to signs, evidence, authority, analogy, and causal relationships. Here is an example:

My cat sleeps a lot during the day. Other cats I have had slept a great deal during the day. Cats must be nocturnally active, as our new kitten coming next week will be, too.

The following arguments, even though they reason from the general to specific, are inductive; their conclusions are at best highly likely rather than certain.

The members of the Williams family are Susan, Nathan, and Alexander—all teenagers, and the newborn baby, Jill. Susan, Nathan, and Alexander wear glasses. The baby, Jill, will also wear glasses as a teenager.

There is no way to know for certain whether the baby, Jill, will wear glasses as a teenager, like her siblings. It is certainly possible, and probably likely that she will. But there is a chance that her genetic inheritance for vision will be better than the vision capability inherited by her brothers and sister.

inductive reasoning
Reasoning from past instances to future predicted occurrences; inductive reasoning offers probability rather than certainty.

inferences
Statements about the unknown made on the basis of what is known.

deductive reasoning
Logical reasoning from premises to conclusions.

validity
In deductive arguments, the situation in which the form or structure of the argument is such that the truth of the premises guarantee the truth of the conclusion. If the premises of a deductive argument are true and the argument's structure is sound, the conclusion is inevitably true, and thus the argument is valid.

Here is yet another inductive argument:

It has snowed in Boston *every* December in recorded history. Therefore, it will snow in Boston this coming December.

Once again, given the history of Boston's weather patterns, there is a strong probability that it will snow there this coming December. But there is no guarantee that it will. The conclusion of this inductive argument is at best highly likely.

Inductive reasoning typically works by looking at a series of examples, not just a single instance—though it can certainly begin with just one. From a group of disparate details, examples, instances, we reason inductively by seeing a pattern of connections, and thereby deriving a general principle, which serves as a conclusion or interpretation of the evidence. Reading a poem or short story is a typical example of inductive reasoning, as the details of the story's or poem's language, structure, characters, setting, plot, and so on, provide the concrete particulars on which we base our interpretation, our understanding of the work's general idea or larger meaning.

In their book, *Philosopher's Toolkit*, Julian Baggini and Peter S. Fosl note that inductive reasoning does not always involve reasoning from the specific to the general. Nor does it necessarily involve reasoning about the future based on observations about the past. Inductive reasoning may reason, for example, from a more general past conclusion, as for example, that no athlete has run 100 yards in under 8 seconds to a more specific past claim that a friend who claims he accomplished this in high school is probably not true.

The process of scientific investigation provides an interesting case of inductive thinking, as scientific experiments begin with empirical observations, with what we notice by means of our senses. Inductive reasoning in the sciences—both the natural sciences and the social sciences—is formalized in a set of processes known as the scientific method. The basis of the scientific method is the gathering, testing, and analysis of data by means of experiment. This experimental data serves as the set of specific observations, the set of instances and examples that form the evidence from which inferences are made, and hypotheses, principles, and theories derived.

Historical investigation follows an analogous process, mostly using primary and secondary source documents rather than experiments as evidence on which to develop conclusions through reasoning inductively about particular instances and arriving at general principles. The particular details of history—historical facts, data, and other forms of information—provide the evidence for the development of inferences and theories of historical explanation.

Both scientific experimentation and historical analysis, however, may begin and often actually do begin, with a theory or an idea—that is, with a generalization the investigator sets out to test, by finding evidence that either supports it or falsifies it. In this case, the process of thought moves from a general idea or concept to specific supporting evidence. Thus, thinking, including scientific and historical thinking, typically involves interplay between inductive and deductive reasoning, moving back and forth between them repeatedly. This process of alternation between concrete and abstract, specific and general, inductive and deductive reasoning—and the logical connections between them—informs sound thinking.

Inductive and Deductive Reasoning Together

In practice, then, inductive and deductive reasoning typically work together. They complement and reinforce each other. Scientists, like other thinkers, use both inductive and deductive reasoning to construct arguments, reach conclusions, and make discoveries.

Consider the following account of the evolutionary connection between long-tongued moths and a species of orchid they pollinate. In a story reported some years ago in the scientific and the popular press, Gene Kritzky hypothesized that a moth with a 6-inch wingspan and a 15-inch tongue had to exist—even though there was no record then of anyone ever having seen one. Kritzky hypothesized the existence of this very long-tongued moth based on the fact that an orchid exists whose nectar lies 15 inches deep in its flowery interior. Other evidence on which Kritzky based his prediction included the following facts:

1. In 1862, Charles Darwin had made a similar prediction about the existence of a moth with a 12-inch tongue. Darwin based his prediction on his discovery of a slightly smaller orchid than the one Kritzky later came to know existed.

2. Darwin's orchid, like the one Kritzky heard about, was found in Madagascar.

3. Neither Darwin's orchid nor Kritzky's could be pollinated by small insects able to crawl into it. The orchids' physical structure prohibits that pollination possibility.

4. Forty years after Darwin made his prediction about the moth with a 12-inch tongue, such a moth was found.

Darwin arrived at his prediction that such a moth existed, in part, from his observation of the deep orchid and in part from his knowledge that the pollinating apparatus of the largest moth known at the time was too short to pollinate such a deep flower. He thus reasoned in traditional inductive fashion from particular circumstances or facts toward a more general claim.

But Darwin also reasoned deductively from the scientific law of natural selection that he himself had formulated. Darwin theorized that species develop and change to enhance their opportunities for continued successful existence. Darwin thought that because moths with slightly shorter tongues pollinate slightly smaller orchids, then, according to the principle of natural selection, a longer-tongued species would evolve to pollinate the deeper flower. Darwin derived his prediction of the longer-tongued moth's existence from a general concept, or theory, exemplifying deductive reasoning.

To reach their respective hypotheses, both Darwin and Kritzky worked from an unstated premise—that insects pollinate orchids. They also worked from the general law that stipulates how insects adapt to their environment. Thus, because Darwin's reasoning has been proven correct with regard to this kind of moth and orchid species, and assuming the same principle applies to Kritzky's larger orchid and moth scenario, there was a great likelihood in such a moth being found. As indeed, it has—in Madagascar.

EXERCISES

5. What kind of reasoning do you find most comfortable, deductive or inductive reasoning? Why?

6. To what extent do you find Kritzky's process of thinking something you could emulate? To what extent does it illustrate deductive and inductive reasoning? Does one type of reasoning seem to predominate—or not?

7. Identify the following arguments as inductive or deductive:

   a. I never win the lottery, even a few dollars. I have never won a raffle. I will never win anything.

   b. Nobody tells the truth all the time. Therefore, I suggest that although you can trust what I say most of the time, there are occasions when you can't.

   c. The life span of human beings has never reached 200 years. It might reach 125 or even 150, but never 200. People's bodies just wear out, internally and externally.

   d. If you drop out of school, you will regret it. People who drop out don't come back and finish their degrees.

   e. I think; therefore, I am.

Syllogisms and Argument

One important and familiar type of deductive reasoning is represented by the syllogism. A syllogism is a type of argument arranged in three parts: a major premise, a minor premise, and a conclusion. The classic example is this:

Major premise: All men are mortal.

Minor premise: Socrates is a man.

Conclusion: Socrates is mortal.

As you can see, the major premise is the more general of the two. If you accept the major premise or statement as true, and the minor premise also as a true statement, then the conclusion follows logically, even necessarily, from it. There is no escaping it; if Socrates is a man and all men (humans) are mortal, then he, too, will surely die, (which, of course, he did, having lived from around 470 BCE till his death in 399 BCE).

Validity and Truth

We speak of an argument as being "valid" rather than "true." We are concerned, that is, with whether the argument adheres to principles of logic in the relationship among its premises. Those premises (or statements) we speak of as "true" or "false." But the logical argument (the relations among the premises and conclusion) is either "valid" or "invalid," depending on a set of rules that govern the relationship and distribution of its premises.

Here's an example of a syllogism whose premises are true and whose conclusion follows from them logically. This syllogism, thus, is valid and its concluding statement is true:

Major Premise: The World Cup soccer tournament champion is chosen from among the semifinalists.

Minor Premise: The four teams in the World Cup soccer semifinal matches this year are all from Europe.

Conclusion: (Therefore), The World Cup Champion this year will be a European team.

The form of this argument suggests that only a European team can win the World Cup, given the truth of the argument's premises. There is no other possibility.

But an argument can be valid even though one or more of its premises or its conclusion is false. Here is an example:

If all mice are green (major premise) and

Mickey Mouse is a mouse (minor premise), then

Mickey Mouse is green (conclusion).

This is a valid argument even though its premises are false. Of course, as we know, all mice are not green. (In fact any green mouse would be an anomaly—something out of the ordinary.) And we also know Mickey Mouse as a cartoon character in black-and-white. Nonetheless, the argument about a green Mickey Mouse is valid "if" he really is a mouse, and "if" all mice are green. Delete the word *if* and the argument is invalid because its premises are false.

Validity concerns the structure of an argument rather than the accuracy of its premises. Truth is concerned with what is the case, with whether or not an argument's premises and conclusion are true—that is, with matters of fact; validity is concerned with whether the conclusion follows logically and necessarily from the premises. Truth is an aspect of statements; validity is an aspect of the structure of arguments. So, "if" all mice are actually green, and Mickey is really a mouse, then Mickey Mouse, too, is green, must be green.

Soundness

An argument is sound if and only if it is valid and if its premises are true. Clearly, the argument concluding that Mickey Mouse is green is unsound because its premises are false. Soundness is important because once we are aware that an argument is sound we have to accept its conclusion as true. In such instances, were we to deny the truth of the conclusion (after accepting its valid form and true premises), we would be saying something false. Moreover, in asserting the truth of a valid argument's premises and yet denying its conclusion, we would be contradicting ourselves. The real challenge in determining the soundness of an argument is in establishing the truth of its premises. This we cannot do by logic alone; we need empirical evidence from observation or experience; we need research in library or laboratory or legwork; and we need conceptual understanding to investigate the factual accuracy of an argument's premises, and ultimately its soundness.

The Problem of Ambiguity

An aspect of syllogisms that may create difficulty is that in purely logical terms, language must be stripped of ambiguity, or inexactness of meaning. There must be absolute clarity as to the meaning of each term in the premises. We find this kind of absolute clarity of meaning, this lack of ambiguity, in mathematics, as for example, in Euclidean geometry, where geometric proofs proceed from one step to the next according to inexorable logical necessity. This kind of linguistic purity and clarity, however, is rare outside of mathematics. The nonmathematical language, of which arguments are typically constructed, allows for ambiguity, and thus for complications. Consider the following argument:

Major Premise: Things detrimental to student learning should be eliminated.

Minor Premise: Tests are detrimental to student learning.

Conclusion: Therefore, tests should be eliminated.

The problems begin with the major premise of this syllogism, with the word *detrimental*. Detrimental, we might ask, in what way(s)? We can also query the first word of the premise, *things*. What things? What kinds of things are we talking about here, we might wonder. And, analogously, we can question the minor premise of the syllogism the same way—"detrimental, how" and "what kinds of tests"? On what basis, we might ask, are tests detrimental to student learning? Always? Inevitably? Unconditionally?

So, even though this syllogism is valid, with its conclusion following necessarily from its premises, the conclusion is not certain. The argument's premises, while not necessarily "false" or "untrue," are clearly complex and open to question and clarification as to just what they mean. The premises need to be clearer and more specific. Yet even with greater specificity and clarity of these premises, we have a syllogism whose conclusion is at best probable, and more likely, simply possible.

Enthymemes

Arguments often do not follow a strict and complete syllogistic form. A newspaper editorial that supports the closing of military bases, or a magazine column that argues for a student-loan program run by the federal government would very likely be presented with the major premise implied rather than explicitly stated.

Syllogisms are often truncated in everyday arguments. We might hear someone argue, for example, that it's time for new technologies to be introduced to college instruction because they can save money and because today's students are technology savvy. This kind of everyday argument leaves out a major premise: That technology provides the best and most successful means of instruction as measured by student learning.

An argument in which the major premise, minor premise, or conclusion is not explicitly stated is called an enthymeme. Here is an example:

> More than half of all varsity football players at State University do not receive a diploma after six years at the university. We have to do something to improve that figure, or we should eliminate the football program at State.

In syllogistic form, the argument looks like this:

> Major Premise: (UNSTATED) Students, including varsity football players, should earn a diploma within six years.

> Minor Premise: More than half of all varsity football players at State University do not receive their diplomas within six years.

> Conclusion: Therefore, we have to improve that figure or eliminate the football program at State.

You may agree or disagree about the reliability of the enthymeme's unstated premise, which, in this case, is an assumption. But the argument is easier to evaluate with that premise explicitly stated. We need to be alert for arguments containing unstated premises; we should try to supply unstated premises to more readily assess their accuracy or reliability. And we need to remember that an argument is only as strong as its premises. If an argument's premises are faulty, or if an argument includes unsupported assumptions, it can be easily refuted.

One of the challenges of identifying the premises and conclusion of an enthymeme is that in everyday speech, premises are often hidden and thus difficult to detect. Sometimes conclusions come first rather than last. Consider the following example:

> Bill: That new Director of Marketing is a real problem. She's nothing like the guy who preceded her. I'm not sure I can work for her.

> Cheryl: But just last week you were talking about how change is good and how you were looking forward to some new challenges at work, including a new boss.

> Bill: Well, I was. But now that I've met her, I'm not looking forward to working with her. You know how women bosses can be.

Here's what this argument looks like in syllogistic form:

All female directors are people who are hard to work for.

　　(All Xs are Ys.)

The new director is female.

　　(Z is an X.)

Therefore, the new director will be difficult to work for.

　　(Therefore, Z is a Y.)

This is a valid argument because its premises guarantee the conclusion. The conclusion, however, is not necessarily true, because its first (major) premise is false. For even though some female directors may be hard for men to work with, this is certainly not the case for all directors who are female. Bill's argument hinges on a stereotype about women supervisors, one that enables us to see the weakness of his claim.

EXERCISES

8. Construct two syllogisms, one valid and one invalid. Explain why each is valid or invalid. Then construct another syllogism, which is valid, but whose premises are problematic.

9. Construct a valid syllogism for each of the following premises.
   a. Cigarette smoke is dangerous to the health of nonsmokers who breathe it.
   b. Walking vigorously for 30 minutes a day provides excellent cardiovascular exercise.
   c. Macy's reported substantial losses in revenue for the last two years.
   d. Speaking a foreign language can enhance one's pleasure when traveling.
   e. Interest rates have declined consistently in the past two years.
   f. Spanish banks are in crisis.
   g. Newspapers and magazines are scaling back print publication and moving to the Internet.
   h. The New York Mets have had late season collapses three times in the past five years.
   i. When in Rome, do as the Romans do.
   j. Laughter is the best medicine.

10. Analyze the following arguments. When necessary, supply the missing premises.
   a. To improve the economy, the president and Congress should create public works projects and increase the number of available jobs.
   b. I'm doing twice as much work today as I did a year ago. I should be paid double what I earned last year.
   c. People should be penalized, by taxation or in other ways, for not looking after their own health.
   d. Harriet is a superb student. She's been on the Dean's List three straight terms.
   e. Guns should be outlawed for civilians. The world has changed radically since the framers of the Bill of Rights included the right to bear arms.

    f. Josh attends the local community college, so he probably didn't get in anywhere else.

    g. Pitching horseshoes should be an Olympic sport because it involves strength, skill, and concentration.

    h. Vegetarians don't eat pork; Gandhi didn't eat pork; therefore, Gandhi was a vegetarian.

    i. Gerry is Canadian. He's used to cold weather.

    j. According to the European Monetary Fund, there will soon be a trend to further lower interest rates. Thus, European banks will be offering lower interest rates for borrowers.

Argument Chains

argument chain
A set of linked arguments, often syllogistic, in which the conclusion of one argument becomes a premise in one that follows.

Two or more syllogisms can be linked or overlapped to create a complex argument. Here is a passage from Aristotle's *Politics*. Identify its two interlocking arguments (syllogisms).

> Every state is a community of some kind, and every community is established with a view to some good; for men always act in order to obtain what they think to be good. But, if all communities aim at some good, the state or political community, which is the highest of all, and which embraces all the rest, aims at good to a greater degree than any other, and thus at the highest good.

Use the word *for* as a key to signal that the clause that precedes it is a conclusion and the clause that follows it is a premise. So, here is what we have so far:

Premise 1: Men always act to obtain what they think to be good.

Premise 2: (Not provided; implied instead).

Conclusion: Every community is established with a view to some good.

To complete the syllogism and the first argument, we need to identify the missing implied premise about the nature of a community. We can state the second premise this way: A community is the product of human action.

Let's return to Aristotle's passage. The opening states: "every state is a community of some kind." This clause also comes before the word *for*; it, too, thus, is a conclusion. But as we already have a conclusion, that conclusion to the first argument becomes a premise in the second argument. Here is what we have so far then in terms of syllogisms and arguments:

Argument I

Premise 1: Men always act to obtain what they think to be good.

Premise 2: A community is the product of human action.

Conclusion: Every community is established with a view to some good.

Argument II

Premise 1: Every community is established with a view to some good.

Premise 2: Every state is a community of some kind.

Conclusion: Every state is established with a view to some good.

We now make this second argument's conclusion the initial premise of the third argument (just as we made the conclusion of Argument I the first premise of Argument 2).

Argument III

Premise 1: Every state is established with a view to some good.

Premise 2: The state is the highest of all political communities and embraces the rest.

Conclusion: The state aims at good to a greater degree than any other community, and at the highest good.

EXERCISE

11. Sort out and outline the two interlocking syllogistic arguments of the following passage.

> It is indeed an opinion strangely prevailing amongst men, that houses, mountains, rivers, and in a word all sensible objects, have an existence, natural or real, distinct from their being perceived by the understanding. But, with how great an assurance and acquiescence soever this *Principle* may be entertained in the world, yet whoever shall find in his heart to call it in question may, if I mistake not, perceive it to involve a manifest contradiction. *For,* what are the aforementioned objects but the things we perceive by sense? And what do we perceive besides our own ideas or sensations? And is it not plainly repugnant that any of these, or any combination of them should exist unperceived?
> —George Berkeley, *A Treatise Concerning The Principles of Human Knowledge*

Categorical Propositions and Syllogisms

A **categorical proposition** is one that affirms or denies that a subject is a member of a class or possesses a particular property. Categorical propositions represent relations of inclusion or exclusion. For example, "Belle is a dog." This categorically affirms that Belle belongs to the class of animals called dogs. If we say about Belle that she is a beautiful golden color, we affirm that she possesses the particular property of the color "golden." Belle is a yellow Labrador retriever. She is not a cat. And she is not black. These last two negative propositions deny rather than affirm. They deny that Belle is a member of the class of animals called cats, and that she is black. Categorical propositions, thus, can deny as well as affirm.

One type of categorical proposition is called a "universal" proposition, one that refers to all members of a class. For example, "All philosophers are wise individuals." And: "No philosophers are wise individuals." In both cases, we completely include or completely exclude philosophers from the category of wise persons.

We can also indicate partial inclusion in a class. For example, we can indicate that "Some philosophers are wise individuals"; and "some philosophers are not wise individuals." We can, thus, distinguish universal propositions about "all" or "none" from particular propositions, which refer to some members of a class. For example, "some people are lazy." (In logic, *some* can mean as few as one or as many as all, though *some* typically refers to more than one.) So, for example, "some dinosaurs were oviparous" leaves open the possibility that they all hatched from eggs.

In abbreviated form, traditionally the four categorical propositions are indicated like this: All S are P.

No S are P.

Some S are P.

Some S are not P.

categorical proposition
Affirms or denies that a subject is a member of a class or possesses a particular property.

Any given categorical proposition involves a combination of a quantifier (all, none, some) and the presence or absence of negation. In traditional logic, moreover, the capital letters A, E, I, and O represent the four types of categorical propositions. These letters are taken from the Latin words for affirm and deny—*affirmo* and *nego*. The chart below shows the four categorical propositions by letter name, type, form, and example:

Name	Type	Form	Example
A	Universal affirmative	All S are P.	All philosophers are wise individuals.
E	Universal negative	No S are P.	No philosophers are wise individuals.
I	Particular affirmative	Some S are P.	Some philosophers are wise individuals.
O	Particular negative	Some S are not P.	Some philosophers are not wise individuals.

categorical syllogism
A syllogism formed with categorical propositions; for example:

1. All major league baseball players make a good salary. R. A. Dickey is a major leaguer pitcher. Therefore, R. A. Dickey makes a good salary.

Categorical syllogisms are formed with categorical propositions. Here are a few examples:

1. All major league baseball players make a good salary.

R. A. Dickey is a major leaguer pitcher.
Therefore, R. A. Dickey makes a good salary.

2. All atheists do not believe in God.

No Christians deny the existence of God.
Therefore, no Christians are atheists.

3. All galaxies contain stars.

Some stars have planets revolving around them.
Therefore, some galaxies have planets revolving around stars.

Categorical Argument Forms

Another example of an argument with the form of 1 earlier is this:

All music groups are entities that spread joy.
The Bedford Duo is a music group.
The Bedford Duo is an entity that spreads joy.

We can outline the form of this argument this way:

All A are B.
C is an A.
Therefore, C is a B.

In our example, A stands for the term music groups; B stands for entities that spread joy; and C stands for the Bedford Duo. We can also represent in this manner such arguments as the following:

All geologists are scientists.
Some geologists are tall.
Therefore, some scientists are tall.

This argument form can be represented like this:

> All A are B.
>
> Some A are C.
>
> Therefore, Some B are C.

In this last example, A stands for geologists, B for scientists, and C for tall.

In their book, *How to Think Logically*, Gary Seay and Susana Nuccetelli offer this summary of some familiar valid categorical argument forms:

1	2
All A are B	Some A are B
No B are C	All A are C
Therefore, No C are A	Therefore, Some C are B

3	4
No A are B	All A are B
All C are A	All C are A
Therefore, No C are B	Therefore, All C are B

5	6
All A are B	All A are B
All B are C	Some A are not C
Therefore, All A are C	Therefore, Some B are not C

EXERCISES

12. Identify which of the following arguments are categorical, and identify the form of each categorical argument.

   a. All living creatures require air. My hamster is a living creature. Therefore, my hamster requires air.

   b. Lawyers are exposed to poor reasoning and misleading information. Carol is a lawyer. Accordingly, she is exposed to poor reasoning and misleading information.

   c. No arid climate is humid. The Mojave is arid. Thus, the Mojave is not humid.

   d. Shakespeare enjoyed comedy. All Renaissance playwrights enjoyed comedy, and Shakespeare was a Renaissance English playwright.

   e. No Idaho farmer grows tobacco, for no western farmer grows tobacco, and Idaho farms are western farms.

   f. There is no human life on other planets. If there were, we would have heard about it by now. And we haven't.

   g. All accountants are good at math. George is not an accountant. Therefore, he is not good at math.

   h. Because no tropical country has ice storms, and because Cuba is a tropical country, Cuba does not have ice storms.

13. For each pair of premises create a valid argument.

    a. Some sports fans love ice hockey.

        All ice hockey fans are emotional about their favorite team.

        Therefore,

    b. All animals have a right to life.

        Disease-bearing mosquitoes are animals.

        Therefore,

    c. No creatures without a nervous system experience pain.

        Only creatures that experience pain possess a right to life.

        Therefore,

    d. Some people are full of ideas.

        Some ideas are worth hearing about.

        Therefore,

    e. All flibbertigibbets are funky.

        No glumquats are funky.

        Therefore,

Hypothetical Syllogisms

hypothetical syllogism
A syllogism that takes the form of "if . . . then;" for example, "If I pass this course with at least a B, I will retain my scholarship."

Hypothetical syllogisms take the form of "If . . . then." An example: If I don't get an A average, I won't get into a top medical school. If I don't get into a top medical school, I won't land a good residency, and I won't get a good medical position. Another example: If I fail this midterm, my course average will suffer. If my average suffers, I might lose my scholarship.

We can put such hypothetical statements into the form of a syllogism. If both premises and the conclusion are in the if-then, or hypothetical form, it is a *pure hypothetical syllogism*. The "if" or hypothetical statement (premise) is called the *antecedent*; the "then" statement is called the *consequent*.

Mapped out, hypothetical syllogisms take this form:

If P, then Q.

If Q, then R.

Therefore, if P, then R.

For example:

If it rains heavily my roof will leak.

If my roof leaks, my carpets will get wet.

Therefore, if it rains heavily, my carpets will get wet.

Where only the major premise is hypothetical, and the minor premise and conclusion are categorical, we have a *mixed hypothetical syllogism*. In positive or affirming mode (Latin: *modus ponens*), the mixed hypothetical syllogism looks like this:

modus ponens
A valid argument that takes the form of If P, then Q; P; therefore Q. For a related logical fallacy, see Affirming the Consequent.

If P, then Q.

P.

Therefore, Q.

For example:

> If there is no God, there are no moral rules or guidelines.
>
> There is no God.
>
> Therefore, there are no moral rules or guidelines.

In negative or denying mode (Latin: ***modus tollens***), the mixed hypothetical syllogism looks like this:

> If P, then Q.
>
> Not Q.
>
> Therefore, not P.

modus tollens
A valid argument that takes the form of If P, then Q. Not Q; therefore, P. For a related logical fallacy, see Denying the Antecedent.

For example:

> If it snows, the roads will be slippery.
>
> The roads are not slippery.
>
> Therefore, it did not snow.

Disjunctive Syllogisms

A **disjunctive syllogism** includes an "either-or" statement, such as "Either the concert tickets are on my desk, or they are in my wallet." Disjunctive syllogisms come in two forms. The first denies one term in the minor premise and affirms the other term in the conclusion. This denial–affirmation form of a disjunctive syllogism looks like this:

> Either P or Q.
>
> Not P.
>
> Therefore, Q.

disjunctive syllogism
A syllogism that includes an "either-or" statement, such as "Either the concert tickets are on my desk, or they are in my wallet."

For example:

> Either the concert tickets are on my desk, or they are in my wallet.
>
> The tickets are not on the desk.
>
> Therefore, the tickets are in my wallet.

A variation of the disjunctive "denial–affirmation" form is to deny Q:

> Either P or Q.
>
> Not Q.
>
> Therefore, P.

For example:

> Either the concert tickets are on my desk, or they are in my wallet.
>
> The tickets are not in my wallet.
>
> Therefore, the tickets are on the desk.

The second form of the disjunctive syllogism does the opposite: It affirms one term in the minor premise and denies the other term in the conclusion. This affirmation–denial form of a disjunctive syllogism looks like this:

> Either P or Q.
>
> P.
>
> Therefore, not Q.

For example:

> The batter will swing right-handed or left-handed.
>
> The batter swung right-handed.
>
> Therefore, the batter did not swing left-handed.

In this disjunctive syllogism in affirmation–denial form, we can also affirm Q and deny P. For example:

> The batter will swing right-handed or left-handed.
>
> The batter swung left-handed.
>
> Therefore, the batter did not swing right-handed.

In this affirmation–denial form of the disjunctive syllogism, P and Q must be considered exclusive of each other. That is, P and Q cannot both occur; it must not be possible for both of them to occur.

EXERCISES

14. Write one example for each form of the hypothetical syllogism: (1) pure hypothetical syllogism; (2) mixed affirmative form; (3) mixed denial form.

15. Write one example for each form of the disjunctive syllogism: (1) denial–affirmation form; (2) affirmation–denial form.

Argument and Authority

Write the Response, Argument and Authority MyThinkingLab

authority
Expert knowledge brought to bear on an argument claim or conclusion; individuals and institutions with demonstrated knowledge, experience, rank, position, and accomplishments.

The persuasiveness of an argument depends on the validity of its structure and the truth of its premises. Yet another aspect of arguments is the extent to which the people who make them are credible and authoritative. Writers gain credibility with readers by demonstrating knowledge, by providing clear and cogent reasoning, and by being fair and reasonable.

An authority can lend credibility to an assertion or claim. Typical **authorities** are individuals and institutions with demonstrated knowledge, experience, rank, position, or accomplishments. Appeals to authority can be persuasive, but they are not always effective. In political advertising, for example, authorities often provide inadequate support for candidates.

In addition, any authority may be wrong in a particular instance. Authorities are fallible, and they can disagree. Equally reputable authorities can—and often do—arrive at conflicting or incompatible conclusions about complex matters. In addition, authorities have their biases as well as their expertise. Medical experts who testify to the safety of a new drug, for example, may be biased, especially if paid by the pharmaceutical company responsible for developing the drug they recommend.

Authorities, moreover, may simply be wrong. Because arguments based on authority are inductive, they are, at best, highly likely. A doctor's recommendation that a particular medication will be effective for us is just that, even though the recommendation is one in which she has a strong belief based on previous knowledge. But there is no guarantee that it will be effective.

Here are a few questions to use in analyzing the use of authorities:

1. What are the authority's credentials and qualifications?

2. Is the authority presenting evidence, information, or judgments within his or her area of expertise?

3. What kinds and amount of evidence does the authoritative expert provide to support a position or judgment being advanced?

4. How sound are the authority's arguments?

Similar to authority is **testimony**—a statement made in support of a fact or a claim. Testimony can be offered by experts or by individuals with specialized knowledge. But it can also be provided by ordinary people. Law courts, for example, typically rely on the testimony of both experts and nonexpert witnesses to ascertain the facts of a case.

testimony
The use of various kinds of spokesmen and witnesses to provide support for an argument or claim.

Testimonials rely on nonlogical attempts to influence decisions. Because athletes and celebrities who appear in advertisements typically receive large sums of money for their endorsements, their testimonials should be viewed with skepticism. This does not mean, however, that the claims made in testimonials are necessarily false. In fact, testimonials are often valuable when used to support arguments—as long as the testimony is credible. To be credible, the person providing the testimony must be operating within his or her area of competence or expertise. The testimony must also be accurate, current, and representative.

EXERCISES

16. Identify the claims and assumptions in the following argument:

    Environmentalists do not underestimate the difficulties the United States faces in trying to wean itself from fossil fuel. Pretty much our entire transportation grid is based on the gasoline engine. Lay rail is one thing we could do. Switch to cars with hybrid engines, increase fuel-efficiency standards, change as rapidly as possible to renewable energy sources—the menu of alternative behaviors is already long and growing. Greenhouse gases can be cut.

17. Find an advertisement that uses an authority to advance its claims. Evaluate the claims of the ad, and consider the extent to which the authority enhances the ad's persuasiveness. Find another advertisement that uses one or more ordinary people to provide a testimonial. Evaluate the claims of the ad, and consider the extent to which the testimonial enhances the ad's effectiveness.

Argument and Analogy

When we argue by **analogy**, we claim that because one state of affairs is like another in one way, it is like it in other ways, as well. Analogical argument is a type of inductive reasoning. If two things are similar in some features, then it is possible, or even likely, that they will be similar in other ways. For example, those opposed to the US war in Afghanistan saw similarities to the US war in Vietnam three decades earlier. Both wars were fought in unconventional ways on foreign territory against enemies that knew their homeland terrain far better than their opponents did. On the basis of these known similarities, those against the war in Afghanistan argued that other similarities would emerge—as for example, that the war would be protracted, that it would be costly in money and in lives, that it would create anti-American feeling around the world, and that it might very well not be winnable.

analogy
A comparison between two different cases to suggest their similarities in the process of making an argument.

The further an analogy can be taken—that is, the more that the two things being compared are truly alike—the stronger the analogy and the more persuasive the argument made with it. The quicker the analogy breaks down—that is, the more readily it appears that major differences exist between the things compared—the weaker the analogy and the weaker the argument made with it. An analogical argument's persuasiveness depends not only on the number of similarities but also on the strength of the similarities. The problem, however, is that what one person accepts as a strong similarity, another may see as weak and unconvincing.

In *How to Think Logically*, Gary Seay and Susana Nuccetelli identify four characteristics of successful analogical arguments:

1. Greater numbers of common features
2. More similarities than dissimilarities
3. Greater relevance of the analogy to the argument claim.
4. Modesty of the hypothesis with respect to the evidence

EXERCISE

18. Consider the following argument by analogy made by George Orwell in his essay "Politics and the English Language."

> It is clear that the decline of a language must ultimately have political and economic causes: it is not due simply to the bad influence of this or that individual writer. But an effect can become a cause, reinforcing the original cause and producing the same effect in an intensified form, and so on indefinitely. A man may take to drink because he feels himself to be a failure, and then fail all the more completely because he drinks. It is rather the same thing that is happening to the English language. It becomes ugly and inaccurate because our thoughts are foolish, but the slovenliness of our language makes it easier for us to have foolish thoughts.
> —George Orwell, "Politics and the English Language"

To what extent does Orwell's analogical argument meet the four criteria outlined by Seay and Nuccetelli?

Commentary

In arguing that the English language is in decline, Orwell suggests but does not identify a group of "political and economic causes." He proposes that an effect (the decline of English) can become a cause furthering that decline. He then introduces an analogy with drinking as a way of supporting his argument about effects becoming causes that further intensify the problem. As readers, we need to be clear, first, about the idea expressed in the analogy and second, about how well the analogy supports Orwell's claim.

Just what does Orwell's analogy say? It says, essentially, that drinking intensifies a person's decline so that the person, as a result, drinks even more—which leads to even greater failure. You can see how Orwell's analogy explains how the effect of a failure can become a cause of further failures. In applying his analogy about drinking as cause and effect, Orwell argues that the English language has declined because some people are sloppy in their thinking and writing, which causes the language to decline further.

But is Orwell's analogy a persuasive part of his overall argument? Does the fact that an effect can become a cause, as the analogy demonstrates, apply to the decline of the English language in the way Orwell suggests? How strong is Orwell's analogy? How relevant is it to his claim about the decline of English? Does it help convince us that a decline was occurring among some users of English? Or does it, instead, simply clarify Orwell's idea, enabling us to better understand his claim?

We can take an analogy only so far before the similarities between the two things compared end and important differences emerge. A baseball double play, in some ways, is like a dance. In other ways, it is not. A heart is like a pump, but only to a degree. The decline of English due to sloppy writing and thinking is analogous to a person's decline through drinking—but only to a degree.

Analogies and Enthymemes

Often we find that a familiar analogy is used to make an argument with very different conclusions. Consider the following political analogy in which a social group—a government or a society—is compared to a ship. Each writer uses this analogy to make a claim, in essence, thereby making a kind of mini argument. Each argument employs syllogistic reasoning; however, each is missing a premise, and is, thus, an **enthymeme**.

enthymeme
An argument with a missing part, more often a missing premise, but sometimes a missing conclusion.

a. "Running a government is like running a ship; we need a strong hand at the helm."

—Thomas Carlyle

b. "Society is like a ship; everyone must be prepared to take the helm."

—Henrik Ibsen

c. "Like the navigator, the statesman may direct the vessel which bears him along, but he can neither change its structure nor raise the winds nor lull the waters that swell beneath him."

—Alexis de Tocqueville

Sometimes, a writer will build an analogy out of another writer's idea. Here is one such example. The first sentence, in English translation, of Leo Tolstoy's novel *Anna Karenina* reads: "All happy families are alike. Each unhappy family is unhappy in its own way." In his book about genetics, *The Violinist's Thumb*, Sam Kean makes the following observation, using an analogy: "Some scientists," Kean writes, "misquote Tolstoy to make this point: perhaps all healthy bodies resemble each other, while each unhealthy body is unhealthy in its own way." Kean uses an analogy to suggest that some scientists believe that each unhealthy body is uniquely unhealthy, just as each unhappy marriage (in Tolstoy's sentence) is uniquely unhappy. Consider some additional examples of analogies Kean makes by doing the following exercise.

EXERCISES

19. Consider whether Kean, in using each of the following analogies, is making a claim—and thus an argument—or whether the analogy functions more as an explanation.

    a. "A gene is really information—more like a story, with DNA as the language the story is written in."

    b. "DNA and genes combine to form larger structures called chromosomes, DNA-rich volumes that house most of the genes in living things."

    c. "Mendel's peas were the Newton's apple of biology."

    d. "As with scientists studying DNA, pilgrims to the Delphic oracle in ancient Greece always learned something profound about themselves when they inquired of it—but rarely what they assumed they'd learned at first."

20. Explain how the analogy in the following passages work—either to clarify an explanation or to develop an argument, or both.

A. History is to the nation rather as memory is to the individual. As an individual deprived of memory becomes disoriented and lost, not knowing where he has been or where he is going, so a nation denied a conception of its past will be disabled in dealing with its present and its future.

—Arthur Schlesinger, Jr., *The Disuniting of America*

B. By far the most exciting of our future technologies are those that enter into a symbiotic relationship with us: machine + person. Is the car + driver a symbiosis of human and machine in much the same way as the horse + rider might be? After all, the car + driver splits the processing levels, with the car taking over the visceral level and the driver the reflective level, both sharing the behavior level in analogous fashion to the horse + rider. Just as the horse is intelligent enough to take care of the visceral aspects of riding (avoiding dangerous terrain, adjusting its pace to the quality of the terrain, avoiding obstacles), so too is the modern automobile able to sense danger, controlling the car's stability, braking, and speed. Similarly, horses learn behaviorally complex routines for navigating difficult terrain or jumping obstacles, for changing canter when required and maintaining distance and coordination with other horses or people. So, too, does the modern car behaviorally modify its speed, keep to its own lane, brake when it senses danger, and control other aspects of the driving experience.

—Donald Norman, *The Design of Future Things*

Argument and Causality

Explore the **Concept**, Argument and Causality— What Happens When you Drop out of School? **MyThinkingLab**

causality
A relationship between or among events in which one event appears responsible for causing others to occur after it; for example, smoking cigarettes causes cancer.

Causality refers to a relationship between or among events in which one event appears responsible for causing others to occur. Smoking cigarettes causes cancer, for example. Taking aspirin reduces pain. Single-cause explanations of complex events, however, often oversimplify, and are almost always unsatisfactory. To reduce the causes of World War I to the assassination of Archduke Ferdinand of Austria or to explain the poor record of a professional football team by isolating its quarterback's weak performance oversimplify more complex situations. So, too, does assigning an explanation for the cause of the depressed job market solely to insufficient government spending. Other contributing factors of the depressed job market include tight credit, business failures, bank and trading scandals, the housing bubble, an escalating national debt, a sliding trade deficit, an increase in consumer debt—and more.

Just as there can be multiple conditions for an event to occur, so too, in other words, can there be multiple causes for something to happen. Those multiple causes can overlap in what we call a "causal chain," in which A causes event B, which causes outcome C, which causes D, and so on. You may have seen one or more of a set of television commercials for satellite TV in which a series of events affect a viewer who subscribes to cable TV. The sequence of interlinked negative outcomes causes him to cancel his cable subscription and subscribe instead to satellite television.

Causal claims can be made as both particular statements and as generalizations. HIV causes AIDS is a particular causal claim. A general claim would be that possessing the genome of a dog causes the puppy, "Belle," to grow up as a dog. It is important to note that in the case of HIV causing AIDS, HIV functions as a necessary cause. That is, HIV is required for AIDS to develop. Without HIV present, AIDS will not develop. But HIV is not sufficient by itself to cause AIDS; other factors are also involved.

In the example of a dog genome causing the development of the puppy into an adult dog, we have both a necessary condition, or cause, and a sufficient condition, or cause. That is, the genome of a dog is all that is needed to achieve the result of an adult dog. It is necessary because without the genome of a dog, a dog will not develop. And it is sufficient because nothing else except the genome of a dog is required. A necessary condition is *required* for something to occur. A sufficient condition is *enough* for something to occur.

In logical terms, a cause C of an effect E is sufficient "if and only if" C always produces E. A cause is necessary "if and only if" the effect E (e.g., AIDS) cannot occur in the absence of the cause C (e.g., HIV). And a cause is both necessary and sufficient "if and only if" C (a dog genome) is the only cause of E (an adult dog).

The criteria for what is considered adequate evidence for causal explanations are not easy to apply. Causality does not usually involve ironclad proof, but rather likelihood or possibility, instead. That's what makes causal arguments inductive rather than deductive.

Causality is rarely easy to establish. Because complex events have multiple causes, identifying those causes and deciding which are most influential often leads to disagreement. Scientists disagree, for example, about the causes of dinosaur extinction. Educators disagree about the causes for the decline in SAT scores. Economists disagree about the causes of slow job growth and what to do about it.

One of the reasons for the difficulty in assigning clear causes to an event, action, or outcome is that complex systems are affected by a web of causation, a network or nexus of causes, which do not operate in a single linear direction. Systems as diverse yet complex as weather patterns and financial markets involve such causal webs. The evolution of life on earth, the continuing evolution of species, including their extinction, involve multiple networks of causes. One of the dangers of causal explanations is that those explanations can be made to appear certain and clear, definite and definitive, when that is anything but the case.

Causality is closely linked with two related concepts, *coincidence* and *correlation*. Let's distinguish among these terms by means of examples. In attending a baseball game, you may wear your "lucky hat," perhaps with the brim facing backward or sideways. If your favorite team wins the game each time you do this, you may think that there is a causal relationship—that is, that wearing your lucky cap that way is related to your team's winning, even that it causes your team to win. This is nonsense, of course. There is no logical relationship—no causal relationship between those two events. It is mere coincidence that your team won its games when you wore your hat sideways. Those two facts—your wearing of the cap and your team winning games—simply occur together; they are coincidental. Coincidence is a particular type of correlation.

A correlation occurs when there is no actual cause-and-effect relationship, but rather a relationship between events that is more tenuous or limited. For example, there is a high correlation between being tall and being a professional basketball player. It's not that every pro basketball player is tall, nor is every tall person a candidate for the National Basketball Association (NBA). Rather, there is an exceptionally high percentage of tall basketball players in the professional ranks, making the correlation between height and being a pro in the NBA a significant one. We might make a similar kind of high correlation between weight and being a professional football player, especially if we restrict that correlation to the weight of linemen and pro players in the National Football League.

EXERCISES

21. Explain the kind of causal reasoning at work in each of the following examples. Decide if the reasoning is valid or not.

  a. Professional cyclists typically have between 5% and 10% body fat. If you decrease your body fat percentage to that low level, you could become a world-class cyclist.

  b. Average SAT scores at highly competitive universities have consistently risen over the past decade. This suggests that high school students taking the SATs have been improving their math, reading, and writing skills.

  c. This newspaper headline has been a familiar one: "Obesity Linked with Depression." In which direction would you draw the arrow between obesity and depression? Why? Is the linkage a correlation or a true cause-and-effect relationship?

  d. Student cheating on tests has been uncovered in Atlanta, Washington, DC, New York, and Boston. This is because moral standards have eroded in the past decade.

22. Identify the causes and effects of two of the following:

  a. The American Civil War

  b. The collapse of the Berlin Wall

  c. The rise in salaries of professional athletes

  d. The demise of the independent bookstore

  e. The popularity of Facebook

  f. The success of Starbucks

  g. The spread of wildfires

  h. The popularity of reality television shows

Looking Back and Looking Ahead

Revisit the learning goals that begin this chapter. Which of these goals do you think you have best achieved? What might you do to reach the remaining goals?

Return to the focusing questions at the beginning of the chapter. How would you answer those questions now? Which of them do you find most interesting and provocative and worthy of following up? Why?

In reviewing the list of resources that follows, identify the two that attract you most. Explain why these books or Web sites interest you. Consider looking into them for further deepening your understanding of careful, logical reasoning.

Take a look, too, at the MyThinkingLab resources on the Prentice Hall Web site. Included there are readings, images, videos, questions, exercises, and other provocations to help you develop your critical thinking prowess.

● ●

Resources

Everything's an Argument, Andrea Lunsford, John Ruszkiewicz, and Keith Walter. Bedford/ St. Martins, 2009.

Good Arguments, 4th ed., Connie Missimer. Prentice Hall, 2008.

How to Think Logically, 2nd ed., Gary Seay and Susana Nuccetelli. Prentice Hall, 2011.

You Must Be Kidding, John Capps and Donald Capps. Wiley-Blackwell, 2008.

Theory of Knowledge, Richard van de Lagemaat. Cambridge University Press, 2006.

The Uses of Argument, Stephen Toulmin. Cambridge University Press, 1969.

The Little Blue Reasoning Book, Brandon Royal. Maven Publishing, 2010.

"Politics and the English Language." George Orwell. In *Essays*. Knopf, 2002.

The Philosopher's Toolkit, Julian Baggini and Peter S. Fosl. Wiley-Blackwell, 2010.

The Violinist's Thumb, Sam Kean. Little, Brown and Company, 2012.

● ●

7
Reasoning Badly: Thinking Fallacies

Bad reasoning as well as good reasoning is possible; and this fact is the foundation of the practical side of logic.

—CHARLES SANDERS PEIRCE

FOCUSING QUESTIONS

- How would you characterize the way most people think? To what extent do you think that most people believe themselves to be good thinkers?

- What errors of reasoning have you noticed that people often make?

- What kinds of errors in reasoning do you find yourself making?

- How might you go about developing ways to avoid making mistakes in thinking?

- What might you do to become a more logical thinker, to improve your ability to reason responsibly and effectively?

LEARNING GOALS

7.1 IDENTIFY different categories of logical fallacies—formal and informal, deductive and inductive.

7.2 RECOGNIZE different types of fallacies, based on faulty induction, presumption, inadequate evidence, and problems with language.

7.3 UNDERSTAND the distinction between necessary and sufficient conditions.

7.4 ANALYZE and explain errors in reasoning fallaciously and understand how to avoid them.

Chapter Overview

This chapter focuses on difficulties encountered in thinking logically; it empha-sizes errors in reasoning—logical fallacies. Key concepts include formal fallacies associated with deductive thinking; informal fallacies associated with inductive thinking; and ways to identify and avoid such reasoning errors. The central theme of the chapter is the need to be alert for thinking errors so as to reason logically in evaluating complex situations and issues, personal, professional, and academic. A corollary concern is to be able to detect fallacious reasoning in the arguments made by others.

How Thinking Goes Wrong

Thinking well poses many challenges. There are many ways we can go wrong with our thinking. Some ways thinking can go awry include the errors we make in deductive thinking, resulting in invalid arguments. Other thinking mistakes involve reasoning errors associated with inductive thinking. These include, among many others, thinking fallacies associated with language, causality, authority, and analogy.

Why should we be concerned about faulty reasoning? For these reasons at least: (1) It is important to learn how to identify thinking fallacies, or errors in reasoning, so that we can avoid them in our own thinking. (2) It is also important to be able to detect fallacious reasoning in the arguments others make so that we can refute those arguments and present better ones that are more logical, better reasoned, and more convincing. In *Attacking Faulty Reasoning*, T. Edward Damer suggests that the main reason we should care about and be aware of fallacies is because they weaken and interfere with good arguments.

Why does making good arguments matter? Damer offers these reasons. First, good arguments help us make better personal and moral decisions. Second, good arguments lead us toward true and defensible beliefs rather than toward unsubstantiated opinion. Third, good arguments raise the general level of conversation and thinking. We should understand and analyze faulty reasoning because we cannot construct good arguments if we are unable to identify bad ones.

Fallacies—Errors in Reasoning

There are two key questions concerning arguments. First, are all the premises true? Second, do the premises support the conclusion? In the first instance, a **fallacy**, or error in thinking, may involve the factual accuracy of the premises. In the second instance, a fallacy may involve the structure of an argument.

As Julian Baggini and Peter S. Fosl explain in *The Philosopher's Toolkit*, all invalid arguments are fallacious, or erroneous, although not all fallacies involve invalid arguments. They explain further that faulty reasoning may involve the form of an argument or it may involve its content. When the faulty reasoning involves an argument's form or structure, the fallacies are "formal" fallacies. When the faulty reasoning involves content, the fallacies are "informal" fallacies. To improve our critical thinking ability, it is helpful to understand these ways thinking can go awry.

Here is an example of a formal fallacy:

Premise 1: If Mary won the Powerball Lottery last night, she will buy her daughter an apartment.

Premise 2: Mary bought her daughter an apartment.

Conclusion: Therefore, she won the Powerball Lottery last night.

A moment's reflection shows why this reasoning is faulty. The truth of the premises does not guarantee the truth of the conclusion. It is possible that Mary bought the apartment even without having won the Powerball Lottery. Perhaps she inherited money; perhaps she borrowed it or attained it by illicit means.

For an example of an informal fallacy—one whose faulty reasoning involves the content rather than the form of an argument—consider this example of the Gambler's fallacy:

In repeated tosses of a coin heads comes up five times in a row.

I assume that the next toss should be tails—because of all those preceding tosses that came up heads.

Watch the **Video**, How Thinking Goes Wrong / Fallacies—Errors in Reasoning **MyThinkingLab**

fallacies
Argument errors or mistakes that occur in making both deductive and inductive arguments.

This conclusion, however, is false. The odds of the next toss coming up heads remain 50/50—the same odds as the previous five tosses (and the odds for all subsequent tosses). The unstated assumption that the odds change from one toss to another is mistaken.

Deductive Thinking Fallacies

Before considering the various types of informal fallacies, we consider some types of fallacies associated with deductive thinking: (1) the four-terms fallacy, (2) affirming the consequent, (3) denying the antecedent, and (4) disjunctive syllogism fallacies.

Four-Terms Fallacy

A valid syllogism consists of three terms—two premises (one major and one minor) and a conclusion. The major term and the minor term are related through the middle term; the conclusion in a valid syllogism connects the major term and minor term. A thinking fallacy occurs if and when a fourth term is introduced.

For example:

All professional basketball players are athletes.

Mike is someone who plays basketball.

Therefore, Mike is an athlete.

Instead of three terms, this syllogism includes four: (1) professional basketball players, (2) athletes, (3) someone who plays basketball, and (4) Mike. The reasoning is problematic here because not everyone who plays basketball is an athlete. Mike can play basketball without being an athlete.

Here is another example:

All professors are academics.

Jane is someone who works in a university.

Therefore, Jane is an academic.

Again, there are four terms in this syllogism: (1) professors, (2) academics, (3) someone who works in a university, and (4) Jane. The reasoning in this syllogism is faulty and the syllogism invalid because Jane might do something else in the university other than academic work. She might be an administrator, a secretary, a cook, a counselor, advisor, fund-raiser, or something else.

Affirming the Consequent

We often engage in hypothetical thinking, also known as conditional thinking—thinking that follows an "if-then" form. For example: "If the paper currency is US currency, then it is green." Why? Because *all* US paper currency is green. Note that we cannot reverse the direction to say that if the bills are green, then it is US paper currency. This is so because some other countries also use green currency.

We can put hypothetical, or conditional, statements into syllogistic form, with the "if" statement the **antecedent** (which comes first) and the "then" statement the **consequent** (which follows after). The structure looks like this, with all three elements of the syllogism exhibiting conditionality (i.e., with each element including an *if*):

antecedent
The first part of a conditional statement; the "if" clause.

consequent
The part of a conditional statement that states what will follow if a condition is met.

If P, then Q.

If Q, then R.

Therefore, if P then R.

FIGURE 7.1   Basketball Player

Here is what the form looks like with a mixed form, that is, with only the major premise hypothetical or conditional, and the minor premise and conclusion categorical statements:

If P, then Q.

P.

Therefore Q.

This valid form of the syllogism, which affirms the antecedent, is called *modus ponens* in Latin. A logical fallacy occurs when the consequent is affirmed in this type of syllogism. This fallacy of "**affirming the consequent**" looks like this:

If P, then Q.

Q.

Therefore, P.

For example:

If I exercise during the day, I feel refreshed at night.

I feel refreshed at night.

Therefore, I exercised during the day.

affirming the consequent
A logical fallacy that treats a necessary condition (the consequent) as if it were a sufficient condition. It takes this form: If P, then Q. Q, therefore P.

What's wrong with this logic? Your feeling refreshed at night might result from something other than exercising. You might have taken an afternoon nap, or had a relaxing day, one with little stress and no strenuous activity. The conclusion, thus, is not warranted by the premises; hence the argument is invalid.

However, suppose we change the major premise to read like this: "If and only if P, then Q." For example: "If and only if I exercise during the day, I feel refreshed at night." Then the argument is valid because we have set a strict limit, or condition, on our "if-then" major premise. It now means that there is only one way I am able to feel refreshed at night, and that is by exercising during the day. Nothing else will give me that refreshed feeling at night—only exercise.

So, unless we qualify an "if-then" statement to an "if and only if" form, we cannot validly affirm the consequent.

Denying the Antecedent

We can also create a valid hypothetical syllogism in negative form, like this:

> If P, then Q.
>
> Not Q.
>
> Therefore, not P.

Notice that in this negative or negating mode, (called *modus tollens* in Latin), it is the consequent (the "then" statement) that is denied.

An error in logical reasoning occurs when the antecedent rather than the consequent is denied. That invalid mixed hypothetical syllogism—"**denying the antecedent**"—looks like this:

> If P, then Q.
>
> Not P.
>
> Therefore, not Q.

For example:

> If it rains tonight, then the streets will be wet tomorrow.
>
> It did not rain.
>
> Therefore, the streets will not be wet tomorrow.

What is the problem with this reasoning? The streets might be wet from other causes. Maybe there was roadwork during the night in which hoses were used to water down the streets. Perhaps there was a break in a water main. It is not necessarily the case that rain was the cause of the wet streets.

However, we can deny the antecedent in this type of syllogism when we qualify the "if-then" statement to make it follow the form of "if and only if—then." A valid syllogism would be:

> If and only if it rains tonight, then the streets will be wet tomorrow.
>
> It did not rain.
>
> The streets will not be wet.

Using "if and only if" excludes all other possibility, thus allowing a denial of the antecedent.

Conditional statements are also described in terms of "necessary" and "sufficient" conditions. A **necessary condition** is a condition (or process or state of affairs) that is essential for something to happen or result. Although a necessary condition must be present for an event to occur, it does not by itself cause the event to occur. That is, it is not sufficient, or enough by itself, for the event to occur. A **sufficient condition**, however, is enough, by itself, to ensure that something will occur. So, as a necessary condition, for example, we must have oxygen to breathe and hence to live. Thus, oxygen is a necessary condition for life. Depriving a person of oxygen

---

denying the antecedent
A logical fallacy that treats a sufficient condition (the antecedent) as if it were a necessary condition. It takes the following form: If P, therefore Q. Not P, therefore Q.

conditional statement
A statement asserting that if one condition is met, then something else will follow from it. For instance: "If you work hard, you will succeed."

necessary condition
A condition that is required for something to be the case.

sufficient condition
What is enough for something to be the case.

CHAPTER 7 Reasoning Badly: Thinking Fallacies

results in death. Oxygen, however, is not a sufficient condition for life. Something more is required.

Sufficient conditions are *enough* for something to be the case. Necessary conditions are *required* for something to be the case. A sufficient condition is one that leads inescapably to a particular outcome or event. Thus swallowing certain poisons results in death. Swallowing poison is a sufficient condition to cause death; nothing else is needed. A necessary condition, on the other hand, while required for a particular outcome, is not enough to produce the effect by itself. In terms of an "antecedent" and a "consequent," the antecedent is the sufficient condition for the consequent; the consequent is the necessary condition for the antecedent.

To say it yet another way: The antecedent (the phrase following the *if*) is the sufficient condition for the consequent (the phrase following the *then*), and the consequent is the necessary condition for the antecedent.

Disjunctive Syllogism Fallacies

Disjunctive syllogisms include an "either-or" statement, as for example, "Either the book costs $10 or it costs $12.50." The form of a disjunctive syllogism looks like this:

> Either P or Q.
> Not P.
> Therefore, Q.

Or, it could take this form:

> Either P or Q.
> Not Q.
> Therefore, P.

For example:

> Either the book costs $10 or it costs $12.50.
> It does not cost $10.
> Therefore, it costs $12.50.

And:

> Either the book costs $10 or it costs $12.50.
> It does not cost $12.50.
> Therefore, it costs $10.

A second form of the disjunctive syllogism takes this form:

> Either P or Q.
> P.
> Therefore, not Q.

And this variant:

> Either P or Q.
> Q.
> Therefore, not P.

For example:

> The professor promised to assign either *Hamlet* or *Macbeth*.
> The professor assigned *Hamlet*.
> Therefore, the professor did not assign *Macbeth*.

And:

> The professor promised to assign either *Hamlet* or *Macbeth*.
> The professor assigned *Macbeth*.
> Therefore, the professor did not assign *Hamlet*.

In all of these forms and in each example, the syllogism is valid only when P and Q are considered to be exclusive of each other—that is, they cannot both occur.

Sometimes, however, *or* is used in an exclusive sense when in reality the *or* may be nonexclusive—that is, when both things could actually occur. Consider the following example:

> "Either Bill went to the gym or he went to the museum."

But isn't it the case that Bill could have gone to both the gym and the museum—just not at the same time? And, we would have a similar problem if the professor in the earlier example broke his promise to assign "either" *Hamlet* "or" *Macbeth* and instead assigned both plays, perhaps to be read in successive weeks. In both of these cases, the more common exclusive meaning of "either-or" is undermined.

EXERCISE

1. Identify the fallacies in the following arguments.

   a. If this truck has not been inspected, then it may be unsafe to drive. This truck may be unsafe to drive. Therefore, it has not been inspected.

   b. If Mickey Mantle was born in Arkansas, then he was not born in New York. Mickey Mantle was not born in Arkansas, and so then he was born in New York.

   c. Either we will slow our carbon emissions or global warming will increase. We are slowing our carbon emissions; therefore, global warming will not increase.

   d. Everybody in this room is a baseball card trader. Some baseball card traders are people who play poker. Jerry is a person who plays poker. Therefore, Jerry is a baseball card trader.

   e. All people in this room are musicians. Some musicians are serious cooks. Therefore, some people in this room are serious cooks.

   f. Either Marilyn Monroe married Joe DiMaggio or she married Arthur Miller. She married Arthur Miller. Therefore, she did not marry Joe DiMaggio.

   g. If Eric Trimmer is a talented actor, then he performs in live theater. Eric Trimmer does not perform in live theater. Therefore, Eric Trimmer is not a talented actor.

   h. The concert was being performed on Friday or Saturday. The concert was performed on Saturday. Thus, it was not performed on Friday.

   i. All professors at this university are teachers. Michelle Smith is someone who teaches at this university. Therefore, Michelle Smith is a professor.

Informal Fallacies

Informal fallacies involve defects in arguments resulting from patterns of error most often in their content. There are a great many kinds of informal fallacies. They can be organized in various ways. In *How to Think Logically*, Gary Seay and Susana Nuccetelli organize them in the following way: (1) *fallacies of induction*, (2) *fallacies of presumption*, (3) *fallacies of relevance*, (4) and *fallacies of language*. This division represents one grouping of informal fallacies; other groupings are possible because some fallacies can be considered under more than one of these categories.

Fallacies of Induction

In this section, we focus on informal fallacies that reveal deficiencies in inductive thinking, a reasoning process that typically works from particular observations to general concepts and claims. We illustrate the following fallacies of induction, or inductive thinking: *hasty generalization, weak or false analogy, false or illogical causality, slippery slope, appeal to ignorance*, and *appeal to unqualified authority*.

Hasty Generalization

A hasty generalization relies on inadequate evidence in making an inductive generalization. Jumping to conclusions on the basis of insufficient information is one type of hasty generalization. For example:

> The mechanic who took care of my car is German, and he didn't fix the car properly. I'll never take my car to a German auto mechanic again.

There might be more than one explanation for the car's not having been properly repaired. Even if the fault was the mechanic's, his German nationality or heritage wasn't the cause; his skill and competence in fixing cars was the problem. Other German auto mechanics are competent, and some are brilliant at their work.

One specific type of hasty generalization is stereotyping, or making assumptions about people, places, and things based on a small sample of evidence. For example:

> Don't visit Mexico City unless you want to take a chance on getting killed. It's an incredibly dangerous city.

Mexico City may indeed be less safe than many other large cities. But the conclusion that a visit is life endangering goes too far, as there are parts of the city that are perfectly safe, and precautions can be taken to increase one's safety.

You can avoid hasty generalizations by recognizing that **stereotypes** are oversimplifications of a more complex reality. You can also remember that to generalize to a claim about "all" or even "most" of something, it is wise to ensure that you are basing your generalization on a broad enough and large enough sample—whether you are sampling evidence in science, history, psychological or economic behavior, or everyday experience.

stereotype
A widely held but oversimplified belief about the members of a group, such that all group members are considered to possess the same character or behavior trait.

Weak or False Analogy

A weak or false analogy misleads by comparing situations that differ more than they are similar. False analogy is sometimes also based on irrelevant similarities.

> If we add a foreign language requirement to the undergraduate program, we will deter students from attending this university, just as we did when we added a math requirement two years ago.

There is no connection between the requirement for math and for foreign language. And there is an assumption that the math requirement put in place earlier was a deterrent, though there may be no evidence for its truth. Other factors, including a rise in tuition or a declining student population pool might have been involved.

Consider an example from the world of political life. Political pundits make analogies between political campaigns run by Democrats and Republicans from one era to another. In the 2012 campaign, for example, the Republican campaign was described as being unsympathetic to the middle class and as presenting a set of positions that favored not only the wealthy, but also white Americans. The analogy made was to a party of the past, whose limited focus, scope, and scale did not represent twenty-first century America. Supporters of particular candidates made other kinds of analogies, including that Mitt Romney's work at Bain Capital was, on one hand, destructive to companies and workers—yet on the other hand, a model for how to create jobs and improve the economic circumstances of Americans. The arguments in each of these situations involved a suggestion that what had been done in the past was analogous to what would happen in the future. This, of course, is not necessarily the case, and thus fallacious.

False or Illogical Causality

False cause, or illogical causality, results from assuming that because one event happens after another, the first event caused the second to happen. This fallacy is also known by its Latin name, *post hoc, ergo propter hoc*, which means "after this, therefore because of this."

> After I saw a black cat in the morning, I knew I was in trouble. And just as I expected, my bike was stolen that afternoon.

There's no logical connection between the two events. Seeing the black cat did not "cause" the bike to be stolen. Their occurrence on the same day is coincidental.

Another way of explaining the thinking problem here is to note that the only evidence offered for the claim that seeing the black cat "caused" the bike to be stolen is that seeing the cat occurred before the theft of the bike.

Write the Response, Analyzing Causality
MyThinkingLab

false cause
Illogical causality, which results from assuming that because one event happens after another, the first event caused the second to happen; also known by its Latin name, *post hoc, ergo propter hoc*, which means "after this, therefore because of this."

FIGURE 7.2 Republican Elephant and Democratic Donkey

It is tempting to impute a causal explanation when two events occur in close proximity. Consider the way in which economic causes and effects are imputed to policies enacted by reigning political parties in House, Senate, and White House. When the economy starts to stagnate, or conversely, to improve, claims are made by one party or the other to allocate blame or to take credit for the economic result, as if it were simply a matter of one or another newly executed policy. In reality, the causes and consequences of adjustments to the economy involve multiple impacts over longer periods of time—adjustments and impacts that might not be adequately measured or reasonably understood until well after the claims for those responsible for the good or bad economic results have disappeared from the political landscape.

False cause fallacies are sometimes based on weak rationalizing and on blaming others. Here are some everyday examples: "I overate last Sunday because I was being polite at my grandmother's house." Or: "We lost the game because of some bad calls by the referee."

Consider the following scenarios described in Rolf Dobelli's *The Art of Clear Thinking*. People living in a chain of Scottish islands, The Hebrides, experienced head lice as a normal part of life. When the lice left their host, the person became feverish and sick. To get rid of the fever, sick people intentionally put lice into their hair. As soon as the lice had settled in once again, the patient improved. What causes the fever to recede? It seems as if it's the lice, but can that be so? Aren't the lice leaving the host after he becomes feverish—when it gets too hot for them to remain in his hair?

Or, consider how in a city where fires frequently occurred, one study showed that in each blaze, the more firefighters were called out to fight the fire, the greater was the damage the blaze caused. The mayor imposed a hiring freeze and cut the firefighting budget. Why? Because he assumed, falsely, that the firefighters were somehow causing fires to grow larger. But doesn't it make more sense to suggest that the extra firefighters were called out because the blazes were bigger, so that the larger fires were the cause, not the consequence, of adding extra firefighters?

Slippery Slope

Related to both false analogy and false cause is the argument known as "the slippery slope" and also as "the domino effect." The term **slippery slope** refers to an argument that develops by suggesting how if one pathway is selected, that will be only the first step to a dangerous situation. For example, a speaker in a debate might suggest that if marijuana is legalized, then it will lead to a series of more serious uses and abuses of other drugs. He might invoke the slippery slope by saying something like this: "The consequences of legalizing dangerous drugs like marijuana will be horrible for society with people tripping out on pot. And if you legalize pot, how soon will it be before heroin and cocaine are legalized?"

In the slippery slope form of an argument about gun control, a claim might be made that because any type of guns are allowed (the constitutional "right to bear arms"), guns will lead to slaughter with weapons such as AK-47s. Once you allow small handguns, the argument goes, soon you will allow rifles and semiautomatic weapons that can wreak havoc with great speed and carnage. So, therefore, all guns of any type or size should be banned.

The "domino effect" takes its name from the 1970s, when the United States was involved in supplying first military advice, then equipment, and finally soldiers, to fight in what initially was a civil war between what was then North and South Vietnam. The argument was made that the United States needed to intervene significantly to save South Vietnam from the Communists—because if South Vietnam fell

slippery slope
A logical fallacy in which a claim is made that one action will precipitate a successive series of actions, as for example, that legalizing medical marijuana will lead to marijuana addiction and then to other forms of drug addiction.

FIGURE 7.3   Dominoes Falling

to Communism, so too, the argument went, would other Southeast Asian countries, such as Laos and Cambodia—like one domino knocking down another. The domino argument was made because of the geographical proximity of the countries and because of their political instability. In the case of Vietnam and these other countries, the claim proved valid—but the argument, nonetheless, illustrates the slippery slope.

Appeal to Ignorance

In an appeal to ignorance, a person argues that a situation is true because evidence to the contrary is lacking. A claim is considered true because it can't be proven demonstrably false.

> God must have created the world in six days. I know this because scientists can't prove that he didn't.
>
> Or: The devil exists because there is evil in the world. And you can't prove that the devil doesn't exist.

The first statement in each of these examples is nonfalsifiable; there is no way to disprove it. But there is also no way to prove it either. This makes it a matter of belief rather than of knowledge.

In the opposite case, an appeal to ignorance may also occur when someone claims that something is false because it hasn't been proven true. Opponents of evolutionary theory often argue in this manner.

Similarly, some people claim that UFOs, or life on other planets, exist by arguing that no one has ever conclusively proven that they do not. Once again, this is an argument made from the absence of contrary evidence. To believe in UFOs or that life exists on other planets is not supported, as there is no evidence to indicate that they do exist.

Appeal to Unqualified Authority

An argument that appeals to an authority cited outside its field of expertise or one wildly at variance with the general consensus of opinion held by prominent and respected authorities commits a fallacy of appeal to unqualified authority. Common examples of the abuse of an appeal to authority involve celebrities, professional athletes, television personalities, movie stars, famous musicians, and other notables endorsing products outside their special areas of knowledge and expertise.

Throughout the history of philosophy and science, there have been appeals to authority and throughout the history of law appeals to precedent—a form of legal authority. These types of appeals are within reason, though they are not without problems, as the history of thought and the development of science and technology have involved debates and mistakes as well as progress and improvements. In fact, the mistakes have often led to later progress.

People also appeal to books as authorities—some will appeal to this book, and throughout this book, the author has appealed to others as reputable and authoritative guides. Legitimate appeals to authority always involve caution; they involve invoking authorities who have earned credibility whether by having acquired positions of prominence, having earned the respect of their peers, having been published in respected journals and by legitimate and respected publishers, and by having demonstrated skill and knowledge, however acquired.

Beware of authorities misused in political campaigns, in advertisements in the media, in medical and legal situations. Use the following questions as guidelines:

1. What are the authority's credentials and qualifications?

2. Is the authority presenting evidence, information, or judgments within his or her area of expertise?

3. What kinds and amount of evidence does the authoritative excerpt provide to support a position or judgment being advanced?

4. How sound are the authority's arguments?

A final note: Appeals to tradition are also a form of an appeal to authority—the authority of tradition: How things have been done in the past, and thus how, it is believed, they should continue to be done. Often the appeal to tradition occurs within the context of religion, as religions tend to be conservative in practice and institution. Reasoning by appealing to tradition without further consideration of why things should remain as they are is fallacious. Religious practices and beliefs, too, have changed over time; and they will very likely change in the future, so appealing to tradition as authority does not necessarily warrant our assent.

EXERCISE

2. Identify the fallacies in the following statements and arguments.

   a. The chance for economic progress in the European Union is strong. Rock star Bono has just returned from Dublin and Paris and reports that things are looking much better economically in Ireland and France.

   b. Most cancer patients are older people. Thus, cancer is caused by the aging process.

   c. He's from Sicily, so of course he loves pizza and pasta. All Sicilians do.

   d. George Allen smoked a cigar every day and lived to be 100. We shouldn't listen to those who claim that smoking causes lung cancer.

   e. There have been a number of recalls of Japanese hybrid cars in recent months. It must be that Japanese automobile manufacturers are cutting corners to save money.

f. She has never won an academy award, so she can't be that great of an actor.

g. The Secretary of State has argued for cutting the defense and education budgets because those budgets are bloated. She should know because she works closely with the Secretary of Defense and the Secretary of Education.

h. You can't prove that humans didn't evolve from dinosaurs, so I'm confident that those big guys were our ancestors.

Fallacies of Presumption

The fallacies in this next group take something for granted that should not be so considered. These fallacies make unwarranted assumptions or beliefs that have not been proven. Unwarranted assumptions can undermine the reasoning process. Arguments that take for granted assumptions that are in truth debatable commit the fallacy of presumption, or of unsupported belief. We consider the following examples of presumptive fallacies: *begging the question*, *complex question*, *false dilemma*, *non sequitur*, and *accident*.

Begging the Question

Begging the question involves assuming what needs to be proven. In one form of this fallacy, a speaker states a claim and asks to be proven incorrect. Begging the question puts the burden of proof not on the speaker to prove his assertion but on the adversary to prove it wrong.

> Paying a mere fifty cents a day is a small price to pay for insuring your family's livelihood. You are covered for up to $100,000 for accidental injury and death for that small outlay.
>
> This sale is the absolute best opportunity for you to stock up on the school supplies you need. You owe it to yourself to take advantage of our sale to get those school necessities.

In both these cases, the argument claim is unsupported by evidence. In fact, there is simply a repetition of the claim in other words.

In another form of begging the question, circular reasoning is even more evident. To engage in circular reasoning is to assert the same idea in different words, but without any evidence to support it.

> The growing popularity of Twitter and tweeting shows that more people are now interested in communicating this way.
>
> I am making these decisions because I am in charge. And I'm in charge because I make these decisions.

In both of these examples, neither speaker provides evidence to support the claim being made. The second statement in each case, simply reasserts what the first claims.

Complex Question

Related to begging the question is the fallacy of the complex question. This fallacy occurs through including an unproven assertion in an argument as if it were a fact. The classic example is "Have you stopped beating your wife?" Or a variant: "When did you stop beating your wife?" Or "When do you plan to stop beating your wife?" These questions can't be answered "yes" or "no" without indicating that the individual in question did beat his wife or still is beating his wife. Here are a couple of additional examples:

"Why are you being so defensive?"

"Because legalizing marijuana will reduce the crime rate, we have to decide how best to make the drug legal."

In both cases, the claim is assumed—in the first case, that you are being defensive, and in the second, that marijuana legalization will lower the crime rate. What needs to be proven is simply assumed.

False Dilemma

A **false dilemma**, a type of either-or thinking, limits options to just two. All other options and alternatives are ignored.

> Either the Democrats band together behind Governor Johnson, or the Republicans will coast to an easy victory.

There are other options besides these two alternatives. There may be other viable Democratic candidates. And if Governor Johnson indeed becomes the Democratic candidate, the Republicans may or may not win the election.

False dilemmas or alternatives oversimplify a more complex reality. The two alternative positions presented in false dilemmas suggest that these are the only possible outcomes, with no additional outcomes possible, and with no intermediary possibilities.

> Either the use of robots in manufacturing will turn out to be a brilliant way to curtail expenses, remain competitive, and save businesses from failing. Or their use will result in the destruction of jobs and livelihoods all over this country.

Given these false alternatives, there is no allowance for the possibility that robots might actually help preserve jobs and require more sophisticated types of training and higher rates of pay for those workers who manage and program them.

False alternatives insist on "either" this "or" that. You are either attractive or not, intelligent or not—a hero or a bozo, an angel or a devil, a jock or a jerk. People are either satisfied or dissatisfied, happy or sad, lazy or hardworking. Other nations are enemies or friends, right or wrong, with us or against us. We hear such simplistic polarities expressed all the time; we need to insist on their inadequacy as rational and reasonable options.

Non Sequitur

Non sequitur is Latin for *it does not follow*. It refers to any argument in which the conclusion does not follow from the premises. For example:

> I worked hard in this course, so I deserve an A.

Here, an unstated premise—that students who work hard should get an A—is not reliable or warranted. Other criteria, besides hard work, are involved in earning and being awarded an A in a course. For one thing, a demonstration of knowledge and skill through performance is typically required. In addition, an excellent performance on tests and projects is expected.

Accident

The fallacy of accident occurs when some exceptional, unusual, "accidental" aspect of a situation is neglected. An argument that treats a particular instance of a case

false dilemma
A type of either-or thinking that limits options to just two. All other options and alternatives are ignored, fallaciously.

non sequitur
A logical fallacy in which one statement does not follow logically from another.

as exemplary of a general rule when in fact that instance is an exception to the rule commits the fallacy of accident. Here is an example:

> Cats are very independent creatures; they don't snuggle up to their owners the way dogs do. Lucia, a Birman cat, is our new pet. So I expect her not to be very affectionate.

Although it is generally the case that pit bulls are aggressive dogs as compared, say, with Labrador retrievers, it might be the case that the neighbor's pit bull is friendly and not at all aggressive. And although cats tend to be somewhat standoffish, there are exceptions; Lucia may be the cat that loves as much attentive affection as friendly golden retrievers.

EXERCISE

3. Identify the fallacies in the following statements and arguments.

  a. Either our university should take the plunge into fully accredited and open online learning for all students, or it will be out of business within three to five years.

  b. There is no free lunch.

  c. Have you stopped cheating on your taxes?

  d. Do you really want another four years of these failed Democratic (or Republican) economic programs?

  e. My family owns two pianos and three guitars. I guess I will have to choose one of those instruments to study.

  f. Scandinavians have traditionally settled in Minnesota and in Bay Ridge, Brooklyn, NY. I guess the Larsen family must live in one of those places.

  g. Female infanticide is never morally permissible. Therefore, killing infant girls is morally unjustifiable.

  h. John is not to be trusted; therefore, he cannot possibly be considered reliable.

  i. You don't want to miss this opportunity to invest in a sensational timeshare property, now do you? This is the best time to take advantage of our special rates.

  j. Media literacy is essential for good citizenship; therefore, all people should become media literate.

Fallacies of Relevance

⊙▸ Simulate the **Experiment**, Appeal to the Public / Appeal to Force **MyThinkingLab**

Fallacies of relevance contain premises that are irrelevant to the conclusion they purportedly support. Even though a premise may be true, if it is not relevant to the argument being developed—to the claim or conclusion being made—then the argument fails. Often, arguments with irrelevant premises distract attention away from the real issue under consideration. We consider the following examples of fallacies of relevance: *appeal to the public*, *appeal to pity*, *appeal to force*, *appeal to emotion*, *ad hominem* and *tu quoque*, *red herring*, and the *straw man*.

Appeal to the Public

Fallacies **appealing to public** opinion or knowledge assume that because a large number of people accept something as being true, it must be true. The Latin name for this fallacy is *ad populum*, to the people, or as we might say today, appealing to what's popular. Here is another example:

> Lots of people play the lottery with the expectation of getting rich, and many of them play their "lucky numbers." Eventually they will win because they believe so strongly in their prospects.

People tend to believe that their prospects or chances for good fortune are better than they really are. All you have to do is consider the mathematical probability of winning any kind of lottery to see that people's belief in this matter is ill-founded.

Many people believed that the return on investments earned by Bernie Madoff made investing in his company a wise decision. Word spread about the extraordinary profits that accrued through investments with Madoff. And then the house of cards collapsed; the Ponzi scheme was revealed, and billions of dollars were lost, with many people losing their life savings.

The **ad populum** fallacy is also known as the **bandwagon** fallacy, as in "jumping on the bandwagon"—because other people have. Advertisers are especially good at creating appeals using this kind of fallacious thinking:

> Join the millions of satisfied customers of xyz weight loss product—or facial cream, or energy boosters, and so on.
>
> Or: Everyone is signing up for our new Direct TV service; you should too.

Whenever an argument hinges on the fact that "everybody is doing it," and "it's the in/hot new thing"—beware of falling for this fallacy. If we come to a conclusion that many others have also reached, that can be just fine. But we should come to that conclusion based on logical analysis, not on fallacious thinking that just because others do or believe or think something, we need to do, believe, or think it, too.

Appeal to Pity

Fallacies **appealing to pity** (rather than to reason) consist of using sympathy in place of evidence to support the strength of a claim. For example:

> You should donate money to cancer research. The poor people who suffer from this terrible disease, especially children suffer so terribly and their lives are shortened, sometimes drastically.

There are good reasons why we might donate money to facilitate cancer research, including the prospects for arresting if not eradicating various cancers. On the other hand, we might argue that the responsibility for such research lies with institutions, especially government agencies.

Some examples of the appeal to pity are authors seeking favorable reviews of their books, teachers requesting students to review their courses favorably (because tenure is at stake, perhaps), people soliciting money or food in the subway, because they are out of work and living day-to-day—these are all appeals to pity. Students explaining that they "need an A (or at least an A–)" in a course or they won't get into law school or medical school are other familiar examples. In each case, the basis for the judgment or evaluation or response is an appeal to compassion to the suffering that a person is or might undergo—and hence an appeal to pity.

---

appeal to the public
(See *ad populum*.)

ad populum
A logical fallacy that contains an appeal to public opinion to prove the truth of an argument; from the Latin phrase meaning to the people.

bandwagon
A popular term for an *ad populum* fallacy, where popularity is invoked as a means of persuasion.

appeal to pity
A logical fallacy that involves appealing to audience sympathy rather than to logic and rational thinking.

appeal to force
(See *ad baculum*.)

ad baculum
A logical fallacy containing an appeal to force that uses fear and threats to assert the truth of an argument; from the Latin phrase meaning "to the stick."

Appeal to Force

Related to the appeal to pity is the **appeal to force**, known in Latin as **ad baculum** (*to the stick*). Arguments that appeal to force attempt to stimulate feelings of fear rather than pity. They are, essentially, warnings that something unfavorable, potentially horrible, will happen unless a particular course of action is followed.

> If we allow the Republicans (or Democrats) to win in November, many middle-class people will lose their jobs and many elderly people will lose their health care.

Some appeals to force are indirect or even direct threats.

> If you don't hire the new dean's wife for this position in the English department, he will reduce the department's travel funding.

> If you don't support E. J. Distaff for Governor, you will be fired.

In these instances, a more rational and logical approach would be to request that explanations for why the dean's wife should be hired or E. J. Distaff be supported—explanations for why each is the best choice for the job. Not force but evidence is expected. Not threats but logical arguments with claims supported by good reasons are needed.

Appeal to Emotion

To some extent, clearly, the fallacies of the appeal to pity and the appeal to force exemplify appeals to emotion. But we can also describe another type of appeal to emotion that involves neither pity nor fear. The "bandwagon" appeal described under the Appeal to the Public section might be considered as an appeal to excitement about jumping on the proverbial bandwagon—or an appeal to avoid the anxiety of being left out or left behind if we don't. In fact, we might say that any appeal that does not invite logical thinking includes at least some element of an **appeal to emotion**.

appeal to emotion
A logical fallacy that in which logic and rational thinking are ignored in favor of feeling and emotion.

Appeals to emotion may involve the use of images that arouse shock or compassion, horror or sympathy. Public service announcements and other forms of solicitation that depict poor starving children, children malformed by disease and malnutrition, children with cleft lips and cleft palettes—such images evoke viewers' emotions. These appeals are not necessarily to be derided. First, they can be quite effective in arousing emotion, and in stimulating us to donate money or goods to help alleviate the suffering depicted via the images. Second, the emotion stimulated by the images can lead us to do some serious thinking about why we might want to donate to certain charities, whether or not it is to the organizations seeking that response through the images in their advertisements.

Ad Hominem and Tu Quoque

ad hominem
A logical fallacy that contains an attack on an individual's character rather than his or her ideas; from the Latin phrase meaning "to the man."

Ad hominem (Latin for "to the man") attacks on a person are used to deflect attention from issues being debated. The ad hominem fallacy introduces information and accusations that are irrelevant to the discussion. Essentially, such information and accusations are premises that are extraneous and irrelevant to the claim or conclusion being asserted. Ad hominem attacks often impute motives in an attempt to discredit someone. For example:

> Senator Misfit argues that we should control the deficit by cutting spending, but he didn't do that in his own household. His credit score and his credit history are atrocious.

The senator's personal financial history is irrelevant to any proposals he makes for political policy. Those proposals need to be judged on their own merits, not on his personal failures, financial or otherwise.

There can be legitimate debate about the extent to which personal traits are or are not relevant to a politician's candidacy for office. To what extent, we might ask, is it relevant that a man may have divorced and remarried three times and be living now with the wealthiest, the most beautiful, and/or the most celebrated woman of his three-part marital history? Some argued that Newt Gingrich's campaign for the Republican presidential nomination was misguided because of his marital history—and also because of how he spent vast sums of his third wife's millions. Is that a fair criticism—a relevant one—or does it exemplify an ad hominem attack? A more recent example is the case of Anthony Wiener, a candidate for mayor of New York City (NYC), who engaged in "phone sex" with young women and sent them pictures of his private parts. Wiener promised to reform but then went ahead and engaged in more of the same behavior. Were NYC voters justified in not voting for him because of this sex-related behavior?

A special instance of the ad hominem fallacy is *tu quoque* (Latin for *you also* or *you too*). This type of fallacy points to the hypocrisy of a person advocating some position that he violates himself. An example is the politician who asserts the importance of public education and how it needs additional funding and support, while sending his children to expensive private schools. Another example often cited is Thomas Jefferson, who drafted the Declaration of Independence, which asserts that "all men are created equal" and that they "are endowed . . . with certain unalienable Rights." Yet Jefferson was a slaveholder, and has recently been shown to have fathered children by one of his female slaves.

An argument built on this information might take the following form:

Thomas Jefferson proclaims loftily that all men are created equal.

Jefferson, however, was a slaveholder, and thus a hypocrite.

Therefore, we should not honor his claims about liberty and equality. They are false claims.

Another example might be taken from a novel by the Catholic novelist Graham Greene, whose *The Power and the Glory* tells the story of a "whiskey priest," one who violates his vows and lives a less than exemplary life. Yet for all his weakness, the priest fulfills his function as a spiritual guide and provider of religious services and consolations. A *tu quoque ad hominem* argument against this fictional character might assert his unworthiness to even be a priest and, from there, the lack of efficacy of the spiritual works he performs. A counter to that argument would be that in spite of his sins, the "whiskey priest" accomplished much good, and that his works were both valid and efficacious even though he himself lacked the qualities he was expected to possess as a spiritual servant and exemplar.

Red Herring

Introducing a **red herring** into an argument directs it toward irrelevant matters. It directs attention away from the central issue.

> Officer, you shouldn't give me a ticket for parking illegally. There's a lot of serious crime being committed in this city tonight, and you should be out there doing something about it.

That serious crime occurs is a red herring here. What's at issue is not other work the officer might do involving more serious crimes, but rather the offense, minor as it might be, that the individual committed by parking illegally.

red herring
A logical fallacy which relies on distraction from the central issue or problem being addressed.

The red herring fallacy takes its name from the use of this smelly smoked fish as a decoy to distract dogs from following the scent of a fox being hunted. In the same way that the dogs were led away from the prey, criminals later used red herrings to deflect dogs from following their scent when being tracked.

Politicians often try to deflect questions by using the red herring fallacy when they want to avoid providing specific answers to a question. In such cases, they tend to redirect the question or attempt to answer another more general question in such a way that they avoid spelling out any specific details about their position.

Straw Man

straw man
A logical fallacy in which an opponent's position is distorted, exaggerated, or otherwise misrepresented in order to make it more vulnerable to attack.

The **straw man** fallacy involves intentionally representing an opposing argument in a distorted and thus weakened manner—the easier to refute it. A straw man is easy to push over. Presenting an opposing argument inaccurately and in weak form is dishonest when deliberate. It is essentially an act of misrepresentation.

> "The government should liberalize the use of marijuana for recreational as well as medicinal purposes."
> "You are advocating the legalization of dangerous drugs."

In this example, the second speaker has grossly exaggerated what the first speaker has suggested.

Straw man arguments are frequently used with topics such as gun control and immigration. After an incident in which someone brings an arsenal of weapons to a school, a post office, or other public building and starts shooting and killing people, debates are ignited over the extent to which guns should be allowed. In response to someone who argues for banning of semiautomatic weapons, an opponent might suggest that the advocate for banning semiautomatic weapons wants to ban all weapons, and he would attack that position. This is an attempt to distort the original position by exaggerating its claim, an argument that is easier to attack.

Straw man arguments often result in both deflecting attention from the issue at hand and in creating confusion over what is at stake in the argument under discussion. It is thus a fallacy of relevance. In addition, the straw man fallacy is one of misrepresentation, and hence a form of dishonesty.

EXERCISE

4. Identify the fallacies in the following statements and arguments.

    a. Everybody goes to Disneyland. Why haven't you gone yet?

    b. Ezra Pound's reputation as a poet and man of letters is overrated. He was an anti-Semite, and he sympathized with the fascists. He was even put in a hospital for the insane.

    c. It is only a matter of time before there is another world war. Natural resources are diminishing—especially oil and water—and the population is increasing. War is inevitable over these rapidly diminishing resources.

    d. You have no right to demand that public servants live in the districts they serve. You yourself have houses in two states and in another country.

    e. If Freud's theory is right, we will never understand our actions and behavior. So much of what we do is based on the unconscious.

f. Students at Stuyvesant High School and Harvard University, when caught cheating on exams, explained that everyone does it, and they would be at a disadvantage if they hadn't.

g. I am the president of this university, and I insist you teach German literary theory and not French theory. The French theorists are passé.

h. He was under pressure on the witness stand; surely, you can understand why he stretched the truth.

Fallacies of Language

Arguments can also fail because of misuses of and mistakes in using language. Two common language problems that create failure in arguments are *vagueness and ambiguity*. We consider, in addition, the following fallacies resulting from unclear or confused language: *equivocation, composition*, and *division*. First, however, let's consider the problem of vagueness and ambiguity.

Vagueness and Ambiguity

Vagueness results from lack of clarity; it also results from excessively abstract and general language. The solution to vagueness is specificity—providing particular details, examples, facts, and other forms of concrete, specific language. Vagueness, however, is sometimes a conscious choice of writers and speakers, particularly when they do not want to commit themselves to specifics. Politicians campaigning for office frequently resort to vague statements and bland generalities so as not to alienate any particular niche of voters—women, for example, or Catholics, or libertarians. In the 2012 presidential campaign, Mitt Romney was accused of vagueness in not revealing details about his plans to reduce health care costs without raising taxes, yet not cancel popular aspects of national health policy. Politicians are fond of making broad statements about how they have a "comprehensive plan" that includes "a wide range of solutions" to "problems of long-standing." When asked to provide specific details, they blather on in the same kind of vague and general language.

Another domain in which specific details and language is not always forthcoming is medicine. When doctors are asked about the outcome of a surgical procedure—for example, a hip or knee replacement—they sometimes hide the potential risks and dangers behind vague language, such as "Well, the outcomes of this procedure are generally very positive; we get good results with consistency from this surgery; and it is something that the patient needs." In answer to queries about data and statistics and rates of infection, rates of success, specific kinds of recuperative complications and time frames, answers can be exceedingly vague, such as "Every patient is different. There is really no way to tell for sure just what degree of pain, complication, and recuperative process will occur. We'll just have to wait and see. But rest assured that we will do everything possible to ensure a quality outcome." Instead of such vague and bland generalities, we need data, specific facts about outcomes.

Ambiguity is a specific type of lack of clarity; instead of vagueness, ambiguity offers two or more meanings of a word or phrase. For example, if you say that you will "give someone a ring," does that mean you will call him or her on the phone or give her a piece of jewelry? For an example of an ambiguous phrase: "I cannot recommend this person too highly." Does this mean that you wish to recommend the individual very highly and no language you might use can convey just how much you favor his or her candidacy? Or does it mean that you can't and don't want to recommend the person highly at all?

vagueness
In argument, a lack of clarity about what is being claimed or how evidence supports a claim.

ambiguity
Inexactness of meaning; the use of language to mean two different things simultaneously.

Jay Leno, the late night talk host, with the help of some others, compiled a set of ambiguous newspaper headlines. Here are a few of these headlines. See if you can explain their two-sided meanings.

"Drought Turns Coyotes to Watermelons."

"Red Tape Holds Up New Bridges."

"Police Begin Campaign to Run Down Jaywalkers."

These comic examples suggest that someone was not paying close attention to the writing of these headlines.

Ambiguity is not always a problem. Some types of ambiguity are unavoidable, even desirable. Poets frequently employ language in deliberately ambiguous ways, complicating a poem with ambiguity intentionally to enrich and multiply what it means and signifies. Here are a few lines from a seventeenth-century poem that contain double meanings in the form of riddles—a common use of ambiguous language:

I saw a peacock with a fiery tail.
I saw a blazing comet drop down hail.
I saw a cloud with ivy circled round.
I saw a sturdy oak creep on the ground.

A further complication with ambiguity occurs with cross-cultural communication. For example, if an Englishman says that he knocked someone up last night, he means that he called them on the phone. In American English, however, to "knock someone up" means to get her pregnant.

Equivocation

equivocation
Using a word in two different senses to make a claim look more plausible than it is.

Equivocation occurs when a word is used in two different senses. Using equivocal language—using a word with multiple meanings, in different senses—can make a claim look more plausible than it is.

This is the right thing to do in this case. And I have the right to make my own decision in the matter.

The word *right* is used to mean "proper" in the first instance and "freedom and duty" in the next. This kind of verbal equivocation introduces confusion rather than clarity into thinking.

Here is a humorous example:

A judge once said to a husband involved in a divorce case. "Mr. Smith, I have reviewed your case carefully, and have decided to give your wife $3,500 per month. "That's very generous of you," Mr. Smith responds. "I will consider what I might be able to add to the monthly allowance you are so generously providing for her."

In this example, the judge uses the word *give* in the sense of "award." The husband, on the other hand, takes the judge's "give" literally, as if he will provide the monthly dollars himself personally.

Composition and Division

The fallacy of composition involves mistaking the part for the whole, such that as each part has a certain property, then the whole or the group possesses that same property.

For example:

Each player for the New York Giants football team is excellent at his offensive or defensive position. Therefore, the New York Giants are an excellent team and should win the Super Bowl Championship game.

This sounds like a reasonable argument; after all, we might think, excellent players are needed for a winning team. But a team is a different entity, more than a mere sum of its players.

Here is another example:

> Each part of a building consumes a small amount of energy. Therefore, the building as a whole consumes little energy.

This, of course, is patently absurd. Logically, we should add the amounts of energy consumed by each part. In fact the total amount of energy consumed might be quite large. On the other hand, in relation to other buildings, it might indeed be the case that a building that has many small energy-consuming sections might indeed, in comparison with other buildings, consume less. But that needs to be determined. It is simply not the case that because each part of a whole consumes a little, then the whole consumes a little, too.

The fallacy of *division* is the opposite of the fallacy of composition. The mistake of this fallacy involves assuming that what pertains to the whole must pertain to its parts. A property or aspect of the whole, however, is not necessarily ascribed to each of its parts.

For example:

> The New York Mets of 1969 and 1986 were each a special team that bonded together and played as a unit. They were World Champions. Therefore, each member of those New York Mets teams was a special individual, who excelled at his individual position; each was among the best at his position in the entire major leagues.

As with the fallacy of composition, the logic here does not contain premises that support the conclusion. Many Mets players, in fact, were not among the best at their individual positions (though some were among the best). What was special about those teams transcended the performance statistics of each individual player. On these teams, the whole was, as we say, "more than the sum of its parts."

EXERCISES

5. Identify the fallacies in the following arguments.

   a. In a *Seinfeld* episode the character George Costanza reasoned that because he enjoyed watching baseball, eating sandwiches, and having sex with a woman, he should try to do them simultaneously.

   b. The population of the borough of Queens, NY, represents more than 75 world languages. Therefore, the population of Queens represents the world.

   c. My cousin Cheryl is a vegetarian; her brother John is a couch potato. They must have a lot in common because they have a vegetable connection.

   d. Middle-aged men are career minded generally. Michael is middle aged, and so he is career minded.

   e. Donors to the Metropolitan Museum of Art are wealthy socialites. My brother's neighbor donated to the museum, so he must be wealthy.

   f. When you come to a fork in the road, take it. (Courtesy of Yogi Berra.)

6. Identify the fallacies of reasoning in the following arguments. Explain what, if anything, is wrong or illogical.

   a. If we don't do something about the problem of overpopulation soon, the planet simply will be unable to accommodate the spiraling increase in people.

   b. Those who are ignorant of the past are condemned to repeat it.

c. He is the best senatorial candidate: He is tall and imposing, an eloquent speaker, and eminently sociable.

d. Something terrible must have happened. They would have called by now.

e. Joanne's intelligence is her outstanding quality. But I'm afraid her good looks will prevent people from appreciating her intellectual ability.

f. People are not really free. Their lives are determined by forces beyond their control.

g. If you don't buy this car today, it won't be here tomorrow. And prices are likely to increase next week.

h. We should not allow 15-year-old children to work for pay. Soon kids as young as 5 or 6 will be doing it.

i. I haven't received responses from half the student body about our plan to hold a bonfire on Saturday night on the football field. So I believe I can count on their support for the event.

j. We should all take part in the state lottery; it's our civic duty to support state initiatives.

Looking Back and Looking Ahead

Revisit the learning goals that begin this chapter. Which of these goals do you think you have best achieved? What might you do to reach the remaining goals?

Return to the focusing questions at the beginning of the chapter. How would you answer those questions now? Which of them do you find most interesting and provocative and worthy of following up? Why?

In reviewing the list of resources that follows, identify the two that attract you most. Explain why these books or Web sites interest you. Consider looking into them for further deepening your understanding of careful and error-free reasoning.

Take a look, too, at the MyThinkingLab resources on the Prentice Hall Web site. Included there are readings, images, videos, questions, exercises, and other provocations to help you develop your critical thinking ability.

Resources

Good Arguments, 4th ed., Connie Missimer. Prentice Hall, 2008.

Attacking Faulty Reasoning, 6th ed., T. Edward Damer. Wadsworth, 2008.

How to Think Logically, 2nd ed., Gary Seay and Susana Nuccetelli. Prentice Hall, 2011.

Thinking, 4th ed., Gary Kirby and Jeffery R. Goodpaster. Prentice Hall, 2006.

Becoming a Critical Thinker, 6th ed., Sherry Diestler. Pearson, 2012.

The Art of Clear Thinking, Rolf Dobelli. Harper, 2013.

The Little Blue Reasoning Book, Brandon Royal. Maven Publishing, 2010.

The Philosopher's Toolkit, Julian Baggini and Peter S. Fosl. Wiley-Blackwell, 2010.

Do You Think What You Think You Think? Julian Baggini and Jeremy Strangroom, Penguin/Plume, 2007.

8

Analyzing and Constructing Arguments

The aim of argument should not be victory but progress.

—JOSEPH JOUBERT

LEARNING GOALS

8.1 ANALYZE the structure of arguments, including their claims and supporting evidence.

8.2 RECOGNIZE and examine the use of *logos*, *pathos*, and *ethos* in arguments.

8.3 UNDERSTAND how to construct and develop an argument with a consideration of purpose and audience.

8.4 RECOGNIZE the need for concession, qualification, and rebuttal in constructing arguments.

8.5 IDENTIFY and analyze the parts of a classical oration and their relationship to the analysis and construction of arguments.

FOCUSING QUESTIONS

- How might learning how to analyze and understand arguments help you with your academic and professional work?

- What makes an argument persuasive? What aspects of an argument, whether spoken or written, make it convincing for you?

- How might you go about establishing credibility for an argument? How might you go about refuting aspects of an argument you disagree with?

- Why should you improve your ability to construct persuasive arguments?

Chapter Overview

This chapter focuses on rhetorical rather than logical aspects of argument. It provides a series of explanations concerning (1) argument strategies, including *logos*, *pathos*, and *ethos*; (2) the analysis of arguments; (3) the construction of arguments; (4) audience and purpose; (5) objection and concession; (6) argument as conversation; (7) Martin Luther King, Jr.'s "Letter from Birmingham Jail"; (8) the classical oration and Rogerian argument. The purpose of this chapter is to enhance your ability to understand, evaluate, and construct arguments. It is important for understanding how and why arguments are persuasive—or not, because argument and persuasive thinking pervade our lives.

Analyzing Arguments

When we analyze an argument, we take into account the claims it makes and how it supports those claims with evidence. We try to identify the writer or speaker's assumptions. Other considerations include how effectively the argument may use causal analysis or analogy, how well selected and developed are its examples, along with other strategies employed by the writer or speaker to win over the audience.

Let's consider a few examples. We begin with an excerpt from an essay by Mark Twain, "Corn-Pone Opinions."

> I am persuaded that a coldly-thought-out and independent verdict upon a fashion in clothes, or manners, or literature, or politics, or religion, or any other matter that is projected into the field of our interest is a most rare thing—if it has indeed ever existed.
>
> A new thing in costume appears—the flaring hoopskirt, for example—and the passers-by are shocked, and the irreverent laugh. Six months later everybody is reconciled; the fashion has established itself; it is admired now and no one laughs. Public opinion resented it before; public opinion accepts it now and is happy in it. Why? Was the resentment reasoned out? Was the acceptance reasoned out? No. The instinct that moves to conformity did the work. It is our nature to conform; it is a force which not many can successfully resist. What is its seat? The inborn requirement of self-approval. We all have to bow to that; there are no exceptions. Even the woman who refuses from first to last to wear the hoopskirt comes under that law and is its slave; she would not wear the skirt and have her own approval, and that she *must* have, she cannot help herself. But as a rule our self-approval has its source in but one place and not elsewhere—the approval of other people. A person of vast consequences can introduce any kind of novelty in dress and the general world will presently adopt it—moved to do it in the first place by the natural instinct to passively yield to that vague something recognized as authority, and in the second place by the human instinct to train with the multitude and have its approval.

Analysis of Twain's Corn-Pone Opinions

The claim of this passage—its central idea—is stated in the first sentence. The words *a coldly-thought-out and independent verdict* suggest a person who knows and expresses his own views, irrespective of the views of other people. That kind of independent thinking, says Twain, is rare. That's his claim. The remainder of the passage provides supporting evidence in the form of examples, largely from the world of women's fashion, although Twain later extends his argument to religion and politics, suggesting that those domains are also influenced by fashions of thought and belief.

Those clothing examples, of course, are just that—illustrations of Twain's claim about the power of fashion more broadly in our lives. But his argument needs firmer support than mere illustration. This Twain provides with a bit of analysis, a psychological explanation about why we follow fashion and the opinions of the majority rather than thinking for ourselves. This, Twain suggests, is because in addition to our own approval, we crave the approval of others. In fact, he suggests that the approval of others supersedes our own. Twain attributes this need and this craving to the "natural instinct" to yield to authority and the "human instinct" to follow the multitude and "seek its approval." We tend to conform to what others do. We cede to them our autonomy.

EXERCISES

1. How persuasive do you find the argument of "Corn-Pone Opinions?" Why? What additional evidence might you bring to further support it? What evidence might undermine Twain's argument?

2. How does the following passage from another part of Twain's essay support the central claim he makes in the first and longer excerpt?

> A man is not independent and cannot afford views which might interfere with his bread and butter. If he would prosper, he must train with the majority; in matters of large moment, like politics and religion, he must think and feel with the bulk of his neighbors or suffer damage in his social standing and in his business prosperities. He must restrict himself to corn-pone opinions—at least on the surface. He must get his opinions from other people, he must reason out none for himself, he must have no first-hand views.

To what extent does the claim in this excerpt extend or deepen Twain's previously articulated claim? What kind of supporting evidence for the claim does this second passage provide? To what extent are you persuaded by it?

Argument and Rebuttal—Melville's "The Advocate"

When we engage in argument, one thing we must often do is to rebut or counter another's challenge to our own argument. One consideration in analyzing an argument is to see how the writer or speaker anticipates counterviews and responds to them in an attempt to dismiss them as unfounded, irrelevant, or otherwise unwarranted. In the following excerpt from "The Advocate," a chapter from *Moby-Dick*, Herman Melville employs this argumentative strategy in a defense of the whaling industry.

As you read the passage, note how it is structured as a set of challenges and rebuttals of those challenges. Notice the way the speaker responds to each of these challenges, beginning with a repetition of key words and phrases of the various criticisms of whaling.

From "The Advocate"

The whale has no famous author, and whaling no famous chronicler, you will say.

The whale has no famous author, and whaling no famous chronicler? Who wrote the first account of our Leviathan? Who but mighty Job! And who composed the first narrative of a whaling voyage? Who, but no less a prince than Alfred the Great, who with his own royal pen, took down the words from Other, the Norwegian whale-hunter of those times! And who pronounced our glowing eulogy in Parliament? Who, but Edmund Burke!

True enough, but then whalemen themselves are poor devils; they have no good blood in their veins.

No good blood in their veins? They have something better than royal blood there. The grandmother of Benjamin Franklin was Mary Morrel, afterwards, by marriage, Mary Folger, one of the old settlers of Nantucket, and the ancestress to a long line of Folgers and harpooners—all kith and kin to noble Benjamin—this day darting the barbed iron from one side of the world to the other.

Good again; but then all confess that somehow whaling is not respectable.

Whaling not respectable? Whaling is imperial! By old English statutory law, the whale is declared "a royal fish."

FIGURE 8.1 Constellation Cetus

Oh, that's only nominal! The whale himself has never figured in any grand imposing way.

The whale never figured in any grand imposing way? In one of the mighty triumphs given to a Roman general upon his entering the world's capital, the bones of a whale, brought all the way from the Syrian coast, were the most conspicuous object in the cymballed procession.

Grant it, since you cite it; but, say what you will, there is no real dignity in whaling.

No dignity in whaling? The dignity of our calling the very heavens attest. Cetus is a constellation in the South! No more! Drive down your hat in presence of the Czar, and take it off to Queequeg! No more! I know a man that, in his lifetime, has taken three hundred and fifty whales. I account that man more honorable than that great captain of antiquity who boasted of taking as many walled towns.

EXERCISES

3. How would you characterize the tone of the speaker/writer as he repeats the various italicized criticisms of whaling? How do you hear these criticisms? And how would you characterize the tone of his response to each criticism? Why does Melville italicize certain portions of the text? With what effect? How does Melville's use of punctuation and question-and-answer help you "hear" these varied tones of voice in the passage? To what extent do you think the writer/speaker rebuts or refutes the challenges and criticisms brought against whaling as a profession? Are you persuaded by him? Why or why not?

4. Whaling has come under critical scrutiny in modern times for different reasons than those cited by the antiadvocate of whaling, whose views we hear in the excerpted passage. What are these more recent criticisms of whaling, and how do you think Melville, one of whaling's greatest advocates, might have responded to them?

Logic and Rhetoric

In developing an argument, we make use of logic, reasoning carefully with plausible claims and providing strong evidence to support them. We avoid logical fallacies, or errors in inductive and deductive thinking. Our use of logic in argument is grounded in a rational, intellectual approach to an issue or subject.

Complementing the use of logic is **rhetoric**, usually defined as "the art of persuasion." Rhetoric includes logical reasoning, but it goes beyond logic in allowing for appeals to emotion and fellow feeling. And it is also grounded in establishing trust and credibility with an audience.

Rhetoric is both a field of knowledge—an academic subject—like **logic**, and also a practical skill. In Greek, such a skill is referred to as a *techne*, a word related to *technical* and *technique*. Rhetorical skill is skill in getting an audience to agree with us and perhaps to act on what we have persuaded them to consider. In ancient Rome, rhetoricians such as Cicero and Quintilian suggested that rhetoric is concerned with three goals: to teach (*docere*), to move (*movere*), and to delight (*delectare*).

Rhetoric is thus related to logical thinking and reasoning. But it differs in its emphasis on the play of language and on the uses of language (rather than logic) to persuade, move, and delight. Rhetoric entices with appeals to the ear as well as the mind. Rhetoric cares about eloquence, how a thing is said along with what is being said.

Logic has a more academic feeling and flavor. Rhetoric is a more mundane matter. We see and hear it in our courts as prosecutors and defenders make their cases. It appears in our political campaigns as opposing candidates seek to belittle each other's ideas while enhancing their own.

We live in a rhetorical world, one saturated in persuasion. Football coaches use rhetoric in the locker room at halftime to inspire their teams to play their best. Military leaders urge their troops into battle with passionate speeches. Advertisers employ rhetorical maneuvers to persuade us to purchase their products. Parents cajole and sweet talk their children to eat their dinner, do their, homework, and behave themselves. Lovers use rhetoric to seduce and persuade their beloved to all manner of things.

Logos, Ethos, Pathos

Three terms derived from Aristotle highlight different aspects of argument: *logos*, *ethos*, and *pathos*. **Logos** refers strictly to the logical relationships within the parts of an argument. With logos you make a reasoned case; you sound reasonable. **Ethos** refers to the character of the person making the argument. Via ethos, you establish your credibility; you sound sincere. **Pathos** refers to an appeal to feeling in the audience being persuaded. By means of pathos, you evoke the emotions of your audience; you warm their hearts.

Let's take these up briefly in reverse order.

Pathos is sometimes considered unacceptable in argumentation, which, some people claim, should resist attempts to persuade by appeals to emotion, by tugging at the heartstrings. Pathos, however, has long been considered an essential element of persuasive rhetoric (the classical art of persuasion), because it reinforces the logical arguments of logos and the credibility of the speaker (ethos) making the argument. Pathos rouses an audience to assent, making acceptance of the argument not merely an intellectual matter but a matter of passionate feeling as well. The goal under this rhetorical aspect is to secure the emotional assent of the audience.

Watch the **Video,**
Logic and Rhetoric
MyThinkingLab

rhetoric
The use of language and images for the purpose of persuasion. The art of persuasion.

logic
A branch of philosophy that emphasizes reasoned judgment.

logos
An aspect of rhetoric that involves logic and reasoning for the purpose of persuasion.

ethos
In rhetoric, establishing a speaker or writer's credibility or trustworthiness.

pathos
An aspect of rhetoric that relies on an appeal to feeling or emotion rather than to reason and logic.

Ethos literally means "character," in ancient Greek, and is the source of our English word *ethics*, which is derived from the Greek *ethikos*, meaning "moral." The root of *ethikos* is *ethos*. In *Rhetoric*, Aristotle suggests that ethos must be present from the start of an argument, with the speaker or writer demonstrating expertise, knowledge, and moral character. To some extent, ethos is determined by the audience, as it is the audience that makes a judgment about the credibility, knowledge, authority, and moral character of the speaker or writer making the argument. Our job as speakers and writers is to convey that we are worthy of trust and that we speak and write in good faith.

Logos, means "word," "speech," "reason," "account," "plea,"—and more, in Greek. In Aristotle's *Rhetoric*, *logos* refers to arguments from reason, or logical arguments, with an emphasis on logical relationships within the parts of an argument. Aristotle placed logos above pathos and ethos as components of an argument, though allowing an important place for each in argumentative discourse, whether oral or written.

In terms of logos our job is to convince by appealing to the intellectual attributes of the audience. We need to reason in such a way that they can only agree with the evidence presented to support our claim logically and reasonably.

EXERCISE

5. Watch a televised political debate, or view a replay on the Internet. Analyze the dialogue between and among the debaters in terms of its adherence to principles of logic. Identify places in the debate when the debaters employ logos, pathos, and ethos. And evaluate their effectiveness.

Argument and Eloquence—Martin Luther King, Jr.'s "Letter from Birmingham Jail"

One of the most eloquent arguments penned in the twentieth century, or, indeed, any century, is the argument in defense of his actions made by the Reverend Martin Luther King, Jr., in his "Letter from Birmingham Jail." In this Letter, Dr. King responded to a group of Southern clergymen who criticized him for the demonstrations King and the Southern Christian Leadership Conference were responsible for, particularly the demonstrations against segregation that King's group mounted in Birmingham, Alabama, in 1965.

Here is how King begins his letter:

My Dear Fellow Clergymen:

While confined here in the Birmingham city jail, I came across your recent statement calling my present activities "unwise and untimely."

1   Seldom do I pause to answer criticism of my work and ideas. If I sought to answer all the criticisms that cross my desk, my secretaries would have little time for anything other than such correspondence in the course of the day, and I would have no time for constructive work. But since I feel that you are men of genuine good will and that your criticisms are sincerely set forth, I want to try to answer your statement in what I hope will be patient and reasonable terms.

2   I think I should indicate why I am here in Birmingham, since you have been influenced by the view which argues against "outsiders coming in." I have the honor of serving as president of the Southern Christian Leadership Conference, an organization operating in every southern state, with headquarters in Atlanta, Georgia. We have some eighty-five affiliated organizations across the South, and one of them is the Alabama Christian Movement for Human Rights. Frequently we share staff, educational, and financial resources with our affiliates. Several months ago the affiliate here in Birmingham asked us to be on call to engage in a nonviolent direct-action program if such were deemed necessary. We readily consented, and when the hour came we lived up to our promise. So I, along with several members of my staff, am here because I was invited here. I am here because I have organizational ties here.

3   But more basically, I am in Birmingham because injustice is here. Just as the prophets of the eighth century B.C. left their villages and carried their "thus saith the Lord" far beyond the boundaries of their home towns, and just as the Apostle Paul left his village of Tarsus and carried the gospel of Jesus Christ to the far corners of the Greco-Roman world, so am I compelled to carry the gospel of freedom beyond my own home town. Like Paul, I must constantly respond to the Macedonian call for aid.

4   Moreover, I am cognizant of the interrelatedness of all communities and states. I cannot sit idly by in Atlanta and not be concerned about what happens in Birmingham. Injustice anywhere is a threat to justice everywhere. We are caught in an inescapable network of mutuality, tied in a single garment of destiny. Whatever affects one directly, affects all indirectly. Never again can we afford to live with the narrow, provincial "outside agitator" idea. Anyone who lives inside the United States can never be considered an outsider anywhere within its bounds.

King's Letter, the Opening—Ethos and Logos

In his opening paragraph, King refers to the first of the criticisms leveled against him—that his nonviolent protest action is "unwise and untimely." He will answer these criticisms later in his letter; first, however, he establishes rapport with his accusers by calling them "men of genuine good will" who set forth their objections with sincerity. King also presents himself as a "patient" and "reasonable" man, who will take the time and make the effort to explain in some detail why the group of ministers criticizing him is wrong. In this opening paragraph, King establishes an "ethos" for himself.

In his second paragraph, King cites another of the ministers' criticisms by quoting a phrase they use about "outsiders coming in," thereby accusing King of being an "outsider" who doesn't belong in Birmingham. King corrects this characterization, explaining that he came to Birmingham because he was "invited" there. But even more importantly, he explains that his organization has a branch in Alabama, a branch responsible for human rights. And so, King has, as he says, "organizational ties" in Alabama, including ties to the city of Birmingham. Given these two premises, or statements that King makes, the logical conclusion of his implied syllogism is that he has a right—even an obligation to be in Birmingham. In this paragraph, King employs "logos," the logical relationship among premises to substantiate his claim. In addition, he continues to develop his "ethos" as a responsive and responsible leader of an organization dedicated to human rights and the eradication of the inequalities perpetuated by racial segregation, something his audience could both understand and appreciate.

EXERCISES

6. Identify the kinds of argumentative strategies King uses in paragraphs 3 and 4. How is the third paragraph a further development of the argument made in the second? Who does King reference in the third paragraph and why? Why are those people particularly important, given what is at stake in King's argument and given the audience of clergymen he is responding to?

7. How does the criticism of King as an "outside agitator" in paragraph 4 and his response to that criticism connect with his argument in the second paragraph? How does King continue to develop his stance and his presentation of himself (his "ethos," or character)? What statements might be identified as his major and minor premises in this paragraph—and what conclusion is thus implied from those premises?

5   You deplore the demonstrations taking place in Birmingham. But your statement, I am sorry to say, fails to express a similar concern for the conditions that brought about the demonstrations. I am sure that none of you would want to rest content with the superficial kind of social analysis that deals merely with effects and does not grapple with underlying causes. It is unfortunate that demonstrations are taking place in Birmingham, but it is even more unfortunate that the city's white power structure left the Negro community with no alternative.

King's Letter—Causes and Effects

In the fifth paragraph, King shifts his focus slightly. Notice how he introduces the question of causes and effects. King deflects attention from the demonstrations occurring in Birmingham—the consequences or effects—and toward what he calls "the underlying causes" that led up to those demonstrations. He opens up the dialogue and debate over his group's tactics to consider how things got to be so bad that nonviolent protest action became necessary. King also turns the tables on his accusers in this paragraph, suggesting that "the city's white power structure" is ultimately responsible. Why and how, King will explain in detail in paragraphs 6 to 9, and then further in another burst of additional detail in paragraphs 10 to 12.

6   In any nonviolent campaign there are four basic steps: collection of the facts to determine whether injustices exist; negotiation; self-purification; and direct action. We have gone through all these steps in Birmingham. There can be no gainsaying the fact that racial injustice engulfs this community. Birmingham is probably the most thoroughly segregated city in the United States. Its ugly record of brutality is widely known. Negroes have experienced grossly unjust treatment in the courts. There have been more unsolved bombings of Negro homes and churches in Birmingham than in any other city in the nation. These are the hard, brutal facts of the case. On the basis of these conditions, Negro leaders sought to negotiate with the city fathers. But the latter consistently refused to engage in good-faith negotiation.

7   Then, last September, came the opportunity to talk with leaders of Birmingham's economic community. In the course of the negotiations, certain promises were made by the merchants—for example, to remove the stores' humiliating racial signs. On the basis of these promises, the Reverend Fred Shuttlesworth and the leaders of the Alabama Christian Movement for Human Rights agreed to a moratorium on all

demonstrations. As the weeks and months went by, we realized that we were the victims of a broken promise. A few signs, briefly removed, returned; the others remained.

8   As in so many past experiences, our hopes had been blasted, and the shadow of deep disappointment settled upon us. We had no alternative except to prepare for direct action, whereby we would present our very bodies as a means of laying our case before the conscience of the local and the national community. Mindful of the difficulties involved, we decided to undertake a process of self-purification. We began a series of workshops on nonviolence, and we repeatedly asked ourselves: "Are you able to accept blows without retaliating?" "Are you able to endure the ordeal of jail?" We decided to schedule our direct-action program for the Easter season, realizing that except for Christmas, this is the main shopping period of the year. Knowing that a strong economic-withdrawal program would be the by-product of direct action, we felt that this would be the best time to bring pressure to bear on the merchants for the needed change.

9   Then it occurred to us that Birmingham's mayoral election was coming up in March, and we speedily decided to postpone action until after election day. When we discovered that the Commissioner of Public Safety, Eugene "Bull" Connor, had piled up enough votes to be in the run-off, we decided again to postpone action until the day after the run-off so that the demonstrations could not be used to cloud the issues. Like many others, we wanted to see Mr. Connor defeated, and to this end we endured postponement after postponement. Having aided in this community need, we felt that our direct-action program could be delayed no longer.

EXERCISE

8. Read paragraphs 10 to 12, and explain how King argues for the necessity of the demonstrations. What evidence does he provide to support his claim that those demonstrations were necessary? What else does King do in those paragraphs besides justifying the need for the demonstrations? What else do we learn from these paragraphs about King's methods? Why do you think he includes that instructive information? What is its purpose as part of his argument? And what tone does King take as he explains the four aspects of his program of nonviolent resistance?

Notice, too, how at the end of this paragraph King introduces imagery of light and darkness, and of high and low, images that he will develop later, in the second half of the letter.

10   You may well ask, "Why direct action? Why sit-ins, marches, and so forth? Isn't negotiation a better path?" You are quite right in calling for negotiation. Indeed, this is the very purpose of direct action. Nonviolent direct action seeks to create such a crisis and foster such a tension that a community which has constantly refused to negotiate is forced to confront the issue. It seeks so to dramatize the issue that it can no longer be ignored. My citing the creation of tension as part of the work of the nonviolent-resister may sound rather shocking. But I must confess that I am not afraid of the word "tension." I have earnestly opposed violent tension, but there is a type of constructive, nonviolent tension which is necessary for growth. Just as Socrates felt that it was necessary to create a tension in the mind so that individuals could rise from the bondage of myths and half-truths to the unfettered realm of creative analysis and objective appraisal, so must we see the need for nonviolent gadflies to create the kind of tension in society that will help men rise from the dark depths of prejudice and racism to the majestic heights of understanding and brotherhood.

11   The purpose of our direct-action program is to create a situation so crisis-packed that it will inevitably open the door to negotiation. I therefore concur with you in your call for negotiation. Too long has our beloved Southland been bogged down in a tragic effort to live in monologue rather than dialogue.

12   One of the basic points in your statement is that the action that I and my associates have taken in Birmingham is untimely. Some have asked: "Why didn't you give the new city administration time to act?" The only answer that I can give to this query is that the new Birmingham administration must be prodded about as much as the outgoing one, before it will act. We are sadly mistaken if we feel that the election of Albert Boutwell as mayor will bring the millennium to Birmingham. While Mr. Boutwell is a much more gentle person than Mr. Connor, they are both segregationists, dedicated to maintenance of the status quo. I have hoped that Mr. Boutwell will be reasonable enough to see the futility of massive resistance to desegregation. But he will not see this without pressure from devotees of civil rights. My friends, I must say to you that we have not made a single gain in civil rights without determined legal and nonviolent pressure. Lamentably, it is an historical fact that privileged groups seldom give up their privileges voluntarily. Individuals may see the moral light and voluntarily give up their unjust posture, but, as Reinhold Niebuhr has reminded us, groups tend to be more immoral than individuals.

EXERCISE

9. Explain how paragraph 13 functions as a transition between what King has been doing in paragraphs 1 to 12 and especially in paragraphs 6 to 12—and what he presents in paragraph 14.

13   We know through painful experience that freedom is never voluntarily given by the oppressor; it must be demanded by the oppressed. Frankly, I have yet to engage in a direct-action campaign that was "well timed" in the view of those who have not suffered unduly from the disease of segregation. For years now I have heard the word "Wait!" It rings in the ear of every Negro with piercing familiarity. This "Wait" has almost always meant "Never." We must come to see, with one of our distinguished jurists, that "justice too long delayed is justice denied."

King's Letter—Pathos

Paragraph 14 is one of the most powerful in the essay. In this long paragraph (the longest in the letter by far), King explains why the advice of the ministers to "wait" for things to get better is untenable. He links this long paragraph to the transitional paragraph 13, with its equating of "Wait" with "Never." But the real power of the paragraph derives from the specific details King brings forward, particular examples that accumulate with increasing intensity and force in an extremely long sentence that begins "When you have seen," and ends hundreds of words later with "—then you will understand why we find it difficult to wait." King follows that long sentence with two shorter ones. The next-to-last sentence employs a famous biblical image. This sentence, coupled with the paragraph's short final sentence, provides a powerful conclusion for the amassed details about the racial prejudice experienced by King's innocent children.

14   We have waited for more than 340 years for our constitutional and God-given rights. The nations of Asia and Africa are moving with jet-like speed toward gaining political independence, but we still creep at horse-and-buggy pace toward gaining a cup of coffee at a lunch counter. Perhaps it is easy for those who have never felt the

stinging darts of segregation to say, "Wait." But when you have seen vicious mobs lynch your mothers and fathers at will and drown your sisters and brothers at whim; when you have seen hate-filled policemen curse, kick, and even kill your black brothers and sisters; when you see the vast majority of your 20 million Negro brothers smothering in an airtight cage of poverty in the midst of an affluent society; when you suddenly find your tongue twisted and your speech stammering as you seek to explain to your six-year-old daughter why she can't go to the public amusement park that has just been advertised on television, and see tears welling up in her eyes when she is told that Funtown is closed to colored children, and see ominous clouds of inferiority beginning to form in her little mental sky, and see her beginning to distort her personality by developing an unconscious bitterness toward white people; when you have to concoct an answer for a five-year-old son who is asking, "Daddy, why do white people treat colored people so mean?"; when you take a cross-country drive and find it necessary to sleep night after night in the uncomfortable corners of your automobile because no motel will accept you; when you are humiliated day in and day out by nagging signs reading "white" and "colored"; when your first name becomes "nigger," your middle name becomes "boy" (however old you are) and your last name becomes "John," and your wife and mother are never given the respected title "Mrs."; when you are harried by day and haunted by night by the fact that you are a Negro, living constantly at tiptoe stance, never quite knowing what to expect next, and are plagued with inner fears and outer resentments; when you are forever fighting a degenerating sense of "nobodiness"—then you will understand why we find it difficult to wait. There comes a time when the cup of endurance runs over, and men are no longer willing to be plunged into the abyss of despair. I hope, sirs, you can understand our legitimate and unavoidable impatience.

EXERCISE

10. List the details King includes in that long sentence of specifics—the "When . . . then" sentence. Explain how King uses "pathos" in this sentence to persuade his audience that waiting is no longer a viable option.

King's Letter—Just and Unjust Laws

In paragraphs 15 to 20, King develops yet another idea—the idea that not all laws are just, and the corollary idea that unjust laws need not be obeyed. In fact, King argues that from an ethical and moral standpoint, we have not merely the right, but the obligation to disobey unjust laws. This is an interesting argument. And King makes it clearly and directly. Notice how he formulates the distinction between just and unjust laws by asking and answering questions and by patiently developing his explanation in layers, one section or segment at a time. This is Dr. King functioning as teacher rather than preacher, in something of a professorial manner, as he distinguishes between legal and moral responsibility with respect to just and unjust laws.

15   You express a great deal of anxiety over our willingness to break laws. This is certainly a legitimate concern. Since we so diligently urge people to obey the Supreme Court's decision of 1954 outlawing segregation in the public schools, at first glance it may seem rather paradoxical for us consciously to break laws. One may well ask: "How can you advocate breaking some laws and obeying others?" The answer lies in the fact that there are two types of laws: just and unjust. I would be the first to advocate obeying just laws. One has not only a legal but a moral responsibility to obey just laws. Conversely, one has a moral responsibility to disobey unjust laws. I would agree with St. Augustine that "an unjust law is no law at all."

16   Now, what is the difference between the two? How does one determine whether a law is just or unjust? A just law is a man-made code that squares with the moral law or the law of God. An unjust law is a code that is out of harmony with the moral law. To put it in the terms of St. Thomas Aquinas: An unjust law is a human law that is not rooted in eternal law and natural law. Any law that uplifts human personality is just. Any law that degrades human personality is unjust. All segregation statutes are unjust because segregation distorts the soul and damages the personality. It gives the segregator a false sense of superiority and the segregated a false sense of inferiority. Segregation, to use the terminology of the Jewish philosopher Martin Buber, substitutes an "I-it" relationship for an "I-thou" relationship and ends up relegating persons to the status of things. Hence segregation is not only politically, economically, and sociologically unsound, it is morally wrong and sinful. Paul Tillich has said that sin is separation. Is not segregation an existential expression of man's tragic separation, his awful estrangement, his terrible sinfulness? Thus it is that I can urge men to obey the 1954 decision of the Supreme Court, for it is morally right; and I can urge them to disobey segregation ordinances, for they are morally wrong.

17   Let us consider a more concrete example of just and unjust laws. An unjust law is a code that a numerical or power majority group compels a minority group to obey but does not make binding on itself. This is *difference* made legal. By the same token, a just law is a code that a majority compels a minority to follow and that it is willing to follow itself. This is *sameness* made legal.

18   Let me give another explanation. A law is unjust if it is inflicted on a minority that, as a result of being denied the right to vote, had no part in enacting or devising the law. Who can say that the legislature of Alabama which set up that state's segregation laws was democratically elected? Throughout Alabama all sorts of devious methods are used to prevent Negroes from becoming registered voters, and there are some counties in which, even though Negroes constitute a majority of the population, not a single Negro is registered. Can any law enacted under such circumstances be considered democratically structured?

19   Sometimes a law is just on its face and unjust in its application. For instance, I have been arrested on a charge of parading without a permit. Now, there is nothing wrong in having an ordinance which requires a permit for a parade. But such an ordinance becomes unjust when it is used to maintain segregation and to deny citizens the First-Amendment privilege of peaceful assembly and protest.

20   I hope you are able to see the distinction I am trying to point out. In no sense do I advocate evading or defying the law, as would the rabid segregationist. That would lead to anarchy. One who breaks an unjust law must do so openly, lovingly, and with a willingness to accept the penalty. I submit that an individual who breaks a law that conscience tells him is unjust, and who willingly accepts the penalty of imprisonment in order to arouse the conscience of the community over its injustice, is in reality expressing the highest respect for law.

EXERCISES

11. Why does King cite St. Augustine, St. Thomas Aquinas, Martin Buber, and Paul Tillich in this discussion? How does each of these religious thinkers—all theologians—help King to clarify and deepen his argument? Why do you think King cites theologians from three different religious traditions—Catholic, Jewish, and Protestant? How effectively does King work with these references?

12. How persuasive do you find King's argument about just and unjust laws? How do his examples relating to Birmingham, Alabama, clarify his argument?

Do you see any danger in what King argues in paragraph 20? Is "conscience" the best guide to deciding what laws should be considered "just" or "unjust"; should "conscience" be our guide in deciding to break unjust laws? Why or why not?

King's Letter—Questions and Analogy

Martin Luther King Jr.'s "Letter from Birmingham Jail" continues for an additional thirty paragraphs in which King develops and refines his argument. In those paragraphs, he also challenges and questions a number of additional criticisms made against him by the ministers. In paragraph 25, for example, he uses a series of questions to undermine the criticism that even though the actions of King's protesters are peaceful, they precipitate violence. King uses analogy to question the logic of the ministers' argument. In the process, he cites as exemplars Socrates and Jesus, whose peaceful lives led others to violence, suggesting, thereby, that King and his protestors are in good company—exemplars that the ministers themselves would recognize and value for their moral courage.

21   Of course, there is nothing new about this kind of civil disobedience. It was evidenced sublimely in the refusal of Shadrach, Meshach, and Abednego to obey the laws of Nebuchadnezzar, on the ground that a higher moral law was at stake. It was practiced superbly by the early Christians, who were willing to face hungry lions and the excruciating pain of chopping blocks rather than submit to certain unjust laws of the Roman Empire. To a degree, academic freedom is a reality today because Socrates practiced civil disobedience. In our own nation, the Boston Tea Party represented a massive act of civil disobedience.

22   We should never forget that everything Adolf Hitler did in Germany was "legal" and everything the Hungarian freedom fighters did in Hungary was "illegal." It was "illegal" to aid and comfort a Jew in Hitler's Germany. Even so, I am sure that, had I lived in Germany at the time, I would have aided and comforted my Jewish brothers. If today I lived in a Communist country where certain principles dear to the Christian faith are suppressed, I would openly advocate disobeying that country's anti-religious laws.

23   I must make two honest confessions to you, my Christian and Jewish brothers. First, I must confess that over the past few years I have been gravely disappointed with the white moderate. I have almost reached the regrettable conclusion that the Negro's great stumbling block in his stride toward freedom is not the White Citizen's Counciler or the Ku Klux Klanner, but the white moderate, who is more devoted to "order" than to justice; who prefers a negative peace which is the absence of tension to a positive peace which is the presence of justice; who constantly says, "I agree with you in the goal you seek, but I cannot agree with your methods of direct action"; who paternalistically believes he can set the timetable for another man's freedom; who lives by a mythical concept of time and who constantly advises the Negro to wait for a "more convenient season." Shallow understanding from people of good will is more frustrating than absolute misunderstanding from people of ill will. Lukewarm acceptance is much more bewildering than outright rejection.

24   I had hoped that the white moderate would understand that law and order exist for the purpose of establishing justice and that when they fail in this purpose they become the dangerously structured dams that block the flow of social progress. I had hoped that the white moderate would understand that the present tension in the South is a necessary phase of the transition from an obnoxious negative peace, in which the Negro passively accepted his unjust plight, to a substantive and positive peace, in which all men will respect the dignity and worth of human personality. Actually, we

who engage in nonviolent direct action are not the creators of tension. We merely bring to the surface the hidden tension that is already alive. We bring it out in the open, where it can be seen and dealt with. Like a boil that can never be cured so long as it is covered up but must be opened with all its ugliness to the natural medicines of air and light, injustice must be exposed, with all the tension its exposure creates, to the light of human conscience and the air of national opinion, before it can be cured.

25   In your statement you assert that our actions, even though peaceful, must be condemned because they precipitate violence. But is this a logical assertion? Isn't this like condemning a robbed man because his possession of money precipitated the evil act of robbery? Isn't this like condemning Socrates because his unswerving commitment to truth and his philosophical inquiries precipitated the act by the misguided populace in which they made him drink hemlock? Isn't this like condemning Jesus because his unique God-consciousness and never-ceasing devotion to God's will precipitated the evil act of crucifixion? We must come to see that, as the federal courts have consistently affirmed, it is wrong to urge an individual to cease his efforts to gain his basic constitutional rights because the quest may precipitate violence. Society must protect the robbed and punish the robber.

EXERCISES

13. What is King's purpose in citing biblical references in paragraph 21? What important distinction does King make in paragraph 22? Why does he reference Socrates and also the Boston Tea Party? What do those references have in common in King's mind? And why does King cite Adolf Hitler in paragraph 22 and the Ku Klux Klan in paragraph 23? To what extent do these citations help King clarify his thinking about the "legal" and the "illegal," and their relationship to the "moral" and the "immoral"? To what extent do you find these distinctions useful, important, and persuasive?

14. In paragraph 24, identify how King uses imagery and to what effect.

    For paragraph 25, identify examples of allusions, parallel sentence structure (with antithesis or opposition), repetition, and rhetorical questions. Explain what effect King achieves with each of these rhetorical strategies.

15. Read the remainder of King's letter—paragraphs 26 to 50. Identify additional arguments that King makes to support his claim that the demonstrations in Birmingham were necessary. Identify other strategies King uses to shift attention away from the demonstrators. Why and how does he bring much attention to the Christian churches of the South? What criticisms does King level against Southern Christians and particularly against Southern Christian religious leaders? How would you characterize King's tone in the second half of his letter—paragraphs 26 to 50? To what extent and where do you hear the tone change or shift in these paragraphs? With what effects?

26   I had also hoped that the white moderate would reject the myth concerning time in relation to the struggle for freedom. I have just received a letter from a white brother in Texas. He writes: "All Christians know that the colored people will receive equal rights eventually, but it is possible that you are in too great a religious hurry. It has taken Christianity almost two thousand years to accomplish what it has. The teachings of Christ take time to come to earth." Such an attitude stems from a tragic misconception of time, from the strangely irrational notion that there is something in the very flow of time that will inevitably cure all ills. Actually, time itself is neutral; it can be used either destructively or constructively. More and more I feel that the

people of ill will have used time much more effectively than have the people of good will. We will have to repent in this generation not merely for the hateful words and actions of the bad people, but for the appalling silence of the good people. Human progress never rolls in on wheels of inevitability; it comes through the tireless efforts of men willing to be co-workers with God, and without this hard work, time itself becomes an ally of the forces of social stagnation. We must use time creatively, in the knowledge that the time is always ripe to do right. Now is the time to make real the promise of democracy and transform our pending national elegy into a creative psalm of brotherhood. Now is the time to lift our national policy from the quicksand of racial injustice to the solid rock of human dignity.

27   You speak of our activity in Birmingham as extreme. At first I was rather disappointed that fellow clergymen would see my nonviolent efforts as those of an extremist. I began thinking about the fact that I stand in the middle of two opposing forces in the Negro community. One is a force of complacency, made up in part of Negroes who, as a result of long years of oppression, are so drained of self-respect and a sense of "somebodiness" that they have adjusted to segregation; and in part of a few middle-class Negroes who, because of a degree of academic and economic security and because in some ways they profit by segregation, have become insensitive to the problems of the masses. The other force is one of bitterness and hatred, and it comes perilously close to advocating violence. It is expressed in the various black nationalist groups that are springing up across the nation, the largest and best-known being Elijah Muhammad's Muslim movement. Nourished by the Negro's frustration over the continued existence of racial discrimination, this movement is made up of people who have lost faith in America, who have absolutely repudiated Christianity, and who have concluded that the white man is an incorrigible "devil."

28   I have tried to stand between these two forces, saying that we need emulate neither the "do-nothingism" of the complacent nor the hatred and despair of the black nationalist. For there is the more excellent way of love and nonviolent protest. I am grateful to God that, through the influence of the Negro church, the way of nonviolence became an integral part of our struggle.

29   If this philosophy had not emerged, by now many streets of the South would, I am convinced, be flowing with blood. And I am further convinced that if our white brothers dismiss as "rabblerousers" and "outside agitators" those of us who employ nonviolent direct action, and if they refuse to support our nonviolent efforts, millions of Negroes will, out of frustration and despair, seek solace and security in black-nationalist ideologies—a development that would inevitably lead to a frightening racial nightmare.

30   Oppressed people cannot remain oppressed forever. The yearning for freedom eventually manifests itself, and that is what has happened to the American Negro. Something within has reminded him of his birthright of freedom, and something without has reminded him that it can be gained. Consciously or unconsciously, he has been caught up by the *Zeitgeist,* and with his black brothers of Africa and his brown and yellow brothers of Asia, South America, and the Caribbean, the United States Negro is moving with a sense of great urgency toward the promised land of racial justice. If one recognizes this vital urge that has engulfed the Negro community, one should readily understand why public demonstrations are taking place. The Negro has many pent-up resentments and latent frustrations, and he must release them. So let him march; let him make prayer pilgrimages to the city hall; let him go on freedom rides—and try to understand why he must do so. If his repressed emotions are not released in nonviolent ways, they will seek expression through violence; this is not a threat but a fact of history. So I have not said to my people, "Get rid of your discontent." Rather, I have tried to say that this normal and healthy discontent can be channeled into the creative outlet of nonviolent direct action. And now this approach is being termed extremist.

31   But though I was initially disappointed at being categorized as an extremist, as I continued to think about the matter I gradually gained a measure of satisfaction from the label. Was not Jesus an extremist for love: "Love your enemies, bless them that curse you, do good to them that hate you, and pray for them which despitefully use you and persecute you." Was not Amos an extremist for justice: "Let justice roll down like waters and righteousness like an ever-flowing stream." Was not Paul an extremist for the Christian gospel: "I bear in my body the marks of the Lord Jesus." Was not Martin Luther an extremist: "Here I stand; I cannot do otherwise, so help me God." And John Bunyan: "I will stay in jail to the end of my days before I make a butchery of my conscience." And Abraham Lincoln: "This nation cannot survive half slave and half free." And Thomas Jefferson: "We hold these truths to be self-evident, that all men are created equal. . . ." So the question is not whether we will be extremists, but what kind of extremists we will be. Will we be extremists for hate or for love? Will we be extremists for the preservation of injustice or for the extension of justice? In that dramatic scene on Calvary's hill three men were crucified. We must never forget that all three were crucified for the same crime—the crime of extremism. Two were extremists for immorality, and thus fell below their environment. The other, Jesus Christ, was an extremist for love, truth, and goodness, and thereby rose above his environment. Perhaps the South, the nation, and the world are in dire need of creative extremists.

32   I had hoped that the white moderate would see this need. Perhaps I was too optimistic; perhaps I expected too much. I suppose I should have realized that few members of the oppressor race can understand the deep groans and passionate yearnings of the oppressed race, and still fewer have the vision to see that injustice must be rooted out by strong, persistent, and determined action. I am thankful, however, that some of our white brothers in the South have grasped the meaning of this social revolution and committed themselves to it. They are still all too few in quantity, but they are big in quality. Some—such as Ralph McGill, Lillian Smith, Harry Golden, James McBride Dabbs, Ann Braden, and Sarah Patton Boyle—have written about our struggle in eloquent and prophetic terms. Others have marched with us down nameless streets of the South. They have languished in filthy, roach-infested jails, suffering the abuse and brutality of policemen who view them as "dirty nigger-lovers." Unlike so many of their moderate brothers and sisters, they have recognized the urgency of the moment and sensed the need for powerful "action" antidotes to combat the disease of segregation.

33   Let me take note of my other major disappointment. I have been so greatly disappointed with the white church and its leadership. Of course, there are some notable exceptions. I am not unmindful of the fact that each of you has taken some significant stands on this issue. I commend you, Reverend Stallings, for your Christian stand on this past Sunday, in welcoming Negroes to your worship service on a nonsegregated basis. I commend the Catholic leaders of this state for integrating Spring Hill College several years ago.

34   But despite these notable exceptions, I must honestly reiterate that I have been disappointed with the church. I do not say this as one of those negative critics who can always find something wrong with the church. I say this as a minister of the gospel, who loves the church; who was nurtured in its bosom; who has been sustained by its spiritual blessings and who will remain true to it as long as the cord of life shall lengthen.

35   When I was suddenly catapulted into the leadership of the bus protest in Montgomery, Alabama, a few years ago, I felt we would be supported by the white church. I felt that the white ministers, priests, and rabbis of the South would be among our strongest allies. Instead, some have been outright opponents, refusing to understand the freedom movement and misrepresenting its leaders; all too many others have been more cautious than courageous and have remained silent behind the anesthetizing security of stainedglass windows.

36   In spite of my shattered dreams, I came to Birmingham with the hope that the white religious leadership of this community would see the justice of our cause and, with deep moral concern, would serve as the channel through which our just grievances could reach the power structure. I had hoped that each of you would understand. But again I have been disappointed.

37   I have heard numerous southern religious leaders admonish their worshipers to comply with a desegregation decision because it is the law, but I have longed to hear white ministers declare: "Follow this decree because integration is morally right and because the Negro is your brother." In the midst of blatant injustices inflicted upon the Negro, I have watched white churchmen stand on the sideline and mouth pious irrelevancies and sanctimonious trivialities. In the midst of a mighty struggle to rid our nation of racial and economic injustice, I have heard many ministers say: "Those are social issues, with which the gospel has no real concern." And I have watched many churches commit themselves to a completely otherworldly religion which makes a strange, un-Biblical distinction between body and soul, between the sacred and the secular.

38   I have traveled the length and breadth of Alabama, Mississippi, and all the other southern states. On sweltering summer days and crisp autumn mornings I have looked at the South's beautiful churches with their lofty spires pointing heavenward. I have beheld the impressive outlines of her massive religious-education buildings. Over and over I have found myself asking: "What kind of people worship here? Who is their God? Where were their voices when the lips of Governor Barnett dripped with words of interposition and nullification? Where were they when Governor Wallace gave a clarion call for defiance and hatred? Where were their voices of support when bruised and weary Negro men and women decided to rise from the dark dungeons of complacency to the bright lulls of creative protest?"

39   Yes, these questions are still in my mind. In deep disappointment I have wept over the laxity of the church. But be assured that my tears have been tears of love. There can be no deep disappointment where there is not deep love. Yes, I love the church. How could I do otherwise? I am in the rather unique position of being the son, the grandson, and the great-grandson of preachers. Yes, I see the church as the body of Christ. How we have blemished and scarred that body through social neglect and through fear of being nonconformists.

40   There was a time when the church was very powerful—in the time when the early Christians rejoiced at being deemed worthy to suffer for what they believed. In those days the church was not merely a thermometer that recorded the ideas and principles of popular opinion; it was a thermostat that transformed the mores of society. Whenever the early Christians entered a town, the people in power became disturbed and immediately sought to convict the Christians for being "disturbers of the peace" and "outside agitators." But the Christians pressed on, in the conviction that they were "a colony of heaven," called to obey God rather than man. Small in number, they were big in commitment. They were too God-intoxicated to be "astronomically intimidated." By their effort and example they brought an end to such ancient evils as infanticide and gladiatorial contests.

41   Things are different now. So often the contemporary church is a weak, ineffectual voice with an uncertain sound. So often it is an archdefender of the status quo. Far from being disturbed by the presence of the church, the power structure of the average community is consoled by the church's silent—and often even vocal—sanction of things as they are.

42   But the judgment of God is upon the church as never before. If today's church does not recapture the sacrificial spirit of the early church, it will lose its authenticity, forfeit the loyalty of millions, and be dismissed as an irrelevant social club with no meaning for the twentieth century. Every day I meet young people whose disappointment with the church has turned into outright disgust.

43   Perhaps I have once again been too optimistic. Is organized religion too inextricably bound to the status quo to save our nation and the world? Perhaps I must turn my faith to the inner spiritual church, the church within the church, as the true *ekklesia* and the hope of the world. But again I am thankful to God that some noble souls from the ranks of organized religion have broken loose from the paralyzing chains of conformity and joined us as active partners in the struggle for freedom. They have left their secure congregations and walked the streets of Albany, Georgia, with us. They have gone down the highways of the South on tortuous rides for freedom. Yes, they have gone to jail with us. Some have been dismissed from their churches, have lost the support of their bishops and fellow ministers. But they have acted in the faith that right defeated is stronger than evil triumphant. Their witness has been the spiritual salt that has preserved the true meaning of the gospel in these troubled times. They have carved a tunnel of hope through the dark mountain of disappointment.

44   I hope the church as a whole will meet the challenge of this decisive hour. But even if the church does not come to the aid of justice, I have no despair about the future. I have no fear about the outcome of our struggle in Birmingham, even if our motives are at present misunderstood. We will reach the goal of freedom in Birmingham and all over the nation, because the goal of America is freedom. Abused and scorned though we may be, our destiny is tied up with America's destiny. Before the pilgrims landed at Plymouth, we were here. Before the pen of Jefferson etched the majestic words of the Declaration of Independence across the pages of history, we were here. For more than two centuries our forebears labored in this country without wages: they made cotton king; they built the homes of their masters while suffering gross injustice and shameful humiliation—and yet out of a bottomless vitality they continued to thrive and develop. If the inexpressible cruelties of slavery could not stop us, the opposition we now face will surely fail. We will win our freedom because the sacred heritage of our nation and the eternal will of God are embodied in our echoing demands.

45   Before closing I feel impelled to mention one other point in your statement that has troubled me profoundly. You warmly commended the Birmingham police force for keeping "order" and "preventing violence." I doubt that you would have so warmly commended the police force if you had seen its dogs sinking their teeth into unarmed, nonviolent Negroes. I doubt that you would so quickly commend the policemen if you were to observe their ugly and inhumane treatment of Negroes here in the city jail; if you were to watch them push and curse old Negro women and young Negro girls; if you were to see them slap and kick old Negro men and young boys; if you were to observe them, as they did on two occasions, refuse to give us food because we wanted to sing our grace together. I cannot join you in your praise of the Birmingham police department.

46   It is true that the police have exercised a degree of discipline in handling the demonstrators. In this sense they have conducted themselves rather "nonviolently" in public. But for what purpose? To preserve the evil system of segregation. Over the past few years I have consistently preached that nonviolence demands that the means we use must be as pure as the ends we seek. I have tried to make clear that it is wrong to use immoral means to attain moral ends. But now I must affirm that it is just as wrong, or perhaps even more so, to use moral means to preserve immoral ends. Perhaps Mr. Connor and his policemen have been rather nonviolent in public, as was Chief Pritchett in Albany, Georgia, but they have used the moral means of nonviolence to maintain the immoral end of racial injustice. As T. S. Eliot has said. "The last temptation is the greatest treason: To do the right deed for the wrong reason."

47   I wish you had commended the Negro sit-inners and demonstrators of Birmingham for their sublime courage, their willingness to suffer, and their amazing discipline in the midst of great provocation. One day the South will recognize its real heroes. They

will be the James Merediths, with the noble sense of purpose that enables them to face jeering and hostile mobs, and with the agonizing loneliness that characterizes the life of the pioneer. They will be old, oppressed, battered Negro women, symbolized in a seventy-two-year-old woman in Montgomery, Alabama, who rose up with a sense of dignity and with her people decided not to ride segregated buses, and who responded with ungrammatical profundity to one who inquired about her weariness: "My feets is tired, but my soul is at rest." They will be the young high school and college students, the young ministers of the gospel and a host of their elders, courageously and nonviolently sitting in at lunch counters and willingly going to jail for conscience' sake. One day the South will know that when these disinherited children of God sat down at lunch counters, they were in reality standing up for what is best in the American dream and for the most sacred values in our Judaeo-Christian heritage, thereby bringing our nation back to those great wells of democracy which were dug deep by the founding fathers in their formulation of the Constitution and the Declaration of Independence.

48   Never before have I written so long a letter. I'm afraid it is much too long to take your precious time. I can assure you that it would have been much shorter if I had been writing from a comfortable desk, but what else can one do when he is alone in a narrow jail cell, other than write long letters, think long thoughts, and pray long prayers?

49   If I have said anything in this letter that overstates the truth and indicates an unreasonable impatience, I beg you to forgive me. If I have said anything that understates the truth and indicates my having a patience that allows me to settle for anything less than brotherhood, I beg God to forgive me.

50   I hope this letter finds you strong in the faith. I also hope that circumstances will soon make it possible for me to meet each of you, not as an integrationist or a civil-rights leader but as a fellow clergyman and a Christian brother. Let us all hope that the dark clouds of racial prejudice will soon pass away and the deep fog of misunderstanding will be lifted from our fear-drenched communities, and in some not too distant tomorrow the radiant stars of love and brotherhood will shine over our great nation with all their scintillating beauty.

Yours for the cause of Peace and Brotherhood,
MARTIN LUTHER KING, JR.

16. Explain the function of the rhetorical questions King uses in paragraph 25.

Identify King's uses of repetition in paragraphs 25, 31, and 44. Explain what he accomplishes with the repetitions in each of those paragraphs. Which use of repetition do you find most effective? Why?

17. Identify and explain the effect of the rhetorical techniques King employs in paragraph 31. How effective and persuasive do you find them to be? What distinction does he make between different types of and purposes for "extremism"? Who does he refer to as support for the claim that he makes about the kind of "extremism" he believes is necessary? Why does he cite those references?

18. Consider how King employs various kinds imagery in paragraphs 27, 32, 33, 37, and 50. Which use of imagery do you find most compelling? Why?

The Declaration of Independence

The Declaration of Independence is a work of consummate argumentation. The argument of the Declaration is based upon the self-evident truths of equality and the unalienable rights of life, liberty, and the pursuit of happiness. According to the declaration, governments are established to secure these and other rights of individuals.

When a government refuses to do so, or when it destroys these rights, the people have a right to abolish that government. That's part of the progression of thought that launches this famous and influential foundational document. With its careful reasoning, precise use of language, and logically developed argument, the Declaration of Independence is a model of clear writing, elegant organization, and cogent thinking.

EXERCISE

19. Analyze the Declaration of Independence from the standpoint of logos, pathos, and ethos.

Explain how the declaration works as a deductive argument. What are the premises, and what is the conclusion that derives from those premises?
To what extent do you find the argument of the declaration logically valid? To what extent do you find it persuasive? Why?

IN CONGRESS, July 4, 1776.

The unanimous Declaration of the thirteen united States of America,

When in the Course of human events, it becomes necessary for one people to dissolve the political bands which have connected them with another, and to assume among the powers of the earth, the separate and equal station to which the Laws of Nature and of Nature's God entitle them, a decent respect to the opinions of mankind requires that they should declare the causes which impel them to the separation.

We hold these truths to be self-evident, that all men are created equal, that they are endowed by their Creator with certain unalienable Rights, that among these are Life, Liberty and the pursuit of Happiness.—That to secure these rights, Governments are instituted among Men, deriving their just powers from the consent of the governed,—That whenever any Form of Government becomes destructive of these ends, it is the Right of the People to alter or to abolish it, and to institute new Government, laying its foundation on such principles and organizing its powers in such form, as to them shall seem most likely to effect their Safety and Happiness. Prudence, indeed, will dictate that Governments long established should not be changed for light and transient causes; and accordingly all experience hath shewn, that mankind are more disposed to suffer, while evils are sufferable, than to right themselves by abolishing the forms to which they are accustomed. But when a long train of abuses and usurpations, pursuing invariably the same Object evinces a design to reduce them under absolute Despotism, it is their right, it is their duty, to throw off such Government, and to provide new Guards for their future security.—Such has been the patient sufferance of these Colonies; and such is now the necessity which constrains them to alter their former Systems of Government. The history of the present King of Great Britain is a history of repeated injuries and usurpations, all having in direct object the establishment of an absolute Tyranny over these States. To prove this, let Facts be submitted to a candid world.

He has refused his Assent to Laws, the most wholesome and necessary for the public good. He has forbidden his Governors to pass Laws of immediate and pressing importance, unless suspended in their operation till his Assent should be obtained; and when so suspended, he has utterly neglected to attend to them. He has refused to pass other Laws for the accommodation of large districts of people, unless those people would relinquish the right of Representation in the Legislature, a right inestimable to them and formidable to tyrants only. He has called together legislative bodies at places unusual, uncomfortable, and distant from the depository of their public Records, for the sole purpose of fatiguing them into compliance with his measures. He has dissolved Representative Houses repeatedly, for opposing with manly firmness his invasions on the rights of the people. He has refused for a long time, after such dissolutions, to cause others to be elected; whereby the Legislative powers, incapable of Annihilation, have returned to the People at large for their exercise; the State remaining in the mean time exposed to all the dangers of invasion from without, and convulsions within. He has endeavoured to prevent the population of these States; for that purpose obstructing the Laws for Naturalization of Foreigners; refusing to pass others to encourage their migrations hither, and raising the conditions of new Appropriations of Lands. He has obstructed the Administration of Justice, by refusing his Assent to Laws for establishing Judiciary powers. He has made Judges dependent on his Will alone, for the tenure of their offices, and the amount and payment of their salaries. He has erected a multitude of New Offices, and sent hither swarms of Officers to harass our people, and eat out their substance. He has kept among us, in times of peace, Standing Armies without the Consent of our legislatures. He has affected to render the Military independent of and superior to the Civil power. He has combined with others to subject us to a jurisdiction foreign to our constitution, and unacknowledged by our laws; giving his Assent to their Acts of pretended Legislation: For Quartering large bodies of armed troops among us: For protecting them, by a mock Trial, from punishment for any Murders which they should commit on the Inhabitants of these States: For cutting off our Trade with all parts of the world: For imposing Taxes on us without our Consent: For depriving us in many cases, of the benefits of Trial by Jury: For transporting us beyond Seas to be tried for pretended offences For abolishing the free System of English Laws in a neighbouring Province, establishing therein an Arbitrary government, and enlarging its Boundaries so as to render it at once an example and fit instrument for introducing the same absolute rule into these Colonies: For taking away our Charters, abolishing our most valuable Laws, and altering fundamentally the Forms of our Governments: For suspending our own Legislatures, and declaring themselves invested with power to legislate for us in all cases whatsoever. He has abdicated Government here, by declaring us out of his Protection and waging War against us. He has plundered our seas, ravaged our Coasts, burnt our towns, and destroyed the lives of our people. He is at this time transporting large Armies of foreign Mercenaries to compleat the works of death, desolation and tyranny, already begun with circumstances of Cruelty & perfidy scarcely paralleled in the most barbarous ages, and totally unworthy the Head of a civilized nation. He has constrained our fellow Citizens taken Captive on the high Seas to bear Arms against their Country, to become the executioners of their friends and Brethren, or to fall themselves by their Hands. He has excited domestic insurrections amongst us, and has endeavoured to bring on the inhabitants of our frontiers, the merciless Indian Savages, whose known rule of warfare, is an undistinguished destruction of all ages, sexes and conditions.

In every stage of these Oppressions We have Petitioned for Redress in the most humble terms: Our repeated Petitions have been answered only by repeated injury. A Prince whose character is thus marked by every act which may define a Tyrant, is unfit to be the ruler of a free people.

Nor have we been wanting in attentions to our British brethren. We have warned them from time to time of attempts by their legislature to extend an unwarrantable jurisdiction over us. We have reminded them of the circumstances of our emigration and settlement here. We have appealed to their native justice and magnanimity, and we have conjured them by the ties of our common kindred to disavow these usurpations, which, would inevitably interrupt our connections and correspondence. They too have been deaf to the voice of justice and of consanguinity. We must, therefore, acquiesce in the necessity, which denounces our Separation, and hold them, as we hold the rest of mankind, Enemies in War, in Peace Friends.

We, therefore, the Representatives of the united States of America, in General Congress, Assembled, appealing to the Supreme Judge of the world for the rectitude of our intentions, do, in the Name, and by Authority of the good People of these Colonies, solemnly publish and declare, That these United Colonies are, and of Right ought to be Free and Independent States; that they are Absolved from all Allegiance to the British Crown, and that all political connection between them and the State of Great Britain, is and ought to be totally dissolved; and that as Free and Independent States, they have full Power to levy War, conclude Peace, contract Alliances, establish Commerce, and to do all other Acts and Things which Independent States may of right do. And for the support of this Declaration, with a firm reliance on the protection of divine Providence, we mutually pledge to each other our Lives, our Fortunes and our sacred Honor.

The 56 signatures on the Declaration appear in the positions indicated:

Column 1 Georgia: Button Gwinnett Lyman Hall George Walton

Column 2 North Carolina: William Hooper Joseph Hewes John Penn **South Carolina:** Edward Rutledge Thomas Heyward, Jr. Thomas Lynch, Jr. Arthur Middleton

Column 3 Massachusetts: John Hancock **Maryland:** Samuel Chase William Paca Thomas Stone Charles Carroll of Carrollton **Virginia:** George Wythe Richard Henry Lee Thomas Jefferson Benjamin Harrison Thomas Nelson, Jr. Francis Lightfoot Lee Carter Braxton

Column 4 Pennsylvania: Robert Morris Benjamin Rush Benjamin Franklin John Morton George Clymer James Smith George Taylor James Wilson George Ross **Delaware:** Caesar Rodney George Read Thomas McKean

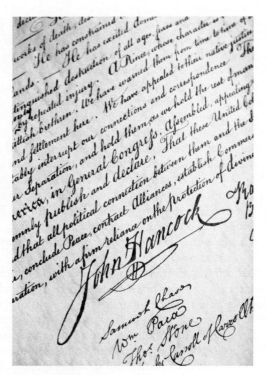

FIGURE 8.2 Signatures on the Declaration of Independence

Column 5 New York: William Floyd Philip Livingston Francis Lewis Lewis Morris **New Jersey:** Richard Stockton John Witherspoon Francis Hopkinson John Hart Abraham Clark

Column 6 New Hampshire: Josiah Bartlett William Whipple **Massachusetts:** Samuel Adams John Adams Robert Treat Paine Elbridge Gerry **Rhode Island:** Stephen Hopkins William Ellery **Connecticut:** Roger Sherman Samuel Huntington William Williams Oliver Wolcott **New Hampshire:** Matthew Thornton

Constructing Arguments

Up till now we have been focusing on how to analyze arguments. Now we turn our attention to how to construct them. We can identify three main types of arguments: (1) arguments of fact, (2) arguments of value, and (3) arguments of policy.

Arguments of fact suggest that something is or is not the case. Often arguments of fact are causal arguments. That is, they explain why something happened, how it resulted from some previous cause or influence. We might claim, for example, that the rise of Amazon.com and Internet book sales generally have resulted in the closing of brick-and-mortar bookstores, both independent bookstores and giant chains, such as Borders. Or we might claim that the state of the economy was or was not the single most influential factor in the 2012 US presidential election.

Arguments of value suggest that something is or is not desirable. These arguments involve judgments about quality; they involve evaluations about the worth of something. Contests and competitions that award prizes are common examples. The Emmy awards highlight music performers and performances of value. The Academy awards call our attention to films we should see. Nobel prizes and Pulitzer prizes, among many others, evaluate and celebrate the contributions of various experts in economics and medicine and literature, for example. Other kinds of arguments of value make claims such as that George Bush's No Child Left Behind legislation improved (or damaged) educational practice in schools throughout the country.

Arguments of policy suggest that something should or should not be done. These kinds of arguments typically include recommendations and suggestions for implementing a policy or practice. That teachers' salaries should be increased; that term limits should be imposed on Supreme Court justices; that psychological counseling and psychiatric treatment should or should not be covered under medical insurance policies—these are a few of the myriad examples of arguments of policy.

Arguments though often primarily of one type, may include elements of the others, or be converted from one type to another. An argument of value, for example, that the No Child Left Behind act was helpful or damaging, can be made an argument of policy such that we might argue that the legislation should be repealed, and it should replaced by a new and different and better educational policy.

Guidelines for Constructing an Argument

What is necessary to construct a good argument? What considerations should we keep in mind when developing arguments, both orally and in writing?

First, we need to be clear about what we are suggesting, or claiming, and why. We need to be clear, that is, about our **purpose** and our point. Second, we need to think about the kinds of evidence required to support our **claim** or idea. Third, we need to consider who our audience is. Fourth, we should consider how to organize or structure our argument. And fifth, we need to imagine objections that might be made to our claim, **counterarguments** that might be advanced against it.

purpose
The goal or aim, along with the practical effect or reason, for which something is attempted or accomplished.

claim
In argument, an assertion or conclusion that requires evidence in its support.

counterargument
An argument that contrasts or opposes another argument.

All of these aspects of argument are evident in Martin Luther King, Jr.'s "Letter from Birmingham Jail." In addition to analyzing King's argument, however, it is necessary to think about these aspects of argumentation in developing our own arguments.

The following list of questions and guidelines was devised by Dr. Donald Pardlow, a professor at Claflin University in South Carolina, for one of his argument-writing classes. It can be used as a framework to begin thinking about constructing an argument. Pardlow uses it for his class's final researched argument assignment. However, his questions can be used for any essay that includes an argument component. Here are Pardlow's guidelines and questions:

1. Choose an issue. Make the issue as specific as possible by answering the following questions:

   • Who or what are you writing about?
   • Why are you writing about this?
   • What kind of thing (what is the essence of the thing) are you writing about?
   • How much of it are you writing about? How does it occur?

2. Consider where you stand on the issue (your position) by answering the following questions:

   • What is the issue?
   • What is the value of this issue?
   • What are the causes and consequences of this issue?
   • What should we do about this issue and why?
   • What is the evidence for your claims about the issue?

3. Consider the audience you are addressing. Use the following questions:

   • Who are my readers?
   • What do they believe?
   • What common ground do we share?
   • What do I want my readers to believe?
   • What do they need to know?
   • Why should they care?

4. Decide on your position on the issue—whether you wish to advocate for or against a particular position. Make this decision after doing the following:

   • Write down 10 reasons to support your position on the issue.
   • Write down 10 reasons not to support your position.

EXERCISE

20. Identify an issue that interests you. Use Donald Pardlow's guidelines and questions to begin thinking through the pros and cons of the issue. These responses provide a form of prewriting, a kind of preliminary thinking useful for writing an argument essay or paper.

Argument as Conversation

In their book, *They Say / I Say*, Gerald Graff and Kathy Birkenstein advise us to think of argumentative writing as a kind of conversation—a serious conversation, in which we engage with others' views with thoughtful consideration. They quote an important passage from the scholar and rhetorician Kenneth Burke, in which Burke describes the ways in which we exchange ideas as a continuing, even a never-ending conversation.

> You come late. When you arrive, others have long preceded you, and they are engaged in a heated discussion. . . . You listen for a while, until you decide that you have caught the tenor of the argument; then you put in your oar. Someone answers; you answer him; another comes to your defense; another aligns himself against you. . . . The hour grows late, you must depart. And you do depart, with the discussion still vigorously in progress.

—*Kenneth Burke, The Philosophy of Literary Form*

Burke's description can serve as a model for the process of engaging in academic discussion and debate generally. It can also serve as a metaphor for the process of constructing arguments—arguments that others will read or hear, and then respond to in speech or writing. By thinking of argument as a kind of conversation, we remind ourselves that others have a say, and that what they say and think will often differ in ways large and small from our ideas.

Considering argument as conversation also encourages us to be both respectful of others and receptive to their points of view. It fosters a more collegial and stimulating form of intellectual discussion than we find with the adversarial "I'm right—you're wrong" approach. It increases the likelihood that others will consider our views thoughtfully. And it enables us to improve our chances of acquiring true beliefs and avoid false ones. In the process of listening to evidence that others provide to support their claims, we come to better understand which of our beliefs and ideas can be justified and which may need to be modified.

EXERCISE

21. What benefits might accrue from conceiving of argument as a type of serious conversation? Do you think there might be drawbacks to seeing argument this way? Why or why not?

Being Reasonable—Purpose and Audience

When we develop an argument in an essay—an argumentative essay—our purpose is to present and defend a thesis, or idea, about an issue so that we can influence the thinking of others. In thinking about our topic or issue, we need to ask ourselves the following questions:

1. What is commonly known, said, argued about it?
2. What has become predictable, stale, clichéd?
3. How can we take a fresh and interesting approach to it?
4. How can we add something new while addressing the expected and considering what is most important, even urgent about the topic?

Arguments require careful attention to audience; we need to know who will be hearing or reading what we have to say. And so, we need to ask ourselves the following questions about audience:

1. Who is the audience? What do audience members know about the topic, and what is their likely perspective on it?
2. What type of approach and what kinds of evidence are they likely to find persuasive?
3. What is our goal—to give them something to think about, to agree with our claim, to take up some action?

Martin Luther King, Jr., knew his audience of religious leaders and chose his language and his examples carefully. For instance, he references religious figures and thinkers whose lives and ideas would resonate with the ministers he was addressing in his letter. Like King, our goal in making an argument is to convince our audience to adopt a particular point of view, to agree with us about our claim and argument. Showing a concern for how our audience and others might think about an issue and how they might react can serve us well in winning them over to our point of view. Adopting a reasonable tone, a willingness to acknowledge an issue's complexity, an ability to represent fairly conflicting viewpoints—all are essential to constructing a successful argument.

Aspects of Audience

Although it is not always easy to determine the various attitudes, perspectives, beliefs, values, and points of view of a diverse audience, it is useful to consider some of the possibilities. The audience for a talk or for a piece of writing can represent various levels of agreement with our ideas. Here are some possibilities along such a spectrum.

- People who agree with our purpose and goal.
- People who agree with our goal and our way of achieving or approaching it.
- People who agree with our goal or end, but not with our means or approach.
- People who agree with our goal, but see it as a means to some other end; they might have (their own "agenda").
- People who agree with our approach or means, but who would use those means to achieve different ends—their own "agenda" ends.

It is often more important to have a sense of our audience and their various perspectives when we are speaking directly to them than when we are writing or conveying ideas by video. And it is important that if there is to be a question and answer session following a direct speech to an audience, that we try to anticipate some of their questions both in terms of content and in terms of their tone, attitude, and point of view.

Some Additional Questions about Audience

- Who is the audience?
- How much or how little do you know about this audience?
- How varied is the audience?
- What side of the issue under consideration are members of the audience likely to be on?
- Is the audience likely to be skeptical and critical, sympathetic and trusting, brimming with questions?
- How much does the audience know about the topic? Are they experts? Novices?
- What do we want them to know, think, believe, or do as a result of our argument?

EXERCISE

22. Find a passage from the second half of Martin Luther King, Jr.'s "Letter to Birmingham Jail" (paragraphs 26–50), a passage that reveals King's reasonableness. Identify how he achieves his reasonable tone in that passage. How does King demonstrate an understanding of his audience?

Anticipating Objections

One reason for identifying possible objections to an argument we are making is that it shows that we are aware of opposing views—that we understand and admit that there are, indeed, other conclusions that might be drawn. It shows us as willing to acknowledge those opposing views rather than avoiding them or sweeping them under the rug. This approach is more likely to enhance our credibility, as it ensures our reasonableness.

◉ Simulate the **Experiment**, Anticipating Objections / Making Concessions **MyThinkingLab**

Identifying potential objections also show that we are capable of considering our audience, of seeing them as thoughtful and caring about the issues under consideration. It suggests that we can find ways to respond to those objections, perhaps by rebutting them, perhaps by accommodating them in some kind of compromise or modified position. It indicates that we are confident enough about our views that we are willing and able to defend them against counterarguments.

A third reason for acknowledging and identifying opposing views is that we can contrast them with our own argument. It helps us clarify our claim and the support we provide for it. And a fourth is that it enables us to go on the offensive, to preempt the opposition by anticipating objections before others can raise them.

Making Concessions

Closely allied with identifying opposing arguments is a willingness to make concessions—to note that a counterargument has some validity, enough validity and strength that we need to give some ground to the opposition. Often when making a **concession** (or conceding a point), we will want to acknowledge some part of the objection or counterargument, while rejecting other aspects of it.

concession
An acknowledgment that some part of an opponent's argument is valid or true.

It is a good idea to try to refute the weaknesses in an opponent's counterargument when there is a need to concede part of it. Under certain circumstances, we might demonstrate the irrelevance of an objection or counterargument to our topic, even while acknowledging that it is valid in some respects, perhaps in ways that are less important or less relevant to our argument to and claim.

Dealing with rebuttals and with counterarguments is an essential skill. It is also an important part of the success of any argument. Making a concession while simultaneously defending our main idea often involves avoiding an "all-or-nothing" approach. A more "combinatory" approach is often an effective argumentative strategy. Here are a few ways you can use to make concessions while maintaining a position:

- Although I admit that. . . . I maintain that. . . .
- While it is true that. . . . it is also the case that. . . .
- On one hand, I agree with X that. . . . However, on the other hand we must consider. . . .
- Proponents of the view that. . . . are right to suggest that. . . . But they are not convincing in their view that. . . .
- While I agree that. . . . I must take exception to the notion that . . . .

EXERCISE

23. On a topic of your choice, develop an argument complete with a claim, support, warrants, and backing. Anticipate some objections and answer them. Also, try to make some concessions in developing your argument. Use one or another of the suggested ways to make concessions.

Argument and the Classical Oration

classical oration
A form and style of argument in ancient Greece and Rome that includes the following parts: introduction, narration, division, confirmation, refutation, and peroration, or grand conclusion.

One of the strongest influences on the structure of an argument is the **classical oration** developed and used to achieve brilliant effects by the orators of ancient Greece and Rome. The oration was usually an attempt by rhetoricians to persuade an audience in court or in the senate.

The classical oration was meant to win the audience over to one side of a contentious debate. Its organizational structure highlights the ways that the speaker's claim and perspective differ from those of the opposition, and how and why the speaker's argument and claim are the stronger of the two.

Here is an outline of the main parts of the classical oration with a brief explanation of the function of each part.

1. *Exordium.* In this introductory section, the speaker or writer introduces the subject or problem while attempting to secure the audience's goodwill. In *Words Loaded Like Pistols*, Sam Leith notes that this is the place that "the strongest up-front ethos appeal will tend to come."

2. *Narratio(n).* Here, the speaker or writer puts the argument in context, presenting the facts of the situation, explaining what happened, when and where it occurred, who was involved, how and why. As Leith notes, the speaker or writer needs to be reasonable and measured in this section.

3. *Parititio(n).* Next, the speaker or writer divides up his subject, explaining the central issues, the key claim, and in what order the parts of the subject will be discussed. Also included here is where we agree and disagree with our opponents.

4. *Confirmatio(n).* In this section, the speaker or writer provides detailed support through a careful selection of evidence and a logical approach to reasoning. Logos is central here.

5. *Refutatio(n).* The speaker or writer next identifies opposing arguments and refutes them by showing their weaknesses in claims and evidence. More use of logos, this time to rebut and refute rather than to confirm, as in the previous section.

6. *Peroratio(n).* Finally, the speaker or writer summarizes the situation or case and attempts to move the audience to take action. This is a kind of grand finale, in which pathos appeals can reach their height.

EXERCISES

24. Reread the Declaration of Independence. Analyze its argument from the standpoint of the classical oration of the ancient Greek and Roman orators.

25. Use the Declaration of Independence as a model to write your own declaration of intellectual, academic, technological, or some other kind of "independence." You may find on the Internet the "Declaration of Sentiments and Resolutions" by Elizabeth Cady Stanton, and use her feminist statement of independence as the model for your "declaration."

26. Develop an argument about a topic of your choice. Follow the six-part structure of the classical oration. Try to accomplish, in each part, however briefly, what the various parts require. For the sake of clarity for yourself and your readers, number each of the six parts (preferably with a Roman numeral).

27. Read the following pair of speeches from Shakespeare's play *Julius Caesar*. Analyze the two speeches to reveal the ways Shakespeare is indebted to classical rhetoric. Identify which parts of the classical oration each speech emphasizes. Analyze how each speaker makes his argument. In the first speech, Brutus, one of Caesar's murderers addresses Roman citizens to explain why Caesar's execution was necessary and right. In the second speech, Mark Antony, friend to both Brutus and Caesar, provides an alternative view of Caesar's death at the hands of Brutus and his fellow conspirators.

Brutus:

Romans, countrymen, and lovers! Hear me for my cause; and be silent, that you may hear: believe me for mine honour, and have respect to mine honour, that you may believe: censure me in your wisdom; and awake your senses, that you may the better judge. If there be any in this assembly, any dear friend of Caesar's, to Him I say that Brutus' love to Caesar was no less than his. If Then that friend demand why Brutus rose against Caesar, this is my answer,—Not that I loved Caesar less, but that I loved Rome more. Had you rather Caesar were living, and die all slaves, than That Caesar were dead, to live all freemen? As Caesar loved me, I weep for him; as he was fortunate, I rejoice at it; as he was valiant, I honour him; but, as he was ambitious, I slew him. There is tears for his love; joy for his fortune; honour for his valour; and death for his ambition. Who is here so base that Would be a bondman? If any, speak; for him have I offended. Who is here so rude that would not be a Roman? If any, speak; for him have I offended. Who is here so vile that will not love his country? If any, speak; for him have I offended. I pause for a reply.

Antony:

Friends, Romans, countrymen, lend me your ears;
I come to bury Caesar, not to praise him.
The evil that men do lives after them;
The good is oft interred with their bones:
So let it be with Caesar. The noble Brutus
Hath told you Caesar was ambitious:
If it were so, it was a grievous fault;
And grievously hath Caesar answer'd it.
Here, under leave of Brutus and the rest,—
For Brutus is an honourable man;
So are they all, all honorable men,—
Come I to speak in Caesar's funeral.
He was my friend, faithful and just to me:

But Brutus says he was ambitious;

And Brutus is an honourable man.

He hath brought many captives home to Rome,

Whose ransoms did the general coffers fill:

Did this in Caesar seem ambitious?

When that the poor have cried, Caesar hath wept:

Ambition should be made of sterner stuff:

Yet Brutus says he was ambitious;

And Brutus is an honourable man.

You all did see that on the Lupercal

I thrice presented him a kingly crown,

Which he did thrice refuse: was this ambition?

Yet Brutus says he was ambitious;

And, sure, he is an honourable man.

I speak not to disprove what Brutus spoke,

But here I am to speak what I do know.

You all did love him once,—not without cause:

What cause withholds you, then, to mourn for him?—

O judgment, thou art fled to brutish beasts,

And men have lost their reason!—Bear with me;

My heart is in the coffin there with Caesar,

And I must pause till it come back to me.

Rogerian Argument

Another type of argument, one that differs significantly from the classical oration, was developed by psychologist Carl Rogers, who believed that disputes could not be settled without proponents of each contesting side having a good, full, and fair understanding of the other side's position. A number of mid-twentieth century rhetoricians used Rogers' concept and approach to argumentation to create a four-part structure that has come to be known as **"Rogerian argument."**

Rogerian argument
A form of argument, devised by psychologist Carl Rogers, which emphasizes cooperation and common ground rather than contestation and condemnation of an opponent's ideas and claims.

- **Introduction**—The speaker or writer describes a problem, issue, or conflict in ways that show an understanding and appreciation for alternative positions on it.
- **Contexts**—The speaker or writer describes the contexts in which the alternative positions might be considered legitimate.
- **The Writer's Position**—The speaker or writer states his or her own position on the issue, and presents the circumstances in which it would be legitimate.
- **Benefits to Opponent**—The speaker or writer explains how his or her opponents would benefit from adopting the position.

Write the **Response**,
Rogerian Argument
MyThinkingLab

The goal of Rogerian argument is reconciliation and mutual understanding. It strives for common understanding through softening differences and bridging controversial perspectives. The key to a successful Rogerian argument is considering and describing opposing positions and perspectives honestly, accurately, and fairly. Rogerian argument offers an alternative to the more combative and dialectical approach of the classical oration.

EXERCISE

28. Select one of the following contentious problems (or one of your own choosing) and construct a sentence outline following the four-part structure of Rogerian argument. Be sure to include sentences in your outline that clearly reveal your position. Be sure to include some sentences that demonstrate an appreciation and understanding of the opposing position.

    Gay marriage

    Capital punishment

    Abortion

    Assisted suicide

    Amnesty for Illegal Immigrants

Cultural Relativism

Anthropologists have long argued for the concept of cultural relativism, which holds that cultures around the world are diverse and different, that they are historical products of peoples' belief systems, and that the way we perceive the world is embedded in the cultural categories we inherit through customs, beliefs, and language. At the heart of cultural relativism lies the belief that no culture is superior to any other, that no single worldview should be used as a way to evaluate another. Such a belief means that the cultural practices of one culture should be understood in relation to that culture's beliefs and traditions alone rather than in comparison with those of other cultures. From this perspective, for example, the Aztec practice of human sacrifice, the Hindu practice of keeping cows sacred, the use of hallucinogenic drugs, the practice of clitorectomy by different cultural groups, or the practice of capital punishment are valid behaviors within those cultural traditions. A counter perspective holds that some, if not all of these practices, are both morally wrong and socially destructive.

Cultural relativism is closely linked with religious beliefs and ideals, such that certain Islamic traditions require retaliation, including death, against anyone considered to have criticized Muhammad or blasphemed against Allah, or God. A "fatwah" is issued against such an individual. Complicating the concept of cultural relativism today is that cultures no longer exist in relative isolation. As the world has become increasingly globalized and as people from different cultural traditions have lived among each other, these differing forms of cultural behavior have become more noticeable and have resulted in conflict, which sometimes turns deadly. And even when the conflicts are less than lethal, they can cause deep societal tensions and rifts, as with the French political mandate against the wearing of headscarves by immigrant Muslim girls attending French schools, or the prohibition in certain US states of using the Spanish language for public business. Practices such as these provoke debate and argument, some of it rational, much of it, unfortunately, not.

Cultural Universals

The flip side of cultural relativism is the notion of cultural or human universals—of commonalities among all people around the world. In *Human Universals*,

Explore the Concept,
Cultural Relativism
MyThinkingLab

Donald E. Brown argues that all descriptions of peoples studied by anthropologists are "shot through with the signs of a universal human nature." Anthropologists, according to Brown, more often than not downplay the similarities among peoples, when not denying them, so as to show how different from us are the exotic people they study.

Brown does not deny that differences exist among peoples the world over, but he puts far more emphasis on what different peoples share. Among the human universals are the use of fire and tools, a division of labor by sex, and the taboo against marrying close relatives—the incest taboo. Brown also suggests that every culture not only has language, but that in addition to spoken language, all cultures include gesture and facial expression in their communication repertoire. By means of each of these aspects of communication, people of all cultures convey feelings, such as sadness and joy, surprise and disgust, anger and contempt. Different cultures employ different gestures to communicate some of these things, but each culture communicates emotion physically through the body in its own way.

Human universals include ways of preparing for birth and for giving birth, as well as preparing the dead for burial, although, of course, different cultures perform these rituals in their own ways. Along with this sense of common human culture is the idea that each people possesses a singular sense of its own distinctiveness. Ironically, recognizing their own difference from other peoples and judging others in their own terms illustrates how they are like those different others, who reciprocate the judgment and replicate their own sense of uniqueness.

Brown reminds us that all people have a way of socializing the young, incorporating them into a network of family relationships. They also distinguish among close relatives and those more distant, and they commonly treat close kin differently and more favorably than distantly related. Also common across cultures are forms of social organization including the formation of rules, laws, and the establishment of governments and leaders.

Further human universals include the status and prestige that are another common category among peoples worldwide, though different cultures indicate rank and status in varying ways. People distinguish right from wrong, good from evil, acceptable from unacceptable behavior. They have standards of etiquette and hospitality as well as standards of sexual modesty, even though they might not wear clothes. The fact of standards is a cultural universal; the nature of those standards varies among cultures, reflecting differing cultural beliefs, values, and practices.

EXERCISES

29. What do you think of Donald Brown's notion of human universals? Do you agree that the kinds of behaviors he cites are shared universally by people of all cultures? Which of the following do you think might be considered cultural or human universals: music, art, dance, written language, the creation and consumption of alcoholic and caffeinated beverages? Which of the "additional human universals" do you find convincing as common among people? Are you less confident about any? Why?

30. Do you think there is any way to reconcile the conflicting, dialectical notions of cultural relativism and human universals? Is there any common ground between these opposed concepts? To what extent might a Rogerian approach be useful in considering their respective claims? What might a cultural relativist and a cultural universalist say to each other while engaged in a Rogerian dialogue?

31. Identify some common practices that illustrate cultural variation. You might consider how people acquire, prepare, and cook food; how they purchase materials, goods, and services; how they celebrate rites of passage such as birth, coming to adulthood, marriage, and death; how they hold conversations, how they engage or courtship or in sport. Provide two examples of how different cultures use bodily gesture and/or facial expression to communicate feelings and attitudes. What cultural differences exist, for example, in the ways men court women? What commonalities might you find among these differences?

Looking Back and Looking Ahead

Revisit the learning goals that begin this chapter. Which of these goals do you think you have best achieved? What might you do to reach the remaining goals?

Return to the focusing questions at the beginning of the chapter. How would you answer those questions now? Which of them do you find most interesting and provocative and worthy of following up? Why?

In reviewing the list of resources that follows, identify the two that attract you most. Explain why these books or Web sites interest you. Consider looking into them for further deepening your understanding of argument—how arguments are constructed, what makes an effective argument, and why.

Take a look, too, at the MyThinkingLab resources on the Prentice Hall Web site. Included there are readings, images, videos, questions, exercises, and other provocations to help develop your critical thinking and argument skills.

Resources

"The Advocate." Herman Melville. In *Moby-Dick*. Penguin, 2002.

"Corn-Pone Opinions." Mark Twain. In *The Complete Essays of Mark Twain*. Da Capo Press, 1991.

"Letter from Birmingham Jail." Martin Luther King, Jr. In *100 Great Essays*, 4th edition. Ed. Robert DiYanni. Penguin-Longman, 2010.

The Little Blue Reasoning Book, Brandon Royal. Maven Publishing, 2010.

Words Like Loaded Pistols, Sam Leith. Basic Books, 2013.

The Uses of Argument, Stephen Toulmin. Cambridge University Press, 1969.

"They Say / I Say," Gerald Graff and Kathy Birkenstein. Norton, 2009.

Everything's an Argument, Andrea A. Lunsford, John J. Ruszkiewicz, and Keith Walters. Bedford/St. Martin's, 2009.

Julius Caesar, William Shakespeare. Simon and Schuster, 2009.

Human Universals, Donald E. Brown. McGraw-Hill, 1991.

9
Parallel Thinking and Lateral Thinking

If you never change your mind, why have one?

—EDWARD DE BONO

FOCUSING QUESTIONS

- How might parallel thinking— thinking in the same direction together with others at the same time—provide a productive alternative to argumentative thinking?

- What might be the value of using colored thinking hats to direct thinking toward facts and feelings, benefits and drawbacks, creativity and process?

- What might be the value of focus for thinking—general and specific focus?

- Why are concepts and essences important for thinking?

- What tools would you like to have at your disposal to generate fresh thinking in the form of new ideas?

LEARNING GOALS

9.1 UNDERSTAND the concept of parallel thinking in contrast to adversarial thinking.

9.2 IDENTIFY the functions of the six thinking hats and apply them to solve problems.

9.3 UNDERSTAND and explain the concept and value of lateral thinking in contrast to vertical, or logical, thinking.

9.4 ANALYZE and employ the tools of lateral thinking, including focus, challenge, and random entry.

9.5 EXPLORE the idea of concepts and essences to generate fresh thinking.

Chapter Overview

This chapter introduces the work on thinking of Dr. Edward de Bono, who invented the term *lateral thinking* and who popularized the idea of "parallel thinking" with his approach based on "six thinking hats." Included in this chapter are some of de Bono's thinking tools, which were created to help us generate new ideas in addition to analyzing and evaluating ideas we already have. The discussions and exercises in this chapter are designed to broaden our thinking. The chapter provides practical tools for thinking more comprehensively, more confidently, more creatively—and less competitively.

Thinking Tools

Dr. Edward de Bono has pioneered a number of thinking strategies and developed them into practical thinking tools that are used worldwide in schools and businesses. He makes the case for his thinking tools by suggesting that logic and analysis, which have dominated Western intellectual life since the time of the ancient Greeks, do not serve all our thinking needs. Although de Bono acknowledges the value and power of analysis and argument, and though he recognizes the need for a scientific method grounded in analysis and argument, he suggests that the best thinking requires something more. He values logic- and evidence-based reasoning along with analytical frameworks and paradigms. However, he claims that argument as a method of thinking includes some built-in weaknesses. The biggest weakness, he suggests, is that it is based on one side proving the other "wrong." "I am right; you are wrong," is the basic structure of argument, a structure that limits fresh thinking because the goal is simply to "win." In addition, argument tends to be ego-driven and adversarial, argumentative aspects that inhibit creative thinking, which often functions best in more collaborative and collegial environments.

Watch the **Video**, Thinking Tools/Six Thinking Hats **MyThinkingLab**

Six Thinking Hats

As an alternative to argumentative thinking, de Bono devised his "parallel thinking," or "six hats" method. This approach is most fully described in his *Six Thinking Hats*, but an overview is included in his *How to Have a Beautiful Mind*. In **parallel thinking**, six colored hats are aligned with six directions for thinking. A group of people works together to consider a problem, issue, or challenge. Each person participating in the thinking session is obliged to wear (symbolically), in turn, each of six hats. Everyone wears the same-color hat at the same time. Following these two basic rules leads to thinking that is prolific and productive. Because everyone in a group is thinking in the same direction at the same time—wearing the same-color thinking hat—the thinking is collaborative and cooperative rather than argumentative and adversarial.

parallel thinking
A form of thinking in which a group of people think together in the same direction at the same time for a common purpose. An alternative to adversarial thinking.

Why use differently colored thinking "hats"? For these reasons: First, the hat colors remind us to think in a particular direction—to focus on facts, information, and data, for example, when wearing the white hat. Second, the hats take our individual egos out of the discussion. If we are all advancing ideas about what we know or don't know under the white hat, we are cooperating and sharing ideas rather than criticizing and evaluating each other's contributions. We are not trying to outdo each other or prove each other wrong. Third, hats have a natural association with thinking. We are familiar with the expression "put on your thinking caps," an indication that we are being deliberate about thinking. And fourth, the hats make the whole process playful, something of a game—but one with serious intentions: to engender and develop good ideas.

The White Hat

The white hat is the information hat. Information includes both hard, or factual, information, which can be verified, and also softer information, such as rumors and personal experience. Key questions associated with the white hat are these:

- What do we know? And how do we know it?
- What don't we know that we want or need to know?
- How and where can we get the required information?
- How trustworthy is the information we have?

Sometimes, information involves conflicts and disagreements. While thinking under the white hat, we need to include the conflicting "facts." At a later point, it will be necessary to resolve the conflict and identify which version is true, or at least closer to what we believe to be true or what the available evidence best indicates is true.

We often use the white hat in situations that involve making decisions about investing our resources in new initiatives. Before we can make important decisions—whether a personal decision like buying a car or a computer, a professional decision about a new job or project, or any decision involving other people—we need to gather information we can trust. The trustworthiness of information is important, for using unreliable information can lead to bad decisions, errors, and other misfortunes.

As an "objective" hat, the white hat serves as a focus to gather information that can be used as evidence for making a decision, or arriving at a judgment. Complementing the objective direction of white-hat thinking is the more subjective direction of another thinking hat—the red hat.

The Red Hat

The red hat is the emotion, or feelings, hat. This hat also represents intuition. Right away, you might think, "Wait a minute; emotion isn't part of thinking—in fact, emotions cloud rational thinking. And besides, our intuitions can't really be explained—they're subjective feelings at best." And to a certain extent, this is true. The other side of this coin, however, is that our feelings often play a significant role in our thinking, but we tend either to overlook or deny their role. Think, for example, of a major purchase you badly wanted or needed. It's very likely that your feelings—your desires—played a significant role in your purchase. This is not to deny that you may also have gathered data, made a comparative analysis, talked with experts, and the like. But oftentimes, if we are honest with ourselves, we use that data to justify what we want, based on other less analytical and more emotional motives. The real driver of our purchases is often less rational than emotional.

The red hat gives our feelings a place in the discussion. It recognizes their validity and legitimizes them. Under the red hat, we say things like "I don't like this suggestion." Or "This idea makes me nervous." Or "I am very excited by this idea." Or "I'm confused and ambivalent about what we are considering."

With the red hat, there is no need to explain or justify our expressions of feeling or intuition. Rather, we simply acknowledge them and move on. One of the benefits of using the red hat is that it allows a group to clear the air about an issue. People often need a release valve when a controversial issue warrants discussion or decision. Giving them a chance to express their feelings under the red hat provides a controlled venue for them. It also opens the way for thinking in other directions, including the fact-based thinking under the white hat.

Besides including our emotional responses as part of the thinking process, the red hat allows for recognition of our intuition about things. Intuition is a complex form of judgment, one that cannot be fully explained. We are often not completely aware of all the elements or aspects that contribute to an intuition. Knowledge and experience are two broad general components. But no matter how much we know and how deep and wide our experience, our intuitions are not always correct. Being aware of this fact doesn't mean we should disallow our intuitions, but rather that we should be careful in using them. That's one reason we don't rely on intuition alone; instead, we check our intuition against information and data collected under the white hat. Intuition, like emotion, is a factor we consider in the parallel thinking process.

The Black Hat

The black hat is the judgment hat—the critical hat, the skeptical hat, the argumentative hat. The black hat is a very important and powerful hat. Under it we look for what we think of as the "negative" side of an idea, the dangers associated with it, the "worst-case scenarios" that might result from implementing it.

We need black-hat thinking to avoid mistakes, to keep from doing things that might be wrong or dangerous. A company's legal department often specializes in black-hat thinking; its responsibility is to avoid situations that might jeopardize the company financially and legally. The black hat is associated with assessing risk, with being careful and cautious.

The black hat should not be considered a bad hat because of its tendency to look for the pitfalls in a situation. Nor should the black hat be considered any better or worse than the other hats. Its function is important. But it should be neither overvalued nor undervalued, neither overused nor underused.

The black hat can also be used to indicate a logical mistake—a fallacy in thinking, for example. Under the black hat, we identify information gathered under the white hat that is incorrect or only partially accurate. The black hat also points out faults and weaknesses of arguments. It indicates why something may be inappropriate, or how it may become a potential problem.

The black hat can block or stifle thinking because of the various kinds of dangers detected under it. These cautions and dangers need to be balanced by the yellow hat, under which we consider things from an opposite and more positive perspective.

The Yellow Hat

The complementary partner of the black hat is the yellow hat. The yellow hat is associated with the benefits and values of an idea or proposal. Under the yellow hat, we look for the good prospects and possibilities, the best-case scenarios, the positives associated with an idea.

When we wear the yellow hat, we avoid judging ideas. Instead, we consider only their potential benefits—the good that might come from implementing them. Sometimes this is more difficult than identifying potential dangers under the black hat. People often say that it is easier to criticize than to create. It is also, perhaps, easier to offer black-hat criticism than yellow-hat value, to see black-hat dangers than yellow-hat benefits. To find value can sometimes be a challenge, but that's one of the advantages of using the six hats approach to thinking—it challenges us, it stretches us, it develops our ability to go outside the thinking domains we are most comfortable with, and, instead, to think in multiple directions (though always and only in one direction at a time).

If the black hat can be described as something of a pessimistic direction for thinking, the yellow hat is its optimistic counterpart. And while the yellow hat looks for benefits, it also considers feasibility—the likelihood that an idea might work or actually be capable of being implemented.

EXERCISES

1. Put on your red hat first and then your white hat to consider the following question: Should video cameras be permitted in jury rooms when the jury is deciding on a verdict?

   For your red hat, simply provide your gut reaction, your feeling about it—without explanation. Then switch to the white hat as you consider this question. Make a list of what you know, what you don't know and need to know, and how you will get that information. You can do this exercise alone, but it tends to work better with a partner, or with a small group.

2. Let's now put on next the yellow hat and then the black hat with respect to the question about video cameras in the jury deliberation room. List first the potential benefits that could result from having video cameras in the room. Spend perhaps 3 or 4 minutes wearing the yellow hat, looking for the upside, the positive potential of this scenario. Again, you can do this exercise alone, with a partner, or with a small group. Now shift for another 3 or 4 minutes to the black hat. What are your concerns? What cautions would you worry about if video cameras were allowed in the jury room? What are the dangers, and what is the downside of this scenario?

3. Now that you have spent some time thinking through the issue of video cameras in the jury room, you have seen both positives and negatives. You have also garnered some information, but realize that you now want more. In addition, you have expressed a feeling about the issue. It's time to put your red hat back on for half a minute. Is your feeling the same? Has it shifted in any way? No explanation is necessary; just provide a red-hat gut check.

Pairing the Hats

We have been pairing the hats with their different thinking directions. It's easier to remember three pairs of hats and what they stand for than to remember six separate hats and their individual directions for thinking. Pairing the hats also suggests how the different thinking directions balance one another. The white hat's objectivity and fact finding is balanced by the red hat's subjectivity and emotional response. The yellow hat's eager optimism is balanced by the black hat's cautious warnings.

So, we have, then, the white and red hats representing facts and feelings. And we have the black and yellow hats, directing our thinking toward dangers and benefits. That leaves two hats—the blue hat for organization and control, and the green hat for creativity. Pairing the hats also reminds us that critical and creative thinking involve seeing things from more than a single perspective, a key aspect of our next thinking hat—the green hat.

The Green Hat

The green hat is the creative thinking hat—the creative energy hat. If the white hat seeks information and the red hat requests feelings and intuitions, the green hat invites ideas, alternatives, possibilities—even models, images, metaphors, and designs. The green had can be intimidating, but it shouldn't be, because creative thinking is the province of everyone. Each of us demonstrates creativity in our everyday lives. What we do under the green hat is a natural extension of something we all do—exercise practical creativity in dealing with life's ordinary problems and its unusual situations and challenges.

When we wear the green hat, however, we become more deliberate about our creative thinking, more conscious and intentional about thinking creatively. Under the green hat, we make our creative thinking more explicit and more focused. We direct our thinking energies collaboratively toward generating new and fresh ideas. And we allow ourselves to do this without embarrassment and without worrying at first whether the fresh approaches we identify are sufficiently practical to warrant implementation.

Too often when someone proposes a new idea, especially an unusual or creative idea, the instinct of many people is to pounce on it, attack it, show how it couldn't possibly work. (That, of course, is thinking under the black hat—useful and necessary in its time and place, but not when we are wearing the green hat and trying to generate new ideas.) And so, when we wear our green hats together, instead of attacking a new idea—no matter how far-fetched or outrageous it might seem—we build on it instead. We can let it stimulate other ideas without having to worry about another person's premature evaluation, judgment, or condemnation of those ideas.

Under the green hat, we give ourselves permission to be creative. We give each other permission to be creative together. We make a game of it; we enjoy the freedom the game aspect provides and the energy it creates. Whatever ideas emerge from our green-hat thinking can be sifted and selected, judged and evaluated—and improved, later. One wonderful aspect of the green hat experience is that we come to see that even though we may not consider ourselves "creative" types, we can discover new and creative ideas, especially when we bounce ideas off others who are thinking collaboratively with us. This experience is partly a result of being given permission to be creative, partly a result of the overall environment we have established with the six hats approach, and partly a result of allocating some actual time for creative thinking.

When we wear the green hat, one of our major efforts is to consider alternatives and possibilities. Whatever topic, issue, or idea we are thinking about, our goal with the green hat is to think of other ways of approaching it, considering it, doing it. Sometimes, we discover useful and practical alternatives, possibilities that we, and others, recognize as valid and valuable. Other times, we come up with more wild and wacky alternatives that are less immediately useful or practical. But even these more far-fetched possibilities can lead to better ideas once we play with them and build on them. This is one reason to avoid judging too quickly ideas generated with green-hat thinking. For even our less than promising ideas can provoke new directions for our thinking; they might become stepping-stones to better, more practical and useful ideas.

Thinking under the green hat, even more than thinking in the directions of the other hats, requires practice, patience, and perseverance. Green-hat thinking also requires that you learn some specific tools for creativity. Edward de Bono has described some of those creative thinking tools under the rubric of lateral thinking, which we explore in a preliminary way after we discuss the last of the six hats, the blue hat.

The Blue Hat

The blue hat is the organizing hat, the management hat. The blue hat controls the process of using the other hats. The specific functions of the blue hat vary. In the beginning of a thinking discussion, the blue hat is responsible for defining the purpose of the thinking session and its focus. This blue-hat function can be shared with the other members of the group, though most of the blue-hat managing responsibility is assigned to a single person. The initial blue-hat decisions about focus and purpose, though directed by the blue-hat facilitator, need to be accepted if not developed and decided by the group as a whole. This is to secure clarity about what the group will be doing during the thinking session, and why. In addition to clarifying the purpose of the thinking discussion, the blue hat also allows for group buy-in into the process.

A key function of the blue-hat is to set the sequence of hats for the session. This, too, can be a matter of discussion among the group members. But even here, someone has to serve as facilitator to guide that discussion and decide which hats will be used, how often they will be used, and in what order. (In any thinking session using the hats, we need not use all six hats. Nor need we limit our use of any hat to a single prescribed period of time. We can bring back a hat for more work thinking in the direction it represents.)

At the end of a thinking session the blue hat gathers the information, feelings, and ideas that have been generated. The blue hat summarizes the outcomes and also, in conjunction with the group, decides on next steps. The group might decide that more information is needed before a decision can be reached about an issue. There might be an opportunity for some action steps to be taken. Or another thinking session might be required to build on the initial one.

So the blue hat serves three basic functions:

1. It initiates the session and set its direction.
2. It guides the thinking discussion as it develops by keeping the group on track—focused on the issue under consideration and using the hats appropriately.
3. It brings things together at the end.

The blue hat questions associated with these aspects are:

1. What are we here for?
2. How are we engaging in the process; what is emerging from our hat-based discussion?
3. What have we achieved, and what should we do next?

EXERCISES

4. It's time, now, to spend 4 or 5 minutes wearing the green hat. What ideas can you devise and develop for having jury-room cameras? If they were going to be used, to what creative uses could you put those cameras? How would you implement their use?

5. Wearing the blue hat, do a quick summary of what you have come up with regarding the use of video cameras in the jury room. List some next steps we need to take with regard to this issue. Do you think there should be more discussion? Should there be some information gathering? Do we need some expert advice? Do you want another thinking session—perhaps with just three or four of the hats? What's next? You can do this exercise by yourself, with a partner, or with a small group.

Individual Use and Group Use of the Hats

We can use the hats by ourselves, individually. For example, we can use them to think about a personal problem or a work-related project or report. We can use them to think about ways to develop and present that report or project. That is, the hats can be used more than once—for different stages of your individual work, for different tasks along the way to completing a project.

We can also use the hats collaboratively. Small groups of three to five can think both efficiently and productively by using the six thinking hats. And large groups can use the hats by ensuring that there are opportunities for smaller groups to break out and think together before sharing ideas with the entire group. However, as in small groups, so too in large ones, each member must wear all the hats—thinking in their different directions, one direction at a time. Each small breakout group needs to experience the same spectrum of thinking directions with each of the hats. This structured guidance of the six hats process, of course, is done under the direction of the blue-hat leader.

A further point of clarification about the use of the six thinking hats is this: The six hats do not represent six categories or types of thinking. Categories tend to be static and fixed. It is not the goal to "specialize" in black-hat thinking or yellow-hat thinking, for example, to become fixed or fixated on them. It is not productive to think of oneself as a "black-hat thinker" or a "yellow-hat thinker," even though we might have a disposition or tendency toward one or another type of thinking. The hats represent "directions" for thinking rather than categories. We can change direction, and we can move in different directions, which is necessary for developing our critical and creative thinking capacities.

One final note: The six hats parallel thinking approach functions best when time limits are set for each hat in a sequence. The timings are set at the beginning of a thinking session in conjunction with the blue-hat facilitator, who is typically given the responsibility for adjusting the allocated time in the course of the thinking session. And, overall, although the blue-hat facilitator welcomes discussion and suggestions, he or she serves as chair or leader of the group, and in that capacity must make final decisions about matters of process and procedure.

EXERCISES

6. Spend some time doing each of the following.

  a. Use the six hats method to analyze a newspaper or magazine article or advertisement, whether you read it in print or on the Internet. The hats can serve as a comprehensive tool to help you think about what the article says.

  Decide first on what order you will use the hats. And write out your thoughts while using each to guide your thinking.

  b. Use the six hats to think through a challenge you face in your personal or professional life. Consider each of the hats in turn. Write out your thoughts as you use each hat as a separate thinking tool.

7. What associations might you make with each of the hats to help you remember their particular functions? For example, the white hat is a neutral color. It is easy to remember its association with facts and information, which are in and of themselves objective or neutral.

8. To what extent do you think the hats can help you think forward in new directions? To what extent can they provide added value to the kinds of current strategies you use for thinking?

Lateral Thinking

Edward de Bono coined the term *lateral thinking* in 1970 when he published a book with that title. In that book de Bono explains that **lateral thinking** involves the generation of new ideas; it focuses on breaking out of the constraints and patterns of entrenched ways of seeing. He argues that lateral thinking is a necessary and viable complement to vertical thinking, the traditional and more familiar type of thinking. Where vertical thinking is sequential and selective, lateral thinking is nonsequential and nonselective.

lateral thinking
An alternative to logical thinking that emphasizes how to generate ideas and focuses on avoiding the constraints and patterns of entrenched ways of seeing. An alternative to logical, or vertical, thinking.

Using the metaphor of digging a hole deeper (which is what vertical thinking does), de Bono suggests that we dig a new hole in a different place, and perhaps do something else (which is what lateral thinking does). He reminds us that we need both vertical and lateral thinking because vertical thinking refines and develops the ideas that lateral thinking generates.

Lateral Thinking and the Green Hat

The lateral thinking tools for generating ideas are related to the green hat—the creative thinking hat of de Bono's *Six Thinking Hats*. In another book, *Serious Creativity*, de Bono discusses a variety of lateral thinking tools, including among others, *focus, challenge, alternatives, concepts, the concept fan (concept extraction), random input (also called random entry), provocation and movement,* and *harvesting*. Each of these lateral thinking techniques requires not just an understanding of what it is and how it works, but also opportunities for application and practice. Like the six hats tools for thinking, the lateral thinking tools require practice in applying them. We sample a few of the lateral thinking tools in the following sections.

The Creative Pause

The simplest of de Bono's creative thinking techniques is the creative pause. This pause is just that—a deliberate effort to think creatively for a set amount of time—a few minutes, perhaps, during a meeting. The creative pause does not have to occur in response to a question or a problem—though it can be so related. It might simply be a decision, or an intention to pause and do something specifically directed toward creative reflection. The creative pause is a way to direct attention and deflect distractions. The creative pause might be initiated by something as simple as saying to yourself: "I wonder if I can think of a different way to do this?" Or, for a group: "Let's see if we can devote a few minutes to thinking of other ways to do this."

The key to the creative pause is that it is simple, short, and unpressured. There's a casualness about it that makes it easy to do. Its virtue is that it is proactive rather than reactive, like so much of our thinking. One of the benefits of the creative pause is that it makes creative thinking a habit a little bit at a time. Another is that it produces a creative thinking mentality; it helps develop a creative thinking attitude, a creative disposition and habit.

Focus

⊙ **Simulate** the **Experiment**, Focus/General Area Focus and Purpose Focus **MyThinkingLab**

Focus is more intensive than the creative pause. Although most people don't think of focus as a creative act or strategy, it almost always can be. One of the benefits of focus is that it targets and directs our thinking. Another is that it can encourage us to direct our attention to small matters that others haven't bothered to consider. De Bono mentions the inventor of the Black & Decker "Workmate," a workstation for using power tools. While a number of people focused on improving the power tools made by the company and creating new power tools, the inventor of the "Workmate" focused on the place where the tools could be used. He also mentions the inventor of the variable-speed windshield wiper, who focused not on a better way of wiping the windshield, but on varying the speed of the windshield wipers.

Even such simple examples suggest the importance of focus and the need to identify a focus point. Like the creative pause, this kind of simple focus helps us develop a habit of creative thinking—of considering alternatives and possibilities, of directing our attention to a different aspect or element of whatever challenge, problem, or issue we are thinking about.

General Area Focus and Purpose Focus

Deciding on a focus is very important because with the wrong focus, we solve the wrong problem and waste a lot of time and energy, and perhaps money as well. With de Bono's prodding, we can develop our thinking about focus in two ways: (1) around a general or "area" focus, and (2) on a more specific "purpose" focus.

For a **general area focus** it's enough to ask for "some new ideas about" something—restaurants, for example, or coffeemakers, or dormitory housing, or hotels. This general or area focus can be broad or narrow. Here are some examples of a general focus:

- We need some ideas in the area of organizing a school.
- We need some ideas on organizing a middle school.
- We need some ideas on inquiry-based learning in the school.
- We need some ideas about professional development for teachers.

The virtue of this way of asking for ideas is that it keeps idea pathways open. Ideas don't necessarily have to be purpose-driven, practical, or feasible. The only constraint is the general direction of thinking as it is defined. We can see the difference if we recast the request for ideas in another more specific way, as a **purpose focus**. For example:

We need ideas to improve efficiency in organizing our department. This is also a useful direction for thinking—a useful focus. But it differs in being more specific and targeted; it is also directed toward a particular purpose—improving efficiency in organization. Sometimes, however, we prefer to consider broader ways of organizing or even "improving" our target focus. It's not that one kind of focus, the specific or the general, is better than the other; they are simply different and yield different kinds of thinking results. We need them both.

Here are some examples of a more specifically directed purpose focus for creative thinking:

- We need ideas on improving traffic flow on our campus.
- We need ideas to improve customer service in our cafeteria.
- We need ideas to increase the effectiveness of classroom discussion.
- We need ideas to increase participation in extracurricular clubs.

There is much more that de Bono includes in his discussion of focus in *Serious Creativity* and elsewhere. For our purposes, here, however, the critical point is to think seriously about the focus of our thinking—what we are thinking about and why we are, in fact, thinking about it at all.

Challenge

The primary purpose of what de Bono calls "challenge" is to question why something exists as it does, why something is done the way it is. Once we ask those questions, we can begin considering other ways of doing things—other possibilities and alternatives.

When we "challenge" something in this sense, it does not mean that we are finding fault with it, or criticizing it. We are not attacking something when we "challenge" it. We are, rather, questioning why it's done one way rather than another way. It might very well be that the way something is done works not only well enough, but as well as any other way, and perhaps is the best of all possible ways.

general area focus
In creative thinking, focusing on a broad or general category.

purpose focus
In creative thinking, focusing on a specific topic rather than a broad or general category.

Write the Response, Challenge MyThinkingLab

Martha Stewart's method for putting a duvet cover on a comforter has been found by many to be the best possible way to perform that action. Until someone discovers a "better" way to do that, anyone who needs to cover a blanket with a duvet is well advised to follow Martha Stewart's procedure.

What about something very different: the peculiar shape of London taxis? Why are they designed the way they are? What are the benefits? Is there a better design for London taxis? And what of the color of the taxis in New York City? Or of the school buses there? Is yellow a better color for the taxis and buses than red or blue or green? Why or why not? Asking these questions as a form of "challenge" pushes our thinking beyond blind acceptance and toward thoughtful consideration. (Even if we decide that those London taxis are just right the way they are, and the yellow school buses and yellow taxis should remain yellow as well.)

EXERCISES

9. Choose something right now to think creatively about in a 2-minute pause.

   Perhaps you can think about some ways you can begin exercising your creativity.

10. Identify a simple focus for each of the following situations:

    a. Being in a long line at an airport for a security check

    b. Putting stamps on 500 envelopes you are mailing

    c. Sitting in a meeting where everyone's head is down on a tablet or smartphone

    d. Waiting for a slow elevator in a tall building

11. Think of a general area focus and a more purpose-directed focus for the following:

    a. Hotels

    b. Shopping malls

    c. Movie theaters

    d. Supermarkets

    e. Underground trains

12. Identify two things you observe around you that you can "challenge" in this way. Your goal is to ask simply why they look or work the way they do and whether there are other possibilities: Identify some of those other possibilities. Candidates: the training of taxi drivers in a particular city; the preseason preparations of professional sports teams; the traffic patterns in a place; the timing and financing of political campaigns; the use of bicycle lanes and bicycle pickup and drop-off stations in a town or city.

Random Entry

Random entry, which de Bono also calls "random input," is among the simplest of creative thinking techniques to use, but it is also one of the most engaging, and one of the most effective for generating new ideas. A random input or entry is used to generate thinking in a series of unpredictable directions. Consider de Bono's example of a copy machine and a random word association of *nose*. The stimulus of the word *nose* makes us of think of smell. And then we wonder how our sense of smell might be of use with respect to a copier.

What happens in this and any case of a random stimulus is that we begin to make connections between these two seemingly unrelated things—the copier and our nose, via smell. For example various smells emanating from the copier might be used to indicate that the ink needs changing, or that the copier has run out of paper, perhaps even a particular-size paper, as different papers could be linked to different odors or aromas.

The notion here is not that this particular instance of a random word—of *nose* with *copier*—necessarily produces a usable idea either at first or later. It is, rather, that the idea of using various smells to signal some aspect of a machine's workings might be of value with other kinds of machines. Or that another of our senses might serve as indicators of information and interpretation as to the functioning of a different kind of machine. Or that this idea of using smell as a way of diagnosing a problem might be applied in some other very different kind of situation.

The more general point, however, is that the random entry or input, in this case a random word, stimulates ideas that lead us in directions we would not have taken our thinking without the random stimulus. The random word provokes the imagination; it generates fresh ways of thinking in unexpected directions. And that's the real goal—to develop our critical and creative thinking capacities by pushing them in new and unexpected ways.

Concepts

One of the most important of all thinking capacities is the ability to form concepts. We need concepts to reason. We use concepts all the time, whenever we solve problems in everyday life, such as opening a can of paint with a screwdriver and stirring it with a twig when we lack a proper opener and paint stick. The concept in this case is that we need something to open the can of paint and we need something with which to stir it. What could we use if the screwdriver and twig were also not available for use?

One approach is to enlarge the concept from "stirring" to "mixing." Of course, we could shake the paint or roll it around—though shaking yields a better result—as long as the top is securely tight.

Consider, further, how the concept of painting a house inside and out has changed with the development of the paint roller, sleeve, and tray for indoor painting, and the sponge "brush" and the spray-gun system for outdoor painting. The invention of these painting systems, however, has not entirely eliminated the need for paintbrushes. But the inventors of those painting systems considered the larger concept of putting paint on surfaces beyond simply brushing it on. They asked themselves how the surfaces could be covered with paint and not just how they might improve the then currently available tool—the paintbrush. A different concept would be to consider not painting at all, but broadening the concept to "covering." In that case, we would think not about painting a house or a room, but "covering" it—as, for example, with wall paper or stenciling inside, or with aluminum siding outside.

We need to identify concepts so we can find alternative ways to accomplish things. Once we extract a concept, we can also look for ways to improve how to do something, as an alternative to finding other and different ways of doing it. We can seek better ways to make a paintbrush, for example, while also looking for alternatives to bristle brushes, such as those just mentioned. And we can look for alternatives to painted rooms. Then once the new systems are developed, we can seek ways to improve them as well, whether those systems apply paint or wallpaper or fabric or something else.

Another example is the concept of "fast food," as evidenced in a wide range of food establishments, such as McDonald's, Wendy's, Burger King, and Taco Bell. Speed is certainly one concept underlying fast food. And cost is another, as the food is meant to be inexpensive. A third fast-food concept is standardization, and a fourth is franchising, which is linked to standardization. No matter where you go, when you order a Big Mac or a Whopper, you get the same combination of ingredients in the same proportions and cooked the same way with the same equipment.

Other concepts we can extract from the notion of fast food, such as appealing to children, can be extended or challenged. For example, what if we had fast-food restaurants that discouraged children. No kids' meals and no playgrounds in the restaurants, for sure. Or what if we wanted fast food that was of the highest quality, which, of course, would make it much more expensive? We now have another concept. Perhaps high-quality fast or semifast food, perhaps handmade pastas, sauces, and cheeses of the finest ingredients and then packaged (perhaps frozen) that can be served simply by being heated when needed. That's fast for the consumer, but nothing like the fast food served at a McDonald's, Wendy's, Burger King, or Taco Bell.

With any idea, it is often useful (and a good habit) to step back and ask what concepts might underlie the idea. De Bono suggests asking the question: "This idea is a way of doing what?" Starbucks, for example, as has been often remarked, is not in the business of selling coffee. That is not Starbuck's concept. Nor is FedEx in the business of transportation or Apple in the business of selling electronics. Starbucks sells lots of coffee, of course, FedEx transports numerous packages, and Apple sells millions of electronic gadgets.

The concept for their selling success, however, is something other than those products. Starbucks sells "atmosphere"—an upscale place where you can sit and relax, get free Wi-Fi, and drink expensive coffee made from the finest of carefully grown and processed coffee beans. FedEx sells peace of mind via speed and reliability. It gets the packages where they need to go on schedule, and it does it speedily and efficiently through a system operated by a single vendor (itself), which handles pickup, transfer, and delivery. And Apple sells style, elegance, and cachet along with glitz, power, "coolness," and an array of special features. Apple has also reconceptualized and redesigned its stores as not merely places to buy its products but as places to try its products, and as places to play with iMacs, iPods, iPhones, and iPads. In addition, Apple has reconceptualized the entire process of music delivery with its iTunes store, its licensing practices, and its overall business model.

Understanding the basic concept of a business, activity, or enterprise is crucial. In her book, *The Power of Why*, Amanda Lang describes a company that manufactured flight simulators to train airline pilots. Their business was selling ever more sophisticated flight simulators. After a while, the company realized that their product was complex and that training was necessary for it to be used effectively. So they created a subsidiary business in training people in how to use their flight simulators. Shortly afterward, they realized that they could reconceptualize their business model and develop an entirely new business in training people to do complicated jobs that require an understanding of how to use complex systems. Their first concept shift involved a change from making a specific product to training people in using that product. Their second shift of concept involved a broadening of that training beyond the use of flight simulators.

A counterexample is provided by a company that failed to identify its real concept—what it was truly about. Kodak, which for over a hundred years was in the business of making film, disappeared from the business universe with the emergence of digital photography. Kodak didn't realize that it was less in the business of making photographic film than in the business of making photographic memories. Had it recognized the concept of memory making, it might have been more willing and able to abandon the idea that film is the only way to record, capture, and preserve those memories.

Essences

Another way of thinking about concepts is to ask yourself what is the "essence" of whatever you are thinking about. We might ask, for example, what is the "essence" of a college or university education. What is "essential" about it? In an opinion piece a few years ago in the Sunday *New York Times Education Review*, two sociologists asked just this question as they described the many new services offered by US higher educational institutions. They listed an array of administrative functions, from directors of communications, development, collaborative engagement (whatever that is), babysitting (!), to vice presidents for student success and residential communications. They cited advertised positions for coordinator of learning immersion experiences, for risk management specialists, grant writers, coaches, sushi chefs, and even baristas.

What concept of educational institution is implied by this array of functions and services? Consider the question in terms of Edward de Bono's question, "This is a way of doing what?" What is the essence of a university education that lavishes such attention on this range of services, while university departments of biology and modern languages, of philosophy and humanities, are filled with part-time faculty who are paid a pittance? These are questions for critical thinking, for sure. But in thinking about what might be done to improve the situation, they are questions for creative thinking, as well.

Suppose the essence or essential concept of a new marketing strategy is "attraction." The goal is to make a product, whether a university education, a new electronic gadget, a perfume, a wristwatch, an e-reading machine, "attractive." One thing we can do is to think about ideas related to attraction, or examples of attraction. Bees are attracted to honey and moths to light. Magnets attract metal; women attract men. Books attract readers. Products attract customers. Politicians attract voters, and religions attract adherents. College sports programs attract athletes, and Web portals attract visitors. Considering these different kinds of attraction and ways of attracting and being attracted broadens our thinking about the concept. We can then use one or another of the concept essences to think about a topic, problem, issue, or challenge in a new way.

EXERCISES

13. Use a random word to generate fresh thinking about the following:
    a. High schools
    b. College fraternities and sororities
    c. Car dealerships
    d. Medical insurance
    e. Commuter trains
    f. Reality television
    g. Athletic programs
    h. Tuition and fees
    i. Scholarships

    Choose your random word by picking up a newspaper or magazine, turning to the third page and reading the third line of print and choosing the third word.

    Be sure to pick a noun, as nouns tend to be more useful as stimuli for idea generation. Alternatively, you can use one of the words from the accompanying list.

Word List

airport	apple	army	badge	bat	balloon	basket	bed	beetle	bike
bird	boat	book	branch	brick	button	cart	carriage	cake	
carrion	cave	cellar	chain	chair	clock	cloud	coat	cook	cord
cork	crayon	curtain	cushion	desk	dock	doctor	drain	drawer	drum
ear	earth	egg	engine	eye	fan	faucet	finger	fish	fork fridge frog
game	gate	ghost	grape	guitar	gun	hair	hammer	heart	horn horse
house	ice	ink	iron	jail	jewel	joke	journey	kettle	key kite
knife	knot	mailbox	marble	mask	mitten	monkey	nail		
needle	net	nose	nut	ocean	orange	oven	owl	pail	pear pencil pie
pipe	popcorn	prison	quill	quilt	rain	ring	road	river	sail shirt
scissors	sock	shoe	skirt	smile	snake	snow	song	spider	spoon stone
sugar	sun	swing	table	tank	tent	test	thumb	thunder	tiger train
tomato	toothbrush	turkey	umbrella	volcano	volleyball	watch			
wave	wheel	word	wrench	yard	yarn	zebra	zipper	zoo	

14. What concepts are associated with each of the following?

   a. Ladders

   b. Advertising

   c. Umbrellas

   d. Midterm exams

   e. Facebook

   f. Holidays

   g. Bars

   h. Environmentalism

   i. Blogs

15. Select one type of "attraction" and describe it in detail. What does it suggest? How does it work? What values are associated with this kind of "attraction?" How can politicians, for example, attract votes? How can a university attract students? What concepts are associated with being "attracted" to a particular school or university? How can these various forms of attraction be packaged and marketed effectively against the competition?

Concepts as Thinking Tools

In a recent book, *This Will Make Your Smarter*, John Brockman, publisher and editor of *Edge*, a journal devoted to the frontiers of thinking, invited contributors to answer the following question: "What scientific concept would improve everybody's cognitive toolkit?" Brockman notes that "scientific" here has a broad application to knowledge of human and corporate behavior, along with the fate of the planet, as well as concepts in the natural and biological sciences.

We can use Edward de Bono's notions of thinking tools and of concepts to consider some of the answers contributors provided for Brockman's book. We can also think about some of the cognitive tools described there as examples of de Bono's concept of "lateral thinking."

We begin with the concepts of "cognitive tool" and "cognitive toolkit." These, of course, are metaphors. Normally, when we think of tools, we think of things like hammers and screwdrivers, among basic manual tools, and of computer software programs and applications, among electronic and digital tools. Cognitive tools, by analogy, are tools that help us think rather than tools that enable us to do various kinds of work (though thinking is certainly a kind of "work"). And a "cognitive toolkit," is simply a collection of such thinking tools, though with the sense that the toolkit keeps them accessible and ready for use.

The kinds of cognitive tools identified in *This Will Make You Smarter* range widely. Some examples include ideas such as cognitive humility; the uselessness of certainty; the biases of technology; how each of us is ordinary yet one of a kind; how failure liberates success; how humans possess an "instinct to learn"; how creativity is provoked by constraints; how "wicked" problems differ from solvable ones; how we can "design" our minds, and many more.

Brockman asked his contributors to focus on a question that leads to answers that can't be predicted, with the question about cognitive tools serving as a provocation. The question was also meant to stimulate thoughts the contributors might normally not have had—or at least to consider some of their most important ideas in new ways. The cognitive tools the contributors provided are meant to enhance creative and productive thinking.

One of the central themes that emerged from more than 150 contributors' essays is the questioning of basic assumptions. Another is the ways technology is altering culture and social interaction in both positive and negative ways. And still another is how it is necessary to move beyond deductive reasoning to include complementary kinds of holistic and emergent thinking. Collectively, the participants' suggestions for a cognitive toolkit involve thinking about thinking; they provide ways to think about the world and to engage with it more effectively. The ideas presented in the book represent both daring and humility—daring to think differently by challenging conventional ideas and beliefs, and humility at how little is known and how much yet to be discovered.

Three Cognitive Tools

Among the cognitive tools presented in Brockman's book are these three: (1) the Pareto principle; (2) recursive structure; and (3) dualities.

The Pareto principle is named after the Italian economist Vilfred Pareto, who discovered that the richest 20% of a country's population controlled 80% of its wealth. This principle has been applied to many kinds of situations and experiences. For example, 20% of users of an Internet site account for 80% of site activity; 20% of a company's employees account for 80% of its revenue; 20% of the people, papers, books, and other research we consult account for 80% of our work activity; 80% of a deli counter's activity centers on 20% of its products—think roast beef, boiled ham, and Swiss cheese.

As Clay Shirky points out in his essay on the Pareto principle, the pattern replicates itself recursively. Within the top 20% of a Pareto distribution, the top 20% of that distribution typically accounts for a disproportionate amount of whatever is being measured. One major effect of the Pareto distribution is to skew the average far from the commonly accepted notion of an average represented by a bell curve. Instead of an even distribution with the middle of the curve showing an average and a median (midpoint of the system) as the same, there is a strong imbalance reflected in the Pareto distribution percentages. The most volatile or most active element of what is being measured is twice as volatile or active as the second most active element and 10 times as volatile or active as the tenth-most element. Such multiples are seen in the magnitude of earthquakes, the social connections of friends, and the habits of readers and book buyers, to cite just a few examples.

A second cognitive tool, "recursive structure," is one in which the shape of the whole is replicated in the shape of its parts. The tracery of Gothic architectural windows (the thin carved stone partitions that separate a window into small panes) is one example. Another is the way a country or state's coastline reveals the same pattern or shape in increasingly larger or smaller increments, such that its structure is similar at five yards or five miles.

In his discussion of this cognitive tool, David Gelernter suggests that understanding recursive structure helps us identify and comprehend connections between

art and technology. Gelernter claims that aesthetic principles influence the thinking of engineers and technologists, and that the clarity and elegance reflected in those aesthetic principles undergird all kinds of successful design. He further suggests that recursive structure indicates a need for a technology education that includes the aesthetics of design along with a study of the history of arts. One place where this conjunction can be seen is in the work done over the past decade at Apple with its popular products such as the iPhone and iPad. Apple's late CEO, Steve Jobs, emphasized the connections between the arts and technology; he saw himself at working at the crossroads of art and technology. His passion was to make products that were both flawlessly functional in their engineering aspects while also being elegantly beautiful.

A third cognitive tool that can change how we understand the world is the concept of dualities. In their respective essays entitled "Dualities," Stephon H. Alexander and Amanda Gefter each highlight a different aspect of this cognitive tool. Alexander focuses on physics, suggesting that some physical phenomena require an explanation from two different perspectives. The classic example is light, the nature of which cannot be fully explained apart from its particle-like and wave-like characteristics. To ask whether light is essentially particle or wave is to miss its underlying duality as both particle and wave. Alexander suggests that dualities remind us and provoke us to use more than a single analytical lens in our attempts to understand anything.

Amanda Gefter explains that dualities transform the concept of "or" into one of "and." Not either/or, but both/and. She encourages us to move beyond the conventional notion of duality as a dichotomy in which opposites clash. Instead of contradiction and conflict among dual terms such as east/west, male/female, light/dark, Gefter urges us to embrace the contraries and attempt to see how two very different things might be equally true. An appreciation for the power of dualities can serve as an antidote to the kind of adversarial thinking of "I'm Right, You're Wrong" that Edward de Bono urges us to transcend. Using the cognitive tool of dualities, along with those of recursive structure, and the Pareto principle can broaden our perception and enrich our understanding of ourselves and of our world.

EXERCISES

16. To what extent do you find the concepts of "cognitive tools" and "cognitive toolkit" helpful? Do you agree with the values ascribed to them?

17. Which of the kinds of cognitive tools—those about humility, failure, certainty, technology, constraints, ordinariness, wicked problems—catches your interest the most? Why?

18. Of the three cognitive tools—the Pareto principle, recursive structure, or dualities—which do you find most promising and attractive? What interests you about this cognitive tool, and how do you think your thinking might benefit from it?

Looking Back and Looking Ahead

Revisit the learning goals that begin this chapter. Which of these goals do you think you have best achieved? What might you do to reach the remaining goals?

Return to the focusing questions at the beginning of the chapter. How would you answer those questions now? Which of them do you find most interesting and provocative and worthy of following up? Why?

In reviewing the list of resources that follows, identify the two that attract you most. Explain why these books or Web sites interest you. Consider looking into them for further developing your capacity for parallel thinking and for lateral thinking.

Take a look, too, at the MyThinkingLab resources on the Prentice Hall Web site. Included there are readings, images, videos, questions, exercises, and other provocations to help develop your critical and creative thinking skills.

Resources

Six Thinking Hats, Edward de Bono. Back Bay, 1985.

Lateral Thinking, Edward de Bono. Harper, 1970.

Serious Creativity, Edward de Bono. Harper, 1993.

How to Have a Beautiful Mind, Edward de Bono. Ebury Press, 2004.

Edward de Bono's Thinking Course, Edward de Bono. BBC Active, 2005.

The Power of Why, Amanda Lang. Collins, 2012.

This Will Make You Smarter, ed. John Brockman. Harper-Perennial, 2012.

Web sites for Edward de Bono: edwdebono.com; debonogroup.com; debonoconsulting.com

Web site for Edge: Edge.org

10
Finding Ideas through Imaginative Thinking

Imagination will often carry us to worlds that never were. But without one, we go nowhere.
—CARL SAGAN

FOCUSING QUESTIONS

- What do you understand by "imagination," and why do you think it could be important to develop your imaginative capacities?

- Where do you get your best ideas? What serves you as the best kinds of stimulation for your own imaginative thinking?

- What do you think might be the relationship between imagination and creativity and between imagination, creativity, and innovation?

- To what extent do consider yourself a creative thinker? And what might you do to strengthen your creative thinking capability?

LEARNING GOALS

10.1 UNDERSTAND and appreciate the power and value of imagination as the source of creative thinking.

10.2 RECOGNIZE and use the Lincoln Center Education capacities for imaginative thinking.

10.3 IDENTIFY and apply techniques for developing creative thinking, including imagining alternatives, breaking rules, and rethinking your thinking.

10.4 EXPLORE different ways to generate ideas and practice creative thinking techniques in personal, academic, and professional contexts.

Chapter Overview

This chapter highlights the primacy of the imagination. It invites consideration of why imagination is important in our lives and what we can do to develop our imaginative capacities. Taking its cue from Lincoln Center Institute Education outreach, the chapter identifies half a dozen Lincoln Center Education practices to explore. The chapter also explains what ideas are, why they are important, and how to find them by means of a series of strategies, techniques, and exercises inspired by Jack Foster, a former advertising director. The exercises based on Foster's *How to Get Ideas* are designed to develop imaginative thinking skills for generating ideas.

The Priority of Imagination

Albert Einstein once remarked, "Imagination is more important than knowledge." He went on to say, "Knowledge is limited, whereas imagination embraces the entire world, stimulating progress, giving birth to evolution." Imagination is the engine that drives creative thinking.

Central to the mission of Lincoln Center Education, the educational outreach arm of Lincoln Center in New York City, is the conviction that imagination is an essential cognitive capacity that can and should be developed. Cultivating the imagination is essential for these reasons: (1) Imagination leads to creativity, which leads to innovation; (2) economic vitality depends on innovation spawned by imaginative and creative thinking; and (3) imagination enriches our lives and makes us more fully human. Developing our imagination deepens our sense of wonder, enriches our capacity for aesthetic appreciation, and enhances the experience of pleasure we take in life.

We can highlight the importance of imagination by means of an analogy with the economy and real estate. Every four years when there is another U.S. presidential election, a key tagline for voters' primary concern is "It's the economy, stupid!" We might amend that to "It's the imagination,—and let's not be stupid about it." In the same way, a mantra among real estate agents advising prospective property buyers is there are three critical factors for a real estate purchase: "location, location, location." For improving creative thinking it's "imagination, imagination, imagination."

EXERCISE ─────────────────────────────────

1. Imagine a world without imagination. Imagine a world without art and music, without sports and fashion, lacking in discoveries and inventions. Imagine a world with no romance and no magic, no poetry and no stories, no new Internet developments, no new electronic gadgets—and no movies. Consider what would be lost with the absence of just any one of these creations of the imagination.

Imagination First—Unlocking Possibility

Imagination is something we are born with. It's an unalienable right that each of us possesses. And yet it's a capacity that we often let languish, that we allow to atrophy. Why? The answer in part is that as we go through school and "grow up," we receive the message that imagination is not so important; we are told that imagination needs to give way to a hard-nosed, realistic understanding of the world. Imagination is replaced with analysis. The playful and imaginative frame of mind is displaced by the factual and the serious.

In their book *A New Culture of Learning*, Douglas Thomas and John Seely Brown suggest that our ability to participate successfully in the world is governed by the play of imagination. Thomas and Brown speculate that play and imagination are critical for successful living in a world of accelerating change. They argue that being "open to the imagination" and allowing for places where the imagination can be at play are essential conditions for fully developing our minds.

Why Imagination?

Why should we care about our imagination? Why is it so important that we develop our imaginative capacities? We have already suggested that imagination is a source of creativity and a necessary step toward its development. Without imagination,

👁 **Watch** the **Video**, Why Imagination?/Imagination, Creativity, Innovation
MyThinkingLab

creative thinking and creative discovery are impeded. That's the practical answer. But there is another explanation: Imagination is a splendid and amazing human capacity. Like our ability to analyze and reason, our capacity to imagine is a big part of what makes us human. Imagining is also one of life's pleasures; it's a joy to imagine "alternative realities," to conjure up prospective possibilities, to conceive of images, patterns, and ideas. In addition, imagination is necessary to understand and appreciate the ideas and creations of others—artistic, musical, theatrical; philosophical, mathematical, scientific; literary, historical, technological—and more.

EXERCISE

2. Find on the Internet Rene Magritte's painting *Personal Values*. Consider how it reveals an imaginative cast of mind. What has the artist done to transform everyday reality? What surprises and shocks does the work provoke in you? What might be the purpose of such uses of the imagination?

   Magritte himself has noted that through a sense of proportion, or rather "dis" proportion, he establishes a "sense of disorientation and incongruity." He inverts inside and outside, and thereby creates a "paradoxical world that defies common sense." He wrote: "I describe objects and the mutual relationships of objects in such a way that more of our habitual concepts or feelings are linked with these."

Imagination, Creativity, Innovation

The twentieth-century American philosopher John Dewey described imagination as being able "to look at things as if they could be otherwise." Another way of saying this is to consider imagination as having the capacity "to conceive of what is not," in the words of Eric Liu and Scott Noppe-Brandon, authors of *Imagination First!* These writers go further by distinguishing between and among imagination, creativity, and innovation, terms often used interchangeably, sometimes synonymously. Liu and Noppe-Brandon suggest, instead, that we think of creativity as applied imagination, the doing or making of something, sparked by an initial imaginative conception. With the exercise of creativity, or applied imagination, comes innovation, the development of something new, advanced, and useful. The sequence goes like this:

Imagination → **Creativity** (*applied imagination*) → **Innovation** (*new creations*)

Here are some examples. A writer imagines a world where a human being can become a man during one part of the year and a woman during another. She creates this place in an innovative book that describes an alternate world somewhat like our own, yet with distinct differences. The book's people are somewhat like us, but with this unusual gender-switching difference, including the stunning possibility of a person being physically both father and mother to a child. This imaginative work is Ursula K. Le Guin's award-winning 1969 novel, *The Left Hand of Darkness*.

Or take a more recent example: the film *Avatar*, directed by James Cameron, who also directed *Titanic*. Before Cameron could develop the innovations for either of these popular films, he had to imagine what the very different worlds portrayed might be like. These acts of imagining, led him to explore a series of creative possibilities and potentialities. In turning his imaginings into creative realities, Cameron actualized imaginative potential, and he developed innovative techniques to bring his ideas to life on the screen.

Capacities for Imaginative Thinking

What are the elements, the aspects, the components, and characteristics of imaginative thinking? What can we do to develop our capacity for building our imagination, for strengthening this creative mental muscle? Lincoln Center Education highlights the following capacities for imaginative thinking and learning:

- **Noticing deeply**—perceiving layers of detail through patient, careful, and thoughtful observation

- **Questioning**—asking the many kinds of thoughtful questions, including "Why," and "Why not"; "How," and "What if?"

- **Embodying**—experiencing things through our senses and emotions, through physical and psychological engagement

- **Identifying patterns**—identifying relationships among details that we notice; linking them together and grouping them into patterns

- **Making connections**—linking the patterns we notice with prior knowledge and experience

- **Exhibiting empathy**—understanding, appreciating, and respecting the experience and perspectives of others

- **Creating meaning**—developing viable interpretations based on our observations, patterns, connections, questions, and expressing this meaning in our own spoken and/or written voice

- **Reflecting and assessing**—looking back on our actions, learning, and thinking to identify additional challenges and questions

- **Taking action**—acting on what we have learned and interpreted; doing something to further our thinking and learning

- **Living with ambiguity**—Learning to accept uncertainty, complexity, and the volatility of experience both literal and virtual

These capacities for imaginative thinking and learning were originally designed for education in the arts. Clearly, however, they are relevant for all aspects of education—for thinking and learning in all academic subjects, and for thinking and learning beyond the classroom, in every aspect of our lives. Developing these capacities so they become habits of mind leads to deeper understanding, stronger thinking, and enriched experience.

EXERCISES

3. Think of a time in your life when your imagination was stifled or at least constrained—by a parent, a teacher, a counselor, a friend. Very likely, there are such instances, from small-scale examples like being told that you can't color the sky green (or a pictured person's face green), to larger more grievous cases, such as being told you have no talent, no creativity, or no possibility of making it as a _____(fill in the blank). How did that limiting of your imagination affect you? How did you respond?

4. Identify two examples of how imagination was the spur to creativity and innovation in one of the following fields—and then add two additional examples where you think creativity and innovation are badly needed.

   a. Professional sports: baseball, football, basketball, tennis, golf, cycling, soccer

   b. Industry: life insurance, healthcare, banking, electronics, food production

    c. Popular music (including country, blues, rock, hip-hop, etc.)

    d. Classical music, rock music, or jazz

    e. The arts of drawing, painting, sculpture, ceramics, printmaking, collage

    f. Architecture and engineering

    g. Theatre and/or dance

    h. Film and comics

    i. An academic field: mathematics, economics, psychology, history, physics

    j. A public service: transportation, safety, sanitation, water, electricity, politics

5. Which of the Lincoln Center capacities seem new—perhaps even unusual—to you? Which of the imaginative thinking capacities are similar to ideas and strategies you have seen and heard before (including elsewhere in this book)? Which of these capacities do you think can be most useful to you in your everyday life? Which might be most helpful in your work and for your future? Why?

Raising Our Imagination Quotient

So how can we raise our imagination quotient? How can we increase our capacity for imaginative thinking? Eric Liu and Scott-Noppe Brandon lay out 28 1/2 "practices" in their book *Imagination First!* Their practices provide a kind of field-manual or toolkit of strategies to develop the imagination. We sample a few of their practices here. The following practices are designed to stimulate imaginative thinking. They are deliberately playful and provocative, but they also have practical applications.

Cultivate Silence—Eliminate Distractions

One of the great inhibitors of imagination is busyness. We tend to overschedule ourselves; we fill our days with appointments, meetings, and obligations of all kinds. As a result, we have little, if any, time to think. We need to clear our calendars and our heads from time to time just to hear ourselves think—to give ourselves a chance to wonder and to imagine. This is essential. We won't be able to concentrate and focus, which are necessary for imagining, if we can't carve out time away from radio and television, and untether ourselves from our smartphones, tablets, and computers.

This need for quiet, private time is described in detail in an important book, *Crazy Busy*, by a practicing psychologist and consultant Edward M. Hollowell, who argues that our addiction to being busy is shortening not only our attention spans but also our lives. Hollowell concurs with Liu and Noppe-Brandon that cultivating periods of silence is a powerfully important, even life-preserving antidote to the frenzy and cacophony that we experience too much of the time.

Silence, moreover, has long been a staple of religious traditions, particularly in their meditative and contemplative aspects. Christian mystics, Zen Buddhists, Hindu yogis, and Trappist monks are just a few who value the practice of silence in their lives. But it's not necessary to be a religious devotee to benefit from creating even a small oasis of quiet each day, and using that quiet time to reflect, think, and imagine.

Banish Your Fears

We all have fears. Fear prevents us from taking chances, from risk-taking ventures. Fear kills imagination. To think effectively and productively, we need to conquer those fears. How can we do that? One way is to think positive thoughts—to confront the fear directly and address it with a counterattack of positive thinking. Even doing this, we may still have some residual fright. That's understandable. But we need to push ourselves to proceed in the face of that fear.

Liu and Noppe-Brandon recount a story about the choreographer Twyla Tharp, who uses a ritual to banish her fears when she begins creating a new dance. Tharp uses a "stare-down" strategy. She writes down what scares her, and she disciplines herself to confront those fears directly. She writes down her fears, such as, "I won't do it right." "People won't like it; the critics won't like it." "My reputation is at stake." She addresses each of her fears in turn; she counterattacks with positive responses. And then with a sense of purpose and determination, she forges ahead and does her creative work, time after time after time.

Renew Your Narrative

Our lives are guided by stories. The psychiatrist and cultural critic Robert Coles titled one of his books *The Call of Stories*, suggesting their pull or attraction for us. We are always telling and listening to stories. Stories inform and entertain us. They lend coherence and meaning to our lives. The novelist and essayist Joan Didion writes: "We tell ourselves stories in order to live." We love our stories; we cherish them as we live them.

Our identities are shaped by stories. We use narratives to identify our individual selves and our tribal affiliations—of family and friends, of political and religious groups, of social and cultural networks. Stories root us in place and anchor us in time.

But stories can inhibit as well as free us; they can imprison as well as liberate us. We need to examine the stories we tell ourselves to ensure that they are productive narratives, capable of releasing our imagination and not constraining it, of stimulating our thinking and not stifling it. Stories that say, "I always fail at the critical moment"; or "Our team just can't make it into the finals," need to be replaced with more positive and purposeful narratives.

We need positive stories, such as "When the chips are down, I come through"; or "I relish the responsibilities needed to support my family and friends"; or "I have found my passion for learning X, and I am going to pursue it devotedly." And we need to look for ways to sustain our positive and productive narratives. In believing ourselves to be intelligent and creative, and acting as if we are—and developing those capacities purposefully—the prophecy and belief will fulfill themselves. But we need to follow a positive, purposeful, and productive narrative trajectory.

EXERCISES

6. For one week, identify a time in your day that you can escape into silence. It might involve setting your alarm 20 minutes early, going off for a quiet lunch by yourself, finding some dead time between the end of work and dinner, or slipping away from late night television. Choose a time that works best for you. You don't need to make it a long stretch—even 10 to 15 minutes a day can be effective. During this time, daydream, wonder, speculate—think in any direction your imagination takes you. If you like, jot down some of your thoughts. If not, don't bother—the thinking is the goal. At the end of the week, consider to what extent the exercise has been valuable for you. Consider repeating the exercise, and developing a habit of finding this kind of quiet thinking time.

7. Identify two or three fears you have with respect to a project you are working on—or some personal goal you have for yourself that involves taking a risk.

Record these fears in a diary or notebook. Think about why you have these fears. And then think of a positive response you can make to counter them. After doing this, share your thinking with someone you trust. See if they can think of other ways you can counterattack those fears, so that you can imagine your goal and then take the first steps toward bringing it to creative life.

8. Identify a narrative that identifies who you are and where you are heading in your life. Write this narrative out for yourself in a couple of pages (or at least in a couple of paragraphs). If the story is positive and constructive, jot down some things you can do to sustain and strengthen that narrative. If the story is negative and destructive, revise it so that it results in a remodeling of the self you are becoming, a remaking of your identity in a more hopeful and productive direction.

Get to Yes!

negotiation
Mutual discussion with the role of reaching agreement.

So much of our lives involve **negotiation**—balancing time and commitments; arriving at decisions through reflection, discussion, and debate; bargaining in the marketplace and in various personal and professional arenas. And in those negotiations, we make trade-offs and compromises. Sometimes we are happy with the outcomes and sometimes not. Much depends on how we conceptualize those transactions—whether as conflicts and battles with winners and losers, or as discussions and collaborations, with more win-win than win-lose or lose-lose scenarios.

▶ **Simulate** the **Experiment**, Get to Yes! **MyThinkingLab**

Liu and Noppe-Brandon cite the bible for this imaginative kind of negotiation practice, Roger Fisher and William Uhry's book, *Getting to Yes*, which presents creative strategies for mutual gain—those **win-win** outcomes we all hope for. Fisher and Uhry identify four obstacles to achieving those positive outcomes:

win-win
An outcome of a negotiation in which both parties come away with a desired element or aspect of what is being contested.

1. Criticizing a novel approach prematurely;
2. Fixating on a single result;
3. Assuming a fixed pie to be divided;
4. Thinking that resolving the problem is the other side's problem.

Because each of these impediments represents a failure of imagination, the authors of *Getting to Yes* propose four remedies, one for each of those imaginative failures.

First: suspend negative judgment through splitting off inventing from deciding.
Second: multiply outcomes by creating alternatives to an ideal "deal," or varying the scope of that deal.
Third: seek differences that can dovetail.
Fourth: find ways to address the interests of the other side.

fixed pie
In negotiation, the idea that there is a fixed amount of goods or services to be divided or apportioned.

No one says that imagining alternatives using these remedies to overcome the four obstacles will be easy. But the ability to reframe a problem using one or another of these strategies depends on the capacity to imagine things otherwise. To illustrate the third remedy—assuming a **fixed pie** (problem)—along with its remedy—seeking dovetailing differences (solution)—Fisher and Uhry tell about two children fighting over an orange. In a traditional kind of ineffectual compromise that satisfies neither child, they decide to cut the orange in half. Later, after the children talk about their compromise, they realize that one child wanted to eat the fruit and the other wanted to use the peel in baking. In this case, seeking differences could have resulted in a better outcome for both children. Their different needs actually dovetailed; it could have been for them a win-win situation.

Rewrite History

In this imaginative practice, we ask the question "what if something that happened in the past had turned out differently?" Liu and Noppe-Brandon cite Winston Churchill's wondering what would have happened if General Robert E. Lee had lost the battle of Gettysburg (which, in fact, was what actually happened). Churchill employs this counterfactual experiment to create a chain of speculative causal events that include the Civil War ending sooner, America not splitting into two weakened countries; a three-nation alliance with England would not have developed; and England, alone, could not have stopped Germany and its allies in 1914, resulting in a World War.

Churchill used this imaginative "thought experiment" as a persuasive strategy to argue for an Anglo-American alliance to help prevent a second European war (another eventual reality). One outcome for us as we think about such a thought experiment is to realize that what we normally assume is a de facto and determined set of historical forces could have turned out differently. It could have been otherwise. Had it not been for America's intervention in the midst of the Second World War, particularly in liberating France, and had Germany won the war, perhaps French children would be speaking German today and not their native French language.

Counterfactuals are tools that stimulate our critical and creative thinking; they help us develop our imaginations. They unmask assumptions, and they help identify both possibilities and goals we hope to reach. Counterfactuals are based on that essential thinking question: "What if?" Usually, we look to the future with that question. With counterfactuals, we turn that "What if" on the past. Either way, counterfactuals remind us that nothing is certain in human experience, and therefore, we shouldn't take anything for granted—not even history.

Embrace Failure and Fail Well

It's true that we learn from success. And it's also true that we learn from failure. At least there is the possibility that we can so learn from both success and failure. Whether we do or don't so learn is up to us.

Thomas Edison famously said that he never failed in his experiments. Instead, he noted that with each experiment he discovered another way that something would not work—did not lead where he was trying to go. But those discoveries of failed results were useful in ruling out certain possibilities so that he could explore others. Edison is said to have done thousands of experiments en route to inventing the incandescent light bulb. And James Dyson created more than 5,000 prototypes of what eventually became the Dyson Cyclone bagless vacuum cleaner.

Failure is inextricably connected with success. A major league baseball player can lead his league in hitting and frequently does with a batting average in the range of .333. As you can readily see, that successful star hitter is failing at a rate of .667; two-thirds of the time he does not get a hit. The great basketball star Michael Jordan once noted that in his career he missed more than 9,000 attempted shots and his teams lost close to 300 games. Yet even with those numbers, he was an NBA All-Star, a Most Valuable Player, member of championship teams, and an electrifying presence on a basketball court.

One of the great paradoxes of human experience is that we get many things right while we also err in more ways than we can (or would want) to count. We need to get things right simply to survive. And among the multitude of daily decisions we make and interactions we have, we do just that. But experience also shows that we get many things wrong, as well. We are built for error as much as much as we are built for success. It's what we do with our errors, mistakes, mishaps, wrong takes, and screwups that matters.

History is replete with examples of projects or experiments that went wrong, and yet which led, afterward, to discoveries. One of the most famous is the discovery of penicillin, which resulted in part from Alexander Fleming's observation that a mold was growing in some Petri dishes he was using in an experiment. Fleming noticed that something from the mold seemed to have killed off bacteria from the perimeter of a ring that had formed in each of the Petri dishes. Because he was knowledgeable and alert, because he was observant, and because he knew what he was seeing, Fleming was able to understand and then capitalize on an experiment gone awry. He turned error into knowledge by his discovery, though it would take others decades to turn his discovery into the miracle drug we know today as penicillin.

Other famous errors have led to similar kinds of unpredicted and unexpected results. Columbus thought he was finding a route to India when he discovered the Americas. The astronomer Johannes Kepler stumbled on the idea of interplanetary gravity even though his reasons for making that discovery were erroneous.

Another reason we need to get over our fear of making mistakes is that this fear can prevent us from taking risks, and risk-taking is essential to creative thinking and discovery. By remaining in our comfort zone, where there is little risk of failure, we won't stretch ourselves; we won't be able to get beyond what we already can do. To learn a new language, we have to be willing to make mistakes. If we don't try to speak a new language imperfectly—even very badly—we will never learn to speak it half decently, or well. Mistakes are part of the learning curve. The same is true with improving our writing or our skills in the kitchen, on the computer, or with a musical instrument. To get to the next skill level, we need to try to do something we are not yet able to do. Only with that stretching and the inevitable mistakes that accompany the effort, will we have a chance to achieve our goals.

Samuel Smiles, author of *Self-Help*, said "he who never made a mistake never made a discovery." And the modernist writer James Joyce said, "A man's errors are his portals of discovery." (This, of course, is true for women as well as men.) Joyce's insight is important because it suggests that errors present opportunities. But we need to approach errors in a positive frame of mind. Not, "Oh my God, what a tragedy"—or "What an embarrassment"; but rather, "Look at that! How interesting!" "What might I do with that—where can it lead me?"

In an essay "To Err Is Human," the science writer and physician Lewis Thomas argued there that we need errors to direct—and redirect—our thinking, to challenge our assumptions and disorient our comfortable, static habits of mind. Here are a few playful yet serious observations Thomas makes about the value of error: "if it's a lucky day and a lucky laboratory, somebody makes a mistake . . . then the action can begin." And "error . . . opens the way. The next step is the crucial one." And, one more "If it is a big enough mistake, we could find ourselves on a new level, stunned, out in the clear, ready to move again."

Errors tell us when to shift gears or change direction. They provide information we can benefit from. As Edward B. Burger and Michael Starbird point out in *The 5 Elements of Effective Thinking*, mistakes and failure do not indicate weakness, but rather signify strength. We should relish errors rather than lament them; those mistakes are a sign of a creative mind at work; they offer opportunities for success. We needn't fear errors, but instead should embrace them.

EXERCISES

9. Identify a conflicted situation you have had in the past or in which you are currently involved. Apply the "Getting to Yes" analysis of the four possible causes of the conflict. Try to identify which of the four problem causes might be particularly amenable to negotiation. Use the corresponding remedy-solution to see if a more hopeful and productive result can emerge.

10. Choose an event from history—from as far back as the origin of human life to as recently as today's news. Identify a counterfactual, "what if" it had been otherwise situation. Then imagine the set of "otherwise" consequences that might or could result. For example, what if the February 2011 protests in Egypt had resulted in a bloody government crackdown on the order of the Chinese response to protesters in 1989 at Tiananmen Square in Beijing? What if Saddam Hussein had not been captured and executed? What if the European Banking system had not provided support for Greece or Ireland? What if the political leaders of Syria had renounced their power and paved the way for a peaceful transition to a democratic rather than an autocratic state?

11. Describe a time when a set of rules or constraints enabled you to create something you were proud of. Explain what the rules were and how you used them to spur your thinking.

12. Describe a time when you got something wrong—when you were mistaken or you were in error—and something positive resulted from it. Do some research in the library or on the Internet on errors and mistakes in one of the following fields: history, political science, economics, psychology, mathematics, biology, chemistry, physics, or medicine. Explain in a few paragraphs what you discover from this miniresearch exercise into error.

The Limits of Imagination

In a recent essay in the quarterly journal *Raritan*, "Imagination: Powers & Perils," Mark Edmundson explores the virtues and dangers of cultivating the imagination. He identifies a number of ways in which imagination can run amok—through excessive worry and fear, through fantasies that lack all connection with plausibility, and through jealousy and ambition that can result in destructive acts. Yet even with such dangers of letting loose the imagination, he contends that stifling the imagination to the point of eradicating it, is far worse.

Remedies for the abuses of imagination can be found in psychological counseling, in friendship, and in literature, which provides potential antidotes in the form of hopeful possibilities. Edmundson suggests that great novels such as George Eliot's *Middlemarch* or Charles Dickens' *Bleak House* provide "visions of the world we might live if we dared," visions of worlds we could share imaginatively.

A dead imagination is far worse than an overactive imagination. No imagination at all is more of a danger to a rich world of thought than an overactive, even obsessive imagination. Those abuses of imagination can be checked with judgment, with questioning, with cautions. In these and in most cases, imaginative prowess requires the pushback of critical judgment. Authentic imagination balances and blends vision and judgment.

EXERCISE ──

13. To what extent do you agree with Edmundson about the potential "perils" of imagination? To what extent do you think that the dangers of imagination he identifies can be redressed and checked in the ways he describes?

What Is an Idea?

Among the many definitions of ideas, one of the best is included in Jack Foster's book *How to Get Ideas*: "An idea is nothing more nor less than a new combination of old elements." We can ignore the "nothing more nor less" part and get to the core of this definition: "A new combination of old elements." The key word is *combination*; the key concept is linking things, putting them together, associating them, juxtaposing or synthesizing them. Combination. That's the key.

In *The Act of Creation*, Arthur Koestler writes that "creative originality" arises "out of a combination of well-established patterns of thought—by a process of cross-fertilization," which he also calls *bissociation*. And so there you have it again: combination, which in Koestler words is a creative act that "uncovers, selects, re-shuffles, combines, synthesizes already existing facts, ideas, faculties, skills."

Let's add the notion that an idea is something to think about and something to think with. Ideas promote and provoke thought, as they themselves are products of preexisting thought, already melded combinations that further stimulate other additional thought-filled combinations.

The ancient Greek pre-Socratic philosopher Heraclitus wrote: "A wonderful harmony arises from the seemingly unconnected." In fact, what we call thinking is fundamentally an act of making connections, linking ideas, facts, information, experiences—and more—together. When we bring together the same ideas over and over, they become stale, clichéd. When we bring together and associate or link things not normally brought together, we provoke thought—and thus, ideas. Heraclitus had it right more than 2,500 years ago.

Why Ideas Are Important

People in many kinds of work are responsible for generating, developing, and presenting ideas. They might be charged with writing advertising copy or creating commercials. Perhaps they run companies or departments within companies. They might be engineers or account executives; perhaps one of them is a fifth-grade teacher needing to help plan a grade-wide project; perhaps another is a volunteer for the annual church carnival, a hospital worker who sees an opportunity to improve the admitting process, a mother planning a baby shower for her daughter, a school administrator organizing a global conversation on innovation in developing countries. Like these people, the rest of us need to know how to get ideas, as well. Why, we might ask?

One answer is that ideas drive progress and innovation. Without ideas there is no movement; without movement, there is no improvement, no progress. Getting ideas is critical to our success, whatever kinds of work we do, whatever our walk in life. Ideas are important more today than yesterday because work is becoming increasingly computerized. The aspects of work unable to be mechanized or computerized require people like us to do the creative thinking those systems aren't capable of.

Ideas are also important because we are increasingly being inundated with an overflow of information. That information needs to be sifted and filtered, combined and synthesized to form ideas that can help solve problems, ideas that can improve processes and products, ideas that can inspire as well as enrich, enlighten as well as entertain.

Ideas drive creativity and innovation. Ideas are tested by means of analysis and critical thinking. Learning to get ideas is at the heart of creative thinking.

How to Get Ideas

So now that we have a sense of what ideas are and why they're important, how do we go about getting them? We have already explored a number of strategies and tried out various tools for generating ideas in the first part of this chapter based on *Imagination First!* Here we introduce some strategies developed by Jack Foster, who had a successful 35-year career as an advertising writer and director in Los Angeles.

Foster presents a process for getting an idea that includes five steps:

1. Define the problem.
2. Gather information.
3. Search for the idea.
4. Forget about it (get away from thinking about it for a while).
5. Enact the idea.

We might notice that the idea should appear somewhere between steps 4 and 5—so we'll add step (4 1/2)—collect the idea as it "comes to you." We might notice, too, that Foster requires that the idea be used or applied. This echoes Liu and Noppe-Brandon, who emphasize "innovation," the application of creativity as stimulated by imagination.

What is more important, perhaps, about Foster's thinking about creativity is that we can't use his approach—or any approach to gathering or generating ideas—unless we prepare ourselves for ideas. The Lincoln Center Education strategies help us do just that. So too do the 10 strategies Foster presents in *How to Get Ideas*:

1. Have fun.
2. Be more like a child.
3. Become idea-prone.
4. Visualize success.
5. Rejoice in failure.
6. Get more inputs.
7. Screw up your courage.
8. Team up with energy.
9. Rethink your thinking.
10. Learn how to combine.

We focus on Foster's first two and last two strategies.

Have Fun

Foster makes having fun his first idea-getting strategy and his most important one. He makes this claim because his experience in the advertising world confirmed that teams that were having the most fun produced the best results—the best ads, the best billboards, the best television commercials. Foster suggests that having fun led those teams to generate effective ideas. He asks whether we haven't had similar experiences ourselves. After all, he notes, "people who enjoy what they're doing, do it better."

Having fun is both a result and a form of play, and play is an essential aspect of human culture. In his classic study *Homo Ludens*, John Huizinga charts the importance of play throughout history. Huizinga claims that play is a fundamental attribute of our humanity, antedating recorded culture itself. Play is a form of activity, a way of doing things, even of making things. And so *homo ludens*, is akin to *homo faber*, man the maker, the creator, the inventor, the fabulator, the imaginator. It is believed that the earliest human tools, for example, resulted from a form of play—initially with sticks and stones. Play is an important stimulus to creative activity. Someone once defined creativity, in fact, as "intelligence at play."

Foster also quotes authorities in other fields to buttress his claim. He quotes the French poet Paul Valery, who said, "People with ideas are never serious." And science fiction writer and biochemist Isaac Asimov, who noted that new discoveries are often heralded with the remark "That's funny."

Foster makes the related point that humor is a key element in creative thinking, largely because humor relies on combining things not normally put together. The incongruity makes us laugh. The notion of incongruity, however, results in more than humor; it also leads to inventions. And even though it might not have taken a joke to arrive at the following inventions, they share with humor the baseline of surprising or unexpected combination, of putting things together that are not normally considered related. The juxtaposition of two different things is a powerful strategy for invention. Here are just a few of those Foster mentions:

- Putting fire and food together yielded cooking.
- An alarm + a clock = an alarm clock.
- A rag and a stick make a mop.
- A coin punch and a wine press = the printing press.
- Dreams and art conspired to form Surrealism.

A number of books, including Walter Isaacson's biography, *Steve Jobs*, reference the invention of the Swiffer cleaner, which combines a mop stick with a thick absorbent paper-towel, along with a mechanism to deliver small amounts of liquid.

In *Your Creative Brain*, Shelly Carson notes that recent research has shown the value of play and games in stimulating areas of the brain associated with creativity. Developing a playful frame of mind also increases motivation to engage in problem solving. The fun we have in the process of working creatively on a project helps us persevere with it. Our rewards for working on a project with play and game aspects are intrinsic and self-motivating.

In *Creative Intelligence*, Bruce Nussbaum notes how important play was in the lives and education of the founders of many new companies, including Android, Flickr, Instagram, Kickstarter, Tumblr, and YouTube. Google founders Larry Page and Sergey Brin, Amazon founder Jeff Bezos, and Wikipedia founder Jimmy Wales all attended Montessori schools, which use games to stimulate imaginative thinking, inquiry, and discovery. The habit of "playing around" sometimes called "messing around" is central to the concept of play, which differs significantly from the concept of "problem solving." Unlike problem solving, in which we know the problem for which we are seeking a solution, play is experimental and exploratory. It is valuable as much for the questions and problems that need to be identified as the answers and solutions that lead to innovation.

Be More Like a Child

W Write the Response,
Be More Like a Child
MyThinkingLab

Why do you think Foster suggests we each try to be more like a child? What is it about children that nourishes and fosters creativity? Foster writes: "The child is innocent and free and does not know what he cannot or should not do. He sees the world as it actually is, not the way we adults have been taught to believe that it is."

Adults are full of opinions and knowledge of the obvious, with common sense and self-evident truths, which sabotage the freedom necessary for creativity. The French psychologist Jean Piaget recommends that we "stay in part a child, with the creativity and invention that characterizes children before they are deformed by adult society."

Children are curious. Their questions keep coming—until they get older. And the older they get the fewer their questions. Neil Postman, the educator, writes: "Children enter school as question marks and leave as periods." The trick for each of us is to keep learning without losing our enthusiasm for learning and for asking questions. We cannot stress too much the importance of questions, asking the right kinds of questions—open questions, probing questions, provocative questions, authentic questions, questions based on innate curiosity and a passion to know. That passionate curiosity fuels our creative thinking.

Amanda Lang, in *The Power of Why*, claims that thinking like a child involves a few other things as well. She suggests that a child listens without bias and preconceived notions, and that a child accepts mistakes as part of the learning process, as partial successes rather than as abysmal failures. Children don't blame themselves for failure; they just carry on. And they tend to engage themselves fully, completely in whatever they are doing. Play is the name of the game for them, play engaged in with unabashed enthusiasm and joy.

EXERCISES

14. To what extent do you agree with Foster that having fun breeds ideas, and often, good ideas? To what extent is this borne out in your own experience, or in what you know of the experience of others? Provide an example of a time when having fun enhanced your creativity.

15. Think of an example of a good joke that puts together two things not normally expected to exist together. Explain where the surprise of the joke is. That is, identify its incongruity. Provide two ideas for how you can have more fun at work or at home or school—or wherever else fun might be useful.

16. Identify two "inventions" that resulted from the combination of different elements. They could be as humble as the mop and alarm clock, or as influential as the printing press. You might wish to focus on a particular area of interest and knowledge for you, such as sports, entertainment, music, history, art, literature, science, games.

17. Add three questions of your own to those that follow:
    - Why are milk cartons square?
    - Why don't kitchen faucets have foot pedals?
    - Why is the moon round?
    - Why is grass green?
    - Why are squirrels grey (and brown and white and black)?
    - Why do we have dreams?

18. Think of something you could do at work or in your personal life in which being like a child—perhaps acting like a child—can help generate interest, curiosity, and excitement for thinking and learning. Think about some ways to let the child in you come out—and play. Ask yourself how you might approach one of your projects if you were in the fifth grade. Think like a child. Be silly. Have fun.

Rethink Your Thinking

There are no rules for thinking or imaginative thinking. There are guidelines, suggestions, strategies, or provocations. There are tools and tactics and techniques. Rules for thinking, like rules generally, exist to be broken.

Visual thinking differs from our normal approach, which is through language. By "rethink" your thinking, Foster means to come at thinking in some different ways. The first of these alternative routes to creative thinking is to think visually. We think with words; that's our common practice. If we add thinking with images, we gain another way to generate ideas. Among the most famous of all visual thinkers was Albert Einstein. This iconic scientist often thought pictorially; ideas came to him in images that he later converted to words, diagrams, and mathematical formulas. Other scientists who made discoveries through visual means include William Harvey, who "saw" the heart as a pump while watching the exposed heart of a live fish. They include Niels Bohr, the physicist, who envisioned an atom in terms of the solar system, and Sir Isaac Newton who saw in an instant that the moon's gravitational pull and an apple's "fall" were the same.

Among the most famous of these scientific discoveries occurred when the chemist August Kekulé dreamed of a snake swallowing its tail, which inspired his discovery of the chemical structure of benzene. Another example is the visualizing of the double helix shape of the molecular structure of DNA discovered by James Watson and Francis Crick.

Scientists don't have a monopoly on visual thinking that leads to discoveries. The geographer Alfred Wegener recognized how the west coast of Africa fit neatly into the east coast of South America, seeing that all the continents were once part of a single large land mass. The modern artist Man Ray in a wonderfully imaginative image envisioned a woman's torso as the body of a violin. He depicted her from the rear in a seated position. This famous image is widely available on the Internet under the title "*Violon d'Ingres*."

More often than we might be aware, our thinking is constrained because we assume unnecessary limits and restrictions. A second "rethink your thinking" strategy presented by Foster is this advice: "Don't assume boundaries that aren't there." Foster gives the example of being asked to plant four trees equidistant from one another. Our natural instinct is to assume that the trees are to be planted on a level piece of land—a two-dimensional surface. And when we try to plot a solution on paper, it simply does not work. If we break through the limiting assumption of planting the trees on the same plane, we solve the problem: One tree is placed on a higher plane, on top of a hill, with the other three placed equidistant on the sides and below.

Boundaries matter; they make games more interesting and challenging. Yet a third "rethink your thinking" strategy of Foster is to set ourselves some limits. Now that sounds like a contradiction of what we were just saying about not assuming constraints that aren't stipulated. But this time we are deciding to play a different game—the game of working within a set of boundaries. We play tennis with the net up. Basketball is played on a court with boundaries. Football and baseball fields have lines drawn that suggest in and out of bounds, fair and foul grounds. And this is true for most games and sports.

Limitation often spurs imagination. A poet writing a sonnet with a prescribed meter and rhyming pattern can surprise himself or herself with verbal solutions that would not have emerged without the constraints of the sonnet form. Leonardo da Vinci noted that "small rooms discipline the mind," and the great jazz musician, composer, and bandleader, Duke Ellington said that "it's good to have limits," while writing music for specific instrument combinations and for particular players of those instruments. We can surprise ourselves by being creative when confronted with a very real but looming deadline.

Break the Rules

In the previous guideline, setting limits, we spoke of the structure of the sonnet, and how that structure provides enabling constraints. Now we'll say that sometimes you may want to break out of those constraints by breaking the rules of sonnet writing. Robert Frost wrote a number of conventional sonnets, adhering now to the Shakespearean, or English pattern, and now to the Petrarchan, or Italian form. Sometimes, though, Frost combined the two different sonnet forms in a single hybrid sonnet. Sometimes he kept the meter and number of lines of the "regular" sonnet, English or Italian, but rhymed in unconventional ways. Sometimes he wrote sonnets, with slightly shorter line lengths; sometimes he wrote sonnets a line longer than the 14-line standard, and sometimes a line shorter.

Jack Foster presents a list of rule-breakers that include a number of the following examples.

- Vincent van Gogh broke the rules on how to paint a flower.
- Pablo Picasso broke the rules on what a woman's face could look like.
- Pete Gogolak broke the rules on how to kick a football (he kicked it soccer style).
- Ludwig Beethoven broke the rules for writing a symphony—by adding a chorus to the movement of his ninth symphony (among other things).
- Niccolò Machiavelli broke the rules about how a prince should behave toward his constituents.
- Thomas More, in his *Utopia*, broke the rules about how a society should be organized.
- e. e. cummings broke the rules on how poems should be punctuated and how author's names should be printed.
- Louis Pasteur broke the rules on how to treat diseases.
- David Ogilvy broke the rules on how advertising copy should sound.
- Igor Stravinsky broke the rules on how ballet music should sound.
- Charlie Parker broke the rules for jazz by playing "forbidden" notes over fast tempo chord changes.
- Bobby McFerrin broke the rules for singing, by persuasively imitating the sounds of various musical instruments with his voice.
- The Beatles broke the rules on what a music "album" should be.
- Four Seasons Hotels broke the rules about what hotel service can be.
- Apple broke the rules about how music should be delivered and sold—and what a retail store might be.
- Twitter broke the rules about how frequently communication can occur.

Creation and Destruction

Creative thinking is destructive as well as creative. The two aspects of creation and destruction are really two sides of the same coin. When a fire rages through a forest, it burns down the trees, but it also makes way for layers of future growth. When a religious person undergoes a rite of purification, this metaphorically kills off one aspect of the self while allowing another to develop and flourish. The Indian religious philosophy of Hinduism, recognizes this fact by having one of its most important divinities, Shiva, represent both creation and destruction. The image of the dancing Shiva shows both these aspects.

Shiva's upper right hand holds a small drum shaped like an hourglass. The specific hand gesture used to hold the drum symbolizes creation originating from sound. The upper left hand contains *agni* or fire, which signifies destruction. These opposing concepts in the upper hands show the counterpoise of creation and destruction. One way we can become more creative thinkers is to "destroy" or challenge the rules. In doing so, we break out of one pattern so that we can create another new one. As the old adage has it, "rules were meant to be broken." Now we know why. In progressing through this book, we can also see how.

EXERCISES

19. Try to visualize one or more images for the following products that need to be advertised: Master locks; company leadership; solar heat panels; a college or university; a hospital; an insurance company. Ask yourself what the problem or challenge looks like. Try to think in pictures first and in words second.

20. Add two people who broke the rules to Foster's list. Explain what rules they broke, and what resulted from breaking them.

Shiva Nataraja

21. Think of a sport that you know well or have a serious interest in. If you know the history of this sport, you can answer the following questions—and if you don't, you can do a bit of research. How has this sport changed in the past few years or decades—or in the past century (if it's old enough)? What pattern of rules were broken or challenged? Think not only of the game itself, but also of equipment, playing locations and surfaces, attire. Some candidates for consideration: baseball, basketball, football, softball, soccer, swimming, tennis, golf, volleyball.

22. Identify a few rules you follow in your personal, academic, and professional life that you can challenge. They might have to do with when you work and relax; with how you organize your free time; with when and where you do these and other things. Explain the reasons you follow these rules. Think about when you first began following them; consider whether with the passage of time, things have changed and yet you still follow the same rules. Ask yourself whether the original reason for following them still holds true. Identify at least one rule that you think you should change. Consider why you want to make the change and what you plan to do differently.

Looking Back and Looking Ahead

Revisit the learning goals that begin this chapter. Which of these goals do you think you have best achieved? What might you do to reach the remaining goals?

Return to the focusing questions at the beginning of the chapter. How would you answer those questions now? Which of them do you find most interesting and provocative and worthy of following up? Why?

In reviewing the list of resources that follows, identify the two that attract you most. Explain why these books or Web sites interest you. Consider looking into them for further developing your capacity for imaginative thinking and for using Jack Foster's and the Lincoln Center Education tools to generate ideas.

Take a look, too, at the MyThinkingLab resources on the Prentice Hall Web site. Included there are readings, images, videos, questions, exercises, and other provocations to help develop your creative thinking capacities.

• •

Resources

A New Culture of Learning, Douglas Thomas and John Seely Brown. Amazon, 2011.
Imagination First!, Eric Liu and Scott Noppe-Brandon. Jossey-Bass, 2011.
Crazy Busy, Edward M. Hollowell. Ballantine, 2007.
The Creative Habit, Twyla Tharp. Simon & Schuster, 2003.
The Left Hand of Darkness, Ursula K. Le Guin. Penguin/Putnam, 1977.
"Imagination: Powers & Perils," Mark Edmundson. *Raritan*, volume 32, number 2, Fall 2012.
How to Get Ideas, Jack Foster. Berrett-Koehler, 2007.
Creative Intelligence, Bruce Nussbaum. Harper Business, 2013.
The Power of Why, Amanda Lang. Collins, 2012.
Self-Help, Samuel Smiles. Infinite Success, 2012.

The Call of Stories, Robert Coles. Houghton Mifflin, 1990.

Getting to Yes, Roger Fisher and William Ury. Penguin, 1991.

The 5 Elements of Effective Thinking, Edward B. Burger and Michael Starbird. Princeton University Press, 2012.

The Medusa and the Snail, Lewis Thomas. Penguin, 1995.

Homo Ludens, John Huizinga. Beacon, 1968.

Your Creative Brain, Shelley Carson. Jossey-Bass, 2012.

Steve Jobs, Walter Isaacson, Simon & Schuster, 2011.

Lincoln Center Education Web site: lcinstitute.org

• •

11

Creative Whacks and Thinkertoys

Creativity is the ability to look at the same information as someone else and see something different.

—MICHAEL MICHALKO

Be willing to be led astray.

—ROGER VON OECH

LEARNING GOALS

11.1 IDENTIFY how thinking can be inhibited and explore strategies to overcome obstacles to thinking.

11.2 APPLY creative thinking techniques to free up thinking, including the stepping-stone, playing the fool, setting quotas, and using humor.

11.3 IDENTIFY and practice creating, exploring, evaluating, and implementing ideas.

11.4 UNDERSTAND the power of "what iffing" to spark imaginative thinking.

11.5 RECOGNIZE the paradoxical nature of creative ideas, including the concept of "thinking the unthinkable."

Chapter Overview

This chapter includes a variety of strategies and techniques to generate fresh thinking, new thinking, and out-of-the-rut thinking. Two prominent thinkers about creativity—Roger von Oech and Michael Michalko—provide the firepower here for freeing our minds to think in new directions. We sample strategies that von Oech and Michalko use with participants in their creative thinking seminars. Attention is given to ways our creativity can be inhibited—and both how to avoid those impediments to creative thinking and how to overcome them.

FOCUSING QUESTIONS

- To what extent have you been trained to find "the" right answer? Why might a concern for this practice limit your ability to think creatively?

- What part do humor, playfulness, and foolishness assume in your thinking? How might less serious and less practical approaches enable creative thinking?

- How often do you find yourself saying "What if" and "Why not" and "Let's give it a try?" How often do you challenge assumptions?

- What role might paradox and opposition, dialectic and ideas-in-tension play in stimulating fresh thinking and new ideas?

Creative Whacks

◉ **Watch** the **Video**,
Be Practical/Consider
Other Points of View
MyThinkingLab

One of the best things that can happen to us as thinkers, suggests Roger von Oech, is to get "a whack on the side of the head." We need these whacks, he says, because our minds are locked in to various kinds of patterns and frames. A good "whack" jolts us into thinking along fresh pathways. Roger von Oech identifies 10 mental locks that prevent us from thinking creatively:

1. The right answer
2. Being logical
3. Following rules
4. Being practical
5. Not being playful
6. Limiting our territory
7. Being afraid of foolishness
8. Avoiding ambiguity
9. Being afraid of error
10. Thinking we're not creative

To break these mental locks, we need a variety of tactics and strategies (creative "whacks"). A "whack" that jolts us out of our routine patterns of behavior and our habitual ways of thinking, however, can be painful; it might accompany a problem or failure, like losing a job, failing an exam, blowing an interview, or mismanaging a project at work. Often, however, we need to find ways to give ourselves such a metaphorical "whack" as a way to rethink our situation and to ask questions that lead us to better answers. For this, von Oech is a useful guide. We sample a few of his strategies for putting ourselves into a more creative mode of thinking.

As a prelude to the first of von Oech's "whacks," do the following multipart exercise:

EXERCISE

1. Turn the Roman numeral 6 (VI) into a 7 by adding a single line. Turn it into a 4 by moving a single line.

    Turn the Roman numeral 9 (IX) into an 11 by moving a line and the 11 into a 12 by adding one line.

    Now turn the Roman numeral 9 (IX) into a 6 by adding a single line.

    What happened as you made those number conversions? The first few were pretty simple, right? 6 to 7 = VI to VII; 6 to 4 = VI to IV; 9 to 11 = IX to XI; 11 to 12 = XI to XII. But what about turning the Roman numeral 9 (IX) into a 6?

To solve this problem, we need a whack on the side of the head. Why? Because we have been locked into a pattern of moving a single line (I) or adding one line. We have also been locked into the pattern of "Roman numerals." And there is simply no way to add a line to the Roman numeral representing 9 (IX) to convert it to a 6 (VI). If the direction were to move two lines we might solve the problem by moving the I after the X to get XI and then taking the X apart and flipping the bottom half of the X onto its top half to make a V and thus get VI. But that was not the challenge.

Instead, the challenge here is to add a line to IX. And so, we need, as Edward de Bono might say, to stop digging the Roman numeral hole deeper, and instead begin digging a new whole, or as von Oech says, to "do something different."

We need a "shift" of attention—a redirection away from the mental lock of "ROMAN" numerals to something else. We can get there any number of ways, but one of them is simply to think of what, in English, Roman numbers really are. They're letters, aren't they?—I and X and V (and also C and D and M). Now let's use that fact as a lever to help us think differently, or to think in a new direction about what IX can be. What *else* can it be(come). If the Roman numeral nine is composed of the letters I and X, or i and x (lower case), suppose we add an *S* in front to make "SIX," or "six." That's another way to solve the problem.

Now you might want to say—"But wait. You said to add a line, and I was thinking of a straight line—like the Roman numeral I we were adding or moving in the first examples." But an *S* is a line too; it's just not a straight line; it curves, instead. The instruction was not to add a "straight line"; it was rather to "add a line." What many of us probably do in our thinking is to make an assumption that the line must be straight. We tend to make this assumption because we have been working with Roman numerals that use straight lines. In making such an assumption, we add a constraint when that constraint is not warranted. And so, we lock ourselves into unnecessary patterns: the pattern of Roman numerals and the pattern of straight lines.

And both of those "locks" need opening for us to get from IX, as Roman numerals composed of straight lines, to SIX (or six), as English letters (with one curved line). To solve the problem we need a creative whack to go in a different thinking direction—from numbers to letters, and from straight to curved lines. Suppose we had changed the rules and substituted a V for the X to go from IX to VI. That would not really have stayed within the rules of the game. But might there be another solution?

The Right Answer

Let's take this a step further by considering more than a single possible right answer. Rather than being satisfied with our first solution to the IX to six (or 6) problem, consider the value of searching for alternatives.

Let's consider some other ways we can convert IX to six (or 6). Suppose we write it this way Ix or: I x? Or suppose we do it like this: I x ? = 6. That should lead us to I x 6 or I X 6, "one times six." In this case, we have rethought the meaning of X yet again. Previously, X meant 10; thus, XI = 11 and IX = 9. Then we considered X as a letter as in SIX. But now we want X to mean something else—"times"—the multiplication sign, "x." We have changed the "context" of X to make it mean different things: (1) a Roman numeral; (2) an English letter; and now (3) a symbol meaning to multiply. In the process, we have been exercising both our critical and creative thinking capacities. And we have seen that there are alternative ways to solve a problem. Here's another challenge—this one strictly visual.

EXERCISE

2. From the following five figures, select the one that's different from the other figures. Explain how it differs. Then compare your explanation with the answers and explanations of some classmates.

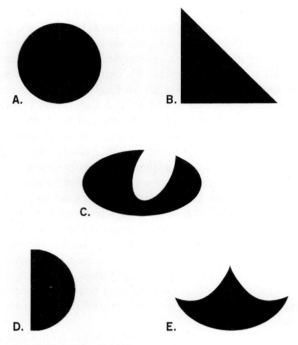

FIGURE 11.1 Odd Shapes

Should we select figure B? Is that correct? It's the only one of the figures with three points. Is A the right answer? It's the only figure of the five with no points. But what if we choose figure C, instead? Is that also correct? Is that the right answer, too? Why? And what about figure D? Is that the correct answer, as well? How about A and E? In fact, they are all correct; they are all "the right answer"—or rather right answers. Plural. And that's the point. There is more than one "right answer."

We are conditioned to think that one answer is the right answer, or the best answer. And that can be the case in some circumstances. But in this instance, there are multiple equally valid correct answers.

We might find some of the "right" answers more interesting than the others, perhaps because we didn't think of them first, perhaps because we didn't think of them at all—because we quit after finding the first (and presumably) the only correct answer. Perhaps we find one or another explanation more compelling for why this figure or that one is also correct. In this context, von Oech quotes the French philosopher Emile Chartier, who wrote: "Nothing is more dangerous than an idea when it is the only one we have." Why? Because we may come to love our idea too much; we may think it's the best approach, maybe even the only really worthwhile approach—in large part, perhaps, because it's *our* idea. In reality, though, to have a good idea, it's wise to have a lot of ideas to choose from. What we need is prolific thinking, fertile thinking, fluent thinking, so we can generate many ideas. The more ideas we can generate, the greater the chance we will discover some good ones.

It is often useful to approach a problem or question from multiple directions. Consider, for example, how each one of the following sports—baseball, cricket, golf, ice hockey, and soccer—might be least like the other four. Let's take these sports one at a time, beginning with baseball. One way that baseball differs from the other sports is that it has no true world or international championship, as its World Series takes place among teams from the United States. The game itself has something in common with cricket in terms of the relatively relaxed pace at which it is played and in terms of pitchers (or bowlers in cricket) throwing a ball that a batter or batsman attempts to hit into a field of defending players. Cricket and baseball, though team sports, differ from soccer and ice hockey, which are also team sports. They are as much like golf, an individual sport, as they are like soccer and hockey.

Other differences include the emphasis on mental effort in addition to physical action that each of these sports requires. How, for example, do baseball and cricket require mental effort? In what ways does that mental effort compare with and differ from the mental work expended in soccer and ice hockey and in golf?

We could go on to catalogue other ways in which each of the sports differs from the other four—in terms of playing surface; in terms of the time of year in which the sport is most frequently played; in terms of the amount of physical contact permitted and the number of players on the field or playing surface; in terms of how scoring works, and how the game is "timed" or otherwise structured. We could compare the various sports in terms of their rules, in terms of punishments for rule violations, in terms of how they are refereed, The important thing is to acquire the habit of considering a variety of approaches, to see the problem or question in various ways, as there are, clearly, many "right answers."

Be Practical

Practicality is the bane of creative thinking. "Be practical," we are admonished. "Be realistic." "You can't do it that way." "That won't work." Our response to these interrelated "don'ts" and "can'ts" should be, first, "Why not?" and "Who says?" and then "What if"?

There is certainly value in being practical, and there is often a need to be realistic. There are times when being practical, taking "reality" into account is necessary. However, there is also a time and place for ignoring those constraints—when you are trying to "think differently," when you are attempting to generate new ideas.

Considering "what if" is necessary to challenge conventional thinking. "What if" questions are an easy and effective way to get your creative juices flowing. "What if" questions are playful and often enjoyable to consider. Having fun, enjoying what you are doing, is a major element in doing it successfully, whatever "it" is—including thinking.

Each "what if" question is an idea generator. Here are some "What if" questions that Roger von Oech provides in his book, *A Whack on the Side of the Head*:

- What if animals became more intelligent than human beings?
- What if men also had babies?
- What if politicians were elected by lottery?
- What if pigs had wings?
- What if human life expectancy exceeded 200 years?
- What if people had to spend every third year living in a different country?
- What if people didn't need to sleep?

And here are a few less whimsical examples from Josh Linkner's *Disciplined Dreaming*:

- What if the police presence doubled in our city?
- What if the legal drinking age was reduced to 18?
- What if we could create a candy that actually had "negative calories" and that helped people lose weight?

Each of these "what if" questions is an idea generator. Each pushes us to think in new directions, to imagine alternatives to the realities we have become conditioned to know.

Consider Other Points of View

Another kind of "what if" strategy to spur our creative thinking is to ask how others might see an issue, problem, or challenge with which we are struggling. This strategy, of course, is helpful in negotiations when we are trying to understand the point of view of "the other side." And it is helpful when initiating a project that involves many different stakeholders. Considering their various perspectives is essential for developing compromises to complex proposals that affect many people with different needs, interests, and values.

The "what if" approach, however, is less about problem solving and negotiation than about taking our thinking in new directions. Von Oech recommends that we think of a particular person, perhaps someone we know, perhaps a figure from history, even a fictional character, and imagine how that individual would respond to a problem we are confronting. Some candidates: Machiavelli, the Pope, the Dalai Lama, Socrates, Confucius, Buddha, Martin Luther King, Jr., Freud, Mozart, Oprah, the Beatles, Mother Teresa, the Three Stooges, Julius Caesar, Joan of Arc, your mother, uncle, cousin, fifth-grade teacher, your best friend, Winston Churchill, Spider Man, Attila the Hun, Huckleberry Finn, Ahab, Holden Caulfield, Hamlet, Lady Macbeth, Romeo or Juliet, Madonna, Beyoncé, Lady Gaga, Justin Bieber, Ice T.

Practicality and the Stepping-Stone

Sometimes when we generate an idea, that idea in and of itself may be unworkable, not really ready for prime time. Those kinds of unusable ideas, however, can lead us to others that will be more useful. Von Oech calls these less-than-useful ideas "stepping-stones" because they provide the impetus and the direction for generating other ideas that may be more workable.

Here is an example. Some years ago, a city in the Netherlands needed to solve a refuse problem because people were littering the streets profusely. After trying some fairly conventional strategies—doubling the fine for littering, adding litter patrols—they decided to "think differently." Reversing their approach, they decided that instead of "punishing" people for littering, they would "reward" them for not littering. This is how they did it.

They asked a "What if question": "What if our trash cans paid people money when they deposited their trash? We could put an electronic sensing device on each can as well as a coin-return mechanism. Whenever someone puts trash in the can, it would pay him."

After careful evaluation of this idea, the citizens of the town decided not to implement it in its original form. But they did not reject it out of hand as "not practical." Instead, they used it as a "stepping-stone" to a more workable idea. They used the concept of rewarding people for putting their trash into cans (a concept they extracted from their initial rejected idea) and asked themselves how else this reward system might work. "What other ways," they wondered "might we use the concept of rewarding people for depositing their trash?"

Their solution was an electronic trash can with a sensing unit on top that could detect when it was opened and trash deposited. This would then activate a tape recorder that played a recording of a joke. Different trash cans told different kinds of jokes—bad puns, shaggy dog stories, crisp one-liners—and the jokes were changed biweekly. Soon people were going out of their way to put their trash in the cans. A bonus was an increase in the city's humor quotient, the amount of laughter enjoyed, and the number of smiles they exchanged.

It seems that a company called Solar Lifestyle has taken the concept of talking trash cans even further, powering them with solar energy. According to Shelley Carson in *Your Creative Brain*, solar-powered talking trash cans in Shanghai thank people for throwing away their trash. Similar talking trash cans in Finland use the voices of celebrities and offer political commentary, as well.

If talking trash cans seems far-fetched, consider a scenario that Michael Michalko describes in *Creative Thinkering*. The city of Cambridge, England, has created park benches that not only talk but also walk. These humanized benches are equipped with mechanisms and sensors that permit them to move and congregate in prescribed ways around a square. The benches move around depending on whether anyone is sitting on them. In inclement weather, they move to drier places. Occasionally, when the benches are occupied, they start singing. Trash bins, similarly equipped with sensors and songs, join in the fun.

EXERCISES

3. Think of a time when you were either forced or shown how to consider alternatives to an idea—a single dominating idea to which you were wedded. What happened to your original idea? What was the result of considering additional alternative ideas—whether you came up with them yourself, you were persuaded to consider them, or you were forced to do so?

4. Where else have you encountered the importance of exploring multiple possibilities before? Why is it important not to be satisfied with the first solution to a problem you find, or the first idea for a project you come up with? What are the benefits of considering alternatives?

5. Answer five of von Oech's and Linkner's "What if" questions. Then answer them again in a different way. Compare your answers with those of one or more of your classmates. Then, add five of your own "What if" questions. Answer three of your questions. Switch papers with a classmate, and answer three of his or her "What if" questions, as that classmate answers yours.

6. Select two candidates from among the various people mentioned earlier to see a problem from their point of view. Focus on a problem or challenge you are dealing with and consider how they would approach it. What assumptions would they make? What special wrinkle would they see? What expertise would they add? What perspective would they bring? What changes might they suggest? And what questions might they ask?

7. To what extent do you think the joking trash cans would work to improve the litter situation in your neighborhood or workplace? Why? To stretch your thinking, imagine another situation—at school, at work, in your community—in which electronic activated jokes (or other sayings) might be of use and value. What adjustments might need to be made for this new application?

8. Give an example from your personal life or from your reading that illustrates von Oech's idea of the "stepping-stone." Explain what the less practical or even impractical idea was and how it led to something more practical and useful.

Playing the Fool

"Don't be foolish," we sometimes hear. "A fool and his money are soon parted," is one of many famous (and wise) observations about fools. And, for certain, we don't want others to see us as foolish. That can be embarrassing, humiliating, or worse. There is, however, another side to foolishness. In fact, the fool has long been considered a stimulus to fresh thinking, as a provoker of laughter, and also as a spur to improved judgment. In Shakespeare's tragedy, *King Lear*, for example, the Fool plays a central role in helping King Lear redirect his thinking, reconsider what truly matters to him. Shakespeare's Fool provokes Lear to a change of perspective through verbal puns, philosophical paradoxes, and outright insults. The Fool's seemingly erratic behavior and his provocative language jolt Lear out of his previously assured ideas. They lead Lear to understand himself and his relationship with others in ways he had never previously considered.

Fools were consulted by Egyptian pharaohs and Babylonian kings, by Roman emperors and Greek tyrants. They had a place among Native American chiefs and Chinese emperors, as well as among European royalty, especially in the Middle Ages and the Renaissance. Fools were needed in these courts because so many in the ruler's entourage were "yes men," constantly flattering the ruler and telling him what he wanted to hear. The fool served as a lightning rod for a jolt of reality, for a "whack on the side of the head." The fool was an antidote to the poison of conformity and groupthink. Every leader needs someone to help shift his perception, broaden his outlook, and help deepen understanding. The fool provided those services.

Von Oech quotes the physicist Niels Bohr, who once said to a colleague: "We all know your idea is crazy. The question is whether it's crazy enough." Was this Bohr's way of playing the fool—in this case jolting his colleague, himself, and the others involved so they would take the crazy idea seriously? Who is to say whether the fool or the wise man is the one in possession of real wisdom?

Here are a few examples of how what seems foolish, silly, even crazy may actually be just the opposite. In Isaac Bashevis Singer's short story, "Gimpel the Fool," what looks like crass stupidity on the part of the title character in the beginning of the story, has us wondering at the end, whether he might be wiser than he appears, the wisest, paradoxically, of all. Foolishness can be wisdom and apparent wisdom foolishness—more often than we might typically realize.

One of Emily Dickinson's poems begins with what sounds like a foolish notion: "Much Madness is divinest sense . . . Much sense the starkest madness." That's an idea that seems counterintuitive, even downright crazy on first hearing. But the lines serve as a provocation, as we wonder how, and in what contexts, madness might provide insight, and sense might be considered foolishness.

Michel de Montaigne, a French Renaissance essayist, asks: "How do I know that when I play with my cat, she's not playing with me?" Is that a foolish question? Or might there be something to what Montaigne is implying? The fool might ask, if a man is walking a dog on a leash, whether it might be the dog that has the man on a leash and is walking him. "Golden Retrievals," by the contemporary American poet Mark Doty, plays with this idea. In the poem we hear the dog's "voice," as it questions its master silently and challenges his view of the world. Listen to the dog expressing his point of view:

> Fetch? Balls and sticks capture my attention
> seconds at a time. Catch? I don't think so.
> Bunny, tumbling leaf, a squirrel who's—oh
> joy—actually scared. Sniff the wind, then

> I'm off again: muck, pond, ditch, residue
> Of any thrillingly dead thing. And you?

We hear the dog as it refuses to chase after the balls and sticks its master throws. The dog would rather chase after other things, like running squirrels and leaves blowing in the wind. And then the dog seems to ask a challenging question: "And you?" As if to say, "master—what are *you* doing with *yourself?*" Here are the dog's thoughts as if they are being said directly to its master about what his master is doing:

> Either you're sunk in the past, half our walk,
> Thinking of what you never can bring back,
>
> Or else you're off in some fog concerning
> —tomorrow, is that what you call it?

These lines from Mark Doty's poem about walking his golden retriever are playful and witty. They reverse the usual pattern of who seems to be doing what, and of who is taking whom out for a walk. They amuse by virtue of their surprise, by means of the poet's imagination. And along the way, they invite us to question the way we live our lives—thinking about the past and the future ("tomorrow") rather than being alert to the present moment. Is this foolishness, or wisdom? Here is the remainder of the poem; you decide. "My work," says the retriever is:

> To unsnare time's warp (and woof!), retrieving,
> My haze-headed friend, you. This shining bark,
>
> A Zen master's bronzy gong, calls you here,
> Entirely, now: bow-wow, bow-wow, bow-wow.

Doty concludes his poem—a sonnet no less—by playing on the sounds of a dog's bark and comparing it to the sound of a gong that serves as a call to attention entirely in the "now." (The "gong" is metaphorically sounded by the dog's noticing a piece of "shining bark" that attracts his attention.) Doty plays with language as well, especially with the representation of a dog's "bark" (echoed in tree bark) as "woof" (linked with "warp") and the concluding triple "bow-wow." The poem's wit and playfulness amuse us; its wisdom is an added bonus. It is wisely foolish and foolishly wise. It is both playfully serious and seriously playful; and in the process it both delights and enlightens.

The Place of Humor

Laughter is one of the fool's tools. Laughing at something helps us see it in a fresh way. In fact, many jokes are funny precisely because they bring things together in unexpected ways. Humor freshens our perspective; it gives us permission to take things less than seriously. In the process and as a result, we lighten up, loosen up, and see things in a different light. As von Oech notes, "humor may not solve our problems, but it puts us in a frame of mind more conducive to solving them"; humor stimulates not just laughter but the flow of ideas, as well. The surprising connections made in jokes, the use of incongruity and the unexpected, are akin to what happens when we discover a fresh thought, a new idea. The "aha" of discovery, as has often been pointed out, is just one letter different from the "ha-ha" of laughter.

Explorer, Artist, Judge, Warrior

In another of his books, *A Kick in the Seat of the Pants*, Roger von Oech provides an overview of the creative thinking process by identifying four key roles: those of explorer, artist, judge, and warrior. The explorer searches for information and resources. The artist converts and transforms these resources into ideas. The judge evaluates these ideas and decides what can be done with them. The warrior puts the ideas into action.

Each of us assumes these roles when we think critically and creatively. We don't take them up in a linear fashion and perform the sequenced roles just once each. Instead, we move back and forth from one role to another, again and again. The process is recursive, doubling back on itself. Once we have generated ideas and begun to evaluate them in our role as judge, we need to return to our artist role to re-envision them. Or, in our role as artist, we may be developing an idea for which we require more information or other resources. In this case, we return to our explorer mode to acquire what we need. The same goes for an idea that our warrior puts into action. It may need to be revised, modified, or adapted, and so we need to take up again the roles of explorer, artist, and judge.

What is required to assume each of these thinking roles? For exploring, we need to make an effort to get out and look and listen. We also need to take the risk of getting lost or of coming upon something unsettling. In addition, we may have become specialized, an expert; exploring means we need to go beyond our normal boundaries of expertise and comfort. Expert knowledge can be both enabling and disabling. To counter these potential threats to exploration we can adopt a curious outlook. We can leave our turf, both our physical places of routine and our intellectual homes, to do some prospecting. And we can find ways to break out of our normal routines.

Our artist might be impeded by a fear of looking foolish and an equal fear that our ideas might not be useful. We might think in such cases that we have wasted our time. We can also become accustomed to doing things the same way all the time. Habit is another disabler of fresh thinking. To overcome these tendencies and fears, we need to make deliberate and intentional changes in the way we approach our work and our play. We might change the rules we usually apply; we might begin looking at things from different, even strange perspectives; we might simply make a conscious effort to use our imagination more frequently and more openly.

Von Oech describes the artist's "palette" of colorful strategies useful in this phase of thinking. We can shift the context for our thinking—looking at an idea from a psychological or historical perspective, from within a political, economic, or cultural context, for example. We can use our imagination by using "what if" questions. We can reverse our idea, looking at it backward, inside out, or upside down. We can connect our idea, combining it with prior knowledge; we can compare it by using an **analogy** or **metaphor** to think about it. We can eliminate aspects of it, or add aspects to it. We can parody our idea, make fun of it, perhaps even invent jokes about it. We can further incubate our idea, giving it time to grow and develop, perhaps after further reading and talking and listening and thinking.

Our inner judge can kill an idea cold. The role of judgment is vital yet dangerous. There's an art to being a judge of our own or other people's ideas. We have to balance being honestly critical enough to ensure that only really good ideas pass the test, against being so critical that we kill our artist's shaping of those ideas and crush our artist's spirit. We can get stuck in our judge's role for two basic reasons: (1) because it is easy to criticize—much easier than to create and (2) because criticizing ideas involves much less risk than creating them and laying them open for inspection and evaluation.

And yet judgment is necessary for critical and creative thinking. In exercising judgment, we need to be objective and fair, to look for positives as well as negatives in our ideas. We need to consider whether the timing is right to implement an idea, and what the deadline is for deciding. We need to think about whether bias or

analogy
A comparison between two different things to identify their similarities, sometimes as part of developing an argument.

metaphor
A type of comparison in which one thing is asserted to be another; for example: knowledge is power.

arrogance might play a part in our judgment. We also need to identify any assumptions and whether those assumptions are valid and current. We might even consider what another critic might say, and even what a fool might say about the idea. Ultimately, though, we have to render a verdict—to judge the idea and then move on.

In allowing our warrior to bring an idea into reality—to apply it in earnest—we take responsibility for it. Once the idea is put into action, it can be evaluated by our judge, fine tuned by our artist, and further researched and studied by our explorer. And then back again into action it goes. The two biggest enemies of the warrior phase of working with ideas are fear of failure and lack of confidence. The solution is to remain confident, ramp up our courage, confront our demons, and eliminate self-doubt. Henry Ford was reputed to have said, "Whether you think you can or can't, you're right." And he was right about that.

EXERCISES

9. Tell a couple of your favorite jokes to a classmate, friend, or coworker. Then listen to his or her jokes in return. (If you can't think of any offhand, look up a few on the Internet or in a book of jokes.) Then together, analyze just what makes those jokes tick. To what extent does the humor rely on surprise, the unexpected, puns, and other forms of unconventionality? To what extent do you have to "think" to get the joke?

10. Who are some of your favorite comedians, comic film or stage actors? Why and how do they make you laugh? Watch a scene from a comic television show or from a movie you enjoy, and analyze its humor.

11. Identify which of the four roles—explorer, artist, judge, warrior—matches with each of the following. Consider how and why it does so, for each case.

   - Asking "What if" questions;
   - Seeing ideas as stepping-stones;
   - Considering multiple "right" answers;
   - Finding humor in situations;
   - Questioning assumptions.

Thinkertoys

One of the best-known and best of thinking gurus, Michael Michalko, believes that we can will ourselves to become creative thinkers. In his book *Creative Thinkering* (that's not a typo—it's "thinkering" and not "thinking" or "tinkering"), Michalko lists three requirements for the development of a creative frame of mind:

1. Intending to be creative;
2. Cultivating creativity consciously in speech and thought;
3. Acting like a creative thinker every day.

Michalko's books, which include *Thinkertoys* and *Cracking Creativity* in addition to *Creative Thinkering*, contain many entertaining and informative stories about creative people—artists, painters, poets, composers, philosophers, inventors, business tycoons, and others. Michalko's books also provide a number of tools and strategies for emulating these creative geniuses, so that we can become more creative thinkers ourselves. We sample a few of those techniques here.

Michalko calls his thinking tools "thinkertoys" as a way to highlight their playful aspects. Of course, like all thinking strategies, these thinking "toys" have a serious purpose—to promote and produce creative ideas and to help us solve problems. To get started, Michalko suggests that we pump our minds for ideas we already have and that we jump-start our thinking with suggestions we can begin implementing right away. In *Thinkertoys* he offers the following 10 for getting started:

1. Set an idea quota.
2. Get tone.
3. Don't be a duke of habit.
4. Feed your head.
5. Do a content analysis.
6. Create a brain bank.
7. Be a travel junkie.
8. Capture your thoughts.
9. Think right.
10. Keep an idea log.

We briefly consider the first 4 of Michalko's list of 10.

Set Quotas

Michalko remarks that setting a quota forces us to actively generate ideas rather than passively to wait for them. In doing so, of course, we take a step toward becoming thinkers. To become a poet, a dancer, a musician, a painter, a businessperson, a speaker of French—we need to start doing it. It's no different than becoming a thinker. Writers write. Painters paint. Thinkers think. We should then get started thinking. We can set a quota for ourselves—an idea every day or half a dozen every week (Sundays off), for example. As the Nike ad says, "Just do it." Our mantra might be "No day without an idea."

Michalko also notes that the most prominent and prolific inventors used this strategy, most notably Thomas Edison, who held more than 1,000 patents. Edison set himself the quota of a minor invention every 10 days and a major invention every six months. To reach those quotas, Edison generated lots of ideas, most of which were discarded. But the ones that remained and that were refined and developed, changed people's lives, ours included.

Get Tone

By "getting tone," Michalko refers to our ability to pay attention, to notice things, to see better. Seeing well, noticing deeply, being perceptive, is at the heart of all thinking, for we can't say (or think about) more than we can see. We can spend our entire lives improving our ability to notice deeply, a key capacity for developing critical and creative thinking.

The American novelist Henry James was a great observer of human behavior. He filled notebooks with his observations of people's actions and with their conversations, which served as provocations to thought and as ballast for his novels and stories. And the British novelist Joseph Conrad, in the preface to one of his novels, declared that his goal as a novelist was "to make you hear, to make you feel—it is, above all, to make you see." Reading literature by writers like Joseph Conrad and Henry James enhances our ability to really learn to "see."

Break Habits

Habit is another inhibitor of both critical and creative thinking. Habit locks us in, freezes our ways of seeing and knowing and doing things. To generate ideas, habits may need to be "broken." Here are a few suggestions for breaking habits.

- Take a different route to work—or even a different means of transportation.
- Change your sleeping hours—or your working hours.
- Change your music—listen to a different station and different kinds of music.
- Read a different newspaper—and if possible, in a different language.
- Make a new friend. Visit a new city.
- Cook a different recipe. Try a new drink.
- Change the season of your vacation.
- Change your reading—Web to print, or vice versa; magazine to book, or vice versa; nonfiction to fiction, or vice versa; light to heavy, or vice versa.
- Watch a different TV channel or show.
- Take a bath instead of a shower, or vice versa.
- Go to a play or concert instead of a movie, or vice versa.

Habits can also be creative. We can develop positive habits that enable us to become more creative thinkers. It's a process and a set of practices that we can inculcate in ourselves.

Feeding

By feeding our heads, Michalko simply means nourishing our minds with new information and ideas. Reading is one very rich way to do this, and traveling is another. Still other ways include watching informative shows on television, renting documentary videos, interviewing people, taking a walk with a focus on observing what you see and hear. For the moment, though, we'll talk about how to maximize the benefits of this kind of feeding, with an emphasis on reading.

First, we should pick something we are interested in reading, something we are curious about. Second, we need to read with a pen in hand to underline, annotate, and take notes. Third, we should write down some questions after reading for a while. Fourth, we can copy some key sentences we would like to remember. And fifth, we might talk about our reading with a friend or family member. We can select a passage to read to them, and get their response to it. Sixth, and finally, we can make reading a habit—a daily habit.

Challenge Assumptions

Assumptions prevent us from seeing things in new ways. A major problem with assumptions is that they are invisible; we aren't aware of the assumptions we make. Moreover, our assumptions are not always correct or valid. And even when they are, they prevent us from seeing things from other perspectives.

If asked to make a paper airplane, what do we typically do first? Many of us would very likely take a sheet of paper and fold it in a manner we had seen or done before. If we then made a second paper plane by simply crumpling up the paper into a tight ball, which "plane," will travel better when thrown across a room? We assume that a paper airplane can't be made by wadding up the paper, and that it must, instead, conform in some way to a set of predictable folds. But that is simply not the case—though, admittedly, the balled up wad is not nearly as elegant as the more conventional alternative paper airplane; nor does it fly as gracefully. But it might very well fly farther.

In linking the nine dots in the following pattern by means of three lines (without lifting the pencil), we would almost automatically assume that the lines would have to go through the center of each dot. Very likely, we would also assume a frame around the dots—that is, that we could not make our lines go outside the "boundary" of the dots. But both of these assumptions would inhibit us from being able to complete the task, which can be accomplished easily enough by violating those unwarranted constraints imposed because of those two assumptions.

Still other assumptions we tend to make about a challenge like this is that we have to solve the problem in a two-dimensional plane—as it's presented here again.

Suppose, however, we cut out the dots, put them in a straight line, and then draw a line through them, like this:

Or, what if the paper were folded in such a way that the dots lined up in three dimensions? Doing either of these things moves the problem and solution beyond the kinds of assumptions we are inclined to make typically. And we need to make a habit of challenging assumptions to become better thinkers.

What Iffing

We have mentioned the idea of asking "What if" before. This habit, however, is such a crucial one that it is presented here, briefly, once again—this time with Michael Michalko's particular spin. Michalko suggests that we need what he calls "what iffing" as a technique to transcend the possible. It's a playful and nonthreatening way to develop a good imaginative thinking habit. It's a first step toward creativity and innovation.

Here are some of the "what if questions" Michael Michalko proposes to provoke thinking:

- What if we had eyes in the back of our heads as well as the front?
- What if trees could produce large amounts of petroleum?
- What if people slept 23 hours a day and were awake for only 1?
- What if each US adult worker had to adopt and care for a homeless person for a lifetime?

- What if US senators and members of the House of Representatives (along with the president, vice president and cabinet) were required to send their children to public schools?
- What if a pill could be taken to counteract prejudice and bigotry?
- What if as we aged we became younger, living our lives backward?

(This last "what if" serves as the premise for a short story by F. Scott Fitzgerald that inspired the movie, *The Curious Case of Benjamin Button*.)

EXERCISES

12. Which of Michalko's suggestions for breaking a habit and trying an alternative way of doing something appeal to you most? Which one(s) would you like to try today?

13. Read the local newspaper; scan bulletin boards and displays at the supermarket, post office, bank, or school. Let your junk mail collect for a couple of weeks. Scan the movie schedules in nearby towns; scan the television schedules for a couple of weeks. Then identify patterns you see developing. What do you notice about issues addressed? The values implied? The lifestyles portrayed? The attitudes conveyed?

14. You have been asked to develop a new kind of restaurant, something unusual, distinctive, unconventional. Let's begin by identifying some common assumptions about restaurants, which can then be challenged in developing an alternative restaurant concept.

    a. Restaurants have menus.

    b. Restaurants serve food and drinks.

    c. Restaurants charge money.

    Begin by challenging each of these assumptions (or any others you can think of). Then devise a restaurant without menus; another restaurant that does not serve food and drinks; a third that doesn't charge money; and a fourth that doesn't do something else restaurants typically do. Develop a concept for each restaurant such that even though your new restaurant violates the conventional expectations of what a restaurant offers, you can still make it a viable business. Ask yourself what your restaurant needs (other than food, menus, and prices) so that it can be viable. (You might do this exercise with a partner.)

15. Choose two of the "what if" scenarios and play out at least three consequences for each of them. Add two of your own "what ifs," and explore their implications. Discuss with a classmate or a friend.

Using Paradox

A **paradox** is an apparent contradiction that upon closer inspection turns out to reveal an interesting truth. Michael Michalko gives the example of the following statement as uttered by a man from Crete: "All Cretans are liars." What are we to make of this contradictory provocation? If the man is telling the truth, then all Cretans, indeed, are liars. But this includes him, too, because he is from Crete. In that case, then, the statement is false because he is lying, as all Cretans do. If he is being truthful, then he is lying; if he is lying, then he is telling the truth; hence, the paradox.

A visual example occurs in the following image, which depicts simultaneously a rabbit and duck.

⊙ **Simulate** the **Experiment**, Using Paradox/ Thinking the Unthinkable **MyThinkingLab**

paradox
An apparent contradiction that turns out to be true.

FIGURE 11.2   Ambiguous Figure: Rabbit/Duck

The rabbit looks to the right and the duck to the left. So which is it, rabbit or duck? The answer, of course, as you have seen, is both. Not either–or, but both–and. Michalko contends that when we think about paradoxes, we transcend ordinary logical thinking. In suspending logic, we create new ideas, which the "swirling of opposites" stimulates. He gives an example of a paradox in which a person wants to make a lot of money but is lazy and lacks ambition. One solution is to take a vacation to an exotic locale and then write a book about it. (Of course, the book will involve some work, but that work should have some pleasure associated with it because of the topic—the exotic vacation—with the prospect of more, if the concept of vacationing and writing takes hold effectively.)

Another solution to this kind of problem is presented in Mark Twain's novel *The Adventures of Tom Sawyer*. You may remember that Tom had to paint a fence. In this case, his need to have the fence painted conflicted with his desire to avoid the work. His solution: Begin painting the fence and pretend that it's a lot of fun. When his friends ask to join in the fun, he resists for a while, but he finally relents and lets them do it by themselves.

Combining Things

Write the Response, Combining Things
MyThinkingLab

In *Where Good Ideas Come From*, Steven Johnson claims that all new ideas are combinations of former ideas, and that all inventions are based on aspects, elements, and components of things that already exist. Johnson argues that ideas are, almost always, networks of other ideas and that we take the ideas we've found and combine them into some new form. According to Johnson (and many other writers on creativity), the secret to innovation involves combining odds and ends, tinkering with what's available, with what's already around, to make something new.

Making connections, seeing relationships, linking things, as we have noted earlier, is at the heart of all thinking, both critical and creative. We combine objects to make something new, phones with cameras and electronic calendars and Web browsers and e-mail access, and so on. We combine ideas, as with the idea of freedom within structure, which yields among many possibilities, various poetic forms, such as the sonnet and the villanelle. We combine subjects from different intellectual domains, such as the creation of social psychology from sociology and psychology, or bioengineering from biology and engineering. Gregor Mendel developed the laws of heredity by combining the fields of biology and mathematics to create the then new field of genetics.

Using the analogy of two chemicals combining to create a new compound—hydrogen and oxygen forming water for example—we can catalyze creative thinking by looking for combinatory opportunities. Einstein's famous equation $E = mc^2$ combined the concepts of energy, mass, and the speed of light into a new set of relationships. He called his mode of thinking "combinatory play," a telling term, indeed. Closer to home, Fred Smith combined three observations and concepts: (1) a speedy messenger service; (2) discounted jets for sale; and (3) empty skies at night. Putting them together led him to create Federal Express, or FedEx. We can also provoke this king of combinatory thinking with simple exercises, such as the following.

EXERCISES

16. Take one object each from column A and B. This time, list the attributes of each of the two objects, and then randomly combine them. For example, taking the first two items from column A and B, "bedroom" and "automobile," we can make a list of attributes like this:

Column A	*Column B*
Bedroom	Automobile
Bed	Doors
Place to sleep	Passengers
Horizontal	Moving
Stationary	Wheels
Comfort	Speed
Sense of security	Automatic door locks
Headboard	Headrests
Near bathroom	Different colors

As Michael Michalko has noticed, if we combine, for example, "sense of security" with "automatic door locks," we might get to the idea of a master lock mechanism that controls the windows, doors, computers, and more, with a single switch. If we combine "window shades" with "moving," we could get to the idea of shades being raised or lowered automatically with light-sensing technology, according to the amount of outside light.

17. Choose two different attributes for the bedroom/automobile example—two different attributes than the ones explained in Exercise 16. Then explain what new idea for a product or service emerges from them.

Thinking the Unthinkable

In *Creative Thinkering*, Michalko argues that creativity is enhanced when we attempt to think the unthinkable. He suggests that we need ways to "unstructure our imaginations" to go beyond the common and usual ways we think. Michalko provides a number of ways to do this, most of which involve freeing ourselves to allow for "crazy or fantastical ideas." One example he offers was developed by a Red Cross director in the state of Washington who wanted to think of activities for children of soldiers deployed to war zones to keep the kids connected in some way with their dads. One suggestion was to hire actors to play the role of the fathers. The idea was considered laughable. But the director thought about its underlying concept—that of a father substitute. This concept reminded her of a program she heard that was based on a children's book, *Flat Stanley*, in which a character's picture travels around the world in stamped envelopes. (This is akin to von Oech's notion of the "stepping-stone.") This concept then led the director to ask for pictures of the fathers along with their jacket sizes. She had the pictures blown up to life-size, backed them with foam cardboard, and then distributed the pictures to the children at a party. The idea was a big hit with the kids, who enjoyed keeping their "Flat Daddies" with them.

Michalko proposes consciously generating a list of outrageous, crazy ideas about a subject. If we are designing a new office space, a new building, a new ad campaign; if you are planning a party for a child, organizing a dinner for friends, creating a new recipe—for these and many other tasks and challenges—we can start by listing some fanciful, outlandish ideas. These ideas serve as starting points, as thought stimuli. They lead to other more usable ideas by means of extracting their essential notion or concept—as with the concept of "substitute fathers" in the previous example. Putting down randomly a number of far-fetched ideas allows also for unusual combinations, things that might not normally be considered together and that can lead to fresh thinking.

Walt Disney—Dreamer, Realist, Critic

One of the most imaginative thinkers who ever lived was Walt Disney, whose name has become synonymous with creative thinking and fantasy. Think, for example, of his movie *Fantasia*, as well as the many famous animated films, including the classic *Cinderella* and *Snow White and the Seven Dwarfs*, and later, *Beauty and the Beast*, and *The Little Mermaid*, among many others. Walt Disney used a simple system to create, challenge, and evaluate his ideas. First, he would dream up fantasies and visions in an unrestrained manner. He let his imagination soar, without regard for feasibility. After he allowed himself this imaginative luxury, he would bring his fantastic visions down to earth. In this second stage of thinking, he tested them against some realistic considerations. He checked their practicality. He looked for ways to see if they could be made workable. And then, in a third stage of thinking, he played the part of critic. Even if he could make the visionary ideas into something workable, he challenged himself to see if they were actually worth producing. Who would benefit from them? How and why? Could the implemented ideas make money?

EXERCISES

18. Explain how you might go about resolving the contradictions implicit in the following paradoxes. How can you begin to make sense of them intellectually? What might you do with them, or from them, in terms of action?

    a. Lead by following.

    b. Win by losing.

    c. Create order while allowing freedom.

    d. Build a cohesive team but welcome conflict.

    e. Reward team effort while encouraging individual achievement.

    f. Be playful yet serious; serious yet playful.

19. Explain the following paradoxes.

    a. Only the ephemeral is of lasting value.—Eugene Ionesco

    b. We can't leave the haphazard to chance.—N. F. Simpson

    c. Art is a lie that makes us realize the truth.—Pablo Picasso

20. Identify the elements that each of the following products combines:

    a. Automatic coffee makers

    b. GPS tracking systems

    c. Virtual colonoscopy machines

    d. Laparoscopic surgery tools

    e. Solar heat panels

    f. Hybrid cars

21. Generate new ideas from combining one word from each column. Aim for five ideas.

Column A	Column B
Telephone	Toaster
Baguette	Lamp
Dining room	Hammock
Sunglasses	Computer
Vacuum cleaner	Tape dispenser
Parking meter	Sculpture
Mirror	Contact lenses
Sportscar	Book

22. Be like Walt Disney: Play the dreamer, realist, and critic using the following guidelines. Choose a problem or challenge from your personal, academic, or professional life. Imagine that you have a genie that will grant you three wishes with respect to your problem or challenge that would normally not be possible. Select one of your wishes and play the realist by turning the wish into something more practical. Extract a principle or aspect of the wish that appeals to you. Then take this principle or aspect, and engineer it

into a product or service. Finally, assume the role of critic, and look for the downsides of the idea. Once you identify these, you can go back and rework your application; you can select another feature or aspect of the wish that generated it. Or go back to your three wishes, choose another one, and repeat the process. You might like to do this exercise with a friend, family member, coworker, or classmate.

Looking Back and Looking Ahead

Revisit the learning goals that begin this chapter. Which of these goals do you think you have best achieved? What might you do to reach the remaining goals?

Return to the focusing questions at the beginning of the chapter. How would you answer those questions now? Which of them do you find most interesting and provocative and worthy of following up? Why?

In reviewing the list of resources that follows, identify the two that attract you most. Explain why these books or Web sites interest you. Consider looking into them for further developing your capacity for creative thinking and for using the strategies developed by Roger von Oech and Michael Michalko to generate new ideas.

Take a look, too, at the MyThinkingLab resources on the Prentice Hall Web site. Included there are readings, images, videos, questions, exercises, and other provocations to develop your creative thinking prowess.

Resources

A Whack on the Side of the Head, Roger von Oech. Business Plus, 2008.
A Kick in the Seat of the Pants, Roger von Oech. Harper Perennial, 1986.
Disciplined Dreaming, Josh Linkner. Jossey-Bass, 2011.
"Golden Retrievals," Mark Doty. In *Sweet Machine*. HarperCollins, 1998.
Your Creative Brain, Shelley Carson. Jossey-Bass, 2012.
Thinkertoys, Michael Michalko. Ten Speed Press, 2006.
Cracking Creativity, Michael Michalko. Ten Speed Press, 2001.
Creative Thinkering, Michael Michalko. New World Library, 2011.
Where Good Ideas Come From, Steven Johnson. Riverhead Trade, 2011.
Web site for Roger von Oech Web site: creativethink.com
Michael Michalko Web site: creativethinking.net

12
Thinking about Design

Design is where science and art break even.

—ROBIN MATTHEW

Good design is a lot like clear thinking made visual.

—EDWARD TUFTE

LEARNING GOALS

12.1 RECOGNIZE that design is all around us and be able to identify its varied manifestations.

12.2 DISTINGUISH between good and bad design on the visceral, emotional, and behavioral levels.

12.3 UNDERSTAND the principles and the paradoxes of design, including its constraints and compromises.

12.4 EXPLORE aspects of institutional design, architectural design, engineering design, and information design.

12.5 INVESTIGATE and analyze the relationship between and among design, art, truth, and society.

FOCUSING QUESTIONS

- What does the word *design* conjure up for you? What do you think about when you think about design?

- Think of a product that you use whose design you love and another whose design you hate. What aspects of their design stir those responses in you?

- In what ways might you think about your life in terms of design? To what extent does it make sense to talk about the design of your life?

- What other aspects of design occur to you or are important to you?

- Do you think it is reasonable for us all to think of ourselves as "designers"? Why or why not?

Chapter Overview

This chapter introduces aspects and elements of design. It invites consideration of the importance of design in our lives, from the design of everyday things like doors and pens to the design of bridges and houses, ballparks and monuments. Also considered are the design of processes and products, the purposes and paradoxes of design, good and bad design, and why we may all need to become "designers" ourselves. The central idea of this chapter is that design is a pervasive and significant aspect of our lives. Its purpose is to help us think better about the creative aspects of design thinking.

Design and Bridges

When we talk about design, we might think first of things like clothes and cars; we might think of design from the standpoint of products that compete for our attention and our money. We could think, for example of designer jeans and shoes and handbags; designer sunglasses and watches; designer fabrics and furniture, hats and houses, luggage and lamps, rugs, wallets, umbrellas, yoga mats, and more. These and many other things are designed for purpose, pleasure, and profit.

But it is not just fashionable things that are designed. Everyday objects, such as batteries and cup-holders, paper clips and staples, tables and chairs, doors and doorknobs, and thousands more, are also designed. These objects too are designed for a purpose, if not necessarily with a concern for pleasure, most often for profit. And certainly, too, for function.

So, too, with large structures—buildings, for example, and bridges, football stadiums and concert halls. In structures such as these, function and purpose intersect with aesthetics and visual impression. This is particularly so of bridges, which form a link between the practical principles of structural engineering and the aesthetic concern for beauty of design.

Bridges appeal to us for many reasons. Some of these reasons are practical, such as transporting pedestrians and vehicles over spans of land and water. Others are aesthetic, as with the beauty and elegance of suspension bridges, whose towers reach upward and whose cables arc along a visual plane. Bridges impress us with their grandeur; they inspire awe on sight and on reflection as we consider how they were constructed. As David Blockley notes in his book *Bridges*, bridges are central to how we think about ourselves; they image the connection between near and far, the natural and the supernatural, heaven and earth.

Bridges link the known and the unknown, here and there, this place and that. Bridges connect us with other people and places in both literal and metaphorical ways. In fact, we use the metaphor of bridges to convey many kinds of connection, including the bridges of personal and social relationships—people bridges. We use bridge metaphors to suggest the connection between the human and the divine, this life and the next—spiritual or faith bridges. We bridge gaps, burn bridges, build bridges over troubled waters, cross bridges when we come to them—and more.

Bridges are also a form of public art; they become associated with the places where they stand. We associate bridges with their locations: London Bridge, the Brooklyn Bridge, the Potomac Bridge, and the San Francisco Bay Bridge. The inhabitants of those places typically exhibit pride in their bridges. They take pride in the feats of engineering required to build them, in their functionality, and in their formal aesthetic qualities.

EXERCISES

1. To what extent do you think that bridges are a form of public art? What bridges are you familiar with—and how do you respond to them?

2. Look at the images of the bridges on these pages. Which bridge appeals to you most? Why? What qualities of the bridges stand out for you? Do some research on one of the bridges you admire. What does the information you find add to your understanding and appreciation of the bridge?

Design and Everyday Life

Watch the **Video**, Design and Everyday Life/ We Are All Designers **MyThinkingLab**

In *A Whole New Mind,* Daniel Pink suggests that design has become a critically important facet of twenty-first-century experience. He claims that developing a sense of design, a feeling for design, an appreciation of and an ability to create design, is important for success in today's world. Because design differentiates one product from another, design matters greatly. Pink argues that design has become crucial for contemporary businesses as a way to create new markets, and he claims, further, that design's "ultimate purpose" is to change the world.

Design has become democratized, with fashion handbags and their knockoffs, with fashion dresses sold in high-end stores and far less expensive imitations sold in JCPenney, T.J.Maxx, Target, and Marshalls. Moreover, design has become main-streamed, moving beyond the world of commerce and entertainment and into the worlds of government and politics, education and religion, leisure and family life. Design is evident all around us.

If we simply look around at this moment, we notice many things that have been designed. The clothes we are wearing, for example, the chair we may be sitting on, this book being read on computer, Kindle, Nook, iPad, or smart phone. All have been designed, constructed from materials, made through a myriad of choices at every turn. If we are sitting in a room, the room's lighting and ambience, its very space and form have been designed. So, too, is our work area, with its accouterments whether we are at home, in an office, a library, or other public space we may have conscripted as a workspace for ourselves. Our computers and printers, our files and folders both electronic and paper, our desk or table and chair—all are arranged in ways we find comfortable for our needs. We design the personal spaces in which we work, and our way of designing that space differs from the ways our friends or coworkers design their workspaces.

Looking closely at any of the objects around us, we discover that they are made of many parts—parts that have been designed by someone. The shirt or blouse or sweater we wear has been made in parts. Someone designed its buttons as well as its shape, its collar stays as well as its pattern of stripes or plaids.

The light fixtures and bulbs that illuminate our workspaces consist of multiple parts. The watches we wear contains numerous parts—many more than a shirt or a light bulb, for example. And each of those parts has been designed to work in conjunction with other parts, to function effectively and efficiently, accurately and predictably.

Daniel Pink suggests that "we must all become designers." Donald Norman in *The Design of Everyday Things* believes that we already are all designers. Pink and Norman claim that design is not something that only experts do, whatever their field of expertise. Norman suggests that what we arrange and restructure in our home and work environments are forms of design. Pink agrees and adds that we need to get better at understanding and using design to create environments that will both increase our own pleasure and improve the way the world works.

In *Emotional Design*, Norman explains how through individual acts of design, we transform commonplace things and spaces of our everyday lives into personalized and meaningful places. The ways we employ design in our everyday lives enables us to have a small measure of control over our environment; it enables us to exercise a modicum of creativity; it affords us a bit of pleasure.

We are constantly involved with aspects of design thinking. In the same way we design our workspaces, we also design our living spaces. Arranging furniture in dining room and den, living room and bedroom, study and family room and more—these, too, evidence our own everyday efforts with design. We design much more than these everyday spaces and places, however. We fashion ourselves to be seen by others—our public selves. And we fashion, retrospectively, our past, and looking forward, we attempt to design our future.

The Design of Processes

Processes also require design, complex design elements that take into account practical engineering considerations. Bridge designs have to work; they have to support whatever traverses them. Design is not simply about products, about objects. Design is a process and a way of doing things. Design thinking is methodical thinking.

More mundane considerations involve design. Vacuuming a room, for example, involves design choices such as where to start, how to negotiate around furniture (or move it), and where to complete the job. Organizing a physical workout involves design, from the time allotted for the workout, to the selection of exercises included in it, to the sequence, time, and number of repetitions for those exercises. So, too, does making arrangements for a vacation, doing research for a project, report, or purchase, and planning for the future.

We engage in the process of design when we plan a meal, cook and serve its various courses, decide on their order and what beverages should accompany each, and even earlier when shopping for the ingredients to create that meal. The shopping trip we take, the way we negotiate the supermarket, the decisions we make along the way—all involve aspects of design. For these things, we design a process and execute it methodically.

Even the supermarkets where we shop for our meal ingredients have been designed to encourage our movement through its spaces in particular ways. The

◉ **Simulate** the **Experiment**, The Design of Processes **MyThinkingLab**

layout of supermarkets, their organization and displays, the location of different kinds of foods and other nonfood items—all are carefully designed to direct shoppers one way rather than another. Candy and magazines, rather than fruit and toothbrushes, are displayed at checkout counters to stimulate "impulse purchases." Produce and dairy products are placed around the perimeter, often toward the back of the supermarket, requiring that shoppers move past many other products, through long aisles beckoning with numerous seductions. From time to time, supermarkets rearrange the location of items. This prevents us from going directly to the aisle and location where we have been accustomed to finding the products we seek. The result is that we pass through more of the store searching for what we came for, and likely notice something else we either need or simply decide to purchase on impulse. That result has been planned, designed to achieve the desired response.

EXERCISES

3. Make a rough map of a store or other place in which you shop. What do you notice about the placement of various categories of items the store sells— a clothing store, for example? What do you notice about the design of the store? Have the locations of products changed recently? Why and with what effects?

4. Look around the space you are now occupying. List at least 20 things that have been designed. Select two of them and try to identify their various parts. How well designed are they? How might their design be improved?

5. To what extent do you agree with Daniel Pink and Donald Norman that we all need to be "design thinkers"? To what extent do you think it is possible for most people to absorb and act on design principles in their everyday lives? What about you, personally?

6. To what extent do you agree with Pink about the importance of design in the twenty-first century? What specific examples and experiences can you identify that support, qualify, or contradict Pink's large claims for the significance of design? Comment on the following quotation from a BMW executive: "We don't make automobiles." BMW, rather, makes "moving works of art that express the driver's love of quality." What other automakers might make the same claim about their cars? Why? About what other products (and services) might such claims be made and with what degree of persuasiveness?

Good and Bad Design

Write the Response,
Good and Bad Design
MyThinkingLab

Because design is so pervasive, and because effectively designed products and processes have become prevalent, accessible, and affordable, we have become increasingly accustomed to expecting good design, which brings pleasure and beauty into our lives. Well-designed objects are not merely functional, they are beautiful as well. They don't merely do the jobs they were designed for; they also engage our feelings. An electronics executive quoted by Daniel Pink suggests that gadgets have moved from being simply "logical devices" to becoming "emotional devices." The wildly successful suite of Apple products—the iMac, iPod, iPhone, and iPad—represent product designs that are both functionally effective and admirably elegant, products that people have strong feelings about.

The design of cars and clothes and computers, of jewelry and watches, of plates and cups, of forks and knives, and hundreds more things, can be appreciated from both a practical and an aesthetic standpoint. Their utility is complemented by their stylish design. We appreciate the things that we enjoy using on both levels. Designers know this. As a result, every manner of product and service, of object and process we experience is considered from this double perspective. Design, thus, engages both our intellectual and emotional responses; it requires our cognitive, analytical abilities and our affective, emotional responses. The fork you use to eat your fish or twirl your spaghetti has been designed as something more than a functional utensil. If it has been well designed, it should also be pleasing to hold and to use.

Levels of Design

According to Donald Norman, we experience design on three levels: *visceral, behavioral*, and *reflective. Visceral design* involves the appearance of products and processes. We respond positively to things we find beautiful or striking, and we respond negatively to things we consider ugly or boring. *Behavioral design* involves the usefulness of products and the effectiveness of processes. We appreciate products that work well and processes that function smoothly. *Reflective design* involves the ways we rationalize and intellectualize our relationship to products and processes. The reflective aspect of design includes the ways products appeal to our self-image, to our pride in owning and using them.

These three aspects of our relationship to design—*the visceral, the behavioral,* and *the reflective*—involve both our intellectual and our emotional being. They affect and are affected by our thoughts and our feelings. From this interweaving of cognitive and affective elements in design, Norman concludes that any successful design will attempt to engage us on both the level of emotion and the level of reason—our hot and cool responses.

The visceral and behavioral levels of design involve our experience and our feelings when we actually use the product or process. The reflective level, on the other hand, is less about the immediacy of use and more about our past and future relationship to a particular product or process. It is at this reflective level that we identify ourselves with products and processes. Design reflects who we and how we see ourselves. Its value transcends it use; it connects with our sense of self and with how we present ourselves to others.

Design and Human Behavior

In *The Design of Everyday Things*, Norman suggests that well-designed objects are easy to understand and use; they contain visible clues to their effective use. Poorly designed objects, on the other hand, are difficult, even frustrating to use; they provide no clues—or worse, they provide false clues about how they should be used. We might agree with Norman's claim that most things are poorly rather than well designed. We have all encountered objects that can't be easily understood, devices that lead us to make erroneous conclusions about their functionality.

Norman argues that designers have to take account of how people use the products they create and the objects they make. Among the principles he lists as essential to a product's effectiveness is "visibility"—the extent to which its use is evident and apparent simply from looking at it. One example he cites is the door. Which way a door opens should be immediately apparent. We should not have to think twice about whether it should be pulled or pushed, or whether it slides or opens outward, and in which direction it slides or opens. This clarity of design, however, is not always evident. We have all had the experience of approaching a door and not knowing whether to push or pull, slide it or open it, and open it in or out. A well-designed door does not pose such problems. How it opens is clear, even obvious.

Another of Norman's essential characteristics for good design is "simplicity." Among the many objects he criticizes for violating this principle are electronic products, including video recorders, remote control devices, digital watches, and telephone answering systems. To take just one example, a watch that does more than tell time invites problems with the design concept of simplicity. Adding functions, such as date, second hand indicator, alternate time zone indicators, stop functions, and more, compromises a watch's ease of use.

In *Emotional Design*, Norman suggests that "good behavioral design should be human-centered, focusing on understanding and satisfying" people's needs in their use of any product. With this consideration in mind, he recommends that designers create products that provide "tangibility," a quality relating to the way a product feels—for example, the way an e-reader feels in your hands, or the way a smartphone feels as you hold it and put it to your ear.

Another aspect of a product is its usability—how well it works and functions; a well-designed product provides feedback. We need to know, for example, that when we turn on a portable computer, it is actually on. We need to know that when we send an e-mail message, it has actually been sent. We need to understand how our technological gadgets work by how they respond to our touch. We need to see and hear what our gadgets are doing in response to the functions we execute with our hands.

Tom Kelley and David Kelley in *Creative Confidence* reinforce Norman's ideas about human design. They provide a number of examples of how designing with people in mind—designing with empathy for users of what is being designed—makes a difference. One of their most compelling examples is the story of Doug Dietz, who was responsible for designing high-tech medical imaging systems, most famously magnetic resonance imaging (MRI) systems. After completing one such design, Dietz was excited to watch it in operation, as he was pleased with its technical specifications and performance. What he had not anticipated was how children would react to undergoing an MRI scan. It turned out that children who needed to have an MRI were frightened by the large machine, which they had to enter lying down and remain perfectly still while inside its narrow circular chamber. The size and shape of the MRI machine frightened them; the noises it made terrified them. Almost all of them had to be sedated before a technician could perform the MRI procedure.

Dietz was mortified and humbled by what he witnessed, and he resolved to do something to humanize the experience, to take the fear and fright out of it for kids. After shifting his thinking to a more human-centered approach to design, Dietz focused not on the MRI machine's technology, but rather on its external design. He and his team created an MRI experience built around a pirate ship, complete with a large captain's wheel that surrounds the opening of the machine's chamber. The script the design team created has the technician tell kids that while they are inside the ship, they must keep very still. When their voyage is over, they select a treasure from the pirate chest in the MRI room. And to combat their fear of the loud noises the machine makes during the MRI scanning procedure, kids are told to listen for the loud *booming* sounds that signal when the ship is shifting into "hyperdrive."

This reframing of the experience of the MRI scan for children transformed what had been a terrifying experience into a pleasurable one, such that sedation was no longer necessary for all but a few. Some children, after undergoing an MRI, asked when they could return for another trip on the "pirate ship."

Two additional principles of design thinking are worth mentioning with respect to the "pirate ship" MRI machine. The first is that Doug Dietz did not do it alone. He worked with a cross-functional team to address the problem of how his machine was perceived and experienced. Diversity of expertise helped solve the problem. Collaboration across that diversity of expertise was key. So was listening—both to Dietz's team collaborators and to the end users—especially the children. Empathy was a key component in motivating Dietz and enabling his eventual success.

In addition to what we might call "shared innovation" was a determination to get things right. Persistence, perseverance, and patience were all involved. And those dispositions were exercised in Dietz's willingness to do field research, which took him to a day-care center, a pediatric care center, and a local children's museum, to see how children reacted to their environment and how they interacted with technology, as he learned more about their needs and their fears. That kind of variegated research helped Dietz develop prototypes for what he dubbed an "adventure scanner," which he piloted in a children's hospital. Out of that experiment, Dietz and his team found their way to design the "pirate ship" MRI experience.

EXERCISES

7. Identify two products or objects whose design you admire and enjoy using. Explain what you like about these objects or products, especially from the standpoint of how they have been designed. Identify two objects or products whose design you deplore. Explain what you dislike about these products or objects from the standpoint of how they have been designed.

8. Keep a design notebook for one week. In your notebook, make a list of objects and products, processes and experiences that you encounter that have been particularly well or badly designed. Note things about them that you find especially interesting or surprising.

9. Think of some product you own and use that is of value to you. Explain its visceral appeal, its behavioral utility and functionality, and its reflective value. That is, use Norman's three aspects of design to consider why this product appeals to you, how it is valuable for you, and the manner in which it relates to how you see yourself.

10. Consider some experience you have had that was particularly frightening or unpleasant. How might it be redesigned to make it more tolerable, even if not necessarily something pleasurable?

11. Imagine how one of the following experiences might be redesigned:
    a. Buying a car
    b. Exchanging gifts
    c. Commuting to work
    d. Getting lunch

Designing for Error

Many of us have had the experience of locking our keys in the car. This is one example among many that Norman sees as an indication that designers should factor in human error into their designs. He recommends that designers make it possible to reverse an action like locking our keys in the car. He also suggests that designers anticipate the errors that will inevitably occur with their products and processes so that they can then make them easier for people to correct when they make mistakes in using them.

Among the things automobile manufacturers can do to prevent people from locking their keys in the car is to design the locking system so that the key must be used and that the doors cannot be locked without them. Warning systems such as buzzers, lights, and bells going off might be bypassed or otherwise ignored. Norman encourages designers to think of error as natural, as common, and as part of the inevitable outcome of a person's relationship to a machine. He suggests that designers should design systems not punish errors, but rather find ways initially to prevent them and, alternatively, to remedy them.

Another practical creative thinker and problem solver concerned with error is Henry Petroski, an engineer, who considers, specifically, the kinds of errors made by engineers. Petroski identifies three kinds of common errors. He describes errors of *assumption*, errors of *calculation*, and errors of *interpretation*—of arriving at conclusions. *Errors of assumption* are common not just in engineering but in many aspects of life. How many times have you said to someone, "But I thought you wanted to do this rather than that. Why didn't you tell me?" Or "But you always do it this way; I just assumed that's the way you would do it again, now." For engineers, it is a case of assuming something is true without testing it, without checking.

Errors of calculation might be as simple as making a mistake in arithmetic, or they might involve leaving out a step, omitting a term or number in a formula, or reversing an element in an equation. *Errors of interpretation* involve the misinterpretation of evidence, something vastly different from a calculation error or an unwarranted assumption. Mistakes are forgivable. But those mistakes must be caught in time and before they can do damage—especially if they form a critical step or stage in a multistage process, such as erecting a building, flying a jet, or performing open-heart surgery.

Paradoxes of Design

One of the paradoxes of design is that if something is too easy to use, it can become boring, and the user can actually use it badly, can misuse it, ignore it, or even neglect to use it at all. Two examples are driving a car and flying a plane. When driving becomes so easy that we don't have to think about what we are doing, it can become dangerous. We can become distracted such that we do other things, like listening to the radio, daydreaming, or talking to someone on the phone or in the passenger seat. When we are alone and driving we can find ourselves on "automatic pilot," so to speak, a situation where we don't have much to do. With all the automatic functions of cars today, it's as if they drive themselves.

Something similar happens with pilots of airplanes because so many controls are computer regulated. Pilots of long-distance flights sometimes find themselves bored and tired and with very little to do, which increases the danger of accidents. Ironically, making driving our cars seem more dangerous might actually make the process safer. And giving pilots more to do (though allowing for the complication of "human error") could reduce the kinds of errors airline pilots make from boredom or sleepiness.

Another type of design paradox mentioned by Norman involves *risk homeostasis*, a term regularly used with regard to safety. *Homeostasis* refers to the maintenance of an equilibrium or constant state, as for example, a constant state of safety. If the environment appears safer, people tend to take more risks. Adding seat belts and air bags to cars, providing antilock brakes and other kinds of accident-avoidance technologies for cars can actually induce people to drive more carelessly. Requiring cyclists to wear helmets and keeping roads in good repair might encourage people to drive faster than they should. Norman suggests that one way to counteract these behavioral tendencies is to reverse things, such that people have to pay more attention to what they are doing because it appears more dangerous. One example he provides is eliminating traffic lights, signs, and road markings, and mixing traffic flows so that people have to regulate their driving behavior instead of having it regulated for them.

In *The Design of Future Things*, Norman describes a set of scenarios in which our gadgets become increasingly intelligent, so smart that they make decisions for us. An example is the way cars are now primarily computers on wheels, computers that calibrate fuel intake, navigate routes to our destinations, entertain us while we drive, protect us with airbags in accidents, decide when and how much to brake, whether we should shift lanes—and more. Norman, however, takes issue with the notion that machines, such as cars, are intelligent. He argues, instead, that "intelligence is in the mind of the designer." It is the designers of the various automated features of our machines who are responsible for imagining how we humans will interact with them. The designers have to imagine the unexpected and plan for its various manifestations.

He also explains the concepts of "swarms" and "platoons," which result from the increasing automation of the automobile industry. *Swarming* refers to behavior in which there is no leader, no external guidance, and that requires each individual in the swarm to regulate his or her behavior in accordance with the mass behavior of the swarm. We see swarming behavior in schools of fish, flocks of birds, and swarms of bees. The bees, birds, and fish move together seamlessly in synchrony. They don't collide or get confused. They glide and swoop smoothly, splitting to avoid obstacles. They keep close without touching. How they do it is something of a mystery, except that we understand that their communication is instantaneous and based on sense experience including sight, sound, smell, and air pressure. In addition, it is the outliers in the swarm, or flock—those flying at the edges or front— that make the first move, which is sensed instantaneously by those closest to them and then by those further toward the center.

With this knowledge of swarming behavior, automotive engineers are beginning to design automobiles that "behave" like animals in a swarm. Computer programs are being developed that allow cars and other road vehicles to self-regulate so as to avoid collisions. This is one more way in which our machines are becoming "smarter"; it's another way in which individual human decision-making and autonomy is being compromised—some would say for the better, while others would argue for the worse, because it diminishes human agency. In simple terms, we are losing control over our machines.

EXERCISES

12. What kinds of errors have you made with machines—computers, for example—that were not reversible? To what extent have your errors with machines been reversible, correctible, remediable—able to be corrected? How do you feel about correctible mistakes when using products and processes?

13. To what extent has your experience with doors been similar to Norman's? Do you think he is right about the extent to which bad design prevails in the objects we encounter in our everyday lives? From the standpoint of touch, tangibility, "feel"—describe your experience good and/or bad with a product you own. How do you respond to what Norman says about the ways we relate to our gadgets—and to the principles he suggests that designers employ when they create new products?

14. What do you think of Norman's idea of reversing risk by making driving appear more dangerous than it actually is? Do you think people would be more careful if they had fewer external forms of guidance and warning? To what extent do you think that our cars are "overautomated," that they do too much for us and leave us too little to do? To what extent do you think increasing automation of functions in cars (and in other areas of our lives) is affecting our ability to make critical decisions quickly and effectively?

15. How much do you think our cars should do for us? And how much should we do for ourselves? Norman asks us to imagine a swarm of cars fully automated. How would the cars "know" how to avoid each other? If the cars were not fully automated, how would the drivers regulate their behavior to account for the other cars in the swarm? Imagine now a big traffic circle with cars coming from three or four directions. Complicate the scenario with pedestrians crossing the circle in different directions. What might be the benefits and dangers of such a situation?

Principles of Design

To increase the likelihood of products and processes having good and effective designs, Donald Norman recommends the following guidelines:

1. Make it easy to determine what actions are possible. Make use of constraints.
2. Make things visible, including alternative actions and their consequences.
3. Make use of natural relationships by acknowledging the natural behavior of people and the natural properties of the world.
4. Make sure the user can figure out what to do.
5. Keep instructions minimal; make the design intuitive and user-friendly.
6. Keep things simple.
7. Design for error.

Design Constraints and Compromises

Design involves a shaping and reshaping of our environment. Daniel Pink defines design as "utility enhanced by significance." Donald Norman suggests that design involves both cognitive and affective aspects—what a particular designed product or process does, and how it makes us feel. Norman suggests that the design of anything from a book to a baseball park, a fence to a freeway, a pizza box to a piano, involves a trade-off between usability and utility on one hand, and form and beauty on the other. In *Small Things Considered*, Henry Petroski explains that design inevitably requires "satisfying constraints, making choices, containing costs, and accepting compromises." Engineering design always involves trade-offs.

Petroski uses the term *satisficing* to indicate that engineering design problems almost always involve some kind of imperfection that has to be accepted as inevitable. The term *satisficing* combines the word *satisfying* and *sufficing*, which indicates good enough conditions rather than the best of all possible conditions. Satisficed conditions are those that are acceptable, those that work well enough, those reached through various kinds of compromises. In fact, Petroski at one point defines engineering as "the art of compromise."

In an ideal world, compromise and satisficing would not be necessary. In the real world we inhabit, however, the world of imperfection, compromise is a reality and satisficing a necessity. Some engineers, Petroski notes, think of the creative aspect of their work as "design under constraint." Those constraints include things like the resistance of materials, the constraints of budgets, political realities, and the limitations of the people who will use what the engineers build—with all potential errors those users can be expected to introduce—and more.

Antidesign

In an innovative and entertaining book, *Catalogue d'objets introuvables* (*Catalogue of Unfound Objects*), Jacques Carelman presents an array of objects that are impossible to use. His designs for outlandish variations of common things like keys and coffeepots, scissors and saws, sofas and chairs, bicycles and ladders are whimsical and witty. Carelman's unfound objects represent a kind of antidesign, even a form of self-punishing or masochistic design by means of which the objects would be painful to use when they are not impossible to use.

Consider what you find interesting about the following example of Carelman's coffeepot.

EXERCISES

16. Select two items from Norman's list of guidelines and give an example of a product you have used that would benefit from Norman's suggestions. Explain how following Norman's guidelines would lead to a better design.

17. To what extent do Petroski's remarks about imperfection and the necessity for "satisficing" make sense to you? What kinds of compromises have you yourself had to make in things you have constructed or planned?

18. How do you respond to Carelman's contradictorily designed coffeepot? How do you imagine he might design a rocking chair, a handsaw, a fork, or a tandem bicycle—a "bicycle built for two"?

Design Thinking

design thinking
Thinking directed toward the design of new things and new ways of doing things—the design of products and processes.

Design thinking is a type of creative thinking that looks to the future. Design thinking derives from a dissatisfaction with things as they are and a determination to improve them. We speak of "building a better mousetrap" as a shorthand way of indicating the continuous effort to improve products and services. One example is the portable computer, which has increased speed, memory, processing power, ease of use, number of features, and more. And of course, the personal computer has morphed into the netbook computer, the tablet computer, the smartphone—and who knows what else.

Design thinking is essential not just for architects and engineers, scientists and technologists. Design thinking is important to all of us, largely because we use the products, employ the services, and are at the mercy of the processes designed by others—from the ways our telephones and televisions work to the ways our public buildings and public spaces are designed.

In a post on his blog, Tim Brown, CEO of IDEO, an innovation and design consulting group, wonders how much might be gained if designers had a deeper understanding of science, including robotics and nanotechnology. He asks whether designers might help scientists better see the implications and opportunities of the technologies they develop. He suggests that the more scientific knowledge and the more awareness designers have, the better chance they would have to be able to challenge the scientific assumptions or reinterpret them in innovative ways.

Like Norman and Petroski, Brown seeks a more continuous and better-informed conversation between the analytical and the creative mind, between the methodology scientists typically employ and the less structured, more creative approach of designers. Brown wonders whether scientists might ask more interesting questions if they were comfortable with the improvisatory and instinctive aspects of design.

Institutional Design

Among the many challenges confronting us today—and in the future—are those of institutions. Large-scale public projects and complex procedures often require public support and a network of shared responsibility in designing approaches to successful design. Urban planners confront such challenges as a matter of course. So, too, do those entrusted with the responsibility of designing transportation systems; and those who develop taxation methods, banking regulations, and other financial systems; public health directives; educational and other large-scale provisions with significant social implications.

Pension reform, social security, automotive fuel efficiency, sanitation, global warming, and other large-scale problems—all require design at the institutional level and beyond. These and other macro challenges require practical, creative resolution (and compromises) in addressing, if not always resolving, intractable human problems. And they require political will, whether exercised through democratic or authoritarian principles. These complex or "wicked" problems require an enactment of public policy grounded in a deep understanding of the problems and challenges themselves and also in a set of creative approaches to dealing with them.

One such approach is provided by Richard Thaler and Cass Sunstein in their book *Nudge*, in which they make suggestions for structuring social policies so that government agencies, companies, and charities will make and encourage better choices in using their resources and influencing people's behavior. Thaler and Sunstein aim to influence the design of public and private policies to improve the lives of people, without coercing them. To that end, they present a series of ideas for structuring choices in such areas as energy conservation, investing, insurance, marketing, politics, health care delivery, and more.

One example is their suggestion that employers make 401(k) savings plans automatic—the default—which employees can opt out of, if they wish. The way such plans are typically structured now is that people must sign up for them; they must opt in. Thaler and Sunstein argue that it is good for us to have these automatic savings plans as a protection for our future, and that more of us will use them if they are set as the default. Another example involves the way organ donations are made in different countries. When renewing a driver's license in the United States, we have the option of enrolling in an organ-donor program by checking a box on the form. Opting out is the default. In some other countries, including Poland and France, we would have to check a box to opt out; participation is the default. These examples show how people can be "nudged" in the direction of policies regarded by many as socially beneficial. The choice is still theirs, but the decision about how to provide and execute that choice differs.

Another set of design challenges is discussed by Jean François Rischard in *High Noon: 20 Global Problems and 20 Years to Solve Them*. The core design challenge described by Rischard involves creating international cooperation among all the world's countries to address global problems such as world poverty, industrial pollution, water and food shortages, deforestation, infectious diseases, illegal drugs, terrorism, and intellectual property rights.

Rischard's 20 Global Issues represent planetary challenges. They are urgent. They are tough politically. They are becoming worse by the year and increasingly difficult and more expensive to solve. Current ways of dealing with them are inadequate: treaties and conventions, intergovernmental conferences, global multilaterals, G8-style meetings. One direction toward a solution that Rischard proposes is networked governance in the form of "Global Issues Networks." These could be designed in three phases: (1) a constitutional phase; (2) a norm-producing phase; and (3) an implementation phase. What's needed for this designed approach, according to Rischard, are imagination, determination, and fully committed collaboration.

Architectural Design

Design thinking, not surprisingly, is also a critical aspect of architecture. In *Why Architecture Matters*, Paul Goldberger explains how buildings affect us emotionally as well as intellectually through their design. He explains why some buildings lift our spirits and others depress us, why we are delighted to behold and experience certain buildings while being bored and even pained by others. Like Donald Norman and Henry Petroski, Paul Goldberger emphasizes how architectural design is limited by physical and financial constraints and by the demands of function and use. Buildings, he reminds us, serve practical purposes; they cannot be considered purely aesthetically—though it is their aesthetic properties that move us. Their proportions and scale, their texture and materials, their shapes and forms, their use of space and of light—these are the elements we find appealing, or not.

Architects confront design problems every day—whether they are designing homes or office buildings, churches or theaters, monuments and memorials or shopping centers and public parks. With its manifold purposes and designs, architecture exists, as Goldberger notes, "to challenge, not to coddle." He suggests that architecture "often expands human possibility," sometimes in troubling, even shocking ways. In the process, architecture breaks through conventions, changing and enlarging our ideas about what a culture is able to create. He cites recent attention to the concept of "evidence-based design," as architects look to make greater connections with nature through their structures, as they seek ways to give the users and occupiers of those structures more choices in their use of facilities and a more pleasant environment in which to live and work.

Another architect, Matthew Frederick in his *101 Things I Learned in Architecture School*, offers some practical advice for design thinking. Here are a few of his 101 suggestions and observations: #18: "Any design decisions should be justified in at least two ways."; #37: "Any aesthetic idea is usually enhanced by the presence of a counterpoint."; #97: "Limitations enhance creativity."; #100: "When you come up with a concept . . . give it a name." Through these and other bits of practical design advice, Frederick brings design concepts down to earth and close to home. He specifies and concretizes architectural principles and practices; in the process, he shows how abstract architectural design concepts can become living architectural realities.

We can illustrate innovative architectural design with the work of two contemporary architects—Jeanne Gang and John Portman. Ms. Gang is best known for re-inventing the skyscraper with her Aqua building in Chicago. The distinctive feature of this unique skyscraper is its use of curvilinear form. At 82 stories and over 1.9 million square feet, Aqua Tower is one of few high-rises in the world that creates a

community on its façade. Its outdoor terraces—which differ in shape from floor to floor based on criteria such as views, solar shading and dwelling size/type—create a strong connection to the outdoors and the city, as well as form the tower's distinctive undulating appearance.

The design of the Aqua building was inspired by the striated limestone outcroppings common in the Great Lakes area. This sinuous shape is more than a mere formal gesture; it is also a way to extend the views and maximize solar shading.

John Portman is known for the design of hotels and public spaces, including the Shanghai Center and the Hyatt Hotel and other buildings at the Embarcadero Plaza in San Francisco. Portman is widely known for popularizing hotels and office buildings with multistoried interior atriums. He has had a significant impact on the cityscape of his hometown of Atlanta, with the Peachtree Center area, which includes Portman-designed Hyatt, Westin, and Marriott hotels. Portman's designs are widely recognized for their drama and their wow factor. His hotel interiors are scaled with high open spaces. They are designed with a blending of rectilinear and curvilinear planes. And they mix materials and low-key colors to form harmonious concepts that have been described as "cinematic" and "symphonic," suggesting their energy and grandeur. Glass elevators, lighted columns, and cascading fountains create an extravaganza of space and light, which is clearly exemplified in the atrium of the Hyatt Hotel in the Embarcadero Center in San Francisco.

EXERCISES

19. Who should be responsible for developing and implementing the principles of "institutional design"? To what extent should institutional design be the primary or even the sole responsibility of institutional leaders? To what extent should institutional design practicalities be shared with and distributed among various stakeholder and participant constituencies? Give an example of an institution with which you are familiar—in terms of shaping its future direction, purpose, goals, and strategies for achieving them.

20. To what extent do you agree with the strategies for creating "default" positions advocated by Thaler and Sunstein with regard to shaping public policy decisions? To what extent might it be dangerous to have government officials deciding what the default conditions are for such things as licenses and health plan contributions?

21. Which of the ideas referenced in the discussion of "architectural design" do you find most interesting and most useful? Why?

22. What matters most to you about the buildings you live and work in? What impresses you most about public buildings you frequent? What do you like and dislike about each of these kinds of buildings? Why?

Engineering Design

Engineering is intimately implicated in design. There is no escaping that fact. And one of the most important aspects of engineering design is its necessary connection with failure. The foremost engineer who has written about engineering design and failure, Henry Petroski, titled his first book, published in 1985, *To Engineer is Human: The Role of Failure in Successful Design*. Note that the failure is linked not with bad or unsuccessful design but rather with good or successful design. The central notion is that engineering a product or a process involves considering ways that product or process can fail—and testing products and processes to include failures.

In a more recent book, *To Forgive Design: Understanding Failure* (2012), Petroski continues to explore the intimate connections between failure and engineering design. He contends that not only are engineering design failures inevitable, but that failure is actually what drives the field of engineering design forward. It is the failures that force new thinking and that lead to improved products and processes.

Among the examples Petroski includes are the insulating O-rings on the booster rocket that launched the Challenger Space Shuttle. Those O-rings failed in the unexpected cold, leading to the disastrous explosion in 1999 of the spacecraft in flight. Petroski also cites the collapse of the Tacoma Narrows Bridge in Washington State in 1940. More recent examples of engineering design failures from which engineers learned include the failure of the New Orleans levees during Hurricane Katrina, collapsed buildings during the earthquakes in Japan and Haiti, and the Deepwater Horizon oilrig catastrophe.

Information Design

In *The Economics of Attention*, Richard Lanham directs our attention to how design is critical in the age of information, and how design is inextricably intertwined with information. Lanham gives the example of fighter-plane cockpits, in which a profusion of data has to be absorbed quickly and accurately for near immediate action. One design technique used in these cockpits is to superimpose information on the cockpit Plexiglas window so the pilot has access to the information projected there, while simultaneously viewing the physical world outside the window. Pilots toggle back and forth between the window and the outside world, flipping attention from one to another nearly instantaneously.

Information design includes the design of flight simulators, videogames, and motion-based theme park rides. It encompasses computer-interface design, Web site design, and numerous examples of military "theater of operations" simulations.

The Army and Marine branches of the US military services have been using a video game to help train soldiers for combat. In fact the military has become a major influence on the growth and development of the video game industry because of its need for and use of increasingly sophisticated simulators and computer-based war games. Some of the features of these digital game tools include the importation of detailed aerial and satellite imagery to replicate in 3-D images the environment to which soldiers will eventually be transported. The games simulate small arms fire and the explosion of IEDs on terrain that mimics, in great detail, the actual locations in Afghanistan and Iraq where the soldiers have been deployed.

EXERCISES

23. To what extent do you agree with the notion that failure is not only inevitable but is also necessary for success? What complicating factors are involved with failures of engineering design as compared say with failures in designing a new smartphone application? To what extent are the failures associated with smartphone applications "acceptable"—such as those that occurred with the voice recognition system and the maps used with the Apple iPhone5, or the software glitches that accompanied the introduction of Microsoft's Surface tablet?

24. What do you think about the idea of using simulators and computer-based war games as training for soldiers preparing to enter combat zones? What other kinds of digital tools do you think would be useful to soldiers in the field? Why?

Design, Art, and Society

Design is an essential feature of any work of art—poems and paintings; novels and novellas; songs and symphonies; dances and dramas; movies and monuments. Design is an integral aspect of concert performances, art exhibitions, and film festivals. We see aspects of design evident in award ceremonies, such as the Oscars, in sports competitions, such as the Olympics, in many kinds of annual events such as local flower and antiques shows, in auto and technology shows, and the like. Design is essential for creating, developing, and organizing religious and civic ceremonies, such as weddings and installations, funeral services, and other forms of memorializing lives and achievements. There is no escaping design and its association with creative thinking.

Let's consider for a moment a few ways design functions in some kinds of artworks, large and small, long and short. Whether a novel or a short story, a work of fiction exhibits a formal design, a structure of organization, a patterned form. This is so whether the fictional work is related to the life of the author autobiographically or not, whether it has some connection to history or not, whether its design follows a traditional plot structure or takes a nonconventional approach. The same is true of works of poetry, whether they be epics like Homer's *Odyssey*, Dante's *Divine Comedy*, and Milton's *Paradise Lost*, or lyric poems of a few lines or stanzas, such as Japanese *haiku* and *tanka* poems written centuries ago or as recently as today.

Consider the design of *The Divine Comedy*, an epic poem written in Italian during the late thirteenth century. Dante divides his *Commedia*, as he called it, into three major parts: *Inferno* (Hell), *Purgatorio* (Purgatory), and *Paradiso* (Paradise). Each of these is divided into an equal number of cantos or chapters—33 cantos for each of the 3 parts, plus 1 additional canto of introduction that Dante includes with the first part, *Inferno*. Altogether 100 cantos make up the complete *Divine Comedy*. That's one aspect of the work's design. Another design element is its structure as the story of a journey, a pilgrimage that begins on earth, descends into hell, treks up the mountain of purgatory, and then soars into paradise. The events that occur along the journey Dante describes reflect and represent beliefs held by medieval Catholics about life, death, and the afterlife. Dante's design in creating the work illustrates these beliefs concretely through image and story. They link the world we know with what can only be imagined; they take us on an imaginative journey from here to eternity.

Theatrical works—plays and operas, musicals and monologues—also offer a wide range of design options and opportunities. Consider any play you have ever seen performed, whether as live theater or in a filmed version, in school or in a professional production. How many elements and aspects of design were involved? These at least—a script, designed to be memorized by actors; costumes, designed for the particular performance; staging sets with props; music and other sound effects; lighting; a curtain or other separating device; design of spaces for the performers onstage, for any musicians needed, for the audience to be seated—and much, much more. For films, these elements of design are multiplied many times. (Think of the long list of credits that flows across the screen following the showing of a contemporary movie.)

Design affects our lives in small and large ways, from the way we organize time into days, weeks, months, and years, to the ways we design our lives to achieve our goals and create purpose and meaning for ourselves and in our relations with others. Design tests our will; design exercises our skills. As Robert Gudrin notes in *Design and Truth*, design gives our lives order, shaping and channeling energy productively. In this shaping and ordering of our energies, we discover and create meaning.

Design and Truth

Gudrin suggests further that the design of objects conveys something important about them. The way things are designed says something about not only their purpose but also their value and their intent. Enlightened designs—those carefully and thoughtfully created with people's needs and the common good in mind—delight and enliven our experience. Debased designs—those in which shortcuts are taken, inferior materials are used, slipshod workmanship is allowed—deform the objects made and debase their value.

There is, then, an ethics as well as an aesthetics of design. Effective design requires not only a concern for beauty and elegance but also a desire for honesty and truth. Inadequate design cheats as it cheapens; its inadequacies are symptomatic of its dishonesty. True and honest design provides opportunities for pleasure and understanding, as well as for a direct and productive engagement with the world. Good, honest design adds value and aids understanding. It enhances and enriches our experience of life.

EXERCISES

25. What other examples of design can you think of with regard to public events and ceremonies? What design structures do they exemplify?

26. To what extent do you think that there is an ethics of design? What do you understand by this notion? What examples can you cite that uphold or violate an ethics of design?

Looking Back and Looking Ahead

Revisit the learning goals that begin this chapter. Which of these goals do you think you have best achieved? What might you do to reach the remaining goals?

Return to the focusing questions at the beginning of the chapter. How would you answer those questions now? Which of them do you find most interesting and provocative and worthy of following up? Why?

In reviewing the list of resources that follows, identify the two that attract you most. Explain why these books or Web sites interest you. Consider looking into them for further developing your capacity for design thinking to generate fresh ideas and new concepts.

Take a look, too, at the MyThinkingLab resources on the Prentice Hall Web site. Included there are readings, images, videos, questions, exercises, and other provocations to help you develop your appreciation of and capacity for creative design.

Resources

Small Things Considered, Henry Petroski. Random House, 2004.

Bridges, David Blockley. Oxford University Press, 2010.

A Whole New Mind, Daniel H. Pink. Riverhead Trade, 2006.

Catalogue d'objets introuvables, Jacques Carelman. Le cherche midi éditeur, 2003.

The Design of Everyday Things, Donald A. Norman. Basic Books, 2002.

The Design of Future Things, Donald A. Norman. Basic Books, 2009.

Emotional Design, Donald A. Norman. Basic Books, 2005.

Creative Confidence, Tom Kelley and David Kelley. Crown Business, 2013.

Nudge, Richard Thaler and Cass Sunstein. Penguin, 2009.

High Noon, Jean François Rischard. Basic Books, 2002.

Why Architecture Matters, Paul Goldberger. Yale University Press, 2011.

101 Things I Learned in Architecture School, Matthew Frederick. MIT Press, 2007.

To Engineer Is Human, Henry Petroski. Vintage, 1992.

To Forgive Design, Henry Petroski. Harvard University Press, 2012.

The Economics of Attention, Richard Lanham. University of Chicago Press, 2007.

Design and Truth, Robert Gudrin. Yale University Press, 2011.

13

Thinking about Innovation

Every truth passes through three stages: First, it is ridiculed. Second, it is violently opposed. Third, it is accepted as self-evident.

—ARTHUR SCHOPENHAUER

FOCUSING QUESTIONS

- How do you define innovation? What is the relationship between and among imagination, creative thinking, and innovation?

- Why might it be important to understand basic principles of innovation?

- What conditions are necessary for innovation to occur?

- To what extent are you an innovator in your everyday life?

- What might you begin to do to foster your ability to become a more innovative thinker?

LEARNING GOALS

13.1 UNDERSTAND the concept of innovation in relation to creativity and imaginative thinking.

13.2 RECOGNIZE and identify key conditions, characteristics, and principles of innovation.

13.3 EXPLORE the value of accident, error, adaptation, and combination, for innovation.

13.4 INVESTIGATE examples of innovation past and present.

13.5 EXAMINE the conditions that thwart and kill innovation and those that foster and nurture it.

Chapter Overview

This chapter introduces the concept of innovation and raises questions about its nature. It identifies dispositions and practices that foster innovative thinking, along with attitudes and practices that inhibit it. Numerous examples of applied innovative thinking are discussed, including the innovations created by Steve Jobs at NeXT Computer, Pixar Studios, and Apple at the beginning and end of his career. The purpose of the chapter is to stimulate thinking about how we can become more innovative thinkers.

What Is Innovation?

Watch the **Video**,
What Is Innovation?
MyThinkingLab

innovation
A significant positive change usually brought about by the creation of something new, which is often based on combining things that already exist.

"**Innovation**" is usually defined as "significant positive change." The change typically involves something new being brought into being (from the Latin word *novum*). What's new, however, is almost always built upon what already exists. Our computer keyboards, as Scott Berkun notes in *The Myths of Innovation*, are composed of typewriter, electricity, plastic, written symbols, operating systems, circuits, USB connectors, and binary data. Besides recognizing the "oldness" in the newness of an innovation, we should also note that we typically recognize innovations as productive changes, at least initially. Any innovation, however, ultimately bears both beneficial and detrimental consequences for different people and groups. That is, some people and groups of people benefit from innovations more than others. Some, in fact, may be harmed by certain innovations.

In an opinion column written for the *Wall Street Journal* in October 2010, Matt Ridley describes the value of importing ideas for innovation. His prime example is the Italian Leonardo Fibonacci, who was born c. 1170 in Pisa. Fibonacci is best known for identifying a sequence of numbers, called the Fibonacci series, which describes, among other things, the mathematical proportions behind the seed spirals of sunflower heads and the shape of nautilus shells. What is not as well known is that Fibonacci spent time in the Arab city of Bugia in present-day Algeria, where he learned to use Arabic numerals. We owe the use of Arabic numbers to Fibonacci (a significant improvement in practicality over Roman numerals), and it is largely to Fibonacci that we also borrowed the powerful mathematical concept of zero.

Fibonacci thrived in part because he moved around, living in different cultural environments, exposed to a variety of perspectives and a wide range of ideas. He was also fortunate to live in states that allowed the free exchange of ideas at a time when world capitals such as Baghdad and Paris were under the sway of religious systems, Islam and Catholicism, respectively, that encouraged uniformity of thinking.

Human progress depends on keeping ideas moving to avoid their being suppressed and thus prevented from being able to mingle and combine with other ideas. Geography helps to spread ideas by means of trade routes that cross countries, continents, and cultures. Political systems also affect the spread of ideas. Centralized systems discourage innovation by imposing uniformity of thought, belief, and behavior; decentralized systems allow for greater variety of thought and an increased possibility for diversification and exchange.

As Ridley notes in a subsequent *Wall Street Journal* article in May 2011, the primary spurs to innovation are trade and urbanization. These stimuli are as important if not more important than money, governmental support, or individual genius (though it would be hard to argue against the importance of these other factors, as well). Trade in commodities leads to exchanges of ideas. Learning other ways to do things and to think about things encourages fresh approaches and stimulates new ideas. Urbanization contributes volume to the equation; more people congregated doing more things leads to different ways of thinking and also to acquiring the critical mass needed to gain recognition for new ideas and fresh ways of thinking.

Ideas follow a process of natural selection, a thought that Ridley further develops in his book *The Rational Optimist*. He explores a link between the evolution of ideas and biological evolution, claiming that for cultural evolution trade is related to culture in the way sex is related to biology. Cultural and economic progress depend on ideas coursing among each other, which drives what he calls "cumulative evolution."

Ideas need to be exchanged, borrowed, modified, and developed so that further ideas can be built from them. When this occurs, new ideas emerge. The collective intelligence of people, their accumulated human ingenuity, leads to positive change and creative problem solving, the basis for Ridley's brand of "rational optimism" and the source of his hopes for the future.

Creativity is an important aspect of innovation. The various characteristics of innovation that Ridley describes played out historically in the ancient history of Babylon. In his book, *Babylon*, Paul Kriwaczek identifies four characteristics that account for the success of the ancient Sumerian city. He argues that creativity was evident throughout the ancient Babylonian empire, with its major cities and extended empire serving as a laboratory for early science, law, literature, and technological invention, while trade and war created a networked web of nations within the empire.

Along with creativity, Kriwaczek attributes what he calls "nonethnicity" as a second significant factor, with its combination of peoples, ideas, styles, beliefs, and behaviors merging into a single continuous cultural tradition woven out of many and varied strands. According to Kriwaczek, these two factors resulted in two others—longevity and continuity—which, enabled the Mesopotamian world, inflected in Sumerian, Akkadian, and later Assyrian forms, to exist as a single civilization with one unique cuneiform writing system for 2500 years.

Principles of Innovation

In "The Discipline of Innovation," an article from the *Harvard Business Review*, reprinted in *The Innovator's Cookbook*, longtime management guru Peter Drucker describes innovation as being both perceptual and conceptual. He notes that although a change in perception does not alter facts, it does change their meaning. Changing one's perception from seeing obstacles to seeing challenges and opportunities exemplifies such a shift.

Innovation also involves thinking imaginatively as well as analytically, laterally as well as logically. And although innovations might involve complex systems, the innovative idea itself needs to be clear, simple, and focused. An innovation in retrospect should elicit the response—"Why didn't I think of that"? Or "Yes, of course" and "How logical," and perhaps even, "How simple."

Innovation requires talent, for sure. But it also involves knowledge and ingenuity, along with a willingness to take risks. Innovation involves imaginative thinking, certainly. But it also requires expertise and motivation—deep knowledge of the right kinds of questions to ask, along with a personal drive to get to the bottom of things. It requires an ability to evaluate ideas as well as to generate them. Innovation, in short, requires both critical and creative thinking.

An additional crucial characteristic for innovative ideas to flourish is "intellectual space," a network of potential directions for imaginative wondering. For creative thinking to emerge, there needs to be space in which ideas can play out. For creative thinking to be productive and efficacious, the raw materials of expertise and creative aptitude need to be complemented by discipline and determination. These accumulated resources for thinking are essential for problem solving and critical to success. Underlying them must be motivation in the form of a natural desire to navigate the complex maze of volatility, uncertainty, complexity, and ambiguity, which inevitably appear during nearly all efforts to innovate.

Conditions of Innovation

Whether a committed innovator is running a streak or is deeply immersed in a new idea, certain conditions for innovation need to be in evidence. In *The Myths of Innovation*, Scott Berkun identifies six conditions that lead to innovation; he sees these factors as providing a stimulus for innovative thinking generally.

One: hard work in a single, specific direction, exemplified by the creation of Google, the discovery of DNA, and the development of the computer mouse.

Two: hard work with a shift or change of direction, exemplified by the development of Teflon and Post-it notes.

Three: curiosity, which has led many inventors to their discoveries, with Leonardo's and Edison's inventions being famous examples, though the discovery of Velcro by George de Mestral is another.

Four: money, which motivates, stimulates, and nurtures innovation. The pursuit of wealth and the need for funding drive much contemporary innovation, especially Internet-based innovation, as exemplified by Google, Facebook, and Amazon.

Five: necessity, which is commonly described as "the mother of invention," and which can be exemplified by the creation of Craigslist, which grew out of Craig Newmark's desire to exchange information with friends living in different cities.

And *six:* what Berkun calls "*combination*," and which is on everyone's list of innovative practices. Combining previously existing elements to make something new is an essential practice and driver of innovation, from the humblest ideas to the grandest.

In the same way, Leonard M. Greene in his book *Inventorship*, suggests that everyday experiences contain opportunities for each of us to exercise our innovative potentiality—as long as we have developed "the necessary awareness." He encourages us to make full use of our knowledge and experience. And he urges us to become ever more observant and to open our minds to new possibilities. The motivating innovation question for Greene is "Why not?" For example, if sprinkling clothes with water makes them easier to iron, "why not" find a way to put the water into the iron? If we can't always be available to take our phone calls or watch TV shows, "why not" create a machine to answer the phone and record a message, and one to record those TV shows? A targeted "why not" question prompts innovative thinking, whether or not an actual new device results directly from that question.

EXERCISES

1. To what extent do you think Ridley's notion of the movement of ideas across borders remains relevant today? Do you think some countries are more or less likely to be sources of innovation than others? Why? To what extent do you think we have reason to be optimistic about the future for the reasons Ridley suggests?

2. How do you think each of the following innovations may have come about? Do some research on two innovations that interest you.

   a. The development of the sonnet poetic form

   b. The use of stream-of-consciousness as a narrative technique in novels

   c. The forward pass in football

   d. The stolen base in baseball

   e. The three-point shot in basketball

   f. The use of the sustain pedal for piano composition and performance

   g. The discovery of photosynthesis

   h. Scotch tape

   i. Panty hose

   j. Post-it notes

   k. The electric guitar

   l. Tea bags

   m. Crazy glue

   n. The thermometer

   o. The pacemaker

3. Think of an area of knowledge or of a hobby, sport, or other skill that you are familiar with and know a good deal about. Identify two innovations that have occurred in that area of knowledge, hobby, sport, or skill. Explain how those innovations came about. Perhaps you could consider something from the world of fashion, cooking, entertainment, music, art, cars, books, computers, real estate, home construction, electronics, or life insurance.

4. What common themes do you find among the drivers of innovation presented by Ridley, Berkun, Greene, and Kriwaczek? Select one of the drivers of innovation mentioned by Ridley, Berkun, Greene, or Kriwaczek, and explain why you think it is important for generating new ideas. What mechanisms do you think might be involved with one of these innovation drivers?

5. Think of a time when you presented an idea, proposal, or other novel approach at home, at school, or at work. How did you respond when you met with one or another negative comment or obstacle?

Innovation and Resonance

Steven Paley refers to the "resonance" of innovative ideas in his book *The Art of Invention*. Paley suggests that although many ideas may circulate in our minds, only those that "resonate," only those that become stronger, more insistent, or more ingrained, are worthy of action. Paley recognizes five sources of innovation: (1) application of life experience; (2) making the familiar new; (3) applying physical principles; (4) chance and accidental observation; and (5) learning from nature, an approach he shares with Leonardo da Vinci. But whatever the source of an innovative idea, and however resonant it might be, to bring it to light and life, to make it a practical invention, it must possess three qualities: *simplicity, elegance*, and *robustness*.

According to Paley, *simplicity* can be profound. Simplicity is compact; it contains much in a small amount of space; it can do much with little. Einstein's basic equation for relativity, Newton's formula for gravitation, and Euclid's basic postulates of geometry provide some examples. Making something simple, however, is not easy. It requires a deep understanding of the tools, methods, mechanisms, and processes involved.

Scientific formulas and mathematical equations that illustrate simplicity can just as well illustrate *elegance. Elegant simplicity* is a way of getting the most from the least. Elegance also refers to the beauty of an idea, the attractiveness of a concept. According to Paley, aspects of elegance include, besides *ingenious simplicity, flexibility, adaptability, self-regulation*, and *further development through use*. And, finally, an idea's *robustness* refers to its strength and its redundancy, along with its ability to manage failure and heal itself when necessary.

These attributes and requirements for practical invention echo and overlap with those of other invention-prone writers cited in this chapter, including Steven Johnson, who takes things further in *Where Good Ideas Come From*. Johnson notes that innovation flourishes in particular kinds of environments while being stifled in other kinds. Two such environments, the city and the Web, are conducive to innovation largely because they are dense networks with many participants of varied and diverse needs, skills, and talents. Johnson also mentions the coral reef as such an environment, a place where biological life teems with variety in a sustained and irrepressible way.

For each of these environments, however, Johnson adds the cautionary note that we need to consider them not just in the short term, but also with a long "zoom." In the short run, competitiveness among individuals and organizations may be the norm for success; in the long term, though, cooperation and collaboration in shared networks can breed more useful and lasting ideas for innovation. Connection is a more useful strategy for innovation than protection. Ideas, Johnson suggests, want to cross conceptual borders to complete each other more than they want to compete.

Innovation Myths and Innovation Drivers

In *The Power of Why*, Amanda Lang discusses a number of myths about innovation. Among the myths she cites are these:

1. *Innovation is about the latest new thing.* It isn't, she suggests. Most innovation is incremental, a slow set of improvements on things that already exist.

2. *Innovation is a private, solo affair.* Mostly, it's not, with some exceptions of course, for special geniuses. But even those unique mavericks often need others to refine and implement their innovations.

3. *Innovation cannot be taught.* Yet unleashing a person's natural curiosity and passion for learning can tap into his or her capacity for innovation.

4. *Innovation is a top-down linear process.* It mostly does not happen that way. Good ideas can and do come from anywhere in an organization—from the margins and from people in the trenches doing the nitty-gritty day-to-day work.

5. *Innovation can't be forced.* There is a measure of truth to this familiar belief. However, when common assumptions are jettisoned, and people are invited to contribute their ideas freely—and given assurance that those ideas will be heard and valued—innovative ideas emerge.

6. *Innovation isn't for everyone.* To the contrary, innovation is, indeed, for everyone— even though our innovations may involve creativity with a small c rather than the large-scale world-changing innovations of Creativity with a capital C.

The main drivers of innovation can be gleaned from the chapter titles of her book:

1. What Happens to Curiosity?
2. Forget What You Think You Know.
3. Question Yourself.

4. Figure Out What No One Else Is Doing.

5. Dream Big.

6. Borrow, Don't Just Follow.

7. Be Prepared to Change Course—Frequently.

8. Get Engaged.

9. Play Well (A Little More Roughly, That Is) with Others.

10. Talk to Strangers.

11. Don't Stop Thinking about Tomorrow.

EXERCISES

6. Which of Paley's conditions of innovation resonate the most for you? Which of them makes the most sense? Why? Which of his qualities of good ideas do you find most compelling, and why?

7. To what extent do you agree with Johnson that innovation in the long term, his "zoom," requires collaboration more than competition?

8. Which of Amada Lang's innovation myths and drivers do you find most persuasive? Why? Which of her chapter titles most intrigues you? Why?

Inadvertent Discoveries

Many innovations were based on discoveries and inventions that came into being almost by accident. In many instances a product was developed by noticing an effect or outcome that was not being looked for in the original research. Among many examples is the laser, which was developed by its inventor because he was simply interested in splitting light beams. The reputed inventor of the laser, Charles Townes, as reported by Nassim Nicholas Taleb in *The Black Swan*, had no ulterior motive; Townes was simply curious about how to split light. His colleagues, says Taleb, were reported to have teased him about the irrelevance of his invention. Ironically, the laser has been found to have many uses, among them microsurgery, eyesight correction, compact disc technology, data storage and retrieval—and who knows yet what else to come?

We can also consider the most influential of modern inventions, the computer, to be in this category of a tool that was invented and designed for one purpose, but which, afterward was found to have many additional applications. It is these additional, unforeseen uses that enable innovative thinkers and companies to capitalize on and develop new products, in short, to monetize them into viable businesses.

The computer, for example, was not designed to allow mathematicians to develop visualizations of complex algebraic, geometric, and other mathematical applications. Nor was it designed for architects and automobile designers to create 3-D computer models. And it was certainly not originally intended for the multiple and complex computer animation effects that have been created by various innovators in film animation and design. Yet, the computer has been used for these and many more widely diversified applications, whose end is not yet in sight. One of the great ironies of the computer, is that when computer technology first emerged more than half a century ago, Thomas Watson, IBM founder, predicted that there would be little if any need for more than just a few computers (which at that time were room-sized machines that had only the tiniest fraction of the capability of today's basic smartphone). What required a large room then fits snugly into purse or pocket today, with our minicomputers vastly more powerful than those earlier monstrous machines.

Achieving Insights

In *Seeing What Others Don't*, Gary Klein analyzes ways that we can develop insights—and also ways that insights can be obstructed. Klein suggests that insight is related to intuition in being unexpected but differs from intuition in terms of the radical shift of understanding that insight brings us. Intuition relies on previously learned patterns; insight discovers new patterns. We achieve **insight** in the search for better, more accurate and comprehensive explanations—stories that explain in ways we were previously at a loss to understand. Insights, Klein suggests, are disruptive; they change our understanding, our feelings, and sometimes even our perspective on life or our beliefs about how the world works.

We gain insights through *making connections, observing coincidences, noticing contradictions*, and *following our curiosity*. Most often, two or three of these ways of achieving insight occur together, so that noticing a coincidence arouses our curiosity, which leads us to ask questions, investigate further, and follow an enticing lead. Or we might make a connection between two things we had not previously put together, and then wonder what further connections, led by our curiosity, we might make. Curiosity is the key.

An additional path toward insight is something Klein calls "creative desperation." This path or trigger for intuition differs from the others in being more dramatic and more ingenious. Klein provides a number of examples, the most dramatic of which is the way a firefighter, Wagner Dodge, saved his life by starting a small fire that encircled him and then diving headfirst into its ashes. In the process the gigantic roaring forest fire that would have incinerated him, instead raced past him without harm. Horribly, his companion firefighters who tried to outrace the fire could not outrun it to safety, and perished in its violent flames. None of those men innovated on the spot, as did Dodge with his counterintuitive lifesaving measure. Dodge's creative act, born of desperation, saved his life.

To improve our chances to gain insights, Klein suggests that we tune our thinking and behavior differently for each of the paths toward gaining insights. In *noticing contradictions*, for example, we need to be willing to be surprised, even shocked by the unexpected. We need to take contradictions seriously even when they violate our normal patterns of belief and understanding.

In *making connections*, we need to be open to new possibilities and ready to explore the unfamiliar. *Creative desperation* necessitates that we examine our assumptions and act in a way that might violate our usual patterns of behavior. As Klein reminds us, an insight is a jump—an imaginative leap—to a different way of understanding how things work. It surprises us in that it is not the result of deliberation, analysis, or conscious thought.

Group and Solo Innovation

In their respective books, *Group Genius: The Creative Power of Collaboration*, and *Quiet: The Power of Introverts in a World That Can't Stop Talking*, Keith Sawyer and Susan Cain, respectively, emphasize group and individual creativity and innovation. Sawyer argues that every major innovation and many minor inventions involved

Simulate the **Experiment**, Achieving Insights **MyThinkingLab**

insight
A radical shift in understanding that relies on a break with previous patterns of thinking.

Write the **Response**, Group and Solo Innovation **MyThinkingLab**

more than a single individual, not just a solitary genius working in splendid isolation. Examples include Charles Darwin's discovery of evolution through the mechanism of natural selection, which was triggered by his reading of Thomas Malthus on population, a reading that sparked Darwin's insight that competition provided the struggle for survival that lies at the heart of his theory. On a simpler and less grand scale, Sawyer cites the development of the board game, *Monopoly*, which was invented by a group of Quakers, extended to other players, offered to Parker Brothers, the game company, and eventually codified with a set of rules, a standardized board and set of game pieces—thimble, hat, iron, and others that derive from humble Quaker origins. The Frisbee and the mountain bike, radio and television, the Internet and social networking—all involved multiple people working together and apart.

While acknowledging that many kinds of discoveries and inventions build on the work of predecessors, Susan Cain emphasizes, instead, the need for individuals to spend time in isolation, thinking things through before they can advance knowledge and spark innovation. She laments the contemporary emphasis on brainstorming, on group activities, excessive collaboration, and the design of workspaces so open that they impede contemplation, reflection, and considered thought. She stresses the link between an emphasis on group activity and extroversion, claiming that American business prides itself on the collaborative nature of creative thinking leading to innovation. What is ignored, or at least downplayed, according to Cain, is the extent to which creative thinking and innovation begin with an individual working obsessively on something he or she loves—Steve Wozniak on developing a small computer, for example. And while acknowledging that Wozniak and other introvert types working in isolation eventually need to share their ideas with others and be spurred to further thinking in conversations, arguments, and debates, Cain argues that those introverted types need to return to their private places to explore and experiment on their own, undistracted. She celebrates the kind of workplaces and workspaces that combine opportunities for people to share ideas with opportunities to retreat to their private lairs where they do their advanced thinking.

Cain calls attention to the dangers of what she labels the "new groupthink." She suggests that groups thinking together are impeded by "social loafing," the tendency for any single individual to do less in proportion to the size of the group. In addition, thinking in groups faces two additional obstacles, particularly for those who are shy and reticent (and high on the introversion scale): (1) apprehension about what others think and hence a fear of looking foolish and (2) productive thinking being limited to whoever boldly holds forth, losing good ideas to their not being voiced by the timid and the shy.

Sawyer acknowledges these limitations to group creativity. He counters, however, with a set of advisory strategies that minimize obstacles and maximize individual contributions to the thinking of the group. These strategies include using jazz musicians and improvisational theater actors as innovative models for how group-thinking sessions can be conducted to generate fresh thinking. Specific strategies include close listening to one another, building on what others say, blending individual egos with the group, ensuring equal participation and communication, and keeping the thinking moving forward toward a focused goal. Sawyer also strongly advises that groups be diversely composed so that different perspectives, points of view, skills, and expertise are included. In addition to balancing diversity, he suggests that there should also be familiarity among the members of a group—but not so much familiarity that it breeds too high a level of comfort and too consistent a measure of ideational conformity. Sawyer cites the example of collaborating on Broadway musical theater productions, in which people with different domains of expertise work together over time on multiple projects. The most creative outcomes typically occur when there is some overlap and repetition among individuals working together on new productions, but when there are also new voices and perspectives mixed in. Blending diverse perspectives and balancing the comfort of the familiar with the discomfort and provocation of the different and unfamiliar make for a successful recipe for creative thinking and innovation.

EXERCISES

9. What other examples of inventions or discoveries initially designed for one particular use can you identify that were later used and developed for very different applications?

10. When you gain an insight, an "aha" moment of understanding—how, for you, does it occur? Does one of the pathways identified by Gary Klein seem to capture how you achieve insights? Or is there, perhaps, some other explanation for how they occur for you?

11. To what extent do you think Sawyer with his group collaboration emphasis, or Cain with her emphasis on individual thinking, is closer to how innovation typically happens? Why? How might it be possible to reconcile the disparate perspectives and emphases Sawyer and Cain bring to explaining how innovations occur and what sparks them?

Where Good Ideas Come From

Steven Johnson identifies seven factors that allow us to capitalize on our potential for innovative thinking. Good ideas emerge, through: (1) the adjacent possible; (2) liquid networks; (3) the slow hunch; (4) serendipity; (5) error; (6) exaptation (adaptation); and (7) platforms (layers of innovation). Johnson argues that the more an environment includes these characteristics, the richer its potential for innovative ideas to emerge. Each of these factors is discussed in detail in Johnson's book *Where Good Ideas Come From*. We will consider each of them briefly.

The Adjacent Possible

The concept of "the adjacent possible" is rooted in the everyday, the matter-of-fact, in using what's at hand to improvise a solution to a problem. Johnson tells the story of incubators that were sent to Meulaboh, a city in Indonesia, following the tsunami of 2004. Just four years later, all eight incubators supplied by relief agencies were no longer functioning. One reason was that the hospital staff could not read the English repair manual. Another was that spare parts were in short supply, and a third was that the incubators were not easy to fix when something went wrong with them. The solution, hit upon by an MIT professor, Timothy Prestero, was to create an incubator that, when it broke down, did so in ways that could be repaired by the local population—by its auto mechanics, for example. Prestero and his colleagues got their idea from Jonathan Rosen, a Boston doctor who noticed that in various places he had visited in the developing world, cars were somehow always kept running. So Rosen suggested to Prestero that perhaps an incubator could be made from automobile parts. It was an effective solution for two reasons: first, it relied on locally available parts; second, it relied on local knowledge for the repairs that would eventually be needed.

Other "adjacent possible" ideas cited by Johnson include sandals made from automobile tires, a form of cheap footwear available from something no longer useful in its original form. Johnson notes that these early-stage, or first-order, examples of innovation via the principle of the adjacent possible open the door to other potential innovations. The limits of this kind of piecemeal, improvised creativity are those of the available parts, objects, and circumstances. But even with these limitations, "the adjacent possible" reminds us to explore the environment around us—to look at its borders and edges to see what alterations, adjustments, and combinations might be interesting and potentially useful or productive. The French have a term for this kind of ad hoc improvisatory innovation with at-hand materials: *bricolage*. The improvising individual adept at *bricolage* is a *bricoleur*.

One way to increase the potential value of exploring the adjacent possible is by creating a varied environment—or ensuring that we expose ourselves to varied environments. The goal is to encounter a variety of "spare parts," things lying around, so to speak, that might be put to use. Nurturing varied friendships is one way to do this in the social realm. Reading books and magazines from different fields, disciplines, and on a variety of subjects is a way to do it in the intellectual realm. Having a storehouse of varied parts of toys, machines, tools, and the like is a way to create the possibilities of discovering the adjacent possible in the more hands-on world of the physical. Exposure to a wide range and variety of perspectives and points of view stimulates fresh thinking.

An especially successful example of the adjacent possible is the scene from the film *Apollo 13* when the engineers on the ground realize that the astronauts circling the earth will die before getting back unless they can devise a filter for the carbon dioxide they are exhaling. There are no "spare parts" and no obvious way to create the filter. The astronauts have only what's available to them in the lunar module, which they are using as an alternate vehicle for their return, due to a damaged spacecraft. The movie is worth reviewing with a focus on the scenes where a team of engineers sorts through a pile of material—things like duct tape, stowage bags, hoses, and canisters—that are available to the astronauts. It's a wonderful illustration of innovative thinking via *bricolage* within the confines of the adjacent possible. And it's a model of collaboration fueled by an urgent need to solve a life-threatening problem quickly, of necessity.

Liquid Networks

✳ **Explore** the **Concept,**
Liquid Networks
MyThinkingLab

Johnson's second characteristic for innovation-stimulating environments is what he calls a "liquid network." By this he means an environment that is densely populated and able to change shape and form, an environment that allows for the possibility of forming new links of connection and association. New ideas emerge in liquid networks because in them many possibilities are allowed for; there are many chances for something to connect with something else, for new configurations to form. Johnson reminds us that our brains consist of dense networks of neurons with trillions of neuronal connections. An idea involves the firing of millions of neurons across the synapses in our brains. It is the connections between and among the neurons that allow ideas to occur, connections crucial for developing new ideas.

Liquid networks are fluid networks; their tendency is toward ideas flowing from one mind to another and back, and then to flow to yet other minds and back yet again, reciprocally. The flow of the ideas is important, as it enhances their ability to become modified in that fluid exchange. And so, movement is critical for idea development. Not much happens to ideas without movement.

Liquid networks are dense networks that capitalize on the sheer numbers of people available for thinking. That's why cities are a good breeding ground for ideas. The artistic flowering that occurred in Renaissance Italy, especially in Florence and Rome, is a prime example. Those Italian cities, like London shortly after, and Boston, New York, and Silicon Valley centuries later, were ripe for innovations of all kinds. Not only did the Renaissance Italian cities have sizable populations for the time, but they also had in place a banking and financial system, which aided and abetted innovations in the arts. One of the innovations in banking in the Renaissance was "double-entry" booking, or accounting, which seems to have developed in a collaborative way, rather than to have sprung from the mind of an individual genius.

Johnson offers an important warning here, however. For even though double-entry accounting and many other inventions and discoveries were made collectively (whoever may have received credit), he does not offer these examples as evidence of a "hive mind," or a "global brain," a kind of super brain far stronger than our efforts to control it. Instead, as he points out, ideas occur within the minds of individuals, whose minds are "invariably connected to external networks." Large densely populated networks increase the number of minds available for discovering and refining, exploring and shaping good ideas. The wisdom of the *crowd* is not a collective wisdom, according to Johnson, but rather "the wisdom of *someone* in the crowd." Actually a series of "someones." It is not the network that is smart, but individuals whose brainpower increases because they are connected to one another through the network. It is the spillover of ideas of individuals across the network that makes for creative thinking and the spread of good ideas.

EXERCISES

12. Which of Johnson's sources of innovation discussed so far do you find the most interesting? Which seems the oddest or strangest? Which do you think might be the most fertile sources of innovation? Why?

13. Think of a time when you had to improvise a solution to a problem, perhaps to make something out of what was available in a particular time and place. Perhaps it involved improvising a meal for a surprise visit from friends, or a costume for a party, or a way to earn some money quickly. Describe how you took advantage of the adjacent possible.

14. Watch the scenes in *Apollo 13* in which the engineers and astronauts work together in space and on the ground to solve the problem of the carbon filter. How do they do it? What processes do they use? What obstacles do they have to overcome? Why do they succeed? To what extent do you think their success is attributable, in part at least, to collaboration? What other factors contribute to their success?

15. Think of a network to which you belong (social, cultural, familial, religious, political, occupational, academic, or other) in which you have experienced the exchange of ideas that led to fresh thinking on your part—or on the part of another person you know in the network. Describe how the network enabled the development of ideas. Consider whether there were any impediments or blocks to new ideas by members of the network. To what extent and how might the network structure be improved to foster the development of new ideas?

The Slow Hunch

Good hunches are based on knowledge and experience. Our hunches about things, of course, can be right or wrong, partially accurate, totally on the mark, or completely off. That's why we should neither completely ignore hunches nor give them total credibility. Hunches need to be linked with other information; they need to be connected with other data sources—of information, knowledge, and experience—to become completed. In addition, hunches need time to mature and develop. Hence Johnson's term *the slow hunch*.

New ideas need time to germinate, incubate, gestate. Hunches need cultivation time. Some hunches can linger for years before bearing fruit. Charles Darwin's slow hunch about the sizes and shapes of finches' beaks took form over a period of 10 years before he realized how important those observations were to his ideas about evolution by natural selection. J. B. Priestley harbored his hunch about the nature of oxygen for 20 years.

Johnson tells the story of the hunches a number of people had about the terrorist attacks on the World Trade Center in New York on September 11, 2001. An FBI field agent, Ken Williams, had a hunch that something was amiss when he noticed an unusually large number of people on an FBI investigative list who were registered for courses at Arizona aviation and flight schools. Williams wrote a memo in which he called attention to this fact as something that was a cause for concern. His memo was ignored, branded by a superior as "routine," and described as "speculative" and not of immediate or urgent concern.

One of the sad ironies of the 9/11 debacle was that other FBI agents in Minnesota expressed concerns that a man named Zacarias Moussaiou might fly a plane into the World Trade Center, based on a hunch they had after becoming aware that Moussaiou had expressed a strange and unusual interest in learning how to use a 747 Flight Simulator. This hunch and the report in which it was listed were also ignored. As Johnson points out, there was no mechanism—no network, in effect—that could have allowed those two reports and the hunches on which they were based to be connected. No one made the necessary connections about the reality of the terrorist threat posed by Moussaiou and his coconspirators. If a liquid network had been in effect, there would have been at least a chance to intercept the plot before it was put into action.

Most ideas emerge slowly over time. They are built on layers of information and knowledge accumulated gradually. Many stories of scientific and other discoveries emphasize the "Eureka" moment, the singular event that precipitates a discovery or invention. Often ignored, are the weeks, months, years of preparatory work, of study and experiment, of observation, note-taking, and reflection that precede those discoveries.

In addition to Darwin's slowly evolving ideas about evolution and Priestley's discoveries about oxygen, Johnson mentions an idea that developed much closer to our time—the idea of the World Wide Web. He tells the story of how Tim Berners-Lee nurtured his thinking about the Web during a decade of reflection in a process of accretion, a slow hunch that needed lots of time to mature into an idea that changed the way the world communicates.

Serendipity

A fourth opportunity element for innovation is serendipity. The word *serendipity* derives from a sixteenth-century Italian story, translated from a Persian fairy tale, whose characters made many wonderful discoveries by accident, while looking for something else. The English translation of the tale, *The Three Princes of Serendip*, yields the word *serendipity*, coined by Horace Walpole in the eighteenth century. The word has come to mean a tendency toward making fortunate discoveries by accident.

Serendipitous discoveries have been made many times in science and medicine, especially in chemistry, physics, and pharmacology. Examples of serendipitous discoveries include Alexander Fleming's discovery of penicillin and Friedrich Kekulé's discovery of benzene's chemical ring structure. More homely examples include the discovery of "silly putty" by James Wright during World War II, when he was trying to find a substitute for rubber for the US government. Another is Ruth Wakefield's creation of chocolate chip cookies, which she hit upon accidentally when she lacked the proper chocolate for another kind of cookie and used a broken up chocolate candy bar, for chocolate "chips." In these and nearly all cases of serendipitous discovery, an open mind is necessary. As the French scientist Louis Pasteur once remarked, "chance favors only the prepared mind."

Serendipity arises in environments that contain opportunities for semirandom connections. Serendipity thrives on exchanges and combinations that move across traditional disciplinary boundaries.

Serendipitous discovery is more likely to occur when we are relaxed and when our minds are moving in unpredictable and random ways, making free associations. We can nurture serendipity by creating conditions in which happy accidents are more likely to occur. Going for a leisurely walk can free our minds and promote serendipitous connections. So can taking a bath or a long hot shower—something that relaxes us physically and mentally.

Also of value is reading books and articles on a wide variety of topics in a short time span. The variety of topic creates opportunities for unusual things to combine in our minds. Doing the reading in a short time increases the chances for surprising connections to occur.

A major enemy of serendipity is a closed environment, any environment in which information and ideas are locked up, left unshared, kept secret. Companies, for example, that allow for new ideas to be developed and discussed only within specialized R&D, or research and development units, ironically, limit opportunities for creative ideas to emerge serendipitously.

EXERCISES

16. Think of a time when some kind of "happy accident" occurred in which you thought of something, accomplished something, or discovered something that you were not explicitly seeking or trying to do. Consider the extent to which it was a kind of fortunate or lucky outcome due to circumstances that you didn't so much create, as simply stumble upon, recognize, and then capitalize on.

17. Do some Internet or library research on a few of the following companies to see what you can learn about how they develop new ideas—how they innovate. To what extent do any of them create serendipitous environments for their employees: Google, Apple, 3M, Microsoft, Ford, Sony, IBM, Facebook, Barnes & Noble, General Electric, Nike, Wal-Mart, Starbucks, Pixar, BMW, Twitter, Groupon, Tumblr, Instagram? To what extent do you think some of these companies innovate a little at a time, building the proverbial "better mousetrap?" To what extent do they look for the "next big thing?" To what extent is the next big thing a lot of little things?

Error

Still another source of innovation is error, especially environments in which error is, if not cultivated, at least tolerated. We might think that innovation would occur more consistently and frequently in error-free environments, but the opposite situation is more often the case. Environments in which mistakes are never made, in which accuracy all the time every step of the way is the norm, tend to be places of predictability, even sterility. These perfect environments lack surprise; they don't provide conditions for unpredictable occurrences, for unanticipated discoveries, for unusual concatenations and combinations to occur. For surprising discoveries to be made, imperfection and error are better.

Errors provide pathways and stepping-stones to discovery. We don't normally create errors deliberately, intentionally, or purposefully. Nor should we agonize over errors and lament them. Instead, we should see what can be learned from error, how error might lead us to a new place we didn't know we wanted to go. As Johnson notes, "mistakes are an inevitable step on the path to true innovation." To this effect he quotes Benjamin Franklin: "Perhaps the history of the errors of mankind, all things considered, is more valuable and interesting than that of their discoveries." This, in large part, is owing to that fact that, as Franklin noted, "Error is endlessly diversified." We should embrace error rather than fear it. Error is the road to success. For as Winston Churchill said, "Success is the ability to go from one failure to another with no loss of enthusiasm."

Exaptation

Exaptation refers to the way a trait designed for one purpose becomes modified over time for another. One example is bird feathers, designed by evolution for warmth, which, over time, became "exapted," or adapted beyond their originally intended purpose. In Johnson's words "natural selection begins sculpting those feathers to make them more aerodynamic." Feathers designed for warmth can be perfectly symmetrical; those exapted for flight become increasingly asymmetrical.

A very different kind of example is the screw press, which was used by the Greeks and Romans to press the oil from olives. The utility of the screw press helped it survive for many centuries. It was one of a set of objects that Johann Gutenberg had available when he created the printing press. As Johnson points out, many scholars have recognized how Gutenberg's printing press was "a classic combinatorial innovation," with the key elements that made it possible—movable type, ink, paper, and the screw press, all developed before Gutenberg came along to combine them into the invention of the printing press.

Another interesting facet of Gutenberg's invention is his expertise as a goldsmith, which enabled him to modify the metallurgy involved in the system of movable type. This kind of adaptation provides yet another instance of an innovation that builds not only upon the multiple developments of previous innovators, but also upon the deep expert knowledge of the inventor. Gutenberg's exaptation resulted from his putting the screw press to use in a way that had nothing to do with its original purpose. This is the normal process of invention; it's a common occurrence in the history of innovation.

The Internet remains one of the most interesting, the most versatile, and the most important of recent innovations. The Internet was originally created to share information and research in a hypertext format. Since its design by Tim Berners-Lee 20-plus years ago, the Internet has undergone a wide range of adaptations; it has been adapted, as Johnson notes "for shopping, and sharing photos, and watching pornography"— along with numerous other uses, creative and destructive, dangerous and productive.

As a sidebar, we might note that Tim Berners-Lee created the Internet on a NeXT computer designed by Steve Jobs, whose computer company failed in the marketplace, but nonetheless spurred the innovative thinking of Berners-Lee. (We might note, further, that the operating system devised for Jobs's NeXT computer was used in the next Apple Mac computers he developed when he returned to the company, including the Macbook Pro laptop, on which this book is written.) Jobs's NeXT computer failure, clearly, also involved considerable success.

Cities are a fertile breeding ground for exaptations, primarily because they are places were many subcultures of specialized interests and skills collide, connect, and combine. So are workplaces that harbor and harness diverse people, places that reflect a spectrum of viewpoints, experiences, and kinds of expertise. As Johnson notes, exaptations thrive "where a diverse mix of distinct professions and passions overlap." When J. B. Priestley discovered oxygen and Benjamin Franklin experimented with electricity, the coffeehouse was the breeding ground for the exchange of ideas that led to new ideas, including the new idea of democracy.

When people like Franklin and Priestley and their friends gathered for drinks—whether caffeinated, effervescent, or alcoholic—the real energy and passion was around ideas. The drinks provided a stimulant to the conversation that fueled further individual thinking as each man went his way and then later corresponded until they could gather together again. They were creating a network, an exchange, a synergistic factory of ideas, all without the express intention of doing more than engaging in stimulating intellectual inquiry. And it was all done in an informal way, before the establishment of a firmly entrenched systematic set of analytical procedures that would later come to be known as the scientific method.

Today, the coffeehouse atmosphere of the past is not replicated in today's coffee bars, in Così and Starbucks, for example. In contemporary coffee emporiums, too many people isolate themselves with their headphones, smartphones, tablets, and computers. Today, the rich soil for the growth and nurturing of ideas exists in Silicon Valley, in companies like Google and Apple. Apple's and Google's various and diverse units meet regularly to share ideas, update each other on progress and challenges. The diverse perspectives brought by design, manufacturing, product development, marketing, and other units create a vibrant atmosphere of multiple differing perspectives that, together, yield many new ideas.

Platforms

We know a platform as something to stand upon. Platforms are built so that people can be seen and heard from a distance by crowds. Here, however, we will consider two other kinds of platforms—first a platform of once living things that, as they die off, serve as a base for other live animals, and second, a metaphorical platform, the platform as a concept.

Steven Johnson tells the story of how, when Charles Darwin and his mates voyaged on the research ship *The Beagle* in the 1840s, he was amazed and baffled by why they encountered an apparently buried volcanic island that had risen just a few feet above sea level. Darwin knew that had the island been formed from an extinct volcano, the rock he stood on would have been volcanic—obsidian and pumice. But it wasn't. And so Darwin pondered the question of what could have formed the island atoll. After a number of years of mulling it over, he decided that the island had not been formed geologically, but rather had been created by a living organism. That organism was a particular kind of tiny reef-building coral polyp, which, during its life, builds a protective exoskeleton for its soft body. After the polyp dies, its exoskeleton remains intact for hundreds of years. Out of millions of these tiny animals' skeletons, a coral reef is formed. This was the stuff of which the atoll Darwin stood on was made.

Johnson describes in some detail how a coral reef is built and how it becomes a platform. Briefly, what happens is that the coral reef is built upon an extinct volcano that became submerged under the ocean. As the mountain slowly subsides, coral build their reefs around the periphery of its crater. The coral keep adding "floors" as the mountain descends slowly over time. And as the original peak descends into the ocean, the older reefs that die off continue to provide structural support for the new, living reefs above them. Darwin predicted that fossil coral would extend nearly a mile below the sea's surface, a prediction that was confirmed a hundred years later.

The importance of the coral reef as a platform lies in two things: (1) the proliferation and profusion of life that it generates—the biodiversity that it makes possible and (2) its value as a metaphor for innovation and the spread of living ideas.

It has been estimated that somewhere between one million and ten million species live in coral habitats, which Johnson describes as an "an undersea metropolis of immense diversity." He considers the coral polyps responsible for the reefs equivalent to "ecosystem engineers," much as beavers do when they transform their forest environment with their dams into microwetland environments where other water-based species can flourish.

As a key example of a metaphorical platform, Johnson cites the story of satellite technology, particularly its use for global positioning, the now familiar GPS. It began when the military asked the physicists William Guer and George Weiffenbach to use their knowledge and experience of the Doppler effect, of waveform frequency changes, and of the Russian satellite Sputnik's emission of a steady signal as it orbited the earth, tracking the location of submarines. The work these men did to solve that problem became a kind of metaphorical platform for later work that led to the many uses of GPS today, including automobile navigation systems, smartphone navigation, and tools to locate skiers stranded in avalanches.

But the most significant platform in our time is the one that continues to be built for various Web-based technologies. When Tim Berners-Lee designed the World Wide Web, he was able to build on the platform discoveries and inventions of others. And when the creators of YouTube developed their service, they built upon not only the Web proper but upon other technologies, such as Adobe Flash. This kind of continued development of new technologies built out of previous ones, Johnson calls "platform stacking." It's a process that requires shared and open resources, along with the circulation of information and ideas, key ingredients of innovation.

A further interesting aspect of the Web is the type of ecosystem it has become. In Johnson's words, it "started as a desert," and it has been "steadily transformed into a coral reef." Just as in the actual coral reef, where various species of plants and animals feed off and nourish each other, so in the Web information and innovations circulate through the system. In the process, they are put to new uses. Music is swapped and photos and videos shared, as the energy of information undergoes continuous transformation.

EXERCISES

18. What has been your experience with error, with mistakes? To what extent have you been able to let errors lead you to see something valuable and useful that you wouldn't have discovered without them? What do you think we can do to enable ourselves to become better at capitalizing on error, on using error productively?

19. Using the model of the ecosystem, identify one other metaphorical or actual ecosystem in which a central source creates something out of which many other elements grow and flourish. How, for example, might the world of book or newspaper publishing be viewed as an ecosystem? The world of children's movies? What about the invention of a new product or service?

Creating Innovators

In his book *Creating Innovators*, Tony Wagner argues that innovators can be cultivated and fostered. He believes that innovation involves both nature and nurture—that it requires a certain amount of inborn talent to be sure, but that it is also developed through a sequence of conditions and opportunities. He identifies three critical factors for developing innovative thinkers: (1) *play*, (2) *passion*, and (3) *purpose*.

Play is important from an early age—free and open play that allows for imaginative thinking. Playing with simple toys and even with objects adapted as toys allows children to develop their imaginative capacities. Wagner argues that play should be unconstrained and that there should be ample opportunity for freedom to explore, imagine, and invent.

Passion is critical for innovative thinking to develop. When we are passionate about something—playing soccer, surfing, learning a language, cooking unusual meals—we devote ourselves to it. We don't think or worry about the time we commit to it, or the difficulties encountered and challenges to be overcome in the process of doing it. We love what we are doing, and we become caught up, even lost, in the learning. Passion keeps us going when those without such passion would quit.

A third aspect—*purpose*—is necessary for the long haul. Without a sense of purpose and meaning, we would have little incentive to carry on for long stretches. Having a purpose for what we are passionate about gives it meaning, makes it matter to us and to others.

Wagner's trinity of *play, passion*, and *purpose* overlaps with and echoes another triad for creative work proposed by Daniel Pink in his book *Drive*. Pink argues that there are three conditions necessary to motivate us to achieve anything at all: *autonomy, mastery*, and *meaning*.

By *autonomy* Pink simply means that we have control to make choices about what we invest ourselves in. Others cannot make this determination for us. His second criterion, *mastery*, refers to our ability to become progressively better at what we are doing—to become highly skilled at it. And finally, like Tony Wagner, Daniel Pink insists that for us to be driven to excellence and to passionate performance, what we do must be meaningful to us—and to others we care about.

Doing vs. Knowing

Tony Wagner also suggests that for innovative thinking to develop there must be an emphasis on doing and not just on knowing. Knowing that and knowing why are, of course, important. But for innovation to occur, there needs to be a more active element—the conversion of knowing to doing, the application of knowledge in a process of action. As Gary Marcus notes in his book, *Guitar Zero*, it's not so much what we know, but how we use our knowledge that allows for progress, improvement, and innovation. Marcus illustrates his point with knowing a few basic guitar chords and a few simple strumming patterns. We can do a great deal with those few chords and strumming patterns if we experiment and if we practice. For example, we can find many ways to combine chords and strums, play them at different tempos, with different plucked and fingered right-hand patterns, with different combinations of single and multiple notes sounding simultaneously.

Tony Wagner posits a set of six criteria that are essential for developing innovative thinkers. He highlights the significance of these criteria by contrasting them with six opposite characteristics. Wagner identifies the following set of contrastive productive and destructive qualities linked with nurturing (and inhibiting) innovative thinking. The first term of each pair fosters innovation; the second term inhibits it.

1. Collaboration vs. individual achievement
2. Multidisciplinary learning vs. specialization
3. Trial and error vs. risk avoidance
4. Creating vs. consuming
5. Intrinsic motivation vs. extrinsic motivation
6. Liberal arts vs. STEM subjects (science, technology, engineering, math)

One important qualification must be made regarding the last item—liberal arts vs. STEM subjects. Wagner values *both* science-related thinking and subjects *and* humanities subjects and thinking. He argues that innovation occurs when individuals are able to combine the approaches, ways of thinking, and ways of doing across the sciences/humanities divide. One recent spectacular example is Steve Jobs, whose interest in things technical and computer-related meshed, merged, and melded with his strong interest in arts and humanities, with a concern for how people would use the products he and his teams developed, and his passion for making his products not just functional but also beautiful. Perhaps, as someone has suggested, we need not just STEM subjects but STEAM, with the arts adding the A and converting STEM to STEAM in a stimulating synergy that leads to greater innovation.

EXERCISES

20. How important to you are the qualities for the development of innovative thinking that Tony Wagner identifies—play, passion, and purpose? Which of the three has meant and/or continues to mean most to you today? What kinds of play do you enjoy most? What is your passion? If you could do one thing with your time, energy, and effort what would you do and why would you do it?

21. What drives you to put effort into those things you work hard at? To what extent are you in accord with Daniel Pink about his three "drivers": autonomy, mastery, and meaning? Which of Pink's three motivators is most important to you, and why?

22. Riff a bit on Gary Marcus's guitar-playing example of doing much with a little knowledge. Provide an example of something you are learning, something you already know how to do, or something you know about that emphasizes the doing. Explain how you can do much with a little knowledge.

23. Review Wagner's contrasting list of oppositions—things that nurture innovations and things that inhibit innovative thinking. Which two stand out most for you—and why? To what extent is it possible for you to shift your focus to the innovation stimulating practices and avoid those innovation inhibitors? Do you agree with Wagner with his assessment and identification of factors that stimulate and suppress innovation? Do you wish to quarrel with any of the items from his chart? Why or why not?

Zig-Zag Innovation

In his book, *Zig Zag: The Surprising Path to Greater Creativity*, Keith Sawyer presents a manual for developing individual creativity as a pathway toward successful innovation. He argues that we all have the capacity to become more creative, and that we have what it takes to innovate. What's needed to develop our creative capacity is deliberate practice through engaging in focused and purposeful creative thinking habits and exercises that can lead to innovation. Sawyer offers an eight-fold path to creativity:

1. *Ask.* Creative work is grounded in clear and meaningful questions.
2. *Learn.* Continued, life-long learning is essential for developing the habit of creativity—learning anywhere at any time.
3. *Look.* Seeking new experiences and cultivating mindful awareness is essential for seeing the surprising and discovering the unexpected.
4. *Play.* The creative life is filled with play, with time for unstructured activity pursued out of pure interest and with sheer joy.
5. *Think.* Creativity derives from having lots of ideas, many ineffectual ideas that can be discarded, and occasional gems to polish and process.
6. *Fuse.* Making connections, putting things together in unusual combinations, is essential for creative thinking.
7. *Choose.* Creativity and innovation require the ability to select productive idea possibilities, to evaluate ideas with appropriate and effective critical criteria.
8. *Make.* It's not enough just to "have" ideas; we need to make something of them. Making is essential; producing, developing a product—a drawing, draft, model, prototype—a discrete, concrete something, and not simply a good idea that is only talked about.

It's not enough simply to read about creativity. We have to work at it; we have to practice the skills associated with developing our creative thinking. We don't develop our creative capacities in a linear fashion—by simply following through on these 8 steps one at a time, one after the other. Rather, we can zig and zag among them, starting anywhere, and doubling back recursively, as we apply the strategies and techniques as many times as necessary.

Social Innovation

In "The Process of Social Innovation," written for *The Innovator's Cookbook*, a collection of articles on innovation, Geoff Mulgan argues that a great deal of innovative thinking in the past was driven by social factors, including social enterprise, with civil society providing much of the stimulus for social innovation. According to Mulgan, social innovations are social in both their ends and their means. He distinguishes social innovation, which has a great social capacity to act and become diffused through social organizations, from business innovation, which is motivated by profit rather than by social benefit.

Some examples of social innovations include trade unions, microcredit, cooperatives, reading clubs, and philanthropic businesses that develop model towns and model schools. Social innovation, of course, has also been driven by government action—welfare states being the most extensive and prominent examples. In addition, we have the many recent examples of online self-help groups, Wikipedia, the Open University, MIT open courseware, the Khan Academy, neighborhood watch groups, the fair trade movement, and more.

Mulgan believes that the pace of innovation will accelerate in the next decades. And he predicts that a significant amount of the most important innovation in the next 20 or 30 years will follow patterns of social innovation rather than patterns established in domains such as information technology or insurance.

Areas that are in need of social innovation promise to generate the most active enterprise. These include an aging populations that will stimulate new ways of organizing health care, pensions, housing, urban design, and transportation. They also include challenges related to climate change, which requires large-scale responses by governments, businesses, and social agencies. And they include medical issues related to obesity, unhealthy diet, addictions to drugs, alcohol, and gambling, which call for socially innovative measures.

EXERCISES

24. To what extent do you find Sawyer's idea of "zig-zagging" among his eight innovation strategies promising? Which two or three of his eight strategies do you think might hold the most promise for you to zig-zag with? Why?

25. To what extent do you agree with Mulgan about the rising importance of social innovation? Which of the broad areas mentioned seem most in need of social innovation? Which areas seem most likely to inspire successful social innovation in the near term?

What Thwarts Innovation?

One of the greatest obstacles to innovation and the development of new ideas is fear—fear of failure, fear of criticism, and fear of appearing foolish. In addition to fear, which also includes the fear of change, Scott Berkun, in *The Myths of Innovation*, lists the following motives for interfering with new ideas:

- *Ego and envy*—Others may be jealous that they didn't think of your idea.
- *Pride and politics*—Your idea might make others look bad.
- *Personal issues*—You may not be liked, so your idea might lack support.
- *Priority*—There are other equally good or even better ideas to support.
- *Sloth*—People tend to be lazy and unwilling to expend additional effort.
- *Security*—People might see themselves as giving up or losing something.
- *Greed*—Some people might be able to make money rejecting your idea.
- *Consistency*—Your idea might be contrary to another's beliefs or values.

Berkun also provides a checklist of negative comments associated with obstructing new ideas. Some of the more common and familiar ones are: "This will never work." "No one will want this." "People won't understand it." "It won't make money." "It's not practical." "We don't have time for this." "It's not in our budget." "We tried that already." "We don't do it that way here." "We've never done that before." And so on.

Other obstacles to innovation are identified by Steven Paley in his book *The Art of Invention*. Paley reminds us that invention requires both the abstract and the nitty-gritty. The abstract is the idea as it develops in the mind of the inventor; the nitty-gritty is what's necessary to turn the abstract idea into a working reality. Although perhaps a bit exaggerated, Paley contends, "Ideas are easy. Invention is work." And so, we can add to Scott Berkun's list of ways that innovation is thwarted, anything that interferes with getting down to the nitty-gritty, anything from fear of failure to lack of experience, from an unwillingness to get our hands dirty to lack of materials, resources, or perseverance.

Getting Support for New Ideas

As a counter to the various kinds of negative thoughts that thwart innovation, here are a few suggestions derived from Scott Berkun about what to consider when gaining support for a new idea, when trying to get an innovation adopted.

- *Identify the perceived advantage* of the new idea over what is currently in place. Consider convenience, cost, prestige, fashion, and satisfaction.
- *Analyze the amount of effort* involved in transitioning from current practice to your new approach. Consider people's values, habits, and personal beliefs, along with cost factors.
- *Evaluate the level of complexity* involved in the idea or innovation.
- *Estimate how much learning* will be required to implement it.
- *Consider whether it is possible to give the idea a trial* or other small-scale application. Consider whether the idea or innovation can be implemented by a few people, perhaps with a sample group.
- *Imagine the opportunities for visibility* the idea or innovation can gain.
- *Evaluate the extent* to which the idea can be diffused widely so that it is highly visible.

And we should add: Have fun. Take pleasure in the process. More good ideas emerge, more innovative thinking occurs, during times of enjoyment.

Balancing Innovation Factors

In their co-authored book, *Creative Confidence*, Tom Kelley and David Kelley identify three factors that require balancing for successful innovation to occur: *feasibility, viability*, and *desirability*. Let's take up each briefly. First, any innovation involves dealing with technical factors. How *feasible*, technically, is the innovative concept? Can the technical factors provide the basis for a new line of business, perhaps even a new company? The Kelley brothers cite the example of carbon fiber aircraft components, multitouch interactive displays, and minimally invasive surgical tools, as examples of revolutionizing technical advances.

Second, innovation requires scrutiny of the bottom line—attending to business factors. How *viable* is the innovative concept? The main issues with business viability most often involve how to sustain, manage, monetize, and scale up an innovative idea. In providing incubators for hospitals in developing countries, a way must be found to maintain them when they break down. The design of those incubators, therefore, should consider how repairs will be made later.

Third, successful innovation must attend to the human users of the products, processes, and experiences created. These human factors are critical for the success of any innovation. Tom and David Kelley cite the example of a warming cocoon that functions as a primitive incubator for use in poor villages in India. The gauge on the incubating warmer that indicated temperature showed the temperature in degrees to indicate that the device was ready for use. However, the women who used it were fearful of that temperature setting, so they regularly stopped it at a lower temperature, which rendered the device ineffective. The solution, which considered these human users, was to replace the temperature degree number with a light indicating that the warming device was "ready." That illuminated signal of readiness was something the village women could accept, even though the actual "ready" temperature was the same.

EXERCISES

26. Which two of Scott Berkun's innovation thwarters seem most dangerous to you. Why? Which two of Berkun's recommendations for innovation do you think are the most critical for implementing new ideas, and why?

27. How persuaded are you by Tom and David Kelley's three requirements for innovation: feasibility, viability, and desirability? Which of the three do you think tends to get overlooked when innovative ideas and concepts are unsuccessful? Why?

Looking Back and Looking Ahead

Revisit the learning goals that begin this chapter. Which of these goals do you think you have best achieved? What might you do to reach the remaining goals?

Return to the focusing questions at the beginning of the chapter. How would you answer those questions now? Which of them do you find most interesting and provocative and worthy of following up? Why?

In reviewing the list of resources that follows, identify the two that attract you most. Explain why these books or Web sites interest you. Consider looking into them for further developing your capacity for innovative thinking.

Take a look, too, at the MyThinkingLab resources on the Prentice Hall Web site. Included there are readings, images, videos, questions, exercises, and other provocations to help you develop your capacity for innovative thinking.

Resources

The Rational Optimist, Matt Ridley. Harper Perennial, 2011.
Babylon, Paul Kriwaczek. Thomas Dunne Books, 2012.
Inventorship, Leonard M. Greene. Wiley, 2001.
The Myths of Innovation, Scott Berkun. O'Reilly Media, 2010.
The Art of Invention, Steven J. Paley. Prometheus Books, 2010.
The Innovator's Cookbook, Steven Johnson, ed. Riverhead Trade, 2011.
The Power of Why, Amanda Lang. Collins Canada, 2012.

The Black Swan, Nassim Nicholas Taleb. Random House, 2010.

Seeing What Others Don't, Gary Klein. Public Affairs, 2013.

Group Genius, Keith Sawyer. Basic Books, 2007.

Quiet, Susan Cain. Crown, Broadway Books, 2012.

Where Good Ideas Come From, Steven Johnson. Riverhead Trade, 2011.

Steve Jobs, Walter Isaacson. Simon & Schuster, 2011.

Creating Innovators, Tony Wagner. Scribner, 2012.

Drive, Daniel Pink. Riverhead Trade, 2011.

Guitar Zero, Gary Marcus. Penguin Books, 2012.

Zig-Zag, Keith Sawyer. Jossey-Bass, 2013.

Creative Confidence, Tom Kelley and David Kelley. Crown Business, 2013.

● ●

SOCIAL NETWORK

14

Thinking about Technology and Information

It has become appallingly obvious that our technology has exceeded our humanity.

—ALBERT EINSTEIN

True genius resides in the capacity for evaluation of uncertain, hazardous, and conflicting information.

—WINSTON CHURCHILL

Chapter Overview

This chapter raises questions about the nature and effects of technology, including how various technologies affect our lives—the ways we work, learn, think, and act, both individually and socially. Included are views of those who consider themselves advocates for and critics of technology. A key aspect of technology concerns information and communication, which are becoming increasingly challenging for those living in the twenty-first century. The central idea of the chapter is that technology is a creative force with both benefits and drawbacks. The challenge is how to maximize technology's benefits while minimizing its drawbacks, to harness its creative power.

The Creative Power and Promise of Technology

Technology is the engine that drives the train of progress. From the first simple stone tools to the design of our most recent communication devices, technological innovation has changed our lives decisively. In every domain—science and medicine; engineering and design; arts and culture; transportation, communication, industry; business, politics, education; fashion, travel, housing, food—developments in technology have changed how we live. Indoor plumbing, air conditioning, air and land travel, computers and music players, smartphones and heart devices—these and myriad other technological developments, including ways to purify water, treat infection, and prevent disease have extended and improved our lives.

But what about technological consequences that alter our lives in less desirable ways? There is no question about the creative power and productive promise of technology. But is this the only way to think about technology? What about other less beneficial consequences? And what about the speed with which technological change is affecting people's lives? A number of writers have offered perspectives, laudatory and skeptical, about both the nature of technological change and its increasing acceleration.

One way of thinking about technology is to consider what we want to do with it—how we want to use it. Another is to consider how technology uses us—how we are limited by the technologies we use, how those technologies shape our behavior. Half a century ago in *Understanding Media*, Marshall McLuhan argued that we first shape our tools, and then our tools shape us. Recently, in *What Technology Wants*, Kevin Kelly has taken a more hopeful view of the powerful technological changes currently taking hold.

Our word *technology* derives from the Greek word *techne*, which carries complex connotations. The ancient Greeks used the word *techne* to mean skill, craft, or art. *Techne*, for the Greeks, also included notions of subtlety, craftiness, and cleverness, as for example, Odysseus's outwitting of the Cyclops in Homer's *Odyssey*. Kelly points out that Aristotle was the first to join the concept of *techne* with that of *logos*, which in Greek, means *speech*, *thought*, and *word*. From the beginning, then, the word *techne* has embodied a complex range of connotations—the positive connotations of someone accomplished in an art or craft—the art of speaking, for example, or the craft of making things, and, on the other hand, less savory connotations, such as slyness and wiliness, and a kind of concealed and sinister cleverness.

Technology is ambiguous. The ambiguity of technology lies in the inevitable trade-offs associated with it. Every time there is a technological breakthrough or development, it carries with it consequences both constructive and destructive, for the various winners and losers it affects. Some of these consequences, both good and bad, are unintended; we neither know that they will occur, nor are we able to control them.

Watch the **Video**, The Creative Power and Promise of Technology **MyThinkingLab**

technology
The creation, knowledge, and use of tools and techniques to solve problems and make improvements.

Kelly is especially interested in what he calls the *technium*, the totality of technological innovation and cultural creations, including social, cultural, literary, and artistic creations, as well as those we typically think of in terms of applied technologies built around scientific discoveries. He extends his notion to suggest that after 10,000 years of civilization, the *technium* has become a "sustaining network of self-reinforcing processes and parts" with considerable autonomy, thus making it a "complex organism that often follows its own urges." Technology, in this view, has a will and a mind of its own. It has, as Kelly says, "its own wants." These "wants" of the *technium* are, of course, not conscious, deliberate, thoughtful, and intentional wants like our own, but rather tendencies, directions, and trajectories, which, though "unconscious," are nonetheless real and detectable.

What does this view of the totality of technology—Kelly's *technium*—suggest? What are its implications? One implication is that even though we humans have created our technological complex, and even though we have given ourselves dominion over it, it is a system that has generated its own momentum. The *technium* wants what we devise it to want and what we direct it toward. But the *technium* also wants to perpetuate itself and to assemble itself in ways that best preserve and sustain it. In the tension between human control and technological "want" lies our future.

The Internet and Responsibility

The one area of technology that has drawn the sustained attention of both critics and supporters alike is the Internet. In *Virtually You*, psychiatrist Elias Aboujaoude, contends that the Internet is more a curse than a blessing, unleashing our least palatable habits, behaviors, and instincts. In his view, the Internet allows us to do far too easily many things that we shouldn't do: gamble, for example, and overspend, lie about and misrepresent ourselves, and arrange sex with strangers. In allowing us to indulge, even customize our fantasies (and do this anonymously), the Internet makes us impatient with reality, including actual friends and romantic partners. In concealing and modifying our identities, the Internet frees us, if not actually encourages us, to be deceitful. It also rewards self-promotion, cheating, lying, and stealing; it even teaches us how to make bombs and commit suicide.

Such a list of dangerous behaviors, however, ignores all the good things the Internet allows us to do, such as accessing information, sharing ideas, accelerating communication, allowing us to work virtually—and many more. These benefits, however, Aboujaoude claims, pale by comparison with its dangers, which he links to consumer debt, sexually transmitted diseases, racism, cyberbullying, terrorism, and much more.

Another view is presented by Jane McGonigal, a game designer, in her book *Reality is Broken*. McGonigal argues that computers can serve a range of positive social functions, from making us more sensitive to other people's needs, to extending and deepening our global understanding and awareness. She contends that playing computer games can enable us to become more aware of and more willing to work together to solve social problems, such as world hunger. McGonigal sees the Internet as a rich resource for social education, moral instruction, and character improvement. She describes the same Internet as Aboujaoude, but she envisions a very different set of positive potentialities for its use.

EXERCISES

1. What do you think of Kelly's suggestion that the totality of technology—the *technium*—is an organism with the kinds of "wants" he describes? In what ways might the *technium* maximize technology's blessings? In what ways might it accentuate technology's "dark" side? What might Kelly's idea imply in terms of recognizing the powerful force and energy of technology?

2. Whose views about the effects of computer use and the Internet are you more inclined to accept—McGonigal's focus on the promise of technology or Aboujaoude's emphasis on its perils? Why? To what extent do you think that they both are partly right? Are their views incompatible and incommensurate, or is there a way to harmonize and integrate them

Into the Electronic Millennium

We are now a decade and a half into the new millennium. Two decades ago, Sven Birkerts, in *The Gutenberg Elegies*, invited us to consider how electronic gadgets and processes were beginning to alter our lives. Birkerts argued then that a general erosion of language resulted from using the then new communication technologies, and that this erosion would continue. He also described a general flattening of historical perspective, as people read fewer books, and he predicted that there would be a "waning of the private self."

As evidence for the first of these claims, Birkerts looks to the ways our use of electronic devices for communication has resulted in less complex writing, writing that is more telegraphic and less nuanced than formerly. With the shift from print culture to electronic culture, the serious reading of books and longer articles has declined. These trends have accelerated with the use of smaller devices, such as PDAs, including Droids, iPhones, and Blackberries, for reading and writing.

Birkerts attributes the flattening of our historical sense to an increasing emphasis on network processes for communication, which keeps us focused on the historical present, with little pressure to consider the past. He suggests that we are losing our sense of the "depth and dimensionality" of the past, which is represented in books rather than in blogs and in libraries rather than media centers. Driving this diminution of the historical sense is the proliferation of data, of masses of instantaneously available information that streams constantly before us.

Creating a context for this content, deciding how to value and evaluate it requires time and thought. A content context also requires a standard against which to measure it and a set of values against which to judge it. However, with the contemporary emphasis on immediacy of information access, on processing speed, and on global availability, there is less interest in and emphasis on the knowledge and standards a historical consciousness could provide.

Birkerts also worries that in the twenty-first century, we are in the midst of a "process of social collectivization," something he fears will destroy the ideal of the individual self. With the rapid rise of social networks, most impressively and influentially that of Facebook, and with the ever-present tracking features embedded in Internet search engines, the sense of individual identity and of privacy have been increasingly compromised. The steady emphasis on social networks and on making public our ideas, tastes, beliefs, and values, has changed our lives. What it means to be a private, autonomous self is being altered, perhaps irretrievably, with independent thinking and idiosyncratic ideas diminishing.

Technology Education

Among the most prominent and persistent students and critics of technological developments and their effects has been Neil Postman, author of a series of books that examine the consequences of technology use and technological change. In *Amusing Ourselves to Death*, Postman shines a critical light on television, especially on the wide range of effects—social, political, and educational—it has wrought. In *The End of Education*, he considers, among other topics, just what technology education should encompass. Postman reminds us that technology education is not the same thing as education in the uses of technology. Technology education is more than a technical subject; it is also a branch of the humanities.

Although technical knowledge (knowing how to use technology) is both useful and necessary, we do not need to know the physics of television to study the social and political effects of the medium. Nor do we need to know how our smartphones and navigation systems work to use them. We do need, however, to better understand the personal and social, individual and public consequences of the technologies we use. And though we need not necessarily have either a negative or positive attitude toward technology, it is useful to develop a critical perspective, one characterized by a questioning attitude that inquires into the full range of effects technology has on our lives.

Postman invites us to consider the extent to which the acceptance of technological change is a Faustian bargain, a bargain made with the devil. He asks us to consider, that is, what trade-offs are involved with the various technologies we use. What is gained with each new technological development—and what is lost? What compromises are we making with their adoption and increased use? And how are our lives altered, for better and worse, in the process?

Technopoly

Simulate the Experiment, Technopoly
MyThinkingLab

technopoly
A society in which technologies generate a surplus of information that requires additional technologies to maintain.

A major question about technology is this: To what extent is technological change not simply additive, or cumulative, but rather systemic, or, in Postman's term, *ecological*? To what extent, that is, does technological change result in not merely a change of quantity, but a change of kind? How much, in fact, does technological change alter not just how we do things, but who we become in the process of doing things in new ways? Versions of these questions lie at the heart of Postman's book *Technopoly*, which provides a broad historical consideration of technological developments and how they have changed society irrevocably.

Postman examines three major technologies of the past and raises questions about today's technological developments in relationship to them. He highlights the development of the mechanical clock, the printing press, and the telescope, as three inventions with deep and far-reaching effects. The mechanical clock, which was created to mark the hours of the prescribed times (hours) of prayer for Catholic monks in the Middle Ages, altered how time is measured and work calibrated. What began as an instrument to assist the Catholic Church became something radically different later on—an instrument used to "clock" the time of workers in factories—with the consequences intended and unintended of work "timed" this way.

Postman's second example, the story of the printing press and the profound effects it had on the transmission of knowledge are well known. The first beneficiaries of Gutenberg's invention were Bible readers, for the vast quantity of books first printed were Bibles, initially in the German translation of Martin Luther, and soon after in a range of translations into other European languages.

With the profusion of Bibles available, the monopoly on Church teaching enjoyed by the clergy was lost, as every individual could read his own Bible. The technology that created this opportunity for private Bible reading enabled the rapid spread of the Protestant challenge to the authority of the Catholic Church. The changing landscape of religious authority was only one of numerous consequences the invention of printing created. Others included the dissemination of many kinds of knowledge, from the practical and technical to the theoretical and philosophical.

As with the mechanical clock and the printing press, so too with the telescope used by scientists like Galileo, who challenged the orthodox geocentric view of the solar system, enshrined in Church teaching. The telescope had even greater consequences than the printing press in changing the way people thought about the universe and the place of human beings within it. Once the teaching of the Church about the position of the earth in the solar system was shown to be inaccurate, other challenges followed. Religious authority was a major casualty of this development, as the Church's supremacy was undermined by the practice of scientific observation and the discoveries to which it led.

These historical examples of technological change and the profound social, cultural, and intellectual developments they wrought suggest that today's major technological developments can have equally far-reaching consequences. Today's equivalent of the printing press is the Internet. Today's equivalent of the mechanical clock might be the PDA—our tablets and smartphones and computing devices that keep us tethered to our work 24/7, no matter where we are. And analogous in its effects, if not equivalent to Galileo's telescope, might be Darwin's idea of evolution, which radically altered how human beings see themselves in relationship to the rest of the animate universe.

EXERCISES

3. To what extent do you agree with Sven Birkerts about his concerns regarding the consequences of our developing technologies? Do you agree that language use has been and continues to be eroded? Do you agree that there is less understanding of history now than a decade ago and that historical depth and dimensionality are being lost? And do you think that the private self is being compromised and people's individuality lessened? What might be done to counteract these tendencies?

4. Consider each of the following recent technological developments and advances. What do you think is gained and lost with each?

   Navigation systems in cars

   Wikipedia

   Twitter

   YouTube

   Wireless home-based telephones

   Smartphones

   TV remote controls

   Microwave ovens

   E-books and e-reading devices

   Google Glasses

Technology and Ethics

A number of developments in technology raise profoundly important moral and ethical issues. Among them are scientific discoveries that have enabled animals to be cloned, human beings to be kept alive on respirators, the transplantation of body parts from animals to humans, and the mapping of genes onto chromosomes. Each of these, along with a variety of other technological developments, has been accompanied by questions about whether certain things should be done at all, even if the technology to accomplish them has become or will soon become available. Cloning human beings is one prominent example. Replacing people with robots is another.

In *The Ethical Imagination*, Canadian philosopher Margaret Somerville discusses a series of important ethical questions related to technology. One of her ideas is that developments in the fields of artificial intelligence and robotics challenge our traditional concepts of what "being" is, what a "creature" is, and what kinds and degrees of respect we owe to other forms of life besides the human. Somerville asks how we would characterize a composite creature composed of half human and half robotic elements. She asks, too, whether we should use technological advances in robotics and artificial intelligence to enhance ourselves, in the process making our human selves more machine-like. And if such an eventuality does occur, would people who are enhanced technologically become more important and more powerful than those not so artificially improved? Following such a trajectory of events, would "unmodified (natural) humans" become less desirable and perhaps eventually obsolete?

Somerville mentions a device developed for the military that allows soldiers to receive signals to their brains from cameras and sonar equipment mounted on their helmets. Something called a "Brain Port" links the soldiers' helmets with their tongues, with signals traveling to the brain. She surmises that one day we will be faced with the decision of whether or not to implant such a device in humans' brains rather than in their helmets. She asks whether it is ethical to create "human techno-warriors."

And further, if we were to take the developments in robotics and artificial intelligence, add those in genetics and nanotechnology already underway, and factor in other technologies yet unknown, we would need to consider the possibility of homo sapiens morphing into "techno sapiens" and what the consequences of that would be for humanity. Developments in technology keep coming; they continue on a pace faster than our ability to absorb them and fully understand their implications and consequences. That's one reason it remains important to have people like Margaret Somerville and Neil Postman asking questions about how the new technologies will be used and what kinds of checks and balances should be developed for them.

One area where technological exploration and innovation is under way is that of aging. Scientists are working on ways to prolong human life. What social, political, and economic issues would need to be addressed, for example, in implementing technologies that would enable people to live to an average of 100, 125, 150, or even 200 years of age? What advantages and what drawbacks might there be in living to such an age, both for individuals and for societies? Jonathan Swift's *Gulliver's Travels* (1726), in which he describes the Struldbruggs, sheds some light on this question, as these long-lived beings continue to experience the decline of physical and mental functioning as they age for hundreds of years. Also relevant is Alfred Lord Tennyson's poetic monologue "Tithonus," which describes a mortal being granted his wish for immortality but lacking eternal youth, without which he seeks to have his immortality revoked, as he longs only for death.

Alone Together

A set of related questions about robots is raised by Sherry Turkle in her book *Alone Together*. Turkle examines the implications of robots on human relationships. She describes a series of research studies in which people interact with a variety of robot creatures not just as functional aids for cleaning floors, lifting heavy objects, or washing clothes, but as friends, confidants, even romantic partners. Turkle suggests that technology has become "the architect of our intimacies," with robots only the latest, most fashionable, and most extreme example. She believes that we are at a "robotic moment," when we need to decide just how far we want to allow our relationship with robots to develop. How far is far enough, and how far is too far, she wonders?

Turkle argues that it is not simply a matter of whether or not we can build the robots with sufficient artificial intelligence to assume the roles of friend and lover, caretaker for children and aging parents, and even substitute for children, parents, and friends. Her questions and concerns relate more to whether and what extent we are ready for robots to assume these roles in our lives. She believes that we are coming to the point where we actually want robots as friends and companions, as romantic partners and caregivers. Why? Because it's easier that way. A robot boyfriend or girlfriend, husband or wife, doesn't make demands on us, doesn't challenge or question us, doesn't have its own set of needs, worries, and concerns. Sociable robots, Turkle contends, allow us to avoid conflicts about intimacy, and they also reveal a desire for relationships with limits, a way to be, as she notes, "both together and alone."

EXERCISES

5. Identify two recent or emerging technological developments that have had or are about to have a significant impact on human life and experience. Consider the extent of their impact on social, cultural, and intellectual life. You might consider, for example, the use of neural implants, such as those that help victims of stroke learn to walk, or the hearing impaired hear, but which could also be used to help an athlete focus on perfecting the swing of a tennis racket or baseball bat, or hit perfect basketball free throws or jump shots.

6. How do you respond to Neil Postman's idea that the success of technology in making our lives comfortable and our workplace more efficient has prevented us from seeking other sources of fulfillment.

7. What do you think of the use of robots as friends, companions, or lovers? What about their use as caretakers of children and aging parents? How about their use as parent substitutes? Do you think, for example, that a robot might be programmed to give you better advice about important matters than a parent or a friend? To what extent do you think that virtual social experience degrades our actual social experience?

Social Networking

Perhaps the most significant technological development in the first decade of the twenty-first century is the emergence of remote forms of social networking, with Facebook the dominant example. Numerous news articles and reviews, a number of magazine pieces, a major film, and more than a few books have appeared regarding the phenomenal success of Facebook. Some of these have celebrated Facebook's

✷ Explore the **Concept**,
Social Networking
MyThinkingLab

success; some have been critical of the Web site; still others have raised questions about both how significant the impact of Facebook has been and will continue to be, and what the consequences of that impact might be.

In a review of *The Facebook Effect* in the *New York Times*, Michiko Kakutani quotes Facebook founder and CEO Mark Zuckerberg about how and why his famous website is important. In an op-ed piece for the *Washington Post*, Zuckerberg noted that the Facebook concept is anchored in three notions: (1) that people enjoy sharing information and experiences and like to stay connected to their friends and acquaintances; (2) that if people can maintain control over the things they share, the amount they share will increase; and (3) that as people share more and become more open and connected, the world will become a better place to live.

Since Zuckerberg provided this explanation of Facebook, there have been a number of privacy complaints and some privacy breeches that prompted Facebook to change its networking protocols and practices. One of the big questions about Facebook and similar forms of social networking technologies is the extent to which individual participants can maintain control of their personal information. Another question is whether an increasing transparency in making information available will lead to a more open and tolerant society. And still another concerns the extent to which the information we voluntarily provide to Facebook and other Internet companies, like Google, is sold and used to generate income and profits for them, with nary a penny going to us, the providers of that monetized information.

Social Networking and Friends

One additional consideration to address with respect to Facebook and other social networking sites is what they do to the concept of "friend" and of "friendship." Facebook is perhaps best known for its use of the term *friend* and extending the meaning of "friend" from a person you know well and with whom you have formed a close bond, to a person you have never met face-to-face and whom you hardly know at all—a "Facebook Friend." In addition, there is the shift in the word *friend* from noun to verb, as in *friending* someone in the Facebook way.

For centuries, a friend has been considered a special person in our lives. Along with family, close friends help us weather the storms of life. They share our joys and sorrows. They encourage and support us, deepen our pleasures, lighten our burdens, and enrich our lives. And now, in the twenty-first century, we are invited to consider a new concept of "friendship," the friends on Facebook, for whom none of these experiences is either necessary or relevant.

The concept of "friend," both traditional and contemporary via social networking, raises some important questions. First is the question of sheer numbers. How many friends can a person have—whether these are friends in the old-fashioned sense, or friends in the new social networking sense? Along with this is the consideration of what you need to do to sustain, maintain, manage, develop, and improve your friendships—of both types. An additional consideration is whether you need different categories of friends—"work friends," "play friends," "college or school friends," "weekday" or "weekend" friends, "deep" or "provisional" or "temporary" friends, friends with various kinds of "benefits."

EXERCISES

8. An article in the *New York Times* in 2011 reported that there has been a significant increase in the number of computer science majors at US colleges and universities in the past few years. The article quotes a few students who say they were inspired to select computer science as their major because of Facebook. How do you explain this dynamic?

9. If you are a user of Facebook, what has been your experience in using the site? What are the upside benefits you have experienced? What difficulties, dangers, or other unfortunate consequences have you experienced personally, or have you heard about from others? If you are not a Facebook user, why haven't you signed on? Are you waiting for certain improvements or assurances regarding privacy or other issues? Or do you have other kinds of reservations about the site? If so, what are they? What alternative to Facebook can you imagine that would satisfy the basic need the Web site serves while diminishing, if not eliminating, its negative effects?

10. How do you manage your friendships—both face-to-face friendships and distant, remote, social network friends? Do you have both types of friends, and if so, what do you do to maintain them? What are the advantages and drawbacks of each type of friend? Do you think that Facebook and similar social networking sites have diluted the idea and value of "friendship?" To what extent have these sites provoked you to think more deeply about what "friendship" means to you and what friends can and should be in your life?

11. What television shows are you familiar with that focus on friends? Why do you think there have been in recent years—the past couple of decades, for example—so many shows based on friends, rather than, say on families? To what extent do you think changing social conditions and circumstances, and changing attitudes toward family life and work life and values are related to the ways friends are depicted on television? Do you think such changes in social and cultural attitudes are responsible for the success of social networking sites like Facebook?

12. An article published in 2008 in *Atlantic* magazine was entitled, "Is Google Making Us Stupid?" To what extent might you imagine how using Google can affect us to such an extent that it makes us "stupid?" Do you think Google is as important, less important, or more important a technological advancement than Facebook? Why?

Does Facebook Reduce Life to a Database?

In *You Are Not a Gadget*, Jaron Lanier suggests that Facebook has done to the concept of human friendship what computerized multiple-choice standardized tests have done to education—degraded it by turning it into a database. He argues that computerized analysis of information and computerized engagements of various kinds are fundamentally reductive of more complex human realities. Lanier's concern is that such a diminished concept of student learning and of human friendship is based on a philosophical error—"the belief that computers can presently represent human thought or human relationships." According to Lanier, these are things that computers simply are not able to do now and very likely will never fully be able to do.

A further complicating development from these misguided assumptions, according to Lanier, is that these ideas have real effects on the real lives of actual people—on us. The danger is that we will live our lives in accordance with the models embedded in the various Internet Web sites we engage with daily. If these sites are built on a faulty, weak, inaccurate, or otherwise limited understanding of what it means to be human, our complex selves will become compromised in the process of computer living. The overall effect will be a potential reduction of life itself via a diminution of its richness and complexity. Equally frightening is the possibility that we will hardly notice what is happening to us because so much of our lives will be lived in these environments, because so many others will be engaged in them, and because, increasingly, virtual reality will become "the" reality.

The Implications of Artificial Intelligence

A computer researcher and innovator, Lanier raises a series of additional questions about current developments in technology. Among them are questions regarding artificial intelligence and issues of personhood—what it means to be a person in the twenty-first century. Let's consider first the extent to which machines are "intelligent." Think, for example, about how our purchasing choices on a site like Amazon allow for the site's software to "know" what we like and offer us "choices" it makes for us on subsequent visits. Or consider how GPS navigation systems "know" where we are and can provide directions to get us where we are going when we don't know the way. And, perhaps, seemingly the most amazing of all, consider how an IBM computer named Big Blue was able to defeat a world chess champion, and how another computer, IBM's Watson, defeated two all-time *Jeopardy!* champions. All of these examples suggest that computers can do things we can't, and that, in a way, they are more intelligent than we are. At least that's what some people believe.

But there are other questions that need to be raised with regard to artificial intelligence. First is the question of whether machines have the capability to imagine, to create something new and unpredictable—which is what we do when we problem solve and innovate. Second is the question of whether machines can shift attention, go in another direction, do something different from what they have been programmed to do. Leonard M. Greene notes in his book, *Inventorship*, that with a machine, creating identical circumstances yields identical results. He reminds us that computers, remarkable as they are in many ways, are incapable of being inventive. People, however, are inventive. Computers like Watson can answer questions with amazing speed and accuracy. But they can't create the questions to be asked, even the kinds of questions used for a game like *Jeopardy!*

In a section of his book entitled "The Most Important Thing about a Technology Is How It Changes People," Lanier suggests that the very acts of blogging, wikiing, friending, and twittering not only change how we interact with others but also alter the very essence of who we are. One reason these Internet behaviors change us, Lanier suggests, is because they are based on two interrelated assumptions of digital living: (1) a program that requires us to interact with computers as if they were people asks us to think of ourselves as a programmable entity rather than as a person; and (2) an Internet service edited by a vast and anonymous crowd suggests that that anonymous and random crowd operates as an entity with a credible point of view.

Lanier's primary concern with the implications of our Internet activities and the assumptions that underlie them is in its impact on what it means to be a person today. If contemporary communication occurs on vast scales (think of the numbers of Facebook postings, blog entries, tweets, and the like made daily), and if communication is largely fragmented and impersonal, Lanier wonders whether it has "demeaned interpersonal interaction," and whether it has created a "reduced expectation of what a person can be and . . . become." He is not confident about the prospects.

In a more recent book, *Who Owns the Future?*, Lanier raises additional concerns about these issues. He argues that people should not be equated with machines in our increasingly engineered world. People possess consciousness, something that machines do not and cannot possess. And with consciousness comes the singular, particular, and uniquely distinctive experience that each of us has in the world. Lanier fears, however, that "[b]elief in the specialness of people is a minority position in the tech world." With the loss of this specialness comes a devaluation of the meaningful, the purposeful, and the distinctively human individual—the loss of what is special and distinctive about each of us.

Moreover, there are two versions of each individual on Facebook: the version of ourselves that we "manage" obsessively and the version of ourselves that we don't know about or attend to at all. This second version is the data about us that we don't see and that is sold to third and fourth parties. It is this data, Lanier argues, that generates value to the companies in a position to exploit it. And it is this data—this information about each of us, on Google and Twitter and in our phone records—that is increasingly batched and sold, from which we ourselves, though generating value to others, gain nothing except a loss of our privacy.

Technology and Our Brains

The Internet may be changing not only the ways we interact with one another, but our brains, as well. In *The Shallows* Nicholas Carr cites numerous research studies that indicate how our many uses of the Internet are "rewiring" our brains such that we are becoming more adept at scanning information but less adept at analyzing it. He argues that the Internet, while a wonderful resource for research, is chipping away at our "capacity for concentration and contemplation." His argument is grounded in the reality that the various tools human beings use and the ways we use them have historically altered how we see the world, how we live in it, and how we affect it.

Among the examples Carr cites are the printing press, which introduced vast societal changes, including mass literacy, a decline in the authority of the Church, the spread of information, and much more. What Carr also reminds us of, however, is that with the spread of books and silent reading, with the dispersion of information, came a number of trade-offs, most importantly, the decline of memory. When information is available in books, we don't need to hold so many things in our memories. The result is that our memories atrophy. This deterioration of memory has been exacerbated by the rise of the Internet.

As Socrates lamented nearly 2500 years ago, the deterioration of memory began with the technology of writing, which enabled reading and "research," and which also diminished people's memories. If we can look up information, there is no need, we might argue, to retain it in memory.

Internet reading is very different from book reading; a screen is not a page. We might think, for example, of the kinds of online reading as compared with the kinds of reading we do in books. We should consider our reading process in these different reading environments, using these different technologies, book and computer. Some aspects of the process seem quite similar, while others differ significantly, particularly a tendency when reading online, to follow links, to break away from one page of printed text to visit linked sites, or to break from the electronic printed page to respond to e-mail and Facebook updates. Scrolling up and down electronic pages differs from flipping pages in a book. Many e-book readers now mimic certain actual book features, notably the turning of pages with a flip of the finger.

These observations about reading, however, suggest only minimally what is at stake with our use of the continually evolving electronic technologies for the ways we think and process information. Carr argues that once we turn on our computers we are entering "an ecosystem of interruption technologies" that shortens our attention spans, limits our ability to focus and to think deeply, and, over time, actually rewires the neurons in our brains to make us intellectual jugglers rather than deep thinkers. The frequent interruptions we experience in using our computers—e-mail notifications, Twitter and Facebook updates, ubiquitous advertisements, page crawls, and the like—scatter out thoughts, dilute our concentration, and increase our level of anxiety.

EXERCISES

13. How do you respond to the concerns expressed by Jaron Lanier about the potential diminishment of human experience due to the increased size, scale, scope, and importance of the Internet in our lives? To what extent do you think such sites as "Second Life" or such games as "Fantasy Football" contribute to the potential problems Lanier describes? To what extent do you think digital representations capture the essential aspects, elements, and qualities of life? To what extent might digital representations and simulations be of value to us—in school, at work, in our personal lives?

14. Consider the ways in which we consider computers "intelligent." What are some of the words and phrases we use in describing computers that suggest they have minds? And, conversely, what are some of the ways we talk about ourselves in terms of computers? What do you think of these ways of speaking and thinking about ourselves?

15. How do you respond to the philosopher John Searle's observation that the *Jeopardy!*–specializing computer, Watson—does not understand either the questions, or the answers it provides. Nor does it understand the accuracy of its answers, or that it played the game of *Jeopardy!* and won. Searle contends that Watson doesn't really "understand" anything. To what extent do you agree with what John Searle implies about what Watson "understands," and by implication what he suggests about the limits of artificial intelligence more generally?

16. How do you define a "person," and what does it means to be a person? How do you conceive of what is involved in "interpersonal" relationships? To what extent do you share Lanier's concerns about how contemporary Internet interactions and behaviors might demean personal relationships and diminish our sense of what it means to be an individual person? To what extent do you share Carr's concerns about our use of electronic technology, particularly the Internet? How can you use the Internet megasites in ways that preserve, protect, and promote your distinctive and unique human selfness?

17. To what extent do you stay "connected" electronically during the day? To what extent are you connected during the evening? What would happen if

you limited your connectedness, perhaps turning your devices off for a certain number of hours or days? Do you think people, yourself included, have substituted browsing for reading? What might be the benefits—and drawbacks—of digitizing entire libraries of books?

Digital Citizenship

In their book, *Digital Citizenship in the Schools*, Mike Ribble and Gerald Bailey enlarge the idea of what we might call "Internet etiquette," focusing on what they call "digital citizenship," responsible behavior with regard to the use of technology. Ribble and Bailey identify nine themes of digital citizenship, summarized on their digital citizenship Web site, and explained in greater detail in their book. They are (1) digital etiquette; (2) digital communication; (3) digital literacy; (4) digital access; (5) digital commerce; (6) digital law; (7) digital rights and responsibilities; (8) digital health and wellness; and (9) digital security.

1. *Digital Etiquette.* Digital etiquette refers to electronic standards of conduct and procedure. What constitutes appropriate digital behavior is a matter for discussion and debate. Putting up derogatory comments about people on Facebook pages, sending sexually suggestive images over the Internet, and using blasphemous and scabrous language in e-mails are among the violations of digital etiquette. Schools and businesses are among the entities developing such standards.

2. *Digital Communication.* Digital Communication involves the exchange of information in electronic form. The explosion of digital forms of communication has made it possible for people to keep in constant communication with one another. Questions regarding digital communication include considerations of when to shut off and cut away from the constant digital connectedness, as well as questions regarding the appropriateness of accessing digital connections during business meetings and classes in school.

3. *Digital Literacy.* Digital literacy is the process of learning about technology and its uses, including how to use newly emerging technologies effectively and productively. Information literacy skills are becoming increasingly important, including knowing how to use what's available in digital technology and learning how to use the new technologies for learning.

4. *Digital Access.* Digital access addresses questions concerning availability of and access to digital tools for full participation in society. Digital access issues involve those who may be excluded from participation due to limited access or a lack of knowledge and experience with emerging digital technologies.

5. *Digital Commerce.* Digital commerce involves buying and selling goods and services electronically. An increasing amount of sales activity is occurring over the Internet and via other forms of electronic and digital communication. Learning to become effective consumers in an increasingly digital society is an important aspect of digital commerce. Becoming aware of the dangers of buying and selling goods and services electronically is another important aspect.

6. *Digital Law.* Digital law involves legal responsibility for electronic behavior and deals with the ethics of technology. Ethical responsibility requires at the very least abiding by societal laws. Violations of law involving hacking into others information, downloading copyrighted music, images, and texts, creating destructive viruses, sending spam, stealing people's identities and personal information, and the like.

7. *Digital Rights and Responsibilities.* Digital rights and responsibilities form two sides of a coin; they involve freedoms and constraints extending to all participants in the digital world. Digital rights include those normally extended to citizens in the nonelectronic world, including the rights to privacy and free speech. Behaving responsibly in exercising our own digital rights while simultaneously respecting the digital rights of others is the essence of digital rights and responsibilities.

8. *Digital Health and Wellness.* Digital health involves the physical and psychological well-being of all who participate in the electronic digital environment. Physical considerations involve taking precautions to prevent or avoid repetitive stress syndrome, vision problems, and other bodily ailments. Psychological considerations include situations involving cyberbullying, sexual harassment, and other violations of appropriate digital behavior and their emotional effects on recipients of such actions.

9. *Digital Security.* Digital security involves electronic precautions for self-protection and safety. Taking precautions such as using passwords and locking PDAs and computers is one form of digital security. Others include backing up data, using virus protecting software, and providing surge control for equipment. Digital security remains a challenge for both personal users of digital technology and for large-scale entities, including companies, public services, and countries.

EXERCISES

18. Which two of Ribble and Bailey's guidelines for digital citizenship do you think are most important? Why? To what extent do you agree that it is now time to develop guidelines for how to be a citizen in a digital age?

19. In an article in the *Wall Street Journal* (August 20, 2011), Marc Andreessen, a cofounder of Netscape and early investor in Facebook, Groupon, Skype, Twitter, and other Internet companies, argues that software and software companies are poised to dominate the economy in dollars and in influence. To what extent do you agree with Andreessen? What examples of the prevalence and power of software in various industries can you think of? To what extent is the rapid development of sophisticated software contributing to the replacement of people by machines in various industries?

Technology and Information

Technology has created a number of challenges for those who live in the twenty-first century. One of the greatest challenges confronting us is the tremendous amount of information we have to absorb each day. However useful much of the information we receive may be, there is so much of it that we are simply unable to process it adequately. We have more information available to us than ever before but less time to absorb it, reflect on it, and understand it. The challenge, thus, is not to gather, consolidate, and disperse information, but to analyze and comprehend it, and then to use it productively.

It is often said that we live in an age of information—the "information age," as opposed to the "agrarian age" or the "industrial age." And there is certainly some truth to this claim. However, we might argue that earlier eras were also deeply influenced by information and the technologies available to disperse it. As Robert Darnton suggests in *The Case for Books*, "every age was an age of information," and, further, that in those previous eras, new technologies disrupted the way information was managed and disseminated. For example, in our own time, blogs and wikis, Twitter and Facebook, Google and Apple—all have affected how we communicate, how we create and share information. In previous decades, printed newspapers and magazines were more common than they are today, but the information presented was then and continues to be today, as complex and shifting as the information presented by means of the latest (and ever-changing) technologies.

Information has always been unstable, exhibiting problems of fact and accuracy. Information, Darnton reminds us, should not be viewed as "hard facts" and not considered "nuggets of reality," regardless of the medium of its transmission. We should think of information, instead, as "messages that are constantly being reshaped." In *What Technology Wants*, Kevin Kelly explains that the term *information* means a number of different things, among them, "a bunch of bits," and "a meaningful signal." Kelly suggests that *information* is less a clearly understood term than a kind of metaphor. It seems, then, that we need to be skeptical of all information, even when it is presented on reputable news channels and via highly regarded print and electronic media.

In *The Signal and the Noise*, Nate Silver echoes Kelly's concerns by suggesting that to arrive at a meaningful "signal" we have to sort through vast quantities of meaningless "noise." It takes a long time to "translate information into useful knowledge." Silver reminds us that numbers cannot speak for themselves. As a result, we have to interpret them, give them meaning. In the process of doing that, we most often imbue them with the meaning we want them to have, allowing our subjective predilections to dominate and control our reading of the data.

Nicholas Carr identifies additional challenges we confront with regard to information. He notes in *The Shallows* that the continued reductions in the cost of creating, storing, and sharing information have contributed to the information glut we now experience. And in a *New York Times* op-ed piece from March 2011, "The Digital Pileup," Shelley Podolny laments our reluctance to hit the delete button, with the result that we retain vast amounts of unnecessary information. This unneeded information takes up space on our servers; it clogs our systems, slowing them down and slowing us down, as we wade through vast amounts of inessential information when we need to find something in our files we actually do need. But that's really only a small part of the problem. Even worse are the consequences in terms of decreased efficiency and lost productivity, as we waste time sorting through useless data. Add to this the costs associated with storing information—including information no longer of value—costs in terms not just of dollars, but also in terms of human capital and energy resources.

An additional problem with information is that it isn't always accurate. In *Information Anxiety 2*, Richard Saul Wurman suggests that 99% of information "isn't meaningful or understandable," and that that more and more information is "misinformation." A visit to the Internet to research something you know well—information about yourself, for example—quickly reveals errors, including misspellings of your name, inaccuracies about your domicile or place of employment, and often much information that is simply out of date. Or consider the "information" that was disseminated in the news about the lost Malaysian airliner—especially how often what was offered as "fact" was later changed, corrected, modified, and abandoned.

Still another danger of information is that people tend to value and gravitate toward easily obtainable information, whether that information is accurate, adequate, or necessary. Decisions are often made on information that is easy to obtain rather than on information that is relevant, though harder to acquire.

As Rolf Dobelli remarks in *The Art of Thinking Clearly*, "We prefer *wrong* information to *no* information," an example of a fallacy of thinking that Dobelli characterizes as "availability bias." This problem, really a thinking fallacy, is ubiquitous; it appears everywhere—in medicine, education, politics, economics, psychology, even in science.

Richard Lanham in *The Economics of Attention*, reminds us how information "has annihilated distance," with shopping and school available from our kitchens and bedrooms, and with surgeons able to operate thousands of miles away. Money is less important, he notes, than information about money; political capital resides in the information that can be gathered, analyzed, and manipulated to help candidates get themselves elected. Lanham argues that what we need is new and better structures of attention that enable us to filter information to master and use it. Art and literature, style and rhetoric are forms of attention that can help us notice more deeply and astutely, compel better ways of seeing and thinking, and thus provide useful information filters that lead to more sharper insights and deeper understanding.

The River of Knowledge

We are absorbing information even before we are born, as David Brooks notes in *The Social Animal*. As we grow within our mothers' wombs, we are accumulating genetic information from our evolutionary past. And after we are born, we inherit streams of information that have been in continuous existence for millennia in the form of religion, culture, and family. Our education continues to be a source of information, as are all the myriad forms of advice, warnings, seductions, and opportunities advertised to entice us. It's a rich legacy and a complex one. And, as Brooks suggests, "no one exists, self-created, in isolation this legacy of information."

The psychologist John Bowlby suggests that the ways we respond to information, the value we assign things, how we react to them and make predictions from them are all connected to how we see the world. Bowlby argues that every life situation we confront is interpreted in terms of the models of the world we have in our heads. Information reaching us through our sense organs is selected and interpreted in terms of those models; its significance for us and for those we care for is evaluated in terms of them, and "plans of action conceived and executed with those models in mind." Information is filtered through our perceptual screens, our ways of making sense of reality. There is no other way for information to get through.

EXERCISES

20. Do you agree with Darnton's notion that every age is an information age? Why or why not? To what extent do you think this current age of information might be different from previous ages of information?

21. Of the views advanced here about the challenges of information by Kelly, Silver, Carr, and Wurman, which do you consider most convincing, most interesting, and/or most important? Why?

22. How helpful do you find Lanham's suggestion that art and literature and rhetoric can be used as ways to filter information productively and understand both its potential and its limits?

23. How do you respond to Brooks' notion of the river of knowledge—the various tributaries of information that come our way from before we are born and throughout our lives. Do you think this is an exaggeration? Is there any benefit to this way of viewing information? What kinds of models do you have for selecting, interpreting, and acting on information? Are these models primarily religious, social, familial, cultural, economic—or something else?

24. To what extent do you trust the information that comes your way? What kinds of questions do you have about the various sources of information you use regularly—Google, Wikipedia, and social Web sites such as Facebook and Twitter? How much of the information about you on the Web is accurate? What do you have to do to correct or eliminate inaccurate or no longer desirable information about yourself?

The Trustworthiness of Information

An essential consideration about any type of information is the extent to which it can be trusted as being accurate. An increased awareness of the various aspects of information, especially the trustworthiness of information—its accuracy and reliability—is the subject of *Blur* by Bill Kovach and Tom Rosenstiel. The subtitle of *Blur*: *How to Know What's True in the Age of Information Overload* invites us to consider how we will know what to believe in an age of information profusion. The authors respond by suggesting an approach grounded in what they call "skeptical knowing." How will we decide what information to believe and what sources to trust? How will we make sense of the information that emerges about the next big catastrophe—perhaps the next nuclear or terrorist crisis?

Kovach and Rosenstiel describe how information was released in an orderly and controlled manner when the nuclear accident at the Three Mile Island nuclear facility in Pennsylvania occurred in 1979. And they ask whether in an age of the Internet, talk radio, and rabidly ideological news shows, the presentation and vetting of information for accuracy would be equally forthright, equally concerned with factual accuracy and with the truth of what happens. Their answer, in short, is "no," largely because the gatekeepers of information are disappearing, as journalistic standards of integrity and honesty are being sacrificed to the demands of politics, **ideology**, and profits.

ideology
A set of beliefs and assumptions that informs how we see and experience the world.

As a result, we all need to be responsible for testing evidence and checking sources, for deciding what's important to know and what can be ignored. We need to decide whether the information we find is reliable and complete. We can ask ourselves a few questions as a base from which to start:

1. Where did this information come from?—(the *sources*)

2. What is the evidence for it?—(*support*)

3. Why is this information important to know?—(its *value*)

4. What's missing?—(*completeness*)

As Kovach and Rosenstiel note, the information gap of today is less about who has and who does not have access to information. Instead, it is more about who knows and who does not know how to analyze the abundance of information at our disposal to determine its completeness, its accuracy, its value, and the persuasiveness of the evidence that supports, refutes, or qualifies it.

25. What other questions might you add to the four suggested by Kovich and Rosenstiel for determining the trustworthiness of information?

26. Read the front page of any newspaper you have handy. Select a story from the front page and follow it through to the end. Use the questions provided by Kovich and Rosenstiel to analyze the story: Where did the information come from? What evidence supports it? Why is this information important? What's missing?

Big Data

In their book *Big Data*, Viktor Mayer-Schönberger and Kenneth Cukier claim that the vast volumes of data being collected, processed, analyzed, and applied multiple times over will transform how we think, work, and live. The authors argue that "big data" in the form of information is multiplying at dizzying velocities and orders of magnitude, and it is creating nothing short of a revolution—a revolution equal to the revolutions following the invention of printing from moveable type and the invention of the Internet.

To consider just how much data is being generated, consider that the amount of information being stored is growing at four times the rate of world economic growth. Concurrently the processing power of computers is growing at nine times the rate of the growth of the world economy. These two facts—the acceleration in the amount of data able to be stored and the increasing power of computer processing—account for the prospect of significant change in how information will affect our lives, and in fact is already altering our lives.

Consider the example of Amazon book and music recommendations. Previously human reviewers offered judgments about and recommendations for purchasing books to read and music to listen to. But Amazon executives discovered that the information we ourselves provide through our purchases, our viewing of particular items, and our sharing of our "likes" are better predictors of what we are likely to buy in the future. Computer analysis based on our most frequently visited Web sites, our Facebook activity, and our LinkedIn and Twitter behavior is beginning to drive these and other economic entities to whom our information is made available ("sold") to send us information, including advertisements for their products and services.

What is different about "big data" from the kinds of data gathering and applications of recent decades? The major differences are that the sheer volume of data and the speed with which it is being processed allow for less precision in analyzing data, as for example, in collecting a truly random sample of voter behavior. Gathering a data set of N = ALL or nearly all, allows for some messiness in the acceptance of error, which would be unacceptable with a small data sample.

A further related development with the arrival of big data is that correlation becomes more important than causality. That is, the reasons why and how things are related becomes less important than simply "that" they are related. The authors of big data offer numerous examples of how this correlation effect can be of value in various domains even without an understanding of why the correlations occur. For example, if the analysis of vast amounts of data reveals a consistent pattern that suggests the best time to save money on the purchase of plane tickets or hotel reservations, then that is enough to provide economic value, even if we don't understand the methods used to arrive at the recommended purchase time.

Among the values and benefits of big data are those of the practical applications for which it can be used. One example is the way companies like Wal-Mart can decide what products to sell in particular stores, how much of them to stock, and when to make them available—even where to position them in stores. Wal-Mart has discovered that just before a hurricane is to hit, people buy pop-tarts in large quantities (strawberry is the preferred flavor), and so when the forecast calls for a major storm, Wal-Mart places piles of strawberry pop-tarts near the checkout counters. And UPS used large quantities of many kinds of data to discover which of its trucks were in need of repair before breakdowns occurred, and thus saved considerable money by getting them fixed before the breakdowns resulted in costly countermeasures to get products delivered.

Among the dangers and concerns of big data are privacy, not just in the information we provide directly about ourselves, but in ways that information is shared without our knowledge and potentially misused, also often without our knowledge. How often, for example, when in signing on to use a Web site or a particular feature of a site, do any of us read the long and detailed privacy notice that accompanies permission to use it? Almost never, if we are like most people. And even if we do read them, those fine-print, super-sized notices are written in complex language that is deliberately made difficult to understand—to discourage us from reading and comprehending them. We thus often allow our information to be put to uses, which if we fully understood, we would be reluctant to sanction.

Other risks with the emergence of big data include the way such data is used to make predictions about our behavior based on past performance, on present social relationships, and on a host of seemingly unrelated bits of information, such as where we live, how much money we make, what kinds of brands we "like" and purchase, who our acquaintances ("friends") are, what movies we rent from Netflix, the number of Twitter followers we have, and on and on. Predictive performance is a kind of super-profiling, and it carries with it the same risks and dangers of any stereotyping based on substitution of group behavior for individuality and uniqueness.

Information, Privacy, and Political Control

A major problem with the emergence of new social and information technologies involves the control of information, especially maintaining its privacy. So much information is shared voluntarily that most of us have only a limited awareness of what happens to the information we provide banks and credit agencies, merchants and academic institutions, hospitals and social service organizations, city, state, and federal governments, as well as our employers.

The leader in inducing people to give up information about themselves so far, has been Facebook, though smartphone companies are not far behind. In his book, *The Filter Bubble*, Eli Pariser sounds a warning about what has previously been a largely invisible problem, Pariser describes how Web sites filter information based on our individual Web history. They cater to our likes and to our habits of browsing and buying. This strategy on the part of the big sites, like Google, Facebook, Microsoft, Yahoo—and many others—can be helpful in narrowing down to manageable proportions the massiveness of the Web and the vast number of hits that appear during Web searches.

But this winnowing process also limits our knowledge of information actually available across a much wider range of topics, aspects, and perspectives. The filtering of information keeps us in a kind of bubble of the familiar, limiting us to the perspectives and viewpoints we are accustomed to. Ian Ayres, in *Supercrunchers*, refers to this as "self-filtering," in which we collaborate with the Internet filters

Write the Response,
Information, Privacy,
and Political Control
MyThinkingLab

to get our news personalized, a seeming convenience that has the consequence of self-censorship by means of limited, narrowly conceived preferences. We secure ourselves inside a self-created comfortable information cocoon.

A major problem with this kind of filtering is that we don't know what's been edited out. We don't know the ways in which the selection process, done on our behalf and for our benefit, limits our knowledge and shapes our thinking. We might argue, on one hand, that such filtering is useful for buying things we want—books, for example, or movies—and that it prevents us from seeing ads and receiving information for things we have no interest in. We might think, however, on the other hand, that others are making many such decisions for us, something we might perhaps want to do for ourselves.

The control of information is nowhere more apparent than in totalitarian countries, most notably, perhaps in China, a country with which Google had its troubles over free access to its services. It is well known that China monitors the Web, especially social media services, in an effort to curtail demonstrations and to detain and sometimes arrest their organizers.

One company that turned over information to Chinese security officials is Yahoo, which released information identifying the dissident Wang Xiaoning and the journalist Shi Tao, who sent pro-democracy messages through their Yahoo accounts. Both were convicted of crimes and sentenced to 10-year sentences in prison. Google, on the other hand, after learning that Beijing had hacked into personal Gmail accounts of human rights activists, rerouted its search results through Hong Kong, which is free of censorship.

Information, Meaning, and Knowledge

Albert Einstein is among many who have noted that information is not knowledge. A great challenge, therefore, is how to make information yield knowledge—how to extract from information useful knowledge, how to learn from information by sorting, categorizing, analyzing, and evaluating it. Winston Churchill added to the challenge by suggesting that true genius is required for evaluating uncertain, hazardous, and conflicting information. As Nate Silver notes, "We think we want information when we really want knowledge." We need critical and creative thinking to help us do the actual work of assessing complex and competing information and for converting information into knowledge—to make information meaningful, useful, and productive.

In *Too Big to Know*, David Weinberger refers to what is known as the DIKW hierarchy: data, information, knowledge, wisdom (with data on the bottom and wisdom at the top). As we know, there are massive amounts of data accumulating but not a lot of wisdom, which is much harder to come by. Each corresponding higher layer yields something more useful. Information, for example can be seen as structured data—data given a more usable form. Knowledge, one degree higher, can be seen as actionable information, and wisdom as knowledge deepened by experience and reflection.

There is no end to information. It continues to proliferate at a staggering rate. The various explanations and categories, the warnings and advice, the suggestions for displaying information in useful and productive ways, will continue. As critical and creative thinkers, we need to be conscious of the challenges we face regarding information. Not the least of these is to translate data and information into useful knowledge that can advance collaboration, deepen understanding, and, perhaps even on occasion, lead to wisdom.

EXERCISES

27. What other advantages of big data—what other productive applications for huge amounts of quickly processed data—can you identify? To what extent do you think these positive uses of big data outweigh the danger to privacy and individuality inherent in the ways big data is being used?

28. What do you think about information filtering? To what extent do you agree that this kind of filtering creates a kind of protective bubble? What other implications do you see from feedback loops focused on "me" that Internet filtering creates? Do you agree with those, like Eli Pariser, who suggest that Internet personalization affects our identity, our relationships, our thinking, and even our democracy?

29. To what extent do you think reducing your privacy for the conveniences of social and communication technologies is worth the trade-off? To what extent do you think it is possible to limit the information that you reveal to governmental agencies, merchants, and technology service providers?

30. Through what kinds of lenses do you perceive and negotiate the many forms of information coming your way? What forms of education and training do you think would help you process these various information streams more effectively?

Looking Back and Looking Ahead

Revisit the learning goals that begin this chapter. Which of these goals do you think you have best achieved? What might you do to reach the remaining goals?

Return to the focusing questions at the beginning of the chapter. How would you answer those questions now? Which of them do you find most interesting and provocative and worthy of following up? Why?

In reviewing the list of resources that follows, identify the two that attract you most. Explain why these books or Web sites interest you. Consider looking into them to further deepen your understanding of the complex effects of technology on our lives and the ways in which information in particular presents us with significant challenges for critical understanding.

Take a look, too, at the MyThinkingLab resources on the Prentice Hall Web site. Included there are readings, images, videos, questions, exercises, and other provocations to help you apply critical and creative thinking to questions relating to technology and information.

Resources

What Technology Wants, Kevin Kelly. Viking, 2011.

Reality Is Broken, Jane McGonigal. Penguin Books, 2011.

The Gutenberg Elegies, Sven Birkerts. Ballantine, 1994.

You Are Not a Gadget, Jaron Lanier. Knopf, 2011.

The Ethical Imagination, Margaret Somerville. McGill Queens University Press, 2008.

Amusing Ourselves to Death, Neil Postman. Penguin, 2005.

The End of Education, Neil Postman. Random House, 1996.

Technopoly, Neil Postman. Random House, 1993.

Alone Together, Sherry Turkle. Basic Books, 2011.

Inventorship, Leonard Greene. Wiley, 2001.

The Shallows, Nicholas Carr. Norton, 2011.

Virtually You, Elias Aboujaoude. Norton, 2012.

Who Owns the Future?, Jaron Lanier. Simon & Schuster, 2013.

Digital Citizenship in Schools, Mike Ribble and Gerald Bailey. International Society for Technology in Education, 2011. Web site: digitialcitizenship.net

The Case for Books, Robert Darnton. Public Affairs, 2010.

The Signal and the Noise, Nate Silver. Penguin Press, 2012.

The Economics of Attention, Richard Lanham. University of Chicago Press, 2007.

The Social Animal, David Brooks. Random House, 2011.

The Filter Bubble, Eli Pariser. Penguin, 2011.

Information Anxiety 2, Richard Saul Wurman. QUE, 2000.

Blur, Tom Rosensteil and Bill Kovach. Bloomsbury USA, 2011.

Supercrunchers, Ian Ayres. Bantam, 2008.

Big Data, Viktor Mayer-Schönberger and Kenneth Cukier. Houghton Mifflin Harcourt, 2013.

Too Big to Know, David Weinberger. Basic Books, 2011.

• •

Glossary

ad baculum   A logical fallacy containing an appeal to force that uses fear and threats to assert the truth of an argument; from the Latin phrase meaning "to the stick."

ad hominem   A logical fallacy that contains an attack on an individual's character rather than a response to his or her ideas; from the Latin phrase meaning "to the man."

ad populum   A logical fallacy that contains an appeal to public opinion to prove the truth of an argument; from the Latin phrase meaning "to the people."

affirming the consequent   A logical fallacy that treats a necessary condition (the consequent) as if it were a sufficient condition. It takes this form: If P, then Q. Q, therefore P.

alternative   In creative thinking, an additional choice or possibility that fosters the generation of new ideas.

ambiguity   Inexactness of meaning; the use of language to mean two different things simultaneously.

analogy   A comparison between two different cases to suggest their similarities in the process of making an argument.

analysis   A process of considering the parts of something, including arguments, to better understand their structure and meaning.

annotation   The process of making brief notes within and around a text.

antecedent   The part of a conditional statement that states a conditional or hypothetical situation.

appeal to pity   A logical fallacy that involves appealing to audience sympathy rather than to logic and rational thinking.

appeal to the public   (See *ad populum*.)

appeal to emotion   A logical fallacy in which logic and rational thinking are ignored in favor of feeling and emotion.

appeal to force   (See *ad baculum*.)

argument chain   A set of linked arguments, often syllogistic, in which the conclusion of one argument becomes a premise in one that follows.

argument   The assertion of a claim or conclusion that is supported with evidence in the form of information, data, numbers, or reasons.

assumption   What is taken for granted in an argument.

authority   Expert knowledge brought to bear on an argument claim or conclusion; individuals and institutions with demonstrated knowledge, experience, rank, position, and accomplishments.

backing   Data and other assurances that strengthen the authority of a claim.

bandwagon   A popular term for an *ad populum* fallacy, where popularity is invoked as a means of persuasion.

categorical proposition   Affirms or denies that a subject is a member of a class or possesses a particular property.

categorical syllogism   A syllogism formed with categorical propositions; for example:
All major league baseball players make a good salary.
R. A. Dickey is a major leaguer pitcher.
Therefore, R. A. Dickey makes a good salary.

causality   A relationship between or among events in which one event appears responsible for causing others to occur after it; for example, smoking cigarettes causes cancer.

claim   In argument, an assertion or conclusion that requires evidence in its support.

classical oration   A form and style of argument in ancient Greece and Rome that includes the following parts: introduction, narration, division, confirmation, refutation, and peroration, or grand conclusion.

concession   An acknowledgment that some part of an opponent's argument is valid or true.

conclusion   What an argument asserts; the claim of an argument. Also, the idea or meaning derived from the process of interpretation.

conditional statement   A statement asserting that if one condition is met, then something else will follow from it. For instance: "If you work hard, you will succeed."

connotations   The personal associations words possess rather than their dictionary definitions.

consequent   The part of a conditional statement that states what will follow if a condition is met.

counterargument   An argument that contrasts or opposes another argument.

creative thinking   The purposeful generation and implementation of novel ideas.

creativity   The use of imagination and/or intuition in the production of original things or ideas.

critical thinking   The process of analysis, reflection, and evaluation that leads to reasoned conclusions and judgments.

cross-fertilization   The process of bringing ideas and approaches to thinking from one discipline to bear upon another. Using concepts of physics (gravity, for example) to think about literary characters; or using concepts from the visual arts (color and texture) to describe music.

deductive reasoning   Logical reasoning from premises to conclusions.

denotation   The dictionary definition of a word; a word's agreed-upon meaning.

denying the antecedent   A logical fallacy that treats a sufficient condition (the antecedent) as if it were a necessary condition. It takes the following form: If P, therefore Q. Not P, therefore Q.

denying the negative   A creative thinking strategy that avoids a negative attitude and instead encourages pursuing possibilities.

design thinking   Thinking directed toward the design of new things and new ways of doing things—the design of products and processes.

disjunctive syllogism   A syllogism that includes an "either-or" statement, such as "Either the concert tickets are on my desk, or they are in my wallet."

enthymeme   An argument with a missing part, more often a missing premise, but sometimes a missing conclusion.

equivocation   Using a word in two different senses to make a claim look more plausible than it is; for example: This is the right thing to do in this case, and I have the right to make my own decision in the matter.

ethos   In rhetoric, establishing a speaker or writer's credibility or trustworthiness.

evaluation   The process of considering values—political, social, religious, and the like—during the analysis and interpretation of texts. Also, in argument, a judgment expressing favor or disfavor, approval or disapproval, agreement or disagreement.

evidence   Proof or support for an argument claim in the form of facts, data, information, and reasons.

fallacy   Argument error or mistake that occurs in making both deductive and inductive arguments.

false cause   Illogical causality, which results from assuming that because one event happens after another, the first event caused the second to happen; also known by its Latin name, post hoc, *ergo propter hoc*, which means "after this, therefore because of this." For example: After I saw a black cat in the morning, I knew I was in trouble. And just as I expected, my bike was stolen that afternoon.

false dilemma   A false dilemma, a type of either-or thinking, limits options to just two. All other options and alternatives are ignored; for example: either the Democrats band together behind Governor Johnson, or the Republicans will coast to an easy victory.

fixed pie   In negotiation, the idea that there is a fixed amount for good or services to be divided or apportioned.

general focus (compare purpose focus)   In creative thinking, focusing on a broad or general category.

hypothetical syllogism   A syllogism that takes the form of "if . . . then;" for example, "If I pass this course with at least a B, I will retain my scholarship."

icon   An image that represents a person, place, thing, or idea. An icon may also refer to a popular or well-known object, such as the Eiffel Tower, which stands for France.

ideology   A set of beliefs and assumptions that inform how we see and experience the world.

image   A general term for any pictorial representation.

imagery   Descriptive detail in a text that triggers visual, auditory, tactile, and other sense stimuli.

imagination   The faculty of forming mental ideas, images, or concepts that are not perceived through the five senses.

implication   A possible outcome of the premises and conclusion of an argument.

inductive reasoning   Reasoning from past instances to future predicted occurrences; inductive reasoning offers probability rather than certainty.

inference   A statement about the unknown made on the basis of the known; the recognition of an implication, what is implied or suggested by something noticed.

innovation   A significant positive change usually brought about by the creation of something new, which is often based on combining things that already exist.

insight   A radical shift in understanding that relies on a break with previous patterns of thinking.

interpretation   The concluding stage of the analytical process resulting in an idea about the meaning or significance of whatever is analyzed and interpreted, often, but not always, a text.

intuition   An unexplained understanding that relies less on logic and reasoning than a sense or feeling about things.

justification   The process of providing reasoned evidence to support, or "justify" an argument, decision, or choice.

lateral thinking   An alternative to logical thinking that emphasizes how to generate new ideas and how to break out of the constraints and patterns of entrenched ways of seeing. An alternative to logical, or vertical, thinking.

logic   A branch of philosophy that emphasizes reasoned judgment.

logos   An aspect of rhetoric that involves logic and reasoning for the purpose of persuasion.

metaphorical thinking   In creative thinking, a form of analogical thinking that seeks unusual connections to promote the discovery of fresh ideas.

modus ponens   A valid argument that takes the form of If P, then Q; P; therefore Q. For a related logical fallacy, see Affirming the Consequent.

modus tollens   A valid argument that takes the form of If P, then Q. Not Q; therefore, P. For a related logical fallacy, see Denying the Antecedent.

necessary condition   A condition that is required for something to be the case. (Compare sufficient condition.)

negotiation   Mutual discussion with the role of reaching agreement.

non sequitur   A logical fallacy in which one statement does not follow logically from another.

paradox   An apparent contradiction that turns out to be true.

parallel thinking   A form of thinking in which a group of people think together in the same direction at the same time for a common purpose. An alternative to adversarial thinking.

paraphrase   A restatement or reformulation of an idea, argument, text, or portion of a text, in different words, that follows the order and organization of the original. (Compare summary.)

pathos   An aspect of rhetoric that relies on an appeal to feeling or emotion rather than to reason and logic.

picture   An image meant to resemble its subject but in a simpler, less detailed form.

prediction   A declaration in advance that something will happen; an expectation of something that is to come.

premises   In an argument, statements explicitly asserted or assumed that comprise an argument's reasons; premises provide justification for the conclusion.

purpose   The goal or aim, along with the practical effect or reason, for which something is attempted or accomplished.

purpose focus (compare general area focus)   In creative thinking, focusing on a specific topic area rather than a broad or general category.

quota-of-alternatives   In creative thinking, a technique to push thinking beyond the first things that come to mind with the goal of discovering something surprising and interesting.

rebuttal and refutation   In argument, showing how an opposing argument is deficient, weak, or otherwise unpersuasive.

red herring   A logical fallacy which relies on distraction from the central issue or problem being addressed.

reversing relationships   A creative thinking process that promotes identifying and considering the implications of an opposite perspective or point of view.

rhetoric   The use of language and images for the purpose of persuasion. The art of persuasion.

Rogerian argument   A form of argument, devised by psychologist Carl Rogers, which emphasizes cooperation and seeking common ground rather than contestation and condemnation of an opponent's ideas and claims.

romanticize   The process of idealizing something, such that it becomes both unrealistic and unpersuasive.

scamper   An acronym for a set of thinking procedures to generate ideas: substitute, combine, adapt, magnify (or minify), put to uses, eliminate, reverse or rearrange.

self-regulation   The critical thinking skill by which one monitors one's cognitive activities.

shifting attention   An analytical technique and problem-solving strategy that involves turning one's focused attention from one aspect of a situation, text, or problem to another.

slippery slope   A logical fallacy in which a claim is made that one action will precipitate a successive series of actions, as for example, that legalizing medical marijuana will lead to marijuana addiction and then to other forms of drug addiction.

stereotype   A widely held but oversimplified belief about the members of a group, such that all group members are considered to possess the same character or behavior trait.

straw man   A logical fallacy in which an opponent's position is distorted, exaggerated, or otherwise misrepresented in order to make it more vulnerable to attack.

sufficient condition   What is enough for something to be the case. (Compare necessary condition.)

summarize   The process of condensing and restating in brief form the argument, ideas, and structure of a text. (Compare paraphrase.)

support   The evidence—details, examples, facts, statistics, and the like that provides the "grounds" for the claim.

symbol   A complex icon that represents more abstract concepts, ideas, and values.

system II thinking   A form of deliberative thinking that allows time for analysis and consideration of different approaches and alternative options.

system I thinking   A form of thinking quickly and reactively without careful reflection and consideration.

technology   The creation, knowledge, and use of tools and techniques to solve problems and make improvements.

technopoly   A society in which technologies generate a surplus of information that requires additional technologies to maintain.

testimony   The use of various kinds of spokesmen and witnesses to provide support for an argument or claim.

vagueness   In argument, a lack of clarity about what is being claimed or how evidence supports a claim.

validity   In deductive arguments, the situation in which the form or structure of the argument is such that the truth of the premises guarantees the truth of the conclusion. If the premises of a deductive argument are true and the argument's structure is sound, the conclusion is inevitably true, and thus the argument is valid.

warrant   In argument, a term introduced by Stephen Toulmin to indicate the "bridge" that connects a claim and its supporting evidence; warrants show how the data or reasons supporting a claim are relevant.

win-win   An outcome of a negotiation in which both parties come away with a desired element or aspect of what is being contested.

Credits

Groves." Robert Frost. 1913; p. 62: "I Wandered Lonely as a Cloud" William Wordsworth. 1888; p. 62: "My Love is Like a Red, Red Rose" Robert Burns. 1794; p. 62: Alexander Pope, "An Essay on Criticism", 1711; p. 62: William Shakespeare, Macbeth, 1623.

Chapter 4

Page 75: Manguel, Alberto. 2000. Reading Pictures. Random House; p. 86: Hames, Thomas X. (2003, April 23). War Isn't Fought in the Headlines. New York Times; p. 88: Pound, Ezra and Michael Dirda. (2011). ABC of Reading. New Directions; pp. 88–89: Courtesy of Nadine Gordon-Taylor; p. 90: Courtesy of Maria DeAngelis; p. 91: Courtesy of Dina Hofstetter; pp. 92–93: Courtesy of Lisa Scavelli; p. 94: Scholes, Robert. 1989. Protocols of Reading, Yale University Press; p. 94: Scholes, Robert. 1991. Protocols of Reading. Yale University Press; p. 100: Costanzo, William V. 2004. Great Films and How to Read Them. NCTE.

Chapter 5

Page 102: Adair, John. 2009. The Art of Creative Thinking. Kogan Page; p. 105: First We Read, Then We Write: Emerson on the Creative Process. 2009. Robert D. Richardson, ed. University of Iowa Press; pp. 105, 108: Dillard, Annie. 1989. Teaching a Stone to Talk. Harper Perennial; pp. 108, 113: "Los Angeles Notebook" from SLOUCHING TOWARDS BETHLEHEM by Joan Didion. Copyright © 1966, 1968, renewed 1996 by Joan Didion. Reprinted by permission of Farrar, Straus and Giroux, LLC; pp. 113–114: Zora Neale Hurston, "How It Feels to Be Colored Me" from The World Tomorrow, 1928; pp. 115, 118, 124–125: "About Men," from The Solace of Open Spaces, by Gretel Ehrlich, copyright © 1985 by Gretel Ehrlich. All rights reserved. Used by permission of Viking Penguin, a division of Penguin Group (USA) Inc; 129: Thoreau, Henry David. Walden. Penguin.

Chapter 6

Page 133: Copleston, Frederick. 2003. History of Philosophy, Volume 4. Continuum International Publishing Group; p. 146: Aristotle. Politics. Penguin; p. 147: Berekley, George. 2010. A Treatise Concerning The Principles of Human Knowledge. CreateSpace; p. 154: Orwell, George. "Politics and the English Language." A Collection of Essays. 1970. Harcourt; p. 154: How to Think Logically. 2nd ed., Gary Seay and Susana Nuccetelli. 2011. Prentice Hall; p. 155: Kean, Sam. 2012. The Violinist's Thumb. Little, Brown and Company; p. 156: Schlesinger, Arthur. 1998. The Disuniting of America. W. W. Norton & Company; p. 156: Norman, Donald. 2005. Emotional Design. Basic Books.

Chapter 7

Page 160: Peirce, Charles Sanders. 1998. Chance, Love, and Logic: Philosophical Essays. University of Nebraska.

Chapter 8

Page 184: "Corn-Pone Opinions." In The Complete Essays of Mark Twain. Da Capo Press; p. 185: Melville, Herman. 1851. Moby Dick. Harper & Brothers; p. 188: © 1963 Martin Luther King, Jr.; © renewed 1986 by heirs to the Estate of Martin Luther King, Jr.; p. 206: Reprinted by permission of Donald Pardlow; p. 207: Kenneth Burke. 1974. The Philosophy of Literary Form. University of California Press; p. 211: Shakespeare, William. 2009. Julius Caesar. Simon and Schuster.

Chapter 9

Page 216: de Bono, Edward. 1985. New Think. Avon; p. 238: Lui, Eric and Scott Noppe-Brandon. 2009. Imagination First! Jossey-Bass.

Chapter 10

Page 236: Sagan, Carl. 1997. The Demon-Haunted World. Ballantine Books; p. 239: Lincoln Center Institute for Aesthetic Education; p. 242: Fisher, Roger and William Uhry. 2011. Getting to Yes. Penguin; p. 244: Thomas, Lewis. 1980. The Medusa and the Snail. Penguin; p. 246: Koestler, Arthur. 1995. The Act of Creation. Penguin; p. 247: Foster, Jack. 2007. How to Get Ideas. Berrett-Koehler Publishers.

Chapter 11

Page 255: Michalko, Michael. 2011 Creative Thinkering. Ten Speed Press; p. 256: von Oech, Roger. 2008. A Whack on the Side of the Head. Business Plus; p. 258: From A Whack on the Side of the Head, by Roger von Oech. Copyright © 1983, 1990, 1998 by Roger von Oech. By permission of Grand Central Publishing. All rights reserved; p. 259: Linkner, Josh. 2011. Disciplined Dreaming. Jossey-Bass; pp. 262–263: Mark Doty, "Golden Retrievals" from Sweet Machine: Poems. Copyright © 1998 by Mark Doty. Reprinted with the permission of HarperCollins Publishers.

Chapter 12

Page 275: Hevner, Alan R. 2010. Design Research in Information Systems. Samir Chatterjee. Springer; p. 275: Jarski, Rosemarie. 2007. Words From The Wise. Skyhorse; p. 282: Norman, David A. 2005. Emotional Design. Basic Books; p. 286: Petroski, Henry. 2003. Small Things Considered. Random House; p. 290: Goldberger, Paul. 2011. Why Architecture Matters. Yale University Press; p. 290: Frederick, Mathew. 2007. 101 Things I Learned in Architecture School. MIT Press; p. 290: Frederick, Matthew. 2007. 101 Things I Learned in Architecture School. MIT Press.

Chapter 13

Page 296: Dembski, William A. and Charles W. Colson. 2007. The Design Revolution. IVP Books; p. 299: Berkun, Scott. 2010. The Myths of Innovation. O'Reilly Media; p. 301: Lang, Amanda. 2012. The Power of Why. Collins; p. 305: Johnson, Steven. 2011. Where Good Ideas Come From. Riverhead; p. 314: Wagner, Tony. 2012. Creating Innovators. Scribner.

Chapter 14

Page 320: Peters, Carol, Martin Braschler and Paul Clough. 2012. Multilingual Information Retrieval. Springer; p. 322: Kelly, Kevin. 2010. What Technology Wants. Viking; p. 323: Birkerts, Sven. 1995. The Gutenberg Elegies. Ballantine; p. 329: Lanier, Jaron. 2011. You Are Not a Gadget. Knopf; pp. 333–334: Ribble, Mike and Gerald Bailey. 2011. Digital Citizenship in Schools. International Society for Technology in Education; p. 334: Darnton, Robert. 2009. The Case for Books. Public Affairs.

Index